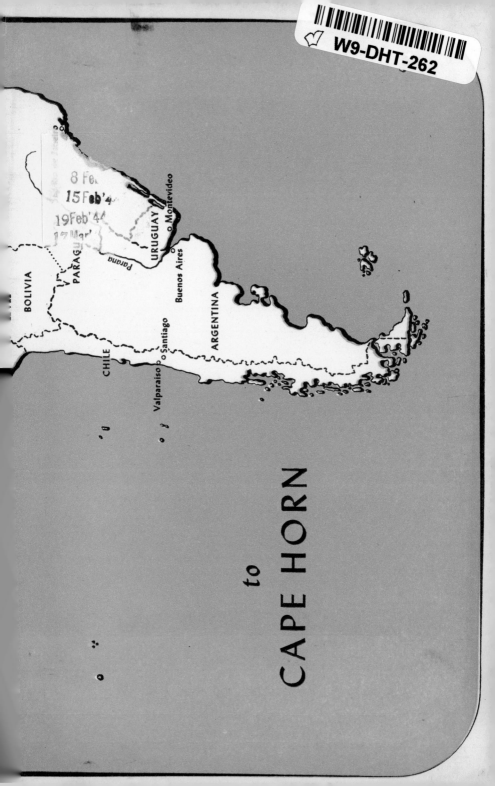

Carleton Beals has lived in Latin America off and on for twenty-five years. His travels have taken him through the mountains and deserts, the valleys and jungles of Mexico and Central America; across the Andes and into the great Amazon basin; along the west coast desert of South America; over the Caribbean beside the silver shores of the Spanish Main. Everywhere he has rubbed elbows with the people. For long periods he has lived among the Indians and the peasants, and he knows many of the intellectual and political leaders of the twenty republics to the south. He was in Villa and Zapata country in Mexico when those two rebels were up in arms and in Nicaragua with Sandino's armies. He saw Batista shoot his way into power in Cuba, witnessed the brutal suppression of the Apristas in Peru, and was at one time a member of the personal staff of President Carranza.

Born in Medicine Lodge, Kansas, then the home town of the famous Carrie Nation and Sockless Jerry Simpson, Carleton Beals was brought up in California. He has served on the faculties of the University of California, the National University of Mexico, and the New School for Social Research in New York City. An advocate of the good-neighbor policy long before it became popular, he believes that before it can become firmly established, we must win over, not merely the governments of Latin America, but the people as well, and that there should be instituted an economic program for the hemisphere which will develop its potentialities, end political and financial imperialism, and make possible the real liberty and independence of all the American republics.

BY CARLETON BEALS

✳

CARLETON BEALS

Rio Grande
to Cape Horn

Houghton Mifflin Company · Boston

The Riverside Press Cambridge

To My Mother

The Riverside Press
CAMBRIDGE · MASSACHUSETTS
PRINTED IN THE U.S.A.

CONTENTS

PART ONE

Panorama

CHAPTER I

Good Neighbors in War Time

BETWEEN México and Guatemala, along part of the frontier, flows the sluggish Suchiate River. Opposite each other on the tropical banks — where the international railroad crosses — nestle two sleepy towns, hot as hinges. Both are primitive and picturesque, predominately Indian. The leisurely life in each appears to be the same, but each community has its own way of doing things.

The first difference to strike the outsider's eye is that the thatched roofs on the Mexican side have less slope; those on the Guatemala side are steeply pitched.

It is an important difference, although it may not figure directly in state papers or Pan-American confabs. Here is almost as reliable an index of annual mean rainfall as a statistician's chart. The traveler has left the dry dusty littoral of Chiapas behind; the train on south now passes through luxuriant vegetation and roars over green-choked streams brimming with quick-rushing water. He is penetrating into one of the world's best coffee regions.

The tropics are far more dominant in the culture of Guatemala than in México. And the geographical change is indicative of a large assortment of divergencies in work, habits, food, speech, dress, institutions, and thought. The steep roofs of Suchiate shed the rain off a people far more placid, methodical, and neat than are the more aggressive, unruly, and imaginative Mexicans. The Guatemalans are more suave and polite; the Mexicans more restless and mordantly ironical. Most Guatemalans, even the upper-class *ladinos* of mixed blood, are more Indian; in México, a more fully mixed breed is the definitely ruling type.

Brown women and girls in loose cotton slips or a cloth around the waist, or not clad at all, tranquilly wash clothes near either bank, rarely with any exchange of greetings. When they dress, the Mexican woman pulls on her embroidered sack-like *huipil*; the Guatemalan woman puts on a blouse with a decided Oriental cut and glinting like the rainbow itself — the famous textiles of Quezaltenango and Huehuetenango. Scarlet plants there are on the Guatemalan side which apparently have never strayed across the border into the drear cactus growth of southern México. At the hip of the leather-clad Mexican ranchero dangles a pearl-handled pistol; but in Guatemala few but designated officials bear arms. Words and speech are different. The Guatemalan swallows syllables; the Mexican drawls each word with precise clarity. In México a turkey is *guajolote* (from the Aztec language); in Guatemala the same fowl is *chompipe* (perhaps a Quiché word), and will not be cooked in the Mexican spicy way at all. This marked regionalism tells of divergent ways of life and thought, some of which go back to ages before the armed soldiery of Cortés overran this corner of the world.

Guatemala is a compact, firmly governed little land. One of the smallest Latin-American countries — though in area almost as large as England — it is tiny compared to México, and is far more closely knit and systematized. And yet even this smaller country presents many varied faces to the visitor. Within it are regions largely distinct from each other, separated areas where the industries, people, and mode of life are radically different. Like a lucky four-leaf clover, it has four important leaves.

Los Altos, the northern highlands, comprise a picturesque land of exquisite handicrafts, marimba bands, brilliant fabrics, village particularism, and a self-sufficient life. The main center is Quezaltenango, seven thousand feet above sea level — for its setting, its architecture, and quaint tilted streets, one of the beautiful cities of the New World.

Next, the great coffee kingdom of German and native *fincas* stretches along the foothills and nestles at the foot of slim snow-capped Santa María, which still erupts and which is still the scene of prehistoric religious sacrifices.

Still another region might almost be another country, so different are its characteristics. The vast jungle of Petén, hot as Central Africa, sticks like a blunt thumb up into México. Here is the main source of chicle, the world's chewing gum. When a young American named Adams called on the exiled Napoleon of México, Antonio López de Santa Ana — the hellion fresh from the Alamo massacre and the Texas war — the former noticed that his host was busily chewing some sort of gum. He captured the idea that enabled him to found a great enterprise and start an industry of many millions on its course. The great American institution of gum-chewing was duly inaugurated, and every American steno thereafter linked by invisible and everlasting bonds to the dark shadows of a Central American jungle, where men toil and sweat, and rot away from the chicle fly, to aid American digestion.

Finally, along Guatemala's coasts are the waving fronds of the prosperous realm (prior to the war) of Baron Banana. In the heart of banana land is set the prehistoric stone city of Quiriguá, a few miles from one of the most famous centers of tropical medicine in the New World, an establishment maintained by the United Fruit Company.

Go into any Latin-American country, and the texture and pattern of life have unique characteristics. The five Central American countries, besides their internal regionalisms, differ radically in race, dress, food, often in politics. In South America differences are even more striking. Why is Chile governed by a Popular Front régime and Paraguay by a military dictator? Why is Colombia, once the host of an endless succession of tyrants, now apparently one of the most democratic lands in the south? Argentina is mostly level pampas; Perú has the highest railroad in the world. The people of one are mostly recent émigrés from Europe; the highland people of Perú trace back to untold centuries before the Conquest, back to the Inca Empire and the Tiahuanaco era and beyond. So many centuries have they lived in that rarefied atmosphere that they have become physically modified by the environment and have on the average twenty-five per cent more lung capacity than ordinary mortals. And so, everywhere to the south, regional and nationalistic highlights stand out sharply and are likely to grow more striking over the years to come.

We North Americans believe that our good-neighbor policy has built one great shining bridge between two outstanding groups of peoples. True enough, there is a common Latin-American culture and also a consciousness of common origin and numerous spiritual ties; there are similar institutions, and an injury to one instinctively is considered an injury to all — but it would be far more accurate to say that we have built at least twenty bridges, each different from the other. The political and economic problems of each southern nation are so unique, the strategic significance of each so determined by different geography and resources, that our policies, within the general scope of the good-will pattern, have had to be adapted to each individual case, and the whole tuned up to harmony like a complicated musical instrument.

Thus we are not so much allied with Latin America at the present time as we are part of a New World community of nations, and to the extent that we have learned to cooperate individually and collectively with the other members of the community, and they with us, to that extent we have laid the basis for future and permanent international good-will and a more decent society among nations.

2

Despite the growth of marked regional and national differences among the South American countries during the past century and more of their independence from Spain, they are today actually closer, with more intimate and ramified relationships than they have ever had before in their history. It may be said that their newly developing differences have brought them together more than their past uniformity under the continent-wide laws of the Indies and Spanish colonial rule.

In colonial times, although the colonies were ruled by the same general laws, and life in México City varied relatively little from that in Lima, Perú, the various regions were separated widely both by poor communications and by royal edict. The numerous Spanish colonies could not trade with each other, often were not allowed to communicate with each other, and only a few specially privileged officials were allowed to pass freely from one to another.

During most of the colonial period Buenos Aires was held in ironclad isolation. It was chiefly a smugglers' port. Argentina was required to ship all her products overland on the backs of Indian peons, mules, or llamas across the high Andes, across the upland plateau of Bolivia, clear to Lima on the far-off Pacific coast, then by sea to Panamá, once more by land across the Isthmus, then by sea to the one Spanish trading port of Sevilla. Losses from storms, official tollhouses, bandits, and delay were enormous. The result was to increase the trend, despite manifold prohibitions, toward local production, hence to foment a growing spirit of independence.

Following independence the contacts of the new countries could scarcely be harmonious. All experience in international affairs was lacking. The international life of the continent was soon featured by war, revolution, and conquest. The dream of continental solidarity promoted by the great liberator, Simón Bolívar, scarcely lasted out enunciation. Petty Napoleonic dictators, with grandiose dreams of conquest; futile rivalries; armament races; vague boundary lines, caused endless bickering and disharmony for the better part of a century. Paraguay was almost exterminated. Chile seized the Peruvian nitrate fields. Border disputes led to endless wars, the recent bloody Chaco conflict being the latest. Argentina has long had a strong imperialist party which has wanted to wrench away western iron deposits from Brazil, and the two countries were long engaged in striving for armament supremacy. Central America was a constant hornets' nest.

The wisdom of Roosevelt's shift of policy toward greater friendliness has become increasingly evident. The good-neighbor attitude helped end the Chaco war; it helped stop war in 1942 between Ecuador and Perú. Brazil and Argentina have become closely cooperative politically and economically. Even before the war, Argentina was selling more goods to Brazil than was England, which earlier had held the bulk of the market, a shift in the world's trade currents of tremendous import. The airplane and better shipping facilities have brought all the countries closer, establishing contacts that never before existed.

Since the war started, interdependency has become still more marked. With European and Oriental markets cut off, the southern countries have had to depend almost entirely upon the United States and each other. The fact that we have agreed to absorb practically all raw-product surpluses, the bulk of which formerly went to Europe, to finance new industrial undertakings and give Latin America a break on priorities, has, with exceptions, strengthened friendliness; both economic and cultural ties have been reinforced. Although these efforts may not as yet provide more than a stopgap solution for immediate problems rather than any well-devised plan for permanent economic development and cooperation, they open the door to wider possibilities in the future.

At the moment, this extreme dependence on us is the only easy way out of the woods for the southern countries; but one and all, they greatly fear the post-war results, when sudden termination of present support may spell economic collapse, and at a time when the sweated plantation products of the British Empire may be brought into ruthless competition with them as a result of some sort of imperial trade *Verein* with the United States. The leaders to the south have sought ways of softening this future blow. And — they ask — is the good-neighbor policy permanent or merely a Roosevelt policy?

Because of necessity and the premonition of serious future difficulties, the southern countries have been trying to promote new manufacturing, diversify production, and increase commerce within the Latin-American bloc itself, apart from trade with the United States. Commercial missions have been hurrying from capital to capital, and the southern countries are surprised themselves at the many products, previously obtained from other continents, that they can procure from each other. This, fortunately, is all part of the necessary foundation for any real hemisphere self-sufficiency. Hence in the long run, this commercial strengthening of Latin America will be beneficial to the United States as well.

Culturally inter-Hispanic rapproachment has been correspondingly marked. As a result of the Spanish civil war and the cutting off of books and periodicals from the mother country, the young republics in this realm also have had to depend more upon their own resources, fortunate at a time when Spain has become a dour Fascist country and the spearhead of Fascist propaganda in the New World. Today Buenos Aires and Santiago, Chile, are rivaling each other for the honor of becoming the publishing center of the Spanish-speaking world. Wealthy new publishing houses have arisen. In 1941 Ercilla in Chile claimed to have published three hundred and sixty-five titles, or a new book a day. Zig-Zag is not far behind. Heretofore the publications of each country found little circulation outside of the national boundaries, unless they also attracted the attention of Madrid, the one large distributing center for the Spanish-speaking world. Now American-made books and magazines circulate more widely over the continent. A brilliant book in one country might go long unheralded beyond the borders, but today the best-seller in one land is apt quickly to become a best-seller in all the others, as happened not long ago with Jorge Icaza's *Huasipunga*, a bitter novel of Ecuadorean Indian life.

The southern countries are now granting scholarships, not only to the United States but to neighbor countries. Bolivia not only invited an American mission to study and exploit rubber developments, but also Mexican agricultural and educational missions to help work out a program for village farming and schools among the indigenous population. Colombia, Brazil, and Central America, which used to cut each other's throats in the international coffee market, increasingly have worked out price and quota arrangements. All this general Latin-American interchange of goods and ideas is quite as much a part of a sound good-neighbor policy as is the American purchase of Guatemalan coffee, or the fact that the Peruvian, Ciro Alegría, won a prize for a novel in the United States.

The changed attitude has a great historical parallel. The stock in trade of ambitious United States politicians in the eighties and nineties consisted of furious attacks on British imperialism and 'the great British gold conspiracy,' whatever that meant. Demands were constantly voiced for the immediate annexation of Canada. Twisting the Lion's tail was sport even for leading personalities of the period. Ill-feeling culminated in the threat of war over the Venezuelan question.

From that moment on, British statesmen, appreciating the danger to them of an unfriendly United States, assiduously set to work to cultivate our good-will. We were quick to respond, and by 1917, or in less than thirty years, this country was allied with England in a world war of vast dimensions, and today American forces are defending the Empire in all quarters of the globe.

In the case of Latin America, our good-neighbor policy, as contrasted to our former policy of aggression and dollar-diplomacy, has already borne important fruits.

3

The policy started to change under President Coolidge, when Ambassador Morrow was sent to México. It was accentuated by President Hoover, who withdrew the Marines from Nicaragua; it became universally applicable after President Roosevelt took office. The results in our present hour of trouble have been gratifying.

During the last war, the Mexican administration of President Venustiano Carranza was almost overtly pro-German. German propaganda was abetted; the government accommodatingly put up what was then the highest wireless station in the world that the Germans might have constant contact with their homeland. Mexican passports were given to spies and *provocateurs* to enter the United States. But today, México has been doing all in its power to assist this country; it was one of the strongest backers of American policy at the Pan-American war conference in Rio, and today it is in the war on the side of the United States.

In the last war Salvador remained stubbornly neutral and pro-German. For a time we allowed no vessels to touch Salvadorean ports. If pressure brought all the other Central American republics into line, nevertheless several, even after declaring war on Germany, did nothing to curb German activities, in fact on occasion lent aid and comfort. But on this occasion the Costa Rican cabinet got up in the middle of the night to beat the United States into the ring in declaring war on Germany; Cuba was slightly peeved that it did not get there first. These attitudes are no pose, but sincere official and popular reaction, which could not have existed, except in a few isolated instances, prior to the good-neighbor policy.

In South America only Argentina has not broken with the Axis or Japan, although there is considerable popular feeling in favor of the United States. Chile hesitated until January, 1943, to break with the Axis. Her exposed geographic position, at the end of the South American stepping-stone islands; her long, undefended coastline; her relative lack of modern armed equipment; her great dependency on imports, were contributing factors in her hesitancy to take a more forthright stand. Not until after the United States had demonstrated that it could block the further advance of Japan in the South Pacific did Chile act.

Reverse causes have contributed to Argentina's militant neutrality. Just as Chile, next to Brazil, is the most strategically exposed country, Argentina, tucked below the Brazilian bulge, knows that she is relatively safe from European attack, for we will have to protect Brazil at all costs. Argentina's safety thereby is automatically guaranteed. On the other hand, the land of the Pampas has done nothing to undermine continental solidarity; she has given the United States and all other American nations the status of non-belligerency; she has expressed constant willingness to cooperate politically and economically provided her interests are properly recognized, and has various American military missions with her armed forces.

Argentina's demands for more extensive cooperation with the United States include provision for proper shipping facilities to take care of Argentina's needs, priority ratings and guaranteed shipments of machinery and other essential supplies, removal of certain prohibitions on Argentine meat, an end of joint pressure by England and the United States to force down the price of meat and wheat; a long-term guarantee as to production and markets for Argentine products.

The United States has made minor concessions with respect to supplies, but has hit Argentina hard by putting all meat-buying in British hands; by restricting shipping still more tightly; by reducing the meat consumption of the people of the United States in order to supply the United Nations, thus destroying a good part of Argentina's outside market; by getting Cuba to seize and condemn Argentine meat as infected. It has created difficulties for the present régime by intensive propaganda inside Argentina and by maintaining friendly official relations with many elements hostile to the present government.

On her side Argentina has bid against the United States for the crude-rubber supplies of South America. The United States has tied up the supply in country after country, with agreements to purchase all available at forty-five cents or less. But Argentina offers sixty cents and up, and the agreements with us naturally are flouted. Other Argentine activities annoy Washington, as for instance her pressure on Bolivia to resist certain demands.

Bolivia as a matter of fact for a time was greatly incensed over our failure to deliver promised lease-lend aid and machinery, and that country rather than Argentina was the real center of Nazi espionage activities. Public feeling in Honduras is very sharply critical of the United States, largely because of the antipathy to Dictator Carías, rather than because of any overt act or oversight by the United States authorities. In Colombia — despite strong anti-American groups — the bulk of the public is wholly anti-Nazi. In Venezuela considerable criticism has arisen over the shipping situation. The very strongly pro-Allied paper, *Acción Democrática*, May 30, 1942, complained that while the subsoil of Venezuela is being rapidly exhausted in supplying oil to the United Nations, that while the companies took out in 1940 a net profit of 325,000,000 Venezuelan dollars, leaving none of this vast sum in the country for new enterprises and relatively little in the way of taxes, Venezuela is quite unable to get goods from the United States which are life and death to her, not even medical supplies. Even a meager seventy thousand tons of products allotted to her were, on that date, still piled up on American wharves for lack of shipping facilities.

In another issue, July 18, 1942, the paper complained that Venezuela, which is the greatest petroleum-producer after the United States, cannot even buy or borrow a ship for essential goods, whereas the United States has given a dozen merchant vessels to Brazil.

In Cuba public sentiment is almost one hundred per cent

behind the United States. The chief criticism has been that the buying up of sugar *en bloc* by the United States Government has prevented Cuba from getting a fair price, that this has benefited 'neither the Cuban nor the American public.' Of late there have been bitter comments about the arrogance and race prejudices of American troops quartered in many parts of the island.

But all told, the situation of Latin America with respect to the United States is far more cheerful than in 1917, when public opinion southward was far more divided than now.

This is not to claim that all is lovely below the Río Grande. There is the constant danger of fifth-column activities. Particularly ominous are the activities of the Falangistas, or Spanish Fascists, who time and again were proven to have been in close cooperation with German, Italian, and Japanese secret agents, whose organizers were frequently trained in Germany by the Gestapo, and who today are the ramrod of anti-United States propaganda and who supply the Axis with information about steamship sailings and other vital matters. Spanish ships, it has been charged, have used their neutral status to provision German submarines on the high seas.

In many quarters in Latin America there are still hold-over unsavory rulers, who played in with the Axis prior to our entry into the war, and who might, in a serious moment of crisis, prove treacherous despite the large funds we have given them and despite the more sincere pro-United States sentiments of their peoples.

A few years ago one of the easier paths to political advancement in Latin America was to bait the United States; and in a number of countries there are still groups who bitterly hate and fear this country. Here and there they gain considerable following because the shift to good-neighborliness, while it has convinced the governments, the newspapers, and the intellectuals, has in many places scarcely penetrated deeply among the masses. In earlier days of marine expansion, not only southern politicians but brilliant writers such as Ugarte, Lugones, and Rodó built their careers on such anti-American activity. A few such still persist; a few who still shout against the United States are not so much pro-Nazi as is so easily charged, but rather are sharpening their spurs for possible future successes in the domestic politics of their own countries. Many such feel that after the war, the United States will become imperialistic, that it will never relinquish the military bases in South America and Central America, that the honeymoon of good-neighborliness will dissolve in a new policy of coercion. A persistent good-neighbor policy, a non-imperialistic attitude, naturally will nullify the efforts of such elements. Only if the United States suffers serious military reverses in the war or fails to make proper provisions for Latin-American economic needs will these antagonistic and frequently self-seeking elements temporarily increase in numbers and vociferousness. But the surge of public opinion is at present definitely in the other direction, and the wings of the enemies of a free and friendly New World are not likely to be spread in very prolonged flight.

All in all, good-neighborliness has proved a workable pattern for both peace and war. If it is reduced merely to wartime expediency, it will founder. It can, however, serve as an example of the possibility of a durable world peace.

4

These developments are gratifying, for today Latin America is far more important than during the last war, when Germany was really blockaded and Japan was an ally and not among the enemies. This time, a shift in fortunes might actually transform the southern continent into a battle-front where the pincers of encirclement of the United States might bite in. The active support of South America is thus a far more decisive factor than it ever has been.

The good-neighbor policy, to the extent that it has been honestly and successfully promoted, has been a mighty weapon to disconcert the common foe. Even in instances, on both sides, where efforts have not been so sincere and were clouded with self-interest, the new gestures, merely as gestures, have been important, for they indicate which way the general tide is now running.

We might successfully fight Japan even if our Marines were still prowling the jungles of Nicaragua, but we would have less right to condemn German occupation of Bulgaria and Greece or Japanese occupation of Indo-China and Thailand. Perhaps the weakest spot in our moral armor with respect to the Southern Hemisphere is that Puerto Rico is in such a terrible economic condition and that the chief Nationalist Party leaders of that country are held in prison in Atlanta. But our general about-face from a policy of imperialist aggression to one of cooperation with weaker neighbors has also buttressed us up morally by proving concretely to the whole world that a concert of independent nations can work out their problems in harmony and peace.

Economically Latin America daily looms more important, and our good-neighbor policy has made it possible for the United States to push swiftly arrangements whereby, if the war is long drawn out, we can supplement our supplies of strategic materials and replace those wholly or partly cut off by Japanese and Axis conquests. The folly of getting the bulk of our tropical products from Asia has become increasingly apparent. Such materials are likely to include all those previously derived from Russia and the Orient, including India; among other things, oils, waxes, fibers, coconut oil and coconut-shell charcoal (for gas masks), tea, Manila hemp, rotenone, tin, rubber, quinine, opium and strychnine, shellac, camphor, antimony, manganese, platinum, graphite, mica, kapok, nickel, chromium, and many less-known commodities.

Brazil promises not only to become anew a great rubber-producer — an adequate labor supply to tackle the millions of wild rubber trees would give us many times the present supply from there — but also the New World tea and silk center. Argentine and Paraguayan *mate* can be treated to resemble Ceylon tea; and someone presently may be making a fortune by importing Mexican *té de limón*, a marsh grass that gives a brew little distinguishable from orange pekoe. Today we know that Guatemala can produce, if as yet in limited quantities, the finest quinine in the world. The feat can be duplicated in Perú, original home of the product. There is nothing particularly revolutionary or strange in protecting industries in friendly countries or for the whole continent, especially when the materials sought are vital, not merely to our prosperity, but to our national security. We have seen to our dismay what a waste of energy and national wealth, and how little national security it has given us to pour out American capital, in obedience merely to the motive of private profit, upon too remote shores where the materials produced become unavailable if an enemy strikes, and in fact then help sustain the enemy in war against us.

Strategically also the United States has benefited by the good-neighbor policy. Numerous countries have given us the unabridged use of air and sea bases. In the case of Ecuador, Guatemala, Brazil, and Costa Rica this has greatly simplified the task of defending the Canal.

And when peace is eventually re-established in the world, the good-neighbor policy will mean, let us hope, that the countries south will have a voice in the final proceedings further to enforce the moral status of Western Hemisphere solidarity, to help determine the sort of world we wish to live in, and to protect their own vital economic and political interests. If their cooperation has been agreeable to this country in wartime, the United States would be less than generous and intelligent if it did not utilize that same cooperation in shaping the world — to the extent possible — in such a manner as to insure peace over a reasonable period of time. The mechanisms already developed for continental cooperation, the spirit of peaceable negotiations, the purposes for which this concert of nations works — all this can well provide the model in many aspects for the world we hope to see established.

5

All this should not reduce us to complacency or permit us to shirk the grave problems that still confront us if we desire to bring about permanent continental solidarity which will endure beyond the war period which has created special necessities. The framework must be ample for development and change. Constant cultivation is the only guarantee of steady growth.

The basis of any solidarity must be that of strong and healthy nations. If we are fighting for the principle of free peoples and their rights, we cannot ignore that need in our own Western Hemisphere. Though the world struggle has made some very strange bedfellows, we should, whatever the *status quo* in Latin America, realize that the spread of democratic processes southward, as well as in our own country, is a *sine qua non* of any faithful alliance and lasting cooperation.

As yet the democratic processes to the south are still very deficient, and spiritually certain chieftains there would be far more at home in the Axis camp than in that of the United Nations, where they have been driven by expediency. The persistence of the military *caudillo* or ruler in Latin America is due to defective economic development, class extremes, the persistence of feudal institutions, the clash of cultures among widely different races, the lack of proper health standards, illiteracy, and lack of education. These conditions have been due, not to racial or national inadequacies, but to the heritage of old régimes, the Spanish conquest, historical circumstances, geographical obstacles, and the prior development of industrial power in the North Atlantic area.

Democracy cannot be conjured out of thin air; it cannot be imposed by force from without; it will arrive only with time and evolution and an intelligent effort to end conditions which keep the masses of Latin America in an intolerable condition of exploitation and servitude, which prevent them from participating in political life, and even prevent them from providing an active and efficient defense of their lands against outside aggression.

Thus, within the framework of Latin America there is, in addition to the opposition to the Axis, a very definite domestic struggle for liberty and democracy, often against the powers that be. International necessity has forced us at all cost to be friends with the governments of Latin America. Unfortunately in a few countries this has made us the enemy of the people. 'How,' asks Luis Alberto Sánchez, head of the great publishing house, Ercilla, 'can Peruvians fight to preserve democracy when in their country they have no democracy to preserve?'

'What is lacking for the formation of a stable inter-Americanism?' asks Raul Haya de la Torre, head of the democratic Aprista movement on the southern continent, and answers: 'Let the American people feel the benefits of democracy.... All of us in Latin America understand that our countries are opposing the Axis powers because they have suppressed liberty. But... Latin-American countries have also suppressed liberty.' He mentions as among the chief sinners against democracy and liberty, the governments of Guatemala, Perú, Paraguay, and Brazil.

6

Among the bases of true democracy are health, prosperity, and education.

Latin-American sanitation, because of limited budgets and other difficulties, is mostly backward, although in the principal cities it has made much progress.

México, since the revolution, has made tremendous advances in health and social hygiene. Today, through a nationwide vaccination program, it has largely stamped out smallpox except for remoter Indian communities. But the death rate is abnormally high, and many serious health problems confront the country.

Doctor Gabriel Ormaechea, of Torreón, writing in *La Opinión* for August 15, 1942, says:

Malaria has cost México half a million lives in the last twenty years. The talk of increasing production in México is just empty words so long as present conditions continue. There is no point to urging our country-people to increase production. Our people are not lazy or indolent but a large part of them are grievously ill. They are badly clad, ill fed, and live in shacks, infected with flies which envelop them. They are dependent for water on putrid ponds. A large part of our workers are trembling with malarial fever. The wealth of the nation consists in its citizens capable of working.

México has lost 501,464 lives by malaria between 1922 and 1942. Year by year, thousands die and 2,000,000 suffer. One-eighth of México is suffering from malaria. Economically this is an incalculable loss to the nation. If each victim loses ten days' labor, this means an annual loss to the nation of 30,000,000 pesos according to the minimum wage as determined by law.

Cuba, following the tradition of Agramonte, Reed, Wood, and others, has carried on sanitation more effectively than most countries. However, it received a severe setback under the Machado tyranny, and the subsequent revolutionary period has resulted in many services never being resumed. Prior to Machado socialized medicine was well advanced in the island, but these efforts were stamped out.

Even in the larger cities in most of the countries, the death rate, in good part due to poverty diseases, is far in excess of that of Europe or the United States, and in some places reaches the terrible proportions of the Orient. Infant mortality is high. In Chile only half of all the inhabitants reach the age of nine. Charles Morrow Wilson in his brilliant survey of Latin-American health problems, *Ambassadors in White*, estimates that at least fifty million people of Latin America, or forty per cent, are suffering from serious ailments and are unable to enjoy medical care — malaria, yellow fever, yaws, beriberi, pellagra, hookworm, Stuks disease, syphilis, fungus diseases, pinta, dysentery, tuberculosis, etc.

Probably an equal number of people are below the civilized subsistence level, are out of the market for nearly all civilized goods, have inadequate diets, and live in unsatisfactory dwellings.

Education has a tradition far older than that in the United States, but illiteracy, according to the country, ranges from twenty-five to ninety per cent. Few universities are equipped with as good elementary physical or chemical laboratories as the small-town high school in the United States, let alone more advanced technical equipment, yet they give degrees for physicians and scientists.

Feudalism, militarism, landlordism, and a parasitical type of ecclesiasticism hold vast populations in semi-serfdom, ignorance, and malnutrition.

Until more headway is made against these basic evils, it is useless to talk about democracy in most of the southern countries or to criticize them for the lack of it. It is relatively useless to send them huge armaments for a defense they can only fumble. True defense requires the active participation of an alert and healthy population. It is useless to hope for democracy to the south while the countries remain in economic subjugation to larger powers. The continent needs industrialization and diversification of production so that the countries will not be obliged, as at present, to sell raw materials, produced by serf-like half-starved labor, at low prices over which they have no control and pay exorbitant prices for foreign manufactured goods. This semi-colonial rôle with respect to the United States and Europe prevents any rise in the general standard of living, blocks education and health efforts, and makes impossible the development of free countries with free democratic governments.

The vast, largely undeveloped riches of the American tropics are a bright bait for all imperial adventurers, a bid for outside aggression — especially as economic resources, petroleum, minerals, and certain vegetable products are the key to the war-making power. Eighty per cent of the South American population still lives within two hundred miles of the seacoast. Until the great vacant stretches, difficult though some of them may be to colonize, are settled up, filled in, and developed, no integral defense of Latin America is possible if it is ever seriously menaced from the outside.

Until the Amazón basin, for instance, which is the very heart and center and pivot of the South American continent, is developed by a coordinated continental plan, South America will not have come of age, and, lacking such economic maturity, cannot find the necessary sinews for self-defense.

The lack of sound democracy south, with the prevalence in many places of large Japanese, German, and Italian colonies, has opened the way for fifth-column elements. Many of the reactionary and ruling cliques of Latin America, despite lip service to continental solidarity, are strongly allied with the Falanx, or Spanish Fascist organization, which postulates a mystic, Pan-Latin, anti-Protestant, religious imperialism, bitterly anti-American.

7

There are, despite the recklessness with which North American millions have been dished out to hungry southern politicians, undercurrents of fear, among truly liberal elements, those whole-heartedly in favor of the United Nations and opposed to Naziism and its fellow-travelers. Will the good-neighbor policy last? Will the military expansion of the United States, the new bases south, the planting of the American flag on the mainland of South America itself, eventually be converted, as for so long in the past, into aggression toward Latin America? Why fight German imperialism, which has threatened Latin America but little, and get American imperialism, of which the southerners already have had such bitter doses? What will happen in the post-war depression period of the United States when the market, wholly controlled by us, goes to pot as it did after the last war? Will it again mean revolutionary collapse in Latin America as on the previous occasion? May not that revolutionary wave this time engulf the whole continent and be far more serious? What is the American program for economic reconstruction and where does Latin America fit into that? Will it be American wheat and cotton and agricultural products that are used to feed the world after the war, while the vast stocks of Latin America rot away for lack of outside markets? After the war will the economic *Verein* of the United States and the British Empire really come to pass so that the products of Latin America will have to compete on an unequal basis already made unequal by the sweated labor of the empire?

These and other questions press for an answer, and upon the answer we give them will depend the enthusiasm for the American cause at this hour and also the permanent success or failure of the good-neighbor policy, and thereby perhaps our own position in the world at large.

The generalized ignorance of the American public concerning Latin-American life and culture and the intimate affairs of the southern countries is a further enormous barrier which does not contribute to intelligent action. All our general reference books need to be rewritten. You may dip into the Encyclopaedia Britannica, for instance, and will find little or no mention of the great leaders of Latin America, some of whom have changed the history of the world, of its writers, artists, jurists, scientists. Doctor Aristides Agramonte, the discoverer of the yellow fever insect carrier, who made the experiments of Reed possible, is not even listed.

If the present status of intercontinental relationships in the New World is far more satisfactory than it ever had been, thanks largely to President Roosevelt, and we are better geared for carrying on outside war, this should not blind us to the immediate complaints which may seriously affect our war efforts or the long-range problems which will beset us when the dust of battle dies away, and which will be all the more serious the longer we neglect them.

CHAPTER II

What's in a Name?

'LATIN AMERICA' is a vague expression. One Western professor attacks the use of it hotly. For years he spent the better part of his academic leisure in crusading for the designation, 'Hispanic America.' This would leave black Haiti, which speaks French, quite out of the picture.

The militant Apristas, an anti-imperialist group, wish the southern realm to be called 'Indo-America.' Such designations as 'Latin America' and 'Hispanic America,' they claim, are musty words, connoting the dead era of Spanish and Portuguese domination, of colonialism, or of cultural tutelage by France. They do not cover the vital native forces of the New World, the new era of independence and self-made culture. 'Pan-America' they have insisted is even worse. This word is official, imperialistic, and represents 'the second conquest' by 'dollar diplomacy.' According to the Apristas, the European and Latin elements in American civilization are amply covered by the word 'America' itself. By calling the southern regions 'Indo-America,' due recognition is given to the basic indigenous elements, whose blood has contributed more to the present-day populations than has Europe, and which will, they believe, eventually provide a greater cultural content as class and racial divisions are broken down.

But this in turn leaves out the vast negro element in Latin America, and the negro has played an enormous part in the development and history of the New World. There are probably fifteen million full-blooded negroes in the southern lands and probably at least twenty-five million other people who are mulattoes or zamboes, or around forty million people, close to a third of the population. It is true, these are largely concentrated in Brazil and the Caribbean and certain hot coastal areas, but they are an inescapable part of the Latin-American world.

One of the first two men ashore in Perú from the Pizarro expedition was a negro, and the astonished natives almost rubbed his skin off to convince themselves his color was real, not painted on. The negro developed the great herds of inland Brazil; his toil carved out the diamonds and platinum and gold; and his sweat irrigated the sugar plantations. He brought his advanced skills with metals and his knowledge of weaving and pottery. Millions of negroes reside in the Caribbean area; their labor largely built the Panamá Canal; they harvest most of the bananas. And the negro has contributed greatly to the music and dance and literature of all Latin America. His buoyant spirit is woven like a song through the living culture of both Americas.

It is not easy, therefore, to frame a whole civilization and a whole continent and a half within the narrow confines of an easy phrase. The vibrant and multiform life of the Americas cannot be shoved into a cubbyhole or put down under one index heading.

Just as 'Indo-America' forgets the blacks, so it is not a particularly apt designation for such countries as white Argentina and white Costa Rica, essentially European in origin. It is out of place for Cuba, where the sons of Chieftain Hatüey, one of the early native martyrs to Christian piety, were largely exterminated as they were in the United States. And so, the happy all-inclusive designation has yet to be discovered; and when it is, it will probably remain pedantic, or people will use it only after generations of scholarly insistence.

2

It is far more important than what we decide to call the world to the south of us — and 'Latin America' is probably the handiest and best designation — to know of what the culture of the folk who are our 'good neighbors' consists — their habits, their thought, their aspirations. Offhand we speak of the twenty free and sovereign republics. The concept is gross indeed. Their freedom and sovereignty are relative, not merely with respect to their internal régimes. The Caribbean countries, and today a goodly part of South America, are definitely subordinated to the needs of North American defense. None of the southern countries have ever demanded naval and air bases or military outposts from us. Cuba has never insisted that we hand over Key West or Miami. Brazil has never asked for a foothold in the Caribbean, though such points are as essential to her defense as other points south that we demand for our own use. This emphasizes the inferior political, economic, and military rôle of all the southern republics. They are still semi-colonial entities with no major rights in the game of power politics.

Farther south, there are other countries affected constantly by their more powerful neighbors. For a century Uruguay has been caught repeatedly in the tug of war between Brazil and Argentina. This has involved her in numbers of wars, and her internal politics are constantly influenced by the political pattern of her two strong neighbors, and often parties there have been a projection of Brazilian or Argentine intrigue. The same pattern holds true to a great extent for Paraguay and Bolivia. Bolivia is divided today into recognized spheres of influence between Argentina and Brazil — much as Persia was divided between British and Russian control, with the United States constantly sticking a finger in the pie. The real factor in precipitating the Chaco War was Argentina, and the conflict ceased when Argentina was ready to have it cease and not before, although the credit for achieving peace was ironically passed to the United States. The internal politics of Ecuador are constantly muddied by *sub-rosa* interventions of Perú and Colombia, with Colombia having the better of it now for a good many years.

But by and large all the southern countries are freer, more independent, than were many of the smaller nations of Europe even before the present world conflict. In many ways, most of the countries of South America have enjoyed more real sovereignty than did Greece or Czechoslovakia or Portugal, and possibly are less subjected to imperialist coercion and pernicious power politics. And as time goes on, the national characteristics of each grow more marked, the culture of each more distinctive.

But in addition to the political and national pattern of Latin America there are definite regional divisions, which to a great extent ignore political boundaries. They are commensurable geographical areas in which different racial groups and different climatic and economic conditions steadily shape a common cultural growth, regardless of the national controls. These basic regional forces were at work long before the coming of the Spaniards, and they still exert a strong and continuous pull on the lives of the peoples. They also will grow stronger as Latin America becomes more self-sufficient and less colonial, as the various countries diversify their industries, promote their well-being, and become less dependent upon foreign trade, hence less compelled to act merely as providers of raw materials for more powerful industrialized nations.

In early days, before the coming of the Spaniards and Portuguese, great empires rose in a number of these compact regions. In prehistoric times the great Inca highways ran parallel to the coast; along the shore on great pilings driven into the shifting sands; along the ridges of the Andes, through tunnels of stone and across high-flung suspension bridges. They ran north into what are now Ecuador and Colombia, south into what are now Argentina and Chile. They spanned a unified economic region, later torn apart by the European conquest when roads and railroads were thrust in from the shore in order to pull out the wealth of the continent for alien lands. The old highways fell into disuse. As a result, Perú today is a country of small, separate economic islands, without intercommunication, each tied to the raw-material needs of the great powers across the seas.

But the older regionalism, in spite of its disruption, still operates, albeit for the time being on a primitive scale. The ancient peoples still move over the broken trails to attend the great native religious festival at Cuzco, the old capital; they still flock to the great markets in Huancayo, Ayacucho, and Cochabamba, even to Salta in Argentina and Riobamba in Ecuador. As Latin America turns away from Europe and the Orient — as this century it has been forced to do repeatedly — the continent again looks inward to its own resources and potentialities. As Europe expires in war and as the Orient becomes a closed system, and as the United States grows industrially powerful, the north-south lines of communication again become more dominant. Soon, instead of stopping at Colombia, the new Inca roads — the Pan-American highway, the Pan-American airways, the steamship routes — run or will soon run clear to the Arctic and south to Cape Horn. And this will mean a revitalization of the mighty highland area once dominated by the Incan Empire.

The counterpart of the South American highland region and culture in the North American continent was the highland culture of México and Central America. These two vast areas, with their great plateaus, follow the line of the massive mountain range which is the dorsal column of the two continents — the Andean-Rocky system. This is the dominant profile of the Americas. It is the great determinant of rainfall, the flow of population, the mixing of races.

The highland culture is strongly indigenous. There, the *mestizos*, or men of mixed blood, are more Indian than white, both in blood and in culture. This Indian-mestizo world stretches from the Mexican plateau into the highlands of Central America. It stretches through the highlands of Colombia, to Venezuela on the east; and on the west, through the lofty regions of Ecuador, Perú, Bolivia, and the Andean regions of Argentina and Chile.

Tropical shores or jungles or deserts lie at the base of these plateaus. Near our own country, those tropical shores are washed by that Mediterranean Sea of the Western Hemisphere, the Caribbean, which, like the two great highland areas and the tropical regions, is an entirely different geographical and cultural expression. Racially as well as culturally, it is remote indeed from the highland world.

Farther south are two great regions, the Pampas of Argentina and Uruguay, and the Green Hell, or the jungle regions of Brazil, Venezuela, Colombia, and the hinterlands of Perú, Ecuador, and Bolivia. Finally there is the west coast of South America, fronting the Pacific, chiefly a long strip of desert from Piura in northern Perú clear down to the mountains and lakes of southern Chile; and this area, too, has its distinctive climatic and regional aspects, although eventually — except in Chile — it will probably be ruled, after long conflict, by the highlanders. The present

rule by the coast, as in Perú, is symptomatic of the alien imperialism that has long twisted Latin America from its true
destiny.

This highland-lowland duality of the continent, highland versus
coast, highland versus jungle, is one of the perpetual motifs of
the history of the southern world. It is a duality that explains
much of the internal political strife of Ecuador, the fierce local
patriotism of coastal-jungle Guayaquil as opposed to highland
Quito; it is a conflict that explains the politics of much of Guatemala's history, where, time after time, the more indigenous men
of Los Altos, the highland folk of Quezaltenango and Huehuetenango, have swept down on the lower valleys and destroyed the
parasitic bureaucracies. It explains the long failure of Perú to
achieve national integration. It partly explains the Chaco War —
the struggle between highland Bolivians and lowland Paraguayans, a recent echo of an eternal conflict. Had the two countries
been under one government, then the story would have been, not
international war, but civil war. It is a pattern that has imposed
itself repeatedly on the politics of Venezuela and which there, too,
existed long before the Spaniards came.

And so in these vast southern regions of the Western Hemisphere are growing into life great new societies, far different from
anything in the United States or Europe, different in race and
creed and family and art. Eventually they will have rich contributions to make to the progress and knowledge of mankind.
Upon our understanding of them, our awareness of them, our
realization of their importance, now and in the future of the world,
may well depend the success or failure of all our efforts to reach
the goal of true hemispheric cooperation.

3

Just as there is a great dance of angels on the pin-point of
what name to call the southern realm, so is there much exegesis
concerning the words 'America' and 'Americans' as applied to
the United States. All Latin Americans, the Indo-Americans,
the Afro-Americans, are also Americans, claim the southerners,
and our usurpation of the generic title is but another instance of

our arrogance and imperialistic spirit. But no one has come forward with a satisfactory substitute.

The whole trouble seems to reside in the fact that our forefathers chose such a prosaic, unimaginative name for our country. Bolivia adapted the name of the great South American liberator, Simón Bolívar, and it is now simple and explicit to say Bolivians. Not addicted (at least theoretically) to the same type of hero worship, we did not call our country Washingtonia, which from the Latin-American standpoint is also fortunate; for if we were now Washingtonians, our southern neighbors would have to accommodate themselves to the letter 'W,' which is not in their alphabet and which they can scarcely pronounce.

Someone has suggested we call ourselves Unisans, but it sounds too much like a raw-carrot sect ever to have much vogue.

To get around the matter, the South Americans have fallen into the habit of calling us North Americans — *Norteamericanos.* This at least narrows us down a bit geographically to one continent, until we can think up some popular designation that will actually describe us for what we are.

Recently in a letter to the Mexican editor and journalist, Felix Palavicini, I used this expression 'North American.' A tart reply came back. Canadians and Mexicans, it seems, are also 'North Americans'; he made no mention of Costa Ricans, or Guatemalans. Instead of such intellectual imperialism, he demanded, why didn't I use the convenient word 'Yankee' as the Mexicans do?

I hastened to reply that although I now live in Connecticut I can never hope to be a Yankee, that Yankees are getting very scarce indeed, mixing their blood with the daughters of immigrant Italians and Poles, and that to call us all 'Yankees' was carrying things to the opposite extreme. If we let ourselves be narrowed down to the little corner of the country that is New England, the first thing we know we will be pushed right off the map. Besides, 'Yankee,' in a Latin American's mouth, has sneering implications.

What's in a name? Perhaps the critics may be right. In the names we use for things often lurk outmoded ways of thought, residues of the unholy past that we should throw aside. A new word freshens us up in thought and deed. But new wine can often also be advantageously put in old bottles. Sometimes the attempt to impose a new word merely smacks of the smart or the pedantic.

Herein I use 'Latin America' almost exclusively because it is convenient, specific — the most comprehensive and precise expression we have at hand. For much the same reason, because of convenience and convention, I use mostly the word 'American' for things and persons of the United States. When I'm feeling South-Americanish, I may stick in a 'North American.' I balk at 'Yankee.' And perhaps if we use the word 'American' with a certain self-consciousness and the full knowledge that it is an accidental usurpation, we may get to feel that we are citizens, not only of the United States, but of a whole New World, a concert of nations that may become free, and are part of a very large geographic and human expression, not merely of an interoceanic band of land occupying less than a fourth of the Western Hemisphere. In the realm of international affairs it is pretty hard and dangerous to call a spade a spade, but, even if we call Unisans 'Americans,' and other Americans, sons of Hispania and France, 'Amerinds,' and Brazilian and Haitian negroes 'Latin Americans,' we shall do our best.

PART TWO

Highlands North

CHAPTER III

Life on the Mexican Mesa

THE great Mexican plateau is a triangular extension of Texas. It is Texas shelving steadily up against the sky. Gradually as the plateau rises to the south, it is pinched in by the lofty coastal mountain ranges that finally meet in the gigantic embrace of Anahuac, the fertile lake-dotted Valley of México. There in a ring of lofty peaks, often snow-clad, lies the sprawling metropolis of México City, with close to two million inhabitants, the fourth largest city in the Western Hemisphere. Beyond are small plateaus in the folds of crisscross ridges, such as the valleys of Cuautla, Cuernavaca, Iguala, Oaxaca, and Guadalajara, arranged like steps leading down to the hot country.

Beyond Oaxaca to the southeast, the plateau breaks down, and the crosscross of mountains suddenly drop swift slopes to Tehuantepec, which lies almost at sea level in a low pass between the two oceans. The plateau rises quickly again in Chiapas and extends on south through Guatemala to Panamá. In Nicaragua and again at Panamá the continents are pierced by low passageways from ocean to ocean.

The border between the United States and México is a long stretch of river and desert, marked in the dry sections by elaborate concrete posts. Over the exact location of the boundary international disputes have arisen. Over the water supply in that arid region, other international disputes have arisen, for water in the northern part of México is all-important; and since most of the rivers, like the Río Grande and the Colorado, rise on the American side, México usually has been the complainant. That vagabond river, the Río Grande, which much of the year is merely a small sluggish mud stream, on occasion becomes a roaring torrent and cuts out new beds to confound the map-makers and the statesmen who want things settled for all time.

But there is a definite border, and at stipulated intervals boundary posts and much barbed wire and armed patrols and customs officials and vaccine and different laws and regulations; but México does not stop at the line any more than the United States does. Both flow over and beyond the limits so arbitrarily set.

At the border, the differences of people, of customs, of ways of thought, come to a sharp focus; and yet the two ways blend, for the border has its own lore and habits, apart from those of either country. Thereabouts people speak differently, dress differently, and eat differently than in other parts of the United States or México. The Texas hat is the first cousin of the Mexican sombrero. As one progresses southward, hat brims widen steadily, till at last one comes upon the huge black Zapatista sombrero, sometimes five feet across, so heavy with silver coins and spangles that only strong men can wear it. Then presently in the loftier Guatemalan highlands, one comes upon the narrow-brimmed little felt hats of the Quichés, looking like the evil gear of a college freshman, and far south in Ecuador and Perú, the misnamed 'Panamá' hats; some of them on tousled heads would be the envy of the lordliest sojourner at Miami Beach.

The so-called Mexican food of Texas is not found in México except in name. Even though its derivation was south of the border, it has become distinctly the product of a different local cuisine. Texas chile con carne bears little resemblance to the dish of that name served in Oaxaca, for, as one goes farther south, the meat content diminishes and the hot content rises, until the concoction becomes mostly pure chile that blazes in the mouth.

One suspects that simple little things like the sun and the kind of plants with which food and clothing are made, rather than the nature of races or the stupidity of man, have consider-able to do with these gradations.

On the Texas side of the border an automobile becomes a *mueble*, 'a piece of furniture,' just another bit of household equip-ment, a sort of walking dresser or an animated bed, and for the

Mexicans frequently it serves as a whole house. But in remoter corners in southern México, it is still a monstrously strange thing, for there are extensive areas in the neighboring republic where even that simple European device, the wheel — unknown to the New World prior to the conquest and settlement — is still wholly absent.

The Texas Mexican goes to the *marqueta* or *marketa* for his supplies; but only a few miles south of the border, the Mexican who hears the word fails to understand it at all, and might even suspiciously believe that his fellow above the border must be talking about an assignation.

On the other hand, some expressions stray far south of the frontier line. The Spanish *ascensor* is lost in the Mexican corruption of an Anglo-Saxon corruption of the Latin — *elevador*. In México City a 'pancake' is nothing else than a cupcake.

2

Probably México and its habits flow over into the United States more than ours flow the other way. One has to jump clear to México City (except for along the Pan-American highway) to find any considerable North American accent on things — new tall buildings, spangled orgasmic movie houses, American-style restaurants, American music, California bungalows, electric gadgets, slot machines, highballs, and sidecars. The California bungalow is really merely a return of an old gift from México, in altered form. The Spaniards originally swiped the design from the Moors; the Cubans modified the Spanish form; the Mexicans borrowed it from Cuba; it was carried northward very early and reshaped and sentimentalized by the Americans, and now it is back again in México — where once more it is being restyled. Of late the new Cuban suburbs began copying the revised Mexican version; a few examples then appeared in Spain; and eventually, I presume, it will be back again among the Moors.

In general the stronger Mexican influence on the American side may be due to the fact that all this border region once belonged to México, taken from her in days when aggression was a

legitimate American custom. Some Mexican families on our side
trace their descent back to the Spanish *adelantados*, to the days
of Coronado and the wandering padres. Some of them claim
descent from Spaniards who founded the oldest town in the
United States, set up long before the *Mayflower* crept into
Plymouth Bay. Quite regardless of war a century ago and the
transfer of sovereignty and being engulfed by an English-speak-
ing world, many Mexicans in Texas are still rooted at the same
old spot. In spirit they are good Americans now, even if some
of them still speak Spanish (New Mexico is officially bilingual),
are proud of their background, and cling to old customs. Also
there are a flood of newcomers, mostly poor folk contracted to
work on railroads, in sugar-beet fields, hotels, and steel mills.
During our depression we booted many of them home in cattle
cars; now we are bringing them back in droves to help save our
wartime man-power problem. Some of the Mexican residents are
political exiles. Some never go back to their native land, but
remain part of the border population and adopt its distinctive
mores.

As one proceeds southward in Texas, México begins to appear
on every hand: flat adobe buildings, broad-brimmed sombreros,
bright shirts and sashes, knives, pistols, swarthy skins. Apparently Laredo, with its tall buildings poking up above the desert,
its neat streets and lawns, its Chamber of Commerce, its Rotary
Club and airplane-spotters, is invincibly North American, but
many ways of México pervade the little city. There is quite a
different bustle to it, a zestful yet leisurely enjoyment of life;
people know how to linger on in the cafés; the colors of clothes in
the modernistic shop windows are brighter, more clashing. At
the very hour when an ordinary small American city would be
closing up the shop doors and people hurrying home to dinner,
folk in Laredo suddenly begin promenading in the traditional
way of old Spain; and many Americans, in that cool moment of
the dying day, promenade, too, 'round and 'round the block and
the public park, where music often plays in the Mexican fashion.

Directly across the border is Nuevo Laredo — New Laredo,
though it seems centuries more ancient than the American town.
Money-exchanges, curious shops with the shoddiest handicrafts,

chromium bars with American names and drinks, give the main street a certain kinship with Niagara Falls. But though many Mexicans live on the United States side of the line, very few Americans live on the Mexican side. They merely pass through as tourists or they visit the rowdy dance saloons. On the Mexican side, therefore, there is far less blending of the two worlds. The town stubbornly follows its own ancient pattern. It is mongrel, unattractive, but it is intrinsically Mexican, far less influenced by American ways than Laredo is by Mexican ways.

It is low, dusty, full of adobe and thatched dwellings. The sanitation is bad. Only the main street is paved for a few blocks. The others are cobblestoned or else just ruts and mud. The tempo of Nuevo Laredo is wholly leisurely and careless, and its folk are ironical of the bustle and haste on the northern side of the river.

3

Just as the two cultures and the people flow over and beyond the arbitrary boundary posts, so does the vegetation. The same cactus and chaparral and mesquite of southern Texas flow on across the dusty miles of northern México, right alongside the straight level surface of the modern Pan-American highway, alongside the route that General Taylor followed and where Villa galloped and Pershing marched. The sparse jagged vegetation stretches on and on across almost trackless wastes to distant purple hills, sharply cut against the sky and often fantastically wind-eroded.

One may cross the border at many points, and if one were to miss the boundary posts and barbed wire, it would be impossible to say where one country ends and the other begins, for north-western México is similarly an extension of Arizona, with the same multicolored buttes sticking out of the sands like inflamed pimples, the same brilliant cactus flowers, the same ribbed stalks of the *palo blanco*. And yet, as one advances still farther south, both mountains and vegetation become harsher, more spiny. The deserts, the mountains, the jagged growths, seem knotted in eternal travail. Nearly everywhere, the mountains are volcanic, with sharp profiles, mostly without enough vegetation properly to hide their bony nakedness. There is ever a cruel quality to the Mexican landscape: twisted rock, saw-tooth crags, jagged points. There is no peace on the Mexican horizon.

This uncouth, untamed quality of the panorama features most of México, but as the traveler proceeds south and higher, the valleys become more fertile and gentle. In the crisscross of mountains, drawing closer together near México City, are verdant oases, where corn and other farm plants leap swiftly into full maturity, stimulated by the violet rays of the more rarefied southern atmosphere. And finally, as one reaches Michoacán to the southwest, in some places the hills, for at least part of the year, roll green and easy as in parts of Pennsylvania. But off to the southeast, about the Mixtec and Oaxacan plateaus, the landscape, save for a few green valleys, is again harsh and cruel and dusty. The growths are curt and spiny. The yuca and pitahaya and organ cactus, growing out of bare rocky slopes, give hill and mountain a rough pincushion appearance, brighter only in the short rainy season with the multicolored gloss of blue and yellow flowers and crimson fruit.

The more the traveler gets away from the American frontier, the more he encounters the authentic indigenous México, less hybrid, more conscious of its own independent destiny. The bulk of the country's population lives on the highlands in the south central portion; in the highlands, too, are the largest cities: México; Monterrey, the steel and iron city; Guadalajara, the garden city; Puebla, the pious city.

Monterrey, only a few hundred miles south of the border, is a disjointed frowsy industrialized place, mostly sordid and ugly. The old seems utterly frayed, and the new seems never to have quite integrated the community into a satisfactory pattern. Many worlds have been laid on there: Indian and Spanish; revolutionary, capitalistic, and proletarian; Mexican and American — but no fire seems to have fused them into one texture. None seems to have grown organically out of the other. They merely butt up against each other. They jangle; cultures jostle. It is as if those numerous layers of many epochs and peoples were waiting for some fiery cataclysm to shape them into granite or treasure.

San Luis Potosí, farther south, for all its dilapidation and numerous scars of the long revolution, is more faithfully Mexican, closer to its hinterland. This is also true of beautiful Guanajuato, though many of its once flourishing silver mines are closed.

Each mile southward, the climate, too, becomes more one texture. The extremes of heat and cold of Texas give way to an eternal spring, the sort of climate California thinks it has. The year is divided, not according to our seasons, but into the rainy and the dry periods of the year, the winter months being dry. The climate in such places as Cuernavaca and Oaxaca, though they lie over the edge in the tropic zone, are more temperate than the temperate zone itself. México City boasts of more than three hundred clear mornings a year. And with the thin quivering air, the glorious wash of sun, the quick glints in the sky, no other place in the world that I know of has mornings so uniformly zestful or so hauntingly beautiful.

In such cities as Guadalajara, Cuautla, Cuernavaca, Oaxaca, and Uruapam, all in the 4000- to 5000-foot level, the range of temperature from day to night is very slight. In Cuernavaca, the yearly variation is only about fifteen degrees. Curiously in those places, especially in Uruapam, one encounters also a cross-section of the fauna and flora of the whole country. There it is not too hot entirely to discourage most growth of the cold mountains, the *tierra fría*; there it is never too cold to discourage most jungle growths. Temperate-climate growths, when transplanted to such spots from more northerly climates, sometimes reveal strange exuberance. I have seen morning-glories turn into small trees. And something of the same exuberance is apt to seize hold of the transplanted human. But other growths sometimes degenerate, and that too happens to outsiders 'going native.'

México has many climates from hot to cold, from that of the dense jungle to pine-clad forests and snowy peaks, and as many different folk. It is correspondingly a country of multiple regionalisms; and love of the *patria chica*, the small fatherland, is strong, so that history has been marked with frequent separatist movements as in Spain and Russia, making it a difficult country to govern. But basically it is the most integrated expression of the highland-tropical culture, the Indian-mestizo culture, in all

Latin America. In theory, at least, México is the most socially advanced nation of the New World.

In Perú, another highland-tropical region, the true development and meaning of its culture have been concealed, its normal growth retarded, by the false rule of the white Creole minority on the coast; but México City is situated, as it always was, in the very heart of the country, in the very center of the plateau country, and over the years more and more has been enfolded into the heartland to become less a city of conquest and more an expression of the country as a whole. One can grasp this in part by trying to imagine the healthy American invigoration that would be given to a Washington transplanted to Kansas.

Thus the Mexican capital, for all its cosmopolitan savor and international influences, is intrinsically a Mexican metropolis. Lima is not truly Peruvian but primarily a colonial and European city. It wears more the air of old colonial México and modern dollar-dominated Havana, double symbol of alien conquest — impressive, artificial, Baroque, overadorned, and without roots. But México City has always been completely exposed to the various cultures, racial expressions, and deep economic and racial currents of the land. México City is rooted in the country and in the nation as are few capitals of the world, certainly much more so than the bureaucratic monstrosity that is Washington.

In Lima one sees only European dress. In México City, though so cosmopolitan and modern, native dress brushes the sleeve of tuxedo and dinner gown. Native sandals swish along the sidewalks; whereas in Perú, they are heard only in the highland villages. In México City, the thatched hut leans against the millionaire's palace. The burros come to market alongside of modern trucks, with airplanes flying overhead.

Despite its lofty situation, México City, with its long siesta and late shopping hours, has a tropical rhythm. And during the wet seasons, the afternoon thunderstorm is a tropical downpour. Although the city does not have, for instance, the continuous deluges of Tabasco, which is a jungle state, nevertheless the tropics touch the highland realm with their languor and grace, like a fevered kiss. The mornings break clear and crisp with limpid skies; the day grows warmer toward noon, and finally after lunch, often during the drowsy siesta hours, the driving thunder-shower breaks fiercely against flat roof and calcimined wall, dancing on the pavements with a swirl of white petticoat spray. The storm clears, a delicate green band stretches along the horizon mountains, and the late sun shoots rose and heliotrope shades into the lingering clouds of a world a bit damp and chill but exhilaratingly fresh and clean.

This afternoon shower is accompanied by a swift drop in temperature, which is a shock even to the habituated organism. It produces marked psychological reactions: a sudden melancholy, and moodiness, a brooding period of quiet memories and expectancy; then, as the skies clear, and the air is left fresh and zestful, never heavy and humid as with New England or mid-Western thunderstorms, the spirit also soars. It is as though each person suddenly felt the effect of all sorts of concentrated vitamins, and the whole city moves out of its lassitude and steps grow quicker and smiles come easier.

The highland world of México, like that of Arequipa or Huánuco in Perú, is an Indian-mestizo world *par excellence*. The altitude in México is not such as to impose the rigid discipline of the loftier Andean highlands, where failure to observe regulations means disaster and death. If the altitude of México's central plateau at times provokes lassitude, it also provides nervous stimulation; and the struggle for existence is not sufficiently severe to impose the ruthless standardization of the Quechua highlands; rather, there is time for leisure, time for play, for art, for revolution. The lassitude imposes brooding and introspection; the Mexican is one of the most sensitive of the Latin-American peoples, with a touchy and often false pride; but along with this introspection, the body gradually gathers force and exhilaration so that the rhythm of highland México is a shuttle from calm acceptance and great repose to spurts of energy and achievement. As a result, the application of energies has less continuity and purposefulness than our own steadier efforts. The Mexican thereby is less chained to habit; he lives more by impulse, is more spontaneous; not the same emotional urge as had the original Spaniard, but something re-compounded of the new environment, the mixing of blood streams and divergent institutions. Just as his country represents a violent extreme of lowlands and highlands, so the Mexican's temperament represents a fusion of great extremes that sometimes shatters into its original components — highland placidity and tropical exuberance, an Indian stoicism and preciseness overlaid with Spanish liveliness and grandiloquence.

4

The Mexican synthesis has its symbol in the eagle with a serpent in its mouth and perched on a cactus, the divine sign which was to indicate to the Aztec nomads, and did so in 1325, the place in the Anahuac Valley to found their great city — Tenochtitlán, the mother of the later Spanish settlement and of modern México City.

Waldo Frank has caught the full meaning of this symbolism. The winged serpent was represented in the native pantheon by Quetzalcoatl, the white god of the wind, of music, joy, and justice — and of thieves. He was the supreme theistic expression of a land of sun. The eagle from the older highlands represented the spirit of death, down from the ice and fire of the crater, the spirit also of conquest. The serpent was fecund, supple, a symbol of life itself in all its multiple forms. Where the eagle devours the serpent — that was the middle ground, the meeting of cosmic forces in full embrace, life and death at the dividing line, the full maturity in the repeated cycle of birth and decay. There where conquest feeds on the vitals of fecundity, there was the rich and fertile highland; there Aztec culture should flourish. And that it might flourish, there was the nopal, the cactus, spined, hostile, but of the earth, and providing multiple needs for a roving people, and a people soon to become settled and strong. This plant and its first cousin, the maguey, were sufficient almost in themselves for the creation of a great civilization. Fruit and leaves could be eaten; the leaves entire served as thatch for wall and roof, or could be distilled for beverages of great potency; the membranes could be peeled off for fine papyrus, and the fibers could be woven into clothing and bags, twisted into ropes; the spines provided needles and pins and surgical instruments for sacrificial bloodletting; the honey juice could make pulque and cured diseases, kept the prostate gland healthy. An insect parasite on the leaves provided dye for cloth and ink for writing; and the white grubs under the leaves furnished a prized food, still eaten and served in the most expensive bars as a rare delicacy. Corn and chile provided the constant base for the native diet, but the nopal, and especially the maguey, became the very pivot of the early civilization, as important as were the *llama* and the potato to the Peruvian highland indigenes. The two Mexican plants were celebrated in song and legend and held sacred as objects of worship.

The Spanish in conquering México broke all native cohesion into fragments. For the Spaniards, the Mexican highlands were the great illusion. More than any other New World country, in coloring, climate and structure, the semiaridity, the clear pulsing air, the sharp sun and shade, all the physiographic characteristics, reminded the Spaniard of his Castilla, his Andalucía, his Extremadura. He named it fondly, 'New Spain.' He overran it far more than he ever did Perú. He felt more at home, and was not baffled as he was by the sterner uplands of the Andes. He worked more mightily in México, built more temples, converted more natives, worked more mines, founded more cities, established more numerous estates. More at home there he became more fused with land and people, and, except perhaps in Chile, interbred more with the native. The result was a quicker unfolding than perhaps anywhere else of a truly mestizan culture. The conflicting problems rushed to a swifter, more violent and dramatic climax. México is today as close to a creative national synthesis and true unfolding of its personality as any other country in Latin America, even though it still remains by far the most complicated of any of the southern lands.

And so, the great Mexican highlands, that vast upland table of plain and harsh volcanic mountains, all sheathed by low tropical coasts, and dropping off into warm acres of sugar-cane, coffee, tobacco, and fruit orchards, is a region set apart in a magnificent setting. It is a realm close to the sky, a paradise of the gods and of strong men and of great deeds. Its mighty acres of corn, its crisscrossed maguey fields, its light fluffy clouds in clear blazing skies — all provide it with a peculiar and beautiful aesthetic unmistakably individualized. Now — with its fusion of old Spanish culture and individualism with the old Indian communalism, and both worked into a new collective norm and driven to new goals by the machine and the pace of the modern world — the culture of the Mexican highlands stands on the threshold of a great new awakening. There has been occurring one of the most interesting social and national experiments to be found anywhere in the world today.

CHAPTER IV

Rainbow Plateau

THE Isthmus of Tehuantepec linking the two oceans is slung like a hammock between the Mexican and Chiapas plateaus. It has the rhythm of the hammock. People rest and sleep and make love in hammocks. The dead are laid to eternal sleep in hammocks. The bellies of the women are like hammocks. Around their heads they wear a fan of stiff lace, like the raised tail of a peacock, but white; about the bottom of their skirts are folds upon folds of stiff lace. Between full blouse and full skirt is the hammock of exposed skin.

It is a matriarchate. The women, with swinging stride, dominate the landscape with their bright colors and their vigor. They weave the fine fabrics, they sell in the market, they command the family exchequer. They rule the Isthmus, although pretending to conform to the legend of male superiority. The men are drones, hammock dawdlers, washed out, not much good.

The Isthmus has long been on the crossroads of trade and war. At one time it was one of the main transit points for gold-rushers on their way to California. Before the Panamá Canal was built, the Isthmus was the scene of great international intrigues. Both England and the United States resorted to many greedy ruses to get possession of it. British capital then planted itself there and ruled, until, with the revolution and the general decline of the empire, the British investments went with the wind. The onetime possessions of the great Lord Cowdray have nearly all been absorbed by México itself.

It is strange that, with all the commotion that has arisen from time to time at Tehuantepec — ever since the marches of Cortés and Alvarado and the China trade, the repeated flow of outsiders into and through the place — the folk there have kept so closely to their own ways and habits and dress and food, their own dances and their own music.

2

South from Tehuantepec stretches the forlorn drouth-stricken coast of Chiapas, but directly behind it, the plateau rises again — sharply. There in the highland towns of Tuxtla, San Cristóbal, Chiapa, Comitán, old Spain lives again, in stately remote isolation, slothfully decomposing, lulled to lassitude by the soft persistent intrusion of Indian-mestizo life, until one day the brittle memory of Spain will break as the hands of a wholly new life choke it off entirely. More dominant and vital are the native life and handicrafts, in color and design akin to those of Guatemala, for here really begin the Central American highlands, another mestizo-Indian region.

The plateau stretches straight on to the beautiful Indian cities of Huehuetenango and Quezaltenango, high above the sea, places of eternal spring, places of a thousand handicrafts and of itinerant marimba players. It is one of the major regions of Guatemala — Los Altos. It is the most integrated portion, socially, of Guatemala, for there the old Indian life still asserts its vitality, lives and breathes, and keeps on creating its own beauty in a world elsewhere grown mechanized and commercialized. From there come the new militant rulers of Guatemala — down from the heights upon bureaucratic Guatemala City, periodically, to cleanse the Augean stables and litter them with new political filth as the old ways of the highlands are forgotten in the lassitude of lower regions.

Below Los Altos are the feudal baron coffee *fincas* and the rolling green foothills. Behind it are the deep festering chicle jungles of Petén. To the Atlantic side are the lush tropical regions of Baron Banana.

The plateau stretches on through the inland portions of Salvador, Honduras, Nicaragua, and Costa Rica. As it comes closer to the Equator, it grows lower and hence also comes closer to the

true tropics. Denser jungles stretch along the coasts; deep croco-
dile rivers flow slowly to the sea. The lowlands are festering hot,
but above them the plateau is warm springtime, without winter,
without summer. There, too, dry and rainy seasons divide the
year. The rain comes down briefly in torrents far heavier than
in México City. The older streets of Guatemala City are small
cobbled river beds, the gutter running down the center. For a
few hours the streets are sometimes brimming full. Swinging
footbridges, pivoted on a center pier, make it possible to get
across.

It is a region of natural violence, a region of earthquakes and
eruptions. Three times the various capitals of Guatemala have
been almost completely destroyed. Just over the hills from Guatemala City is the half-ruined metropolis of Antigua, with old
broken walls, cracked churches, and shattered towers. The new
life flows in and around the old remains.

A railroad now connects Guatemala with Salvador, the only
international road in Central America, but it is a long way around.
The shortest route to the next-door country is a hair-turn automobile road from Guatemala City over the mountains to Santa
Ana, from which a railroad line runs on into San Salvador.

When I made my first trip over this route, a big sign at the
border read: 'The state of a nation's culture is revealed by the
condition of its roads.' Whereupon we hit one of the worst-rutted
roads in Christendom. But today Salvador has the best roads in
all Central America, and a broad paved highway leads in from
the very border.

The train from Santa Ana, a place of mansions of coffee-plan-
tation owners, and of shockingly poverty-stricken Indians, skirts
a lava flow so closely that nearly every year, in that land of
eternal quakes and eruptions, parts of the track have to be relaid.

San Salvador, the capital, is a neat, well-paved little city, one
of the most modern and bustling of all mid-America. It is dominated by its old churches and the medieval barracks.

The plateau sweeps on to Honduras, but the traveler must
follow the coast, by rail to La Unión on the great harbor of
Fonseca Bay, ringed by giant volcanoes. A launch carries one to
the customs island — Amapala — then through a twisting man·

grove channel to the yellow-fever pest-hole of San Lorenzo, where the wise man does not linger overnight in the dirt-floored mud-walled rooms that serve as a hotel, but hastens to go by car back up to the plateau to the healthy mountain-perched Tegucigalpa. It stands in a valley of fireflies, on a slanting slope, like an em-battled fortress. Its cobbled narrow streets tip up and down hill.

To the north, a winding road climbs up and up, then drops fast, down to the broad Comayagua Valley, still part of the plateau, and finally to beautiful Lake Yohoa. This lake again marks the break to lower country. Its high southern mountain-banks are clad with pines, dense forests of temperate-zone ever-greens; below it, toward hot San Pedro Sula, stretches jungle country, and the jolting train leads straight into the banana kingdom again.

Mountainous Nicaragua, in the parts across from Danlí, is definitely an Indian land, still the haunt of people known for their fierceness, independence, and resistance. In older times the belli-cose Indians of northern Nicaragua wiped out expedition after expedition of invading Spaniards. They were wont to cut off the penises of their slain enemies and put the dissevered member in the mouth of the victim, for this symbolized the destruction of enemy virility; it was their primitive V for victory, apparently far removed from our modern boy-scoutism, yet obeying similar instincts.

There in the same locale, Agustus César Sandino fought the American Marines and was never subdued. Many of his men were of the same fierce breed as those who fought earlier subju-gation by the Spaniards, and Marines who fell in battle and whose bodies were not immediately recovered were sometimes treated in the ancient symbolic manner.

The population of the rest of the country shades from the white stock of the Pacific coast to the black workers of the Atlantic banana regions.

In southern Nicaragua, the plateau runs out again, leaving another gap from ocean to ocean. All day is required for the little inland steamer to cross Lake Nicaragua, from port to port, to discharge and take on passengers, to load sugar and coffee and beans. The vessel swings under the tall volcano of Ometepe

Island, a cone that looks just like Fujiyama, with swift rising slopes, minus snow. Glacial scratches have been traced ages ago on the stone face of that mountain, as E. G. Squier, that amazing exploring American consul, discovered more than a century ago.

The little steamer swings into the flat-roofed port of Rivas, where, in plain sight of the pier, men bathe on one side, women on the other, without benefit of bathing suit. The poor things have never had a Texas congressman to advise them that they are immoral.

Here, a low range of hills is all that divides the lake from the Pacific, hills that may some day be pierced by the engineers of a second canal route.

At regular intervals on either of the lake shores rise, tier on tier, little thatched-roof towns, amid glistening luxuriant vegetation. The leaves are polished every morning by fresh showers. At San Carlos, the southeasternmost town of the lake, the waters drain off through San Juan River to the Atlantic.

Save for a stretch of swift rocky rapids, the river flows fairly deep and slow, between matted jungle walls. Here and there are little landings where bananas, cattle, hogs are taken on by the river craft.

Beyond El Castillo, a town on a ledge above the river, the mountains come close and the stream tumbles through a narrow gap, then flows on to its delta at Greytown, where Chinamen fish for sharks.

The plateau slopes up again on the Costa Rican side, beyond the short southern tributaries of the river. But never again does it rise so high. Most of Costa Rica is low enough to be good coffee country, and presently the highlands melt away into the deadly jungles of Panamá, to the third link between the two oceans, the Canal Zone, healthiest spot on earth; and to Darién, the malarial pest-hole of the world.

3

Central America is Latin America in microcosm, and repeats the general racial pattern of the whole southern world. México is Indian and mestizo. The Caribbean is heavily negro; Brazil is a hodgepodge of European, Indian, and negro; Argentina is mostly white European.

In Central America the racial zoning is somewhat similar. Indian-mestizo Guatemala stands at the north. In the center is the mulatto-zambo country of Honduras. To the south is Costa Rica, mostly white European.

But throughout most of Central America the highlands are Indian and mestizan. It is their type of country *par excellence*. They are a part of a great highland culture that starts at the Río Grande and sweeps down to Panamá; part of the similar culture that stretches south through the higher levels of Ecuador, Perú, and Bolivia. It is all temperate-zone country because of the altitude, but conditioned, culturally and economically, by the tropical shore jungles. Its population of mixed blood stands in contrast to the white oases in larger centers and the negro populations of the hot banana lands and the Amazón coast.

Two great forces converge on the men and women of Middle America, as they do on all peoples: tradition and environment. Tradition in this area is chiefly a composite of native and Spanish modes of life, never yet successfully fused and integrated; although this integration is slowly evolving through the emergence of the mestizo as the dominant ruler of the region, the type best adapted to the conditioning environment, the climate, the clash of races and cultures.

CHAPTER V

México Eats Corn

CORNFLAKES can be bought all the way from Eastport, Maine, to San Diego, California. In México, another corn product — the flat unsalted pancake, the tortilla — can be obtained all the way from Encinada, in Lower California, to far southeastern Quintana Roo.

Maize, or Indian corn, from prehistoric times was long the principal New World staff of life. Domesticated from a wild plant, probably thousands of years ago on the Colombian plateau, it was soon widely diffused over the two continents and provided the basic foodstuff for most of the aboriginal population of the Americas, except in Perú, where the potato was early domesticated and became the great mainstay. But even in Perú, corn in the well-stocked Inca granaries served as a source of food for some years for the conquering Spaniards.

Corn also saved many an early American colonist from starvation. John Winthrop, Jr., of New England, soon after the first settlements there, told how it was for a long time the mainstay of the early English planters, and he wrote of its multiple uses.

> The natives call it weachin, and in some southern parts of America 'tis known by the name of maiis or maize. The ear is a span long, composed of eight rows of grain, or more, according to the goodness of the ground, about thirty grains in a row; 'tis of various colors, as red, white, yellow, blue, olive, greenish, black, speckled, striped, etc. . . .; 'tis jointed like cane, is full of sweet juice like the sugar cane, and a syrup as sweet as sugar may be made out of it. . . .

Shades of Karo!

Today, the billion and a half to three billion bushels that we grow in this country constitute our most valuable single crop, worth more than cotton or wheat or tobacco. Most of the output we use ourselves, for food, for fattening hogs, for alcohol, for plastics, for various other industrial purposes; little is exported. But large as corn bulks in our own national economy as a food supply, it bulks far larger in most Latin-American countries. Ours is fundamentally a wheat culture; but corn is still the basic diet of perhaps seventy million people in the New World. For them corn is King. It is life. Corn is as potent a determinant in the lives of those millions of Latin Americans as a few years ago the Ford car was for North American life. By their staff of life, ye shall know them: we and Europe, the wheat-eaters; the Orient, the rice-eaters; the Indian mestizos, the corn-eaters.

The Latin-American peoples call us a regimented, materialistic folk. It seems fair to note, however, that the bulk of México's population has been regimented for untold centuries to a pitifully inadequate diet of corn. It may, in good times, be supplemented with chili for proper vitamins, beans, or occasionally meat, and in the upland plateau with pulque, also rich in vitamins; but the backbone of the diet is corn. So much so that, though México is one of the world's important corn-producing countries, for many generations it has been obliged to import corn. Except in the large centers, efforts to alter or vary greatly the historic diet of the Mexican people have mostly failed. Once I talked with the village priest in far southern Maltinaltepec, a little Tlapaneca settlement on a river ledge, who had tried to convert the natives to the planting and use of barley, rye, buckwheat, and other cereals, but ingrained customs defeated his efforts. 'They and México simply haven't enough fertile acreage to grow sufficient corn,' he told me, 'and we can never be a strong people till we turn to more economical cereals.' The enslavement to a single foodstuff has meant a type of regimentation close to the poverty line; it has meant periods of near famine and economic disturbance; it has narrowed the margin of national independence.

Many factors have been cited to explain the periodic instability of México politics. But corn, not the conflict with foreign capital, or Fascism and the Fifth Column, or the hostility of the

Ch\ .., or military revolt *per se*, has been the real rock upon which stable governments have rested. When corn has been scarce and costly, governments have fallen; when corn is plentiful and cheap, Mexican politics are more apt to flow smoothly. The corn problem lies at the very root of Mexican life and habits.

During my frequent long horseback trips into the wilder interior of México, no sound has ever fallen on my ears with more pleasure than when, on riding into an Indian village at nightfall, I have heard the pat-a-pat-pat of tortillas in the making within the hatched huts. The patting of the dough in the hands to make the flat cake is a very gleeful sound, as of a joyous folk making merry. When it is heard in the villages, it means that bellies, if not full, are not denied food, that people are happy, that life is reasonably secure. Then the visitor is generously fed. When that sound is absent, the village immediately takes on a dour appearance, the outsider is greeted with hostile glances, and every bite is begrudged.

2

So closely and so long has the life of the people been linked with this elementary product that many of the old legends concern corn and miracles relating to corn. One legend tells that the first man was created from a kernel of corn. Another tells how the stars grew from corn sowed in the heavens by a happy god. Many of the native tribes had a god or goddess of corn or both. The first shoots of tender corn were always proffered to the gods, and still are; for, after the coming of Christianity, they were then laid on the altars of the Church with the same reverence. The white man's saint was often merely a disguise for the old deities, the ones able to make corn grow bountifully.

In many parts of México, I have witnessed elaborate corn fiestas — long processions of men in white 'pajamas' and women in blue scarves, *rebozos*, all dancing to music and carrying multi-colored baskets with the first shoots of spring corn. Later in the season, the first scarcely formed buds are similarly laid before this or that saint in the village chapel. Frequently special crosses are made out of cornstalks, interlaced with the orange *zempa-*

suchitl flower, a blossom frequently mentioned by the old chronicler Sahagún as sacred in nearly all pre-Spanish religious rites, and still quite as sacred in the modern Church fiestas. And so from Cuzco in the Andes to Tepoztlán in the Mexican Sierra Madre, the corn plant provides motifs for prehistoric and modern sculpturing and pottery and for post-Conquest church reliefs.

A great deal of the time and labor of the women is taken up with the backbreaking work of preparing corn tortillas. The kernels are soaked overnight in lye-water to remove the tough outer husk, then the corn is ground on a *metate*, made of a black porous volcanic stone, artificially shaped with three legs, the two in front very short, so that it provides a sloping, slightly concave grinding surface. Another stone, in the shape of a rolling-pin, is used to crush the corn. The meal must be ground to a consistency as smooth as pâté de foie gras, so that not the slightest coarseness is perceptible to the touch. This task requires from two to three hours for each meal. Many years ago, the brilliant Mexican writer, Francisco Bulnes, pointed out the anti-social character of this labor and its enslavement of Mexican women. He estimated, if I recall rightly, that the work of one American woman in a modern textile factory was roughly the equivalent in the value of the goods produced of some thirty thousand Mexican women chained to the primitive grinding stone.

Simple grinding machines, run by an electric motor, could do in a few seconds what now requires hours of body-breaking labor. In cities and many towns such machines have been introduced and are generally used, though the husbands sulkily lament that the tortilla does not taste so good. Probably not; it is cleaner, less salted with human sweat.

After the corn is ground, a small ball of dough — without salt or other condiment — is pressed and patted between the hands until it is perfectly round and paper-thin. The patting is done in a rotary fashion; a special dexterity is required. I have tried many times to pat out tortillas, but my results have always been laughable.

The flat cake is flung on the *comal*, a flat tin, and is best if served piping hot. The taste for tortillas stays with one for years, and a chief drawback I find to living in the United States is that I can so rarely get good freshly cooked tortillas.

Stale tortillas are utilized by the good housewife in many ways. They are cut into strips and used as noodles in soup; or they are toasted to make *tortas*, on which are spread chile or a bit of meat, or beans, sliced radishes, onions, and lettuce. A tortilla, smeared with chile or sprinkled with shredded meat and rolled up, is called a *taco*. In many poor rural communities of México, for months on end, the only food is often the tortilla smeared thick with hot chile.

Ground corn, boiled with milk, sugar, and salt, makes the gruel known as *atole*, which is considered very sustaining and especially good for convalescents. This is much like the 'samp' of our early New England colonists, a concoction described by Winthrop, Jr., as 'a very pleasant wholesome diet; this was the most usual diet of the first planters, and is still in use among them, as well in fevers as in health.' The Mexican frequently flavors his *atole* with chocolate, cinnamon, cloves, vanilla, or other ingredients.

When on extended trips through thinly inhabited regions, the native Mexican toasts corn, grinds it fine, and carries the meal in a little leather bag. From this he draws his sole sustenance for many days, often for weeks. Merely by adding water, he makes *pinol*, on which he can live indefinitely and perform the severest physical labor. I once traveled several days with an Indian mail-carrier, from a mining town in the high sierras over the lofty ridges to Tepehuanes in Durango. Most of the way we had nothing to eat but *pinol*. Under other names, it is known throughout the indigenous cultures of the entire New World. The Quechuas of the Peruvian Andes call it *máchica*, although usually they add cinnamon, sugar, and a pinch of quicklime. *Pinol* is little different from the preparation used by our early New England settlers, known as 'nocake.'

All these ingrained dietary habits, dependent upon corn, in existence long before the arrival of the Spaniards four centuries ago, today present a real problem in the national life of México. They definitely complicate agrarian and other economic and political problems.

3

After the 1911 revolution, for the first time in four centuries, México attempted to found its nationality upon native traditions, needs, and methods. With the downfall of Porfirio Díaz in that year, México definitely turned her back upon Europe and its culture to promote a species of neo-Aztecism. It set positively to work to cultivate its own backyard in a spirit of independence and extreme nationalism, almost Boxer in spirit. The foreigner, from that day to this, has been distrusted, often hated.

The long revolution was in good part a reaction against giving away more of the wealth of the country to the outsider. Among the recent highlights of this prolonged attitude were the oil seizures. The revolution became an effort to retrieve land, minerals, and other resources that had fallen into alien hands. Today ninety per cent of the employees of foreign companies must be Mexican. No outside technician can be imported if a Mexican can do the work. Capital export taxes have sought to suck away part of the outflow of profits on foreign investments. Royalties on exported raw materials constantly increase. Strict immigration laws, as tight as those of the United States or the Soviet Union, have been set up.

With outside immigration all but cut off, México must auto-populate itself, and this means automatically increasing emphasis upon Indian blood and culture. Even without these stringent barriers, for a century México more and more had been growing darker in pigment. The number of Whites as well as the percentage of Whites has steadily declined. The last census gave the percentage as but fifteen, and this is undoubtedly a great exaggeration. If the percentage of pure-blooded Indians during the past century has also declined (now about thirty-five per cent), nevertheless in actual numbers they have increased, and the majority of those of mixed blood are more Indian in customs and psychology than White.

With the stoppage of nearly all fresh blood from Europe, the process of mixing, or mestization, among the population is reduced largely to that between those already of mixed blood and the Indians. Thus the Indian quotient in the mixture inevitably must increase until the White contribution to the blood stream is largely reduced. In other words, México has definitely tried to found its new revolutionary structure and present-day life on the Indian, the peasant, the new proletariat, the previously oppressed lower classes, the new mestizo middle class.

This determination to found the nation on the people, the masses — so backward, poverty-stricken, and long so cruelly exploited — has been a herculean task. It is, of course, the only way that México can truly achieve its national destiny, but the effort has created many startling problems.

Not the least of these is linguistic. In the United States, when one buys cornflakes, the storekeeper may use a Yankee nasal tone, a Southern drawl, or Western breezy slang, but the language is everywhere English, though Johnny Bulls might dispute the statement. But in México, if one crosses its entirety in search of tortillas, one will have to ask for them in a dozen different languages and some sixty dialects. Quite some millions of folk still speak native tongues and do not even understand Spanish. More millions are bilingual. In some places in Guerrero and Oaxaca, where a number of native groups have been telescoped together, I have known towns where the people actually speak four languages. All this increases the problem of diffusing a common national culture and of maintaining political unity and stability.

Another immediate problem resulting from the government's effort to base its strength on native rather than foreign precedents resides in the fact that any oppressed group, especially an oppressed racial group, is stubborn against change. The more such a group has been persecuted, the more it clings to traditional mores. This has happened with the Indians of México. Four centuries of oppression have not sufficed to 'civilize' them. They have fought with all the desperation of a conquered people to maintain their group traditions. Some of those traditions are of doubtful value, especially where they conflict with the findings of modern science and sanitation and food requirements, but many others are far more admirable than some we presumptuously call 'civilized,' and much of the revolution has been merely a projection of this old undying loyalty to racial habits and thought, the old Rabbi Ben Ezra story: 'Earth changes, but thy soul and God stand sure.... Potter and clay endure.'

It has, in fact, been a potter-and-clay economy, and the corn diet has been part of that tradition. Being universally eaters of corn, the Mexican peasants are desirous, above all else, of growing corn and very few other products. With corn and a little chile gathered wild in the forests they can survive in elementary independence. Corn therefore is their social security, their insurance against the worst disasters. But this belly-clinging to life complicates the economic headaches of the authorities.

First of all, the peasants, plus all the large estates, can't grow enough corn for proper survival. Neither the peasants nor the country as a whole have enough available acreage to provide an adequate diet if corn is to be the basis. Except in limited localities, México is not properly a corn-growing country at all.

For arable land is definitely limited. Much of the country requires irrigation (much has been done of late years) or expert dry farming. The places that corn grows best are usually more suitable for other products. If in certain regions, two or even three crops of corn can be harvested a year, and corn will grow higher than a rider on horseback, such land is usually better adapted to other more profitable sub-tropical crops, giving better yield, more valuable returns, crops hardier in the face of tropical insect scourges. Nor can México effectively compete with the rich corn-growing regions of the United States. It is true that in the United States our corn yield, owing to our careless waste of soil and reckless methods, has declined all during the century, and notably from 30.3 bushels to the acre in 1920 to only 16.5 bushels in 1936; nevertheless, given México's definite paucity of cultivable soil, the frequently non-level nature of the ground, and the pressing need for other crops, that country cannot compete advantageously beyond a certain point with the mass production by mechanized methods of the Mississippi Valley. México's real agricultural wealth resides in such sub-tropical crops as cotton, coffee, henequén, tobacco, rice, sugar-cane, fruits, rubber, etc.

This has meant that the enormous land acreage seized and being seized by the government and subdivided for the Indians usually reverts to corn cultivation regardless of how the land was previously used. In Yucatán I have seen expropriated henequén fields cut up and given to the Indians, and though the new owners were given facilities for the processing of sisal, they preferred to utilize this semi-arid land, with its indifferent soil properties, for growing very scrubby corn giving a low yield per hectare, and more frequently shriveling to nothing in the hot sun. Part of this obstinacy is due to long-standing habit, and part to the ingrained fear of the outsider who has always oppressed them or tricked them. To have grown henequén would immediately have put them at the mercy of officials, rarely honest, commission agents, and the gamble of world markets. They preferred to grow corn and be independent, even though this provided a mere subsistence.

A crop needs to do two things: provide for the happiness and prosperity of those producing it; secondly, promote the general social and national welfare. If this statement is a tremendous economic oversimplification, it is sufficiently true to indicate that the utilization of good henequén lands for corn-growing, with no relation to the outside market or the national needs, while it may provide a degree of self-satisfaction to the grower, does not necessarily promote his prosperity or the national welfare.

In human terms the matter is quite understandable. Thirty-odd years ago most Yucatán agricultural laborers were serfs; many actually worked with shackles on their legs, and if they tried to escape were hunted down with bloodhounds or armed posses. They were on the Georgia chain-gang level. Certainly the change to a status of a free man has been of immeasurable importance to them and to the nation. But that freedom needs to be a starting point, not a jumping-off place to old inadequate ways of doing things. As with our own negroes, the abolition of previous servitude was too often merely a jumping-off place.

By the time of the Cárdenas administration, about seven million souls had been lifted out of hacienda serfdom to become members of free villages, without, however, securing sufficient acreage, sufficient education, or sufficient technical knowledge properly to support themselves.

Under Cárdenas land distribution was speeded up. More

land was given out in thirty-odd months than during the previous eighteen years. In addition the Cárdenas government struggled to make each rural project truly self-sustaining, with the proper economic basis and with community needs properly guaranteed.

This could be done only in certain model control areas, for otherwise the cost would have been staggering. Elsewhere, most of the land, regardless of what it had produced before, was promptly seeded to corn; in other words, put upon the basis of meager subsistence farming. But whatever the drawbacks of the new system, a great social and agrarian revolution was effected in México, which completely changed the status of the rural worker from what it was in the time of Díaz. If in some places agriculture slid back technically, in others it went ahead. Whatever the outcome, perhaps the old inefficient hacienda unit had to be smashed in order that new life might grow in the country. In some cases the break-up of former large estates had the beneficial result of seeing large areas of former idle fertile lands cleared and brought under cultivation, new communities started, new frontiers opened up — as all through the Tlapaneca region in Guerrero.

But subsistence farming, corn farming, runs counter to many other aims of the Mexican New Deal and counter to sound national economy. The sudden reversal to subsistence farming (though the old feudal estate also attempted to be a self-sufficient unit) helped bridge over a very upsetting transitional period; it quieted down the country; gave occupation to hordes of demobilized soldiers and revolters. But this was just the beginning of the solution of a major problem, and it introduced many new problems.

For the revolution also greatly accelerated the process of urbanization, just as the Civil War did in our own country. In 1910 México City was still a small, semi-rural, sleepy community. Today, with its population of nearly two million, it is highly cosmopolitan. Other Mexican cities have also expanded. Cities require agricultural surpluses; they require diversified agriculture; they require the commercialization of agriculture — unless a country remains purely colonial, which México does not wish to do.

Corn is King in México, but in many spots his robes are shabby.

CHAPTER VI

The Great Turk

MÉXICO has had four great social upheavals. The first was the Spanish Conquest, which tore the native empire to pieces, and reduced the indigenous population to helots. The Spanish régime, firmly established a century before England colonized the Atlantic seaboard, endured for nearly three hundred years.

The second great revolution was the war for independence, a struggle lasting more than a decade. Eventually it turned into a counter-revolution in which the Creoles, or American-born Spaniards, established a rule featured by inefficiency and continuous disorders between the ins and outs, the Federalists and the Centralists. Creole rule was constantly menaced by the growing power of the mestizo and Indian groups, whom the Creoles utilized for their battles, and the mestizos ere long took over the rule of the country, by intermarriage, war, and cunning.

The third great social change was that of the Reformist wars, which first came to a head under Gómez Farías in the eighteen-thirties, and gathered full force with the victory of Benito Juárez in the fifties. Its success was sapped by foreign imperialism, first the joint English-Spanish-French invasion, which resulted in the French (secretly allied with the Papacy) seating Maximilian on the Mexican throne. The Reformation was further sidetracked by the invasion of British and American capital, which, from 1870 on, increasingly seized the resources and wealth of México. Most of the popular benefits of the Juárez revolution were lost, and the general trend was toward the establishment of a semi-bourgeois landed feudalism allied with foreign capital. By the end of the Díaz régime, most of the rural population of México had been driven into enforced serfdom — a cruel class and race subjugation, which had few of the ameliorative features which permitted Spanish rule to survive for so many centuries.

The fourth great upheaval ushered in a species of nationalistic socialism. It began with vague doctrines of the rights of man, deepened to a proletarian-agrarian revolt, sought to recover México's wealth, and ended up more nationalist than socialist. The forces engendered by the long struggle since 1910 are still operative in México, and the social changes are being carried on along a fluctuating line during the twilight period of México's present war participation.

The American State Department fought nationalistic socialism in México long before similar trends made their appearance in Russia, Italy, and Germany. Time and again American troops were massed along the border; Pershing led an expedition into México ostensibly to hunt Villa but in reality to coerce the Querétaro constitutional convention, already threatening the oil rights of large American companies; Marines were landed at Vera Cruz, where in a frenzy of sanitation they tossed the precious archives of the city on the flames, archives which had survived more than a century of previous war and revolution.

Not until the New Deal did the United States really make its peace with Mexican nationalistic socialism. The unpalatable doctrines and acts of the country to the south were condoned for the sake of the general continental good-neighbor policy, and perhaps because of the memory of Carranza's overt pro-German attitude during the First World War. The nationalistic socialism of México, except for its ideas, was never a menace to outside nations, never took the form of international aggression. It was restricted to internal reforms and aggression against foreign property-holders.

Certainly the revolution which began in 1910 — a strange paradoxical upheaval — has reshaped much of the life and thought of our neighboring country. Though its violent aspects have diminished, its ideas still march on, still influence the political leaders of the country. The trend toward Mexican socialism is likely to deepen still more during the dictatorial process of war.

2

The basic demands of the Mexican revolution, some of which evolved only after years of struggle, and many of which have been fulfilled with varying degrees of success, were effective suffrage (or political democracy), abolition of serfdom, land for the peasants, more education, the protection of labor and the raising of wage standards, national control of resources, increased opportunities for the Indians and for women, curtailment of Church privileges, improvement of irrigation and transportation, and the expansion of public works. It was featured by a Boxer-like hatred for foreigners and a general distrust of the United States. Whatever the general philosophy of the revolution, many of these aims, however unfortunate the methods, were highly idealistic and worthy, but until the time of Franklin D. Roosevelt, they were fought tooth and nail by the various Washington administrations, especially when Mexican acts ran foul of the property rights of powerful American companies.

The revolution was repeatedly infected with all the traditional evils of Mexican life, inherited from the days of the Spanish conquest; militarism, feudalism, ecclesiastical corruption, race and class conflict — all went into the blind swirl of events. During the civil strife, many long-standing vicious practices were merely more deeply intrenched to plague the country; but many others were destroyed. Whatever the contradictions, the failures, the hypocrisies, and the abuses, nation-shaking changes occurred, which have forever altered the face of the country.

Land has been widely distributed to the people. Often the immediate economic results were deplorable, but land distribution created new social relationships in contrast to the property-less condition of the rural population under Díaz and the previous system of debt-slavery and peonage. If some *hacendados* or big landowners of the earlier epoch were patriarchal and relatively kind, few were progressive. Most were abusive and backward, knowing little of modern farm techniques.

Whether the farming class as a whole has greatly improved its standard of living is doubtful, but it has become a freer class. Today the bulk of the rural population lives in free villages, which own community lands or *ejidos*. Peasants who still work on large estates cannot be held in debt-slavery and cannot be robbed at company stores, which are forbidden. Farm workers are protected by elaborate labor laws, are guaranteed proper medical care and education. Whatever the abuses in Mexican life — the robbery of the poor by the great, the officials and the military caste — the rural population now has a new status, a new dignity, and undoubtedly a better chance to move on to a better existence.

Also a labor code was written into the constitution to protect urban and factory workers.

A third great achievement was the general implantation of education, especially in rural districts. Schools might lack material equipment; teachers might lack experience; shady politics ever played a part. At one time on horseback I visited hundreds of remote mountain schools. With limited resources, the teachers were mostly imbued with the spirit of a great crusade. Ill-paid, living in difficult circumstances, often in the most primitive places, they poured their very souls into their undertaking. Under Díaz ninety per cent of the population was illiterate. Today at least sixty per cent can read and write, and the tradition of popular education is now too firmly rooted to be torn away.

A fourth important aspect of the era was the anti-foreign or Boxer attitude. Díaz had given the country over to foreign capital. This blocked the development of a strong native capitalist class; it gradually weakened the sovereignty of the country, especially in the days when dollar diplomacy made every penny invested abroad a citizen of the Stars and Stripes. All classes became bitterly imbued with hostility to the outsider. This had several important results: strenuous effort (1) to re-establish the political sovereignty of México, so greatly undermined by the Pershing and Vera Cruz expeditions and by the power of foreign companies; (2) to establish economic control over Mexican resources by Mexicans.

A fifth aspect of the revolution was to re-establish the somewhat faded precepts of the earlier Juárez revolution against the Church, to curtail its power, reinforce the provisions against ecclesiastical land-holding, and take away its near-monopoly of educational facilities.

3

All these and other demands precipitated a titanic struggle, and the personages who stepped forth on the stage were often picturesque, and usually powerful or capable. A few were men of great and unsullied ideals; more often they soon managed to subordinate such ideals to personal gain and personal ambitions.

The revolution was precipitated from general unrest by the mystic little Francisco Madero, son of a wealthy land-holding and mining family of northern México, which by 1910 was losing its shirt in competition with the Guggenheims. Francisco — 'Don Pancho' — was a vegetarian, spiritualist, and idealist, but scarcely practical enough to handle the upsurge of military chieftains, the growing disorders, or the machinations of American Ambassador Henry Wilson. The last was Madero's chief thorn in the flesh, and the Ambassador's meddling, as much as anything else, converted what might have been a facile peaceful transition into prolonged bloody upheaval.

Madero's program was simplicity itself: the rights of man and the abolition of dictatorship through the formula of 'effective suffrage and non-re-election' — in short, 'democracy.' His platform contained one vague reference to agrarian reform, and denounced the abusive treatment of the Yaqui Indians. The forces that rallied behind this queer little man overthrew the mighty Porfirio Díaz at a time when his eighty years could hardly bear the burden of the medals that weighted down both sides of his chest. Thereby Madero also overthrew the powerful clique of 'Científicos' who had been rifling the national treasury and either seizing the country's wealth by force and unjust laws, or taking their cut from foreigners whom they helped to gobble up the country.

Madero's reign was brief. As disorders grew, the bloody, brutal, drunk, but super-astute Indian, Victoriano Huerta, butchered his way to power, and with the cordial assistance of Henry Lane Wilson, was installed in the National Palace. Madero and the Vice-President were promptly assassinated, and Huerta clung to his high post with feline canniness.

In spite of general hatred of Huerta, the Mexican people

deeply resented Woodrow Wilson's meddling efforts to oust him when Huerta played ball with British capital at the expense of American capital. The Pershing expedition and the Vera Cruz occupation aroused Mexican fears and kindled intense patriotism and deep grudges against the United States. Huerta even gained some popularity by his staunch opposition to Yankee coercion. When Wilson massed troops on the border and ordered all American citizens to leave the country, offering to pay third-class fare to all those unable otherwise to leave, Huerta gleefully offered to ship them all out first-class, and kept his word with those who applied.

John Lind of Minnesota was sent down to iron things out. He was a great liberal, but he thought Mexicans a sneaky inferior crowd obligated by some recondite law of benign Providence to obey the slightest whim of the Washington authorities.

Lind never understood México. He was woefully ignorant of the titanic forces surging up. He had no comprehension of the country's cultural heritage or the real wishes of its people. He was a well-meaning, blunt-fingered man suddenly grown too important, and Huerta was politer to him by far than he should have been. Huerta was also adamant and ironical, and Lind went home in a big huff. No greater incompetent ever meddled abroad in the sublime destinies of nations.

4

The revolution moved on its relentless courses. The storm was blowing up. The untutored Zapata was fighting for land. The wild Pancho Villa was harrying the north. The white-bearded Carranza was riding a white horse austerely behind blue spectacles toward the capital. Generals Pablo González and Alvaro Obregón were swinging their armies toward the same goal. All were as angry at Wilson and Americans as they were at Huerta, the bloody dictator they were fighting.

For a time the barbarous Villa became Wilson's protégé. Villa hated Chinese and Spaniards and Americans. He hung Chinamen up by their queues. He slaughtered Spaniards in the plaza. He machine-gunned American miners. He raided an American town and killed Americans — except for inter-border Indian raids, the first outside invasion of American soil since the British burned the capitol in Washington.

Wilson's shift of ground, his decision to recognize Carranza, caused Villa to kill still more Americans. Carranza, if anything, was handicapped by American support, and to recover prestige sharply ordered the American Marines out of Vera Cruz. For Wilson to break with Carranza at this juncture was to confess still another blunder, so the Marines hot-footed it back to their ships. And so, all told, American meddling helped spill a river of blood across México. The red river might have flowed anyway, but we added beautifully to the general confusion without accomplishing anything except to cause the revolution to become more violently revolutionary at the cost of more American lives and property. Our government caused the people to become more intense in demanding the very things it feared they might demand.

Zapata, the agrarian rebel of the south, was making land-distribution a national issue. The labor unions of Vera Cruz became strong enough to write a whole protective labor code into the new constitution drawn up at Querétaro — while American troops were still on Mexican soil. The subsoil mineral wealth was made the property of the nation, and the long tussle over petroleum began. Madero had been merely a political reformer. The revolution was now striking out for far-reaching economic changes.

Stiff, white-bearded Carranza sat like granite in power. As a member of his staff, I had some contact with him. For a Mexican he was strangely cold, a severe, unbending man. He was heavy as a rock, a monolith of purpose. Perhaps he had a slight trace of Indian blood, certainly he was taciturn as an Indian. When he did speak, his words were ponderous, like stones carved out of the cliffs. He sat impassively behind his blue spectacles and ruled.

He shaped the constitutional and legal foundations of the whole revolutionary epoch. He initiated most of the tendencies which were to determine the course of México's life for several decades and more: land reform, petroleum rights, church reform, education. But he could never handle the military crowd. His choices were bad. He picked the sycophants and the grafters rather than the men of ability, of strong will and revolutionary purpose.

He was not a tactful man, and in the disorders of the times could not push any program far enough to please anybody. He initiated some land reform, but not enough to satisfy the aroused countryside. Zapata's rebel watch fires soon glowed on the hills outside México City itself, and though Carranza's General Pablo González finally tricked Zapata into ambush and killed him, the clamor for land was not stilled by that gross treachery. Pancho Villa rode once more in Chihuahua.

Carranza started some schools, and a flock of political vultures stole the funds. When the teachers struck for the pay they should have received, his police mowed them down with clubs and fire hose.

He did not enforce the labor code fast enough to please the *Casa del Obrero*, and soon found himself putting labor leaders in jail. The resultant disorders permitted the greedy militarists to thrive still more. They sucked the treasury dry putting down endless revolts they often abetted. In such a difficult situation Carranza stubbornly fought the American State Department on the oil question. Oil companies soon subsidized 'bandits' in revolt, such as Manuel Pelaez of Tamaulipas.

Deep as was the current hatred of the United States, the oil controversy was in itself not sufficient to restore Carranza's popularity, and when he broke with the main backers who had put him into power, he was done for. His most serious rupture was with Alvaro Obregón, who had already proven himself the ablest general of the whole revolutionary period.

5

Obregón was as genial as Carranza was hermetic. He would have been a great military strategist and tactician in any country. He never fought a battle till he was ready to fight it and the outcome was secure. Villa broke against his barbed-wire barricades at Celaya, and after that the wild chieftain, though he was to

cause headaches for many a year, was a dying cock in the ring.
Obregón lost his arm in that battle, but he acted as though it
were a fine joke on himself. In the darkest moments he never
lost his good humor.

Some people said his name was a corruption of O'Brian — certainly he looked Irish with his florid jovial face — but Obregón
is a name ancient in Spanish history. What was really certain was
that Obregón was part Yaqui Indian. He belonged to the small-
rancher class, as had Carranza, but had more of the intrinsic
qualities of that class: common sense, serenity under great difficulties, soil-wise humor and a touch of the horse-trader. He was
one Mexican leader who really enjoyed opposition because he
could always outwit his enemies.

He outwitted Carranza. Carranza tried to impose a nonentity
as his successor in office. He not only stopped Obregón from
campaigning for President, but put him under arrest. Obregón,
in the company of labor leader Luis Morones, escaped to Guerrero. His legions closed in on the capital swiftly. Down from
the north came the Yaqui fighters that had always been Obregón's
mainstay, and soon Carranza rode to his death in the Puebla
hills, and Obregón rode into the capital in suspenders in the
greatest military demonstration of México's history.

Obregón turned the treasury inside out for schools and more
schools. He set the land program into definite motion. But he
compromised on the oil question — the Bucareli agreements.

6

His protégé was Plutarco Elías Calles, from the same northwest state of Sonora, who in 1924 was made his successor. Four
years later, in 1928, after Obregón was assassinated, Calles inherited full control of the country.

Madero was the great apostle, the Mazzini of the revolution;
Carranza was its great legalist; Obregón was its military genius;
Calles, its great disciplinarian; Cárdenas, its great applier. It
was Calles who, when Obregón first took power, slapped the
rough-and-tumble army into shape and made it obey the laws.
He concentrated the federal power and ruthlessly eliminated all

opposition. The mob of greedy and treacherous generals had respected Obregón because they knew he could outwit them and outfight them. But it was Calles who made them toe the mark. It was Calles who created totalitarian obedience of army, peasantry, and labor — the new trinity.

Calles drove ahead with the land program at a somewhat faster pace, continued the educational expansion, broke anew with the United States over the oil question, headed full tilt into a struggle against the Catholic Church.

Calles, an illegitimate child, began as a poor schoolteacher and ended up as 'the first chief of the revolution,' and the dictator of México — for a time. He was another taciturn, monolithic type, long-faced and long-jawed.

He was born in 1878 near Guaymas, a semitropical seaport in Sonora — the natural son of the well-known Elías family, said to be Syrian in origin. Calles himself was nicknamed 'The Grand Turk.' Certainly Calles has the rectangular, boxlike, secretive face of many Syrian traders. But his cheekbones come high against his narrow slit-eyes, so that many claim that he, like Obregón, has quite a dash of Yaqui Indian blood.

The story has been frequently told that he didn't have money for shoes till he got his first school to teach. However, his mother was granted some income by Elías, and Plutarco's circumstances, if modest, were never penurious. On the other hand, apparently he always hated his father, hence always went by his mother's name.

In 1897, according to a picture in my possession, he was a very dapperly dressed youth in a bat-wing collar, and with smooth-plastered hair. In front of a group of pupils, he is wielding a pointer on a row of figures scribbled on a standing blackboard.

He was still a schoolteacher in 1906 when the great Cananea copper mine strike against the Greene interests occurred, and American troops rushed across the border. If not an actual strike leader, Calles advised the leaders, but luckier than they, he was not shipped off to the San Juan de Ulúa undersea dungeons.

He gained some army experience in the Madero revolt against Díaz, but did not jump into importance until he joined the forces of Alvaro Obregón during the Carranza anti-Huerta revolution.

When in 1914 Obregón led his forces down the west coast into México City to end the sanguinary rule of the Indian dictator Victoriano Huerta, he left Calles behind in Sonora as military governor.

There Calles ruthlessly destroyed all opposition and rapidly consolidated the Obregón-Carranza forces in the state. Though not personally a teetotaler, he gathered notoriety for his death-penalty prohibition edict, and is said to have shot all violators.

After Obregón broke Villa at Celaya and pushed him over into Sonora, Calles swiftly smashed the remnants of his forces.

When Carranza finally was installed as President, Calles was called to the cabinet to head the Ministry of Industry, Commerce, and Labor. Later when Carranza tried to prevent Obregón from becoming President, Calles found an excuse to resign by refusing to countenance the use of troops to suppress a strike in the Río Blanco textile region, where Dictator Porfirio Díaz in 1907 had slaughtered hundreds. Calles hurried back to Sonora to prepare Obregón's revolt in the northwest — the so-called 'Revindicating Revolution.'

Obregón took over, installing Adolfo de la Huerta, the ex-cabaret singer, as provisional President, until elections could be held, whereupon Calles returned to the cabinet as Secretary of War. At once he began slapping back the ears of the generals.

As soon as rubber-stamp elections could be held to seat Obregón 'constitutionally' on the cactus throne, Calles became Minister of the Interior and head of the cabinet. His rôle was similar to that of Postmaster General Farley — to build up the political machine of the new régime and incidentally prepare the way for his own election.

Particularly he favored the labor elements of the Regional Confederation of Labor (CROM) and the Mexican Labor Party. The head of those two organizations, Luis Morones, was given control of the National Munition Works and the Army Supply Department, with a combined budget of thirty million pesos. Celestino Gasca, another Laborite, was made Governor of the Federal District; other important posts and governorships were distributed to that group.

A year before the end of the Obregón term, Calles resigned (as is required of all candidates by Mexican law) to run for President in 1924. He refused all endorsements save that of the Mexican Labor Party.

The conflicting presidential aspirations of Adolfo de la Huerta, who sought to arouse sentiment against the Bucareli oil settlement with the United States, and who also sought to attract the clerical and other conservative elements, precipitated the armed revolt of 1923. While Obregón was crushing this on two fronts, Calles, cooperating with the Labor Party, hurried north to San Luis Potosí to organize worker and peasant volunteers. After a few ticklish situations, the revolt was put down, and Calles was smoothly elected.

Before taking office, he toured Europe, and in Germany took treatment for an ancient illness. The Germans touted him with regal fanfare; Washington largely ignored him. In New York, at Stuyvesant High School, along with Morris Hillquit and Norman Thomas, he addressed Socialists and Laborites. His speech terminated with the ringing phrase, 'Before I will ever betray the proletariat, I will wrap myself in the red flag and hurl myself into the abyss.' The following night at the Waldorf-Astoria he addressed a banquet of America's greatest financial and industrial leaders, promising them security for their investments.

7

Inducted into office December 1, 1924, he promptly showed his intention of carrying the new constitution through on all fronts. He was particularly partial to the Laborites; and labor leader Morones, lover of diamonds, auto-cars, and sundry diversions, was put in charge of the Department of Industry, Commerce, and Labor. Adalberto Tejeda, bitter anti-clerical revolutionist from Vera Cruz, became Minister of the Interior.

Calles started off in radical fashion, with rapid land-distribution and determined enforcement of the labor laws. Two major conflicts soon developed: that with the American and British petroleum interests (when he set aside the Bucareli agreement) and that with the Catholic Church. By August, 1926, the priests were on strike against compulsory registration; armed religious revolts were sweeping five states with death and ruin. Brutal reprisals and counter-reprisals featured the activities of both sides. The worst was the ferocious attack on a Guadalajara train by the Cristeros, who looted it, then set fire to the coaches, burning many people alive and driving some insane. And on the oil question, by the end of 1926, Nervous Nellie Kellogg and Calles had reached an impasse which led the two countries to the brink of war.

President Coolidge hurried Dwight W. Morrow of the house of Morgan into the breach, and both countries backed away from the brink. No man was ever put across with more organized publicity than was Morrow. He ate a ham-and-egg breakfast of friendship with Calles, and within a few weeks he had wangled a Supreme Court decision superficially favorable to the oil companies. Within a short time he effected a compromise.

Morrow's personal intimacy with Calles permitted him to exert pressure on other fronts. One Mexican anthropologist declared, 'He killed the revolution with a smile.' Morrow extracted a promise from Calles to discontinue land expropriation, except with payment in cash instead of in bonds. Since no government funds were available, this meant full paralyzation of the agrarian program.

Despite years of land-distribution, México was still a country of concentrated large holdings. Over 95 per cent of the rural property of the country remained in large estates. Only 2½ per cent of México's rural properties had an acreage over 2500, but that acreage constituted over 84 per cent of the area of all rural property. Property valued per unit at over half a million pesos made up nearly 70 per cent of the total value of México's rural property. This was the sad picture when Morrow stopped agrarian reform.

The Calles Government also dutifully made assaults upon the *ejidos* or communal lands already granted to Indian villages by inaugurating the 'family patrimony,' in order to change such holding from a collective to individual ownership, thus paving the way for them to be stolen away again. Soon peasant leaders were being murdered right and left.

In thus temporarily knifing the land program, Morrow successfully changed the whole outlook and purpose of the Calles régime.

Morrow also forced through a settlement — more of a truce than a permanent peace — with the Church, in which the government got most of the bacon. This was accomplished only after indefatigable patience and secret negotiation, including a never-reported clandestine meeting in the old Ulúa fortress in Vera Cruz, with an outside emissary of the Pope.

Likewise Morrow became the power behind the throne in Mexican finances, subtly directing the operations of Minister of the Treasury Montes de Oca, although toward the end of Morrow's stay, an indiscretion by a former military attaché caused a serious break, and quite overthrew Morrow's plans for financial reconstruction.

Morrow's efforts contributed, at some cost, to temporary peace and stability, but they solved no basic issue permanently. For a brief time he and Calles sidetracked the Mexican revolution. Morrow made the revolution palatable even to Nervous Nellie Kellogg, and overnight the fire-eating Calles became super-respectable in international circles.

Despite Morrow's good efforts, the American petroleum interests, disgruntled, clamped down on their operations, and turned their attention largely to Venezuela and the Near East. Thereby they gave the British interests a chance to regain the overwhelming lead in Mexican production. But Morrow's efforts caused other American capital to gain confidence. The Southern Pacific completed its trunk line in Nayarit and Guadalajara. The I. T. and T. put in a telephone system to compete with the Swedish Erickson phones; the National City and Chase Banks opened up branches; the Electric Bond and Share Company secretly garnered in nearly all the light and power resources of the country. One large banana company secured lands and set out thousands of new trees. New mining investments were reported.

Labor leader Morones now did his share by crushing the independent miners' union of Jalisco, then giving trouble on the property of ex-Ambassador Gerard and to other American interests; he broke the independent railway organizations, and brought most of them under the government wing.

Education also languished.

And so, after 1926, the reformist tendencies in México, except for speech-making, were largely aborted. It appeared that Ambassador Morrow had successfully scotched nationalistic socialism below the border. Subsequent events have revealed that he was merely a King Canute.

8

The shift back to the revolutionary trends now had to wait till the elimination of Calles as the ruling force. Calles, growing older, inevitably had become a wealthy promoter. His private interests soon extended all over the country — factories, lands, gambling resorts, and other speculations. Much of the land benefited by the irrigation works, which most experts considered antieconomical, was in Calles' hands. A man with broad acres is less likely to favor land distribution. A man with tire and electriclight bulb and other factories does not relish labor trouble. Calles, besides being President, militarist, labor leader, and politician, had become a capitalist.

The nationalistic socialist movement was definitely complicated by this erection of a native capitalism. This led to many contradictions. Increasingly it became evident that the government's stern control of the labor and peasant movements had a dual character. The labor movement was necessary to help break the power of foreign capital. Foreign corporations could now be given a triple squeeze through rate regulation, taxation, and labor demands. The trick was to prevent these same devices being used against the new leaders of Mexican capitalism. That was Calles' great rôle during the second half of his administration. Neither his concessions to Morrow nor his concessions to Mexican labor were sincere. The new American capital that dashed into México merely put its head in the noose. Labor was being increasingly regimented to the purposes of the régime.

Both Calles and Morrow looked with trepidation on the unexpected determination of Obregón to return to power. Ambassador Morrow privately expressed to me the hope that Calles would declare himself dictator. For a time Calles did try to block Obregón's aspirations.

Obregón promptly slapped Calles' labor backers, Morones and the CROM, in the face, and boldly reallied himself with the discontented peasant elements. Having been double-crossed by Calles, they now flocked to Obregón's banner. Thus the latter's unconditional promises of land distribution definitely jeopardized the more conservative position of Morrow and Calles. With Obregón's more radical elements were joined queer bedfellows — many of the sundry 'outs' of previous administrations, particularly Carranzistas; American West Coast oil interests with whom Obregón had extensive personal business dealings; and the new group of industrialists from the iron and steel centers in Nuevo León and Coahuila.

Calles found himself in a tense situation and a mounting dilemma. His own confidential group, the Mexican Labor Party, soon broke openly with Obregón. Morones even threatened to take his portly be-diamonded self to the barricades. In Yucatán and Puebla armed fracases occurred. Bullets showered about Obregón. Morones's strong-armed gangs — *La Palanca* — now shot to kill. Obregón's partisans accused the *Laboristas* of sundry crimes. But the edge cut two ways. One morning Morones's auto, coming in from his palatial home in Tlalpam, was riddled with bullets. The police discovered that it was triple-steel lined and had a machine-gun mount.

But though Calles, pushed on by Morrow, exerted under-cover political pressure to block Obregón's return to office, in state after state the pro-Calles gubernatorial candidates, despite unlimited federal aid, were downed by the Obregón candidates in violent elections. The army unmistakably revealed its personal solidarity with Obregón.

Calles bowed to the inevitable, and from then on, though trying to salvage his own labor party, actively prepared the way for Obregón's re-election. Anti-Obregón presidential candidates, Serrano and Gómez, were prodded into premature revolt.

During forty-eight sleepless hours, Calles, his face unshaven, his suspenders dangling, stamped along the terraces of Chapultepec Castle, snapping out orders. Serrano and Gómez were swiftly seized and along with scores of followers were stood up against bloody execution walls without benefit of trial. When an attempt to assassinate Obregón was made in Chapultepec Park, Calles' subordinate, General Roberto Cruz, hastened to execute the supposed aggressors, one of them the priest, Father Humberto Pro, also without a trial.

Apparently Calles wished to prove by such drastic measures that the government and the labor group had no hand in the frustrated attack. If anything the hasty secretive executions gave rise to malicious rumors that the three executed parties were victims of a frame-up to hide the real culprits. The secret evidence against the three victims, never published, but which I have examined, is presumptive, but not at all conclusive, and against Father Pro is scarcely presumptive. Certainly it would not in itself lead to his conviction in any fair court of law.

And so Calles was obliged willy-nilly to prepare the road for Obregón's return to the presidency. Thereby he resigned himself to being a secondary figure in the history of the epoch. But Fate suddenly changed his destiny.

9

In August, 1928, at the Bombilla Restaurant in San Angel, a Catholic fanatic, José Toral, emptied a Spanish repeating pistol into Obregón's back.

A terrific crisis was precipitated. All of Calles' inveterate enemies, all the old backers of De la Huerta, Madero, Carranza, had clambered on the Obregón bandwagon, hoping to get back into office and favor. Having no standing with Calles, overnight they now saw themselves brushed away from the honey-jar of governmental spoils. It was shouted that Morones had killed Obregón, that even Calles was responsible. A governmental upset seemed imminent.

Calles rode out the storm successfully. He saved himself by completely sacrificing the Labor Party, whose candidate he had been. His political friend for a decade, Morones, was thrown to the wolves. For days Morones sulked behind his machine-guns in his secretariat, then resigned and hid out. Calles hastened also to deliver the police investigations of the crime directly into the hands of the Obregón group. Hurriedly he appointed key

Obregonistas to his cabinet. These various measures split the Obregonista opposition, placated much of it, clipped the nails of the rest, and tided over the situation.

For a time Calles seemed even willing to permit the election of a Provisional President from the Obregón opposition, but with the Obregonistas divided, he suddenly produced a dark-horse compromise — Emilio Portes Gil, Governor of Tamaulipas, who, though close to the Obregón faction, was really a Calles supporter. Also he was a hater of Morones but had the active support of the peasant and labor elements in his own state.

Calles, reading a special message to Congress and to all the military commandants of the country, ordered to attend the session, now declared the era of military chieftainship or *caudillismo* was forever ended in México.[1]

On that tense gala occasion, the sacred galleries and roofs of the Chamber of Deputies were ringed with machine-guns. The doors and windows along the streets where Calles was to pass were sealed up tight. The avenues where his car passed were lined with thousands of soldiers. He shot through to the Chamber at high speed. Clearly assassination was in the air.

In the Chamber — with its secret defenses, and a great show of military forces without — Calles stood in the lion's mouth. All the heroic generals of two decades of revolution were seated behind him — and some would gladly have shot him dead. Before him were the bickering Senate and Chamber.

Calles was very uneasy. He started in a husky, almost inaudible voice. Repeatedly he put his hand to his throat with a nervous gesture. But gradually his voice grew calm and strong. His speech cleverly played the politicians off against the militarists and vice versa. He promised that he would never become President again, thus quieting rumors that he intended to declare himself dictator. Only in the event of a grave crisis would he come temporarily to the rescue of the fatherland. The régime, he declared, was strong enough to permit hereafter free political rights, even to Catholics.

Clever showmanship. Even Ambassador Morrow forgot himself and clapped.

[1] This speech was prepared in entirety by Puig Casauranc, Minister of Education.

10

Calles now hastened to found the National Revolutionary Party to weld all so-called revolutionary elements into the totalitarian organization, hoping thus to reconcile laborites, generals, and the professional politicians. The labor organizations and most of the peasant groups held out. The PNR thus created a pseudo-Fascist alliance of generals, politicians and a small minority of workers and peasants. It spelled the death-knell to the Morones elements and to all independent, labor, peasant, and political organizations.

Organizations refusing to affiliate were soon dissolved by propaganda, pressure, or overt police force. The PNR, with insincere Bolshevik labels, was conceived as an organization that would henceforth determine the policies of government. At the same time, the government supported the party by exacting part of the pay of all public employees, thus providing it with a budget of millions to be squandered by favorites. No independent organization could compete, even if such had been permitted any free expression and a free press. Thus the new PNR in reality became a bureau of political control and dictatorship, anything except a party. The new party had one hundred per cent control of all jobs, activities, and elections. One complacent opposition congressman was usually allowed as a show-piece to prove democracy and tolerance. But it was totalitarianism. Even so, the PNR did not put an end to *caudillaje* or military rule.

Soon after Portes Gil took office, Calles was called back to face a new crisis. His close friend, General Escobar (who a few years before on Calles' orders had previously lined up presidential candidate Arnulfo Gómez against a wall to be shot), now tried to prove by armed revolt that unruly chieftainship had not ended. In company with various other military gentlemen, mostly from Sonora, also friends of Calles, Escobar looted the northern banks.

At the moment, Portes Gil's Minister of War, General Joaquín Amaro, the one man who could have handled the situation, was being rushed to the Mayo clinic in the United States, his eye-socket crushed and infected from a blow in a polo match. Calles had to jump back into the breach.

Rapidly he gathered together all loyal armed forces and moved to the front in his radio-equipped railroad car to crush the rebels. Red-headed 'Sandy' McNab, the American military attaché, accompanied him. The marihuana addict, General Eulogio Ortiz, whirled up from Tamaulipas to lend a hand. In Sonora General Lázaro Cárdenas shoved the rebels north toward the border. In a few short weeks the revolters had scampered into the United States.

Calles then dutifully retired to his big Santa Bárbara estate on the Puebla road, to grow alfalfa and chickens, with federal soldiers paid from the public treasury. Portes Gil continued to strike down all independent popular organizations. Calles, still under Morrow's influence, again publicly announced the agrarian program a failure. Portes Gil (afterward, his successor, Pascual Ortiz Rubio) hastened to put an end to what little was left of the program.

Next, finding the railroads in crisis, Calles took over the $50,000 (pesos)-a-year presidency of the national lines and brought in a Canadian expert to untangle them. Next, Calles founded the Bank of Mexico and accepted the honorary presidency for another $50,000 (pesos)-a-year salary.

In spite of the PNR's ironclad monopoly of politics, the anti-Calles elements lifted up their heads. José Vasconcelos, the volatile Hindu scholar and ex-Minister of Education, rallied students and clerical elements behind his candidacy. Within the PNR, Aarón Saenz, who had enriched himself with government contracts, loomed as the official candidate. But though he was Calles' brother-in-law, he was not allowed to have the post, the chief reason being that the arch anti-clerical, Calles, could not stomach a Protestant.

Calles, after meditating on his Santa Bárbara estate, at the last moment yanked the inoffensive obscure adenoidal Ortiz Rubio, Ambassador to Brazil, back from his peaceful sunbaths in Rio de Janeiro, to be the official candidate. Ambassador Morrow tried to help out the weak Ortiz Rubio by sending an emissary to candidate Vasconcelos, offering him the rectorship of the University as a reward if he would abandon his presidential aspirations.

After a little gunplay, Ortiz was duly elected. But as he rode to the National Palace to take office, an assassin put a shot into his jaw — a mysterious affair hushed up and never investigated, though the would-be assassin was captured. After due time, Ortiz's new platinum mandible worked properly, and following a period of ruthless terrorism by several generals, Ortiz restored order and thereafter carried out Calles' orders with considerable dignity and ability.

But bungling of finances shoved the Bank of México and the federal treasury toward bankruptcy. Calles dramatically pulled out of the hat the Calles monetary law. It was pushed through the Senate and Chamber without discussion and with hurrahs of 'Viva Calles!' México was the first country in the world to abandon the gold standard, one of the first to embark on a managed currency. It was a symptom of internal breakdown. But once more Calles had 'saved the country,' wiped out much of its indebtedness, and extricated himself from his own tottering financial situation. The inner group of the régime, knowing what was coming, also made a juicy killing.

Sharp differences, not of principle but of control, now developed between Ortiz and Calles. Ortiz's friend, General Amaro, Secretary of War — now with a glass eye, but with a very good grip on the army — favored throwing off the Calles yoke. He massed troops in the capital.

Calles moved boldly into the Palace. Several thousand armed peasants, led by a loyal chieftain, Saturnino Cedillo, moved in with him. The officers of Amaro's own troops then offered Calles full allegiance.

With a bold sweep and without public explanation, Calles cleared four generals of division out of the 'civilian' cabinet, and he himself, a general of division, took over the Secretariat of War. Amaro scampered to cover as head of the Popotla Military School — México's West Point.

Shortly, Montes de Oca, Minister of Finance, getting the presidential bug, ran foul of Calles, and fearing for his life, made a hurried overnight departure for the United States. Shortly, Ortiz Rubio found it convenient to resign in favor of Abelardo Rodríguez, Calles' close business and gambling associate, a friendship dating from Cananea strike days.

The Mexican revolution had had two armed forces, in the north and the south. The latter, where occurred the more sincere movement, had been represented earlier by Emiliano Zapata, the agrarian leader of Morelos, assassinated by General Pablo González. In previous eras the political dominant region had always been in the more typical rooted south, particularly in Oaxaca, the birthplace of both Juárez and Díaz. But after 1910, the north gained the ascendancy, in part because the population there is more mobile, and because of nearness to the United States, which made possible arms-smuggling. First, the state of Coahuila; Madero and Carranza came from there. Then northwest Sonora snatched the crown of power to become the ruling bailiwick — the new President state. From there came Obregón, Calles, Rodríguez, De la Huerta, most of the high officials, even most of the major revolters, such as Francisco Serrano and Arnulfo Gómez. This shift of political hegemony to the northwest was indicative of the new overriding influence of the United States in all Mexican affairs.

Inevitably, once the revolution became more stabilized, the military and office-holding monopoly of northwest Sonora was challenged. At first this narrow localism in power was widened by taking in other northern areas and absorbing other local ruling groups. Thus, after a time, the Sonora military politicos moved over a few inches for the industrial politicos of the central north — Nuevo León, Coahuila, and Chihuahua, with Monterrey, the iron and steel center, as the pivot. The leaders from that part of the country mostly represented the new 'capitalist' tendencies within the revolution; they copied American methods, even in politics, and like Aarón Saenz and Pérez Treviño and Almazán, waxed wealthy from public works and important industrial initiative rather than following the old Mexican custom of directly looting the treasury.

The pull of the more 'typical' México was first shown by the emergence of new political demands from the Gulf Coast states — Tamaulipas, Vera Cruz, Campeche, Tabasco, and Yucatán — all more 'radical' than the north. This accounted for the growing influence of such pseudo-agrarian radical leaders as Portes Gil, Marte Gómez, De Negri, Adalberto Tejeda, and Garrido Canabal — vivid compromise figures. By making concessions to these elements, a rupture between the Sonora-Monterrey group of the north and the agrarian elements of the south was avoided. The bases of the régime were broadening out.

Perhaps the two most typical Indian-mestizo states of México are Oaxaca and Michoacán. And a new focus of political strength soon developed in Michoacán, birthplace of President Ortiz Rubio, Lázaro Cárdenas, and Minister of War Joaquín Amaro. Both this group and the Gulf Coast group were cleverly used by Calles to offset the influence of his predecessor, Obregón; but after Obregón's assassination, the political aspirations of other parts of the country were again suppressed. Once the difficulties had been bridged, Portes Gil was balked in further political ambitions; Ortiz Rubio was summarily kicked out of the presidency; General Amaro was sidetracked; and Abelardo Rodríguez, a millionaire 'business' President of the north — from Sonora — was put into office. The bases were whittled down again.

Once more Calles retired, now to his new handsome chalet in Cuernavaca in Morelos, cradle of the Zapata agrarian movement, where Zapata's son today does not even have a plot of land.

Erelong Calles again emerged, this time to prevent schism between opposing PNR candidates for the presidency, General Pérez Treviño (still part of the old Obregón faction of northern industrialists) and General Lázaro Cárdenas. Calles forced Pérez Treviño to relinquish his candidacy and to abandon the control of the official single-track party, which was for the moment placed in the hands of another of Calles' close friends and business associates, a man enjoying luscious federal concessions and owning a large share in the notorious Foreign Club gambling establishment.

CHAPTER VII

Socialism on a Platter

By 1934 México had become a land of millionaire Socialists, a land of knight-errant Mexican capitalists. It was a land where the owners of luxurious gambling dens, wealthy members of the inner Calles clique, made throbbing speeches in behalf of the proletariat; a land where Croesus suburbanites lived in fairylike palaces and damned the harsh exploiters of human toil. It was a land where powerful leaders denounced monstrous clericalism and baptized and christened their children and married their daughters off in bootleg Catholic ceremonies they had arbitrarily made illegal.

It was at that time the only country in the world where a group of powerful and wealthy political leaders — those in full control of the government — constantly expressed radical pro-letarian doctrines in cliché Marxian phraseology. The *nouveaux riches* of the revolution, those who had risen to power through several decades of bloody strife, flaunted their riches in tasteless ostentation and the most vulgar pursuits. Men who had become enterprising industrialists, owners of vast estates, promoters of banks, and high and honored office-holders, those were precisely the ones who were insisting that México destroy the Church, inculcate Socialist doctrines among the youth, fight foreign capi-tal, and proceed to reinitiate the radical agrarian program, side-tracked by the blandishments of Ambassador Morrow. They knew quite well that their own large domains and their holdings would not be touched.

This group of collectivist idealists which, with the aid of Calles, then controlled the destinies of our neighbor-country, created for itself one of the luxurious paradises of this continent. In benign Cuernavaca, a place of eternal spring set proudly on the high southern slopes of the Sierra Madre and overlooking a great valley, the successful chiefs of the Mexican revolution laid out lovely gardens and winding boulevards along which they constructed their palatial homes. Near-by was the fashionable De la Selva gambling hall and dance cabaret and a new country club, the latter also fitted up with faro and roulette tables. Around about in Cuernavaca were the slums of folk without proper clothing, their homes without floors, running water, or sanitary appliances. Around about were the hovels of the peasants, even worse equipped. There were the folk the rulers of México were so constantly assisting — in their speeches.

In the swank country club hung a big oil painting of Calles, 'First Chief of the Revolution,' decked out in golf togs and welding a putter. Out on the greens, so softly glowing under the southern light, the rough-hewn creators of México's new liberties now trudged from hole to hole, attended by soldiers as caddies; soldiers cared for their private gardens; soldiers guarded their possessions; soldiers scoured the mountain road to the capital as a precaution against bandits. Cuernavaca had become a fabulous show-place. Maliciously the public named the main boulevard 'the street of Ali Baba and his forty thieves.' This was obviously an unfair blow below the belt at men constantly devising new laws to protect the downtrodden proletariat.

Calles' new home loomed naked on a bald hill. Fearing assassination, he had had all the beautiful trees cut down so no one could sneak up unseen.

The most impressive palace was that of President Abelardo Rodríguez, one of the wealthiest men on the American continent. He had built himself a veritable castle in the midst of long sloping lawns surrounded by a majestic dentated wall. One of México's new and puissant entrepreneurs, wealth had not dried up his great humanitarian instincts. Where else in the world would the President of a country, belonging to his class, put his name to a statement that the only way to end war is for the workers and peasants to become sufficiently well organized to refuse to obey the unworthy commands of their rulers? He is now chieftain of Atlantic coast defenses.

But not so many years ago, Rodríguez was himself a poor workman leading a miners' strike. Not so long ago he was languishing in a Díaz prison. Obviously he could not easily forget such sufferings. As President, with much Socialist rhetoric, he implanted a universal minimum wage of a peso and a half a day (less than forty cents). Presently he announced, although México was not at that time at war, that since the government had so clearly demonstrated its friendliness and generosity to the workers, there was no further excuse for strikes; henceforth work-stoppages would be considered anti-patriotic and seditious. (Two strike leaders had just been packed off to the Islas Marías penal island without benefit of trial to join others in a like predicament.)

A financial intimate of the President brought into existence the local Fascist 'Gold Shirts.' But the chiefs of the revolution soon saw the mistake and put an end to the incipient hoodlumism. Instead, the erratic Oriental revolutionist and despot of Tabasco, Tomás Garrido Canabal, was permitted to organize a national corps of Red Shirts to safeguard proletarian gains and murder priests.

2

The inconsistencies multiplied. Poor people were constantly being killed by the collapse of homes in the México City slums, slums as vile as any in the world; yet nothing whatever was done to regulate housing conditions because powerful officials, who were making ardent speeches in behalf of the proletariat, owned many of the titles. But Rodríguez did lay out a whole new colony of model homes for workers, which even had cement slabs for beds. These could be purchased for ten years of thirty-pesos-a-month payments (eighty per cent of the minimum wage decreed by him). Most of the homes were acquired by petty political favorites, clerical bureaucrats, and secret-police agents.

The government maintained a most enlightened crime-prevention bureau while the most eager and wealthy high proletarian officials erected a million and a quarter peso 'Foreign Club,' one of the most luxurious, vicious, and wide-open gambling joints in the world, a place that soon corrupted all México City, draining poor employees of their wages, subverting honest cashiers, causing embezzlements and desperate suicides.

In another quarter of the city the government was erecting an enormous marble monument to the revolution. Unfair local wags asked which was the real monument, the huge dome at the foot of Avenida Juárez or the Foreign Club. 'See,' they gibed, 'what an impetus the latter has given to revolutionary art!' For the Foreign Club was extensively adorned with frescoes, pornographic and crudely disgusting, but in the modernistic vein. The masterpiece, the central cabaret figure, was a streamlined female form stepping forth, as a modern Aphrodite should, from lavender plumes, entirely nude except for the modesty of scarlet gloves.

In answer to this masterful ostentation in a city flowing with ill-gained wealth, flooded with guzzling tourists, and prosperous in defiance of world depression, sinister rumblings began coming from the hinterland. According to the national deputies the Church was conspiring to stage new revolt. Once more the poverty-stricken peasants were taking their rifles out of their thatched roofs. The workers, slipping out from under the wing of the official P.N.R. into more militant unions, were again demanding that the government make good its many vibrant promises.

Calles, ear close to the ground, hoping to ward off possible trouble over the inauguration of the new puppet president, General Lázaro Cárdenas, began beating the Church harder and again damning the unworthy capitalists. Besides, Ambassador Morrow was gone. The fighting shibboleths of the outgoing administration and the oncoming one were 'anti-clericalism,' and obligatory 'socialist' instruction in the public schools.

There was no one to teach it. There were not half a dozen Marxian scholars in all México. Most of those calling themselves 'socialists' were in the Islas Marías prison. The instruction proposed, and that still theoretically followed, was 'to fight to form a concept of solidarity necessary for the progressive socialization of the means of economic production.'

In practice, the government was rapidly moving away from such socialization. In agriculture it had abandoned any semblance of it. Asked one newspaper that was soon suppressed: 'Will the new instruction in the public schools teach that the flamboyant Babylonic resort of Cuernavaca, symbolic of the ill-gained wealth of México's socialistic leaders, be collectivized as a fittingly beautiful proletarian resort? That was done in Russia. Will it be done here?'

The hypocrisy of the rulers of 'thirty-four had gradually stunted Mexican thought, art, and honesty. The artistic manifestations of the Mexican New Deal had withered away. The original afflatus in painting, which produced, among others, Rivera, Orozco, and Siqueiros, dried up at its source. Tourists were now bringing about the rapid commercialization and resultant deterioration of all handicrafts. Writers were equally frustrated. Capable authors, who might have derived amusement out of the current scene, remained in a blind alley, scribbling stale blood-and-thunder anecdotal chronicles of Villa and Zapata, without psychological nuances or any intelligible social criteria. Everything fundamental was suppressed. Arbitrary control was maintained over the large dailies. Direct orders from a high government office forbade criticism of the Foreign Club, then showering its golden profits into the laps of the leaders of the P.N.R. — no mention of suicides or embezzlements or the swarms of prostitutes among the habitués.

3

What was the meaning of all this contradiction? Several centuries ago the new weapon of the rising mercantile and industrial class of western Europe was democracy. Democracy directed mass force against the feudal lord, liberated the peasant, instituted *laissez faire* and free trade, shifted political control to the cities where demagogy and money could manipulate the electorate.

Today the scene is vastly different. Mere political democracy no longer offers great hope for the masses. The demand is for economic democracy as well. Hence, for a new capitalism to arise in a world of powerful capitalist nations required entirely new weapons. The new bourgeoisie in México had to fight not only the landed fuedalism and the Church, but foreign capitalism as well, and also compete with efficient American mass production.

This could be done only by ironclad control of the state and the sponsoring of an exaggerated nationalism. To combat feudalism, the peasant had to be liberated, peonage destroyed. The best weapon for this was a collectivism corresponding to indigenous, pre-Spanish traditions, and not so remote from the modern Russian trend. To combat foreign capital, it was necessary to promote a labor movement. Thus, for the native bourgeois group to establish itself, it was necessary to invoke not only a pseudo-democracy, but also partial collectivism; it was necessary to grant at the outset some of those mass conquests already made in countries with an existing capitalist economy. Naturally a proletariat, too class-conscious, would simultaneously augment the handicaps of the new native industrialist group.

The contradictions involved could be bridged by thorough control of the state; for through the state and patriotic nationalism, the peasant and labor movements could be controlled. Such control also permitted typical nationalistic protective measures: high tariffs, special subsidies, privileged rates on the state-owned railway, monetary manipulation, judicial leniency, tax-favoritism, plus all the new tricks of managed foreign exchange, barter, etc. typical also of the closed economic systems of Russia and Germany, and in increasing use by all countries. All these weapons helped eliminate foreign competition and foreign economic penetration. It was the property of oppositionists and foreigners that was nationalized, not the big estates and factories of the generals and politicians. This was the acme of national socialism, in a world of supposedly declining capitalist civilization.

But once the diplomatic struggle had been won, especially in connection with petroleum and the Catholic issues, once the régime was no longer menaced by external coercion, it no longer needed to cater so much to the militant radical and peasant movement. Such a movement increasingly endangered the new bourgeois 'revolutionary' group in control of the state.

Hence, by 1928, Calles and the government began to smash

independent and peasant groups and to force proletarian elements into the official National Revolutionary Party — a local version of Mussolini's corporate state. This overhead control and monopolization of all proletarian forces had various advantages. It prevented unpleasant labor trouble's being directed at native enterprise; but it became far easier to engineer crippling strikes against foreign corporations and also local concerns standing in the way of complete monopolization by the small clique in power.

This, in part, explains why the new wealthy industrialists of México continued to hand out socialism on a silver platter, a peculiar Mexican brand of socialism, exceedingly voluble and very, very Fabian. But as the good suburbanites, followed by their soldier caddies, went swinging their golf clubs over the Cuernavaca Country Club links or gambled their new wealth in the De la Selva gambling halls, they had painful moments of doubt. The contradictions jostled each other so vigorously and patently. The forces involved were explosive. The whole situation was charged with dynamite. Calles was holding the lid on, but he was no longer so young, his health not so good. Any bold leader might snatch away the prize by rallying the popular elements on a more sincere program. There were plenty of rumblings. Even the official National Revolutionary Party was threatened with a dangerous split. Would the new shift of power and policy survive? The Mexican people still had to be heard from on the issue.

CHAPTER VIII

Lázaro Cárdenas

EVERY November, the school children of México march thousands strong to commemorate the revolt of Francisco Madero, and the end of dictator Porfirio Díaz's prolonged iron rule over a nation of serfs. A few years ago, the commemoration was invariably celebrated by a military parade. The change to a civilian accent is symbolic of a nation slowly emerging from military rule to that of more active public opinion and civic organization — an evolution toward democracy, though scarcely a democracy of the American pattern.

Whatever the abuses of the millionaire Socialists, momentous changes had been occurring in México.

During the week of the day of the parade, a year after Lázaro Cárdenas was sworn in as President — pledged to carry out a definite Six-Year Plan — the newspapers of México City carried the following items:

1. 'To fulfill the commitments of the Six-Year Plan, the federal government is to spend 150,000,000 pesos in railroad construction.'

[Without digging into the records of the exact figures, it is possible now to say that many millions were spent and many miles of new railroads were built.]

2. 'Beginning in December, the government will spend 19,000,-000 pesos in constructing three dams to make Nazas River water available in the Laguna district where President Cárdenas has been personally directing the distribution of tillable land among

former propertyless farm hands. Equipment has already been purchased in the United States.'

[Thus began a large-scale experiment in collective farming along industrialized lines. The debate over whether the project has been economically sound still agitates many minds, but there is little debate over the fact that housing and living conditions, opportunities for education, health, recreation, have improved.]

3. 'Fifty Yucatán townships are to be provided with sanitary water supplies, part of a vast program of improvement there, planned by President Cárdenas. The villages are to receive cattle breeders and farm implements. A large experimental school will be established. Simple methods of processing sisal, Yucatán's major product, will be taught and applied.'

[During the succeeding years, Cárdenas made numerous trips to Yucatán to inspect the work initiated and the newspapers periodically published reports of progress.]

4. 'One thousand and twenty new rural schools, seventy-five per cent of which have been established in Indian districts, have been founded this year. Two thousand additional schools will be established in 1937.'

[Very nearly carried out, although many schools and teachers were far from satisfactory. This was due, not to intention, but to lack of better resources.]

5. 'Over two thousand plans for new buildings in the Federal District have been approved thus far this year in accordance with new health, safety, and zone-harmony standards. Five thousand tenement-type houses have been inspected and the owners obliged to provide sanitary conveniences.'

[The first large-scale effort in México's history to end slum conditions.]

6. 'The México–Guadalajara highway, to be the most beautiful road in México, will be finished October, 1938, at a total cost of 21,000,000 pesos. A Mexican corporation is in charge of the work.'

[This highway has been completed.]

7. 'Mexican imports for the month of August declined 18 per.

cent from the same month of the previous year; exports increased 41 per cent. The bulk of exports, however, corresponded to raw materials, especially minerals, which so far yield absentee foreign stockholders the larger portions of the profits made.'

[Cárdenas subsequently imposed a 12 per cent export tax on mining products. Laws were passed providing for the retention of a percentage of profits in México for reinvestment within the country.

Various mining cooperatives, contracted by the miners, were started.]

8. 'The Mexican government has bought two million dollars' worth of sugar-refining machinery from the Fulton Iron Works of St. Louis to be installed at Zacatepec, Morelos. It will be one of the largest plants in the world and will be operated on a profit-sharing basis.'

9. 'Laws are being pushed in all states to give the population access to all idle lands.'

[The amount of new lands made accessible by Cárdenas to the rural population exceeded the acreage of all grants by all previous revolutionary régimes combined.]

10. '*Petroleros de México*, the Mexican-owned oil company, signed an agreement raising wages forty per cent. The foreign-owned companies refused to meet union demands. The conflict is expected to be satisfactorily settled by President Cárdenas.'

[The outcome, following the refusal of the oil companies to abide by the decision of the National Labor Board, or, later, the decision of the Supreme Court, was the expropriation of all foreign-owned oil properties. The further outcome was reams of propaganda, incessant attacks upon México and Cárdenas, a diplomatic tangle, the breaking off of relations with Great Britain, and finally a settlement, so far as American oil companies were concerned, imposed by the Federal Government at Washington, most of the funds for payment being provided by the United States; i.e., the oil companies have been reimbursed at the expense of the American taxpayer.]

11. 'Felipe Mungía, the oldest officer of the 1910 Francisco

Madero rebels, in a commemorative celebration held yesterday in Torreón, presented an old-time rifle to President Cárdenas and received a brand-new plow in exchange.'

12. 'All hotels are to be regulated to prevent all "soak the tourist" practices. Most hotelkeepers in México are aliens.'

[The paper might have said that the owner of the luxurious Mancera Hotel was Luis N. Morones, the Calles-controlled labor leader and millionaire office-holder. It might have added that another luxurious hotel was owned by Calles' business associate, ex-President Rodríguez, and that several more of the newest, most sumptuous tourist hotels were owned by high politicos of the Calles régime.]

México was one of the few countries in the world (Turkey was another) building new railroads out of current finances and locally floated bonds. Under Cárdenas, two trunk lines were pushed toward the Pacific, opening up regions hitherto accessible only by long horseback trips. The Vera Cruz line was extended along the hitherto impassable coast marshes and jungles of the Gulf toward Yucatán. A railroad was driven across the burning sands of the Sonora Desert to connect up with Lower California; other minor but difficult and costly connections were pushed through mountain country. These roads had political and economic significance and were also vital for national defense.

These random news items reveal offhand the very pro-Mexican and somewhat anti-foreign tinge of the period. But more important, they revealed a new prosperity, optimism, and rising standards of living. They revealed enormous government initiative in building roads, edifices, railroads, dams, schools, and in the promotion of agriculture, industry, public health, better living conditions. They reflected a new spirit of peace and order. The fact is, all during our own depression (except for a short slump in 1932) México's production was expanding in all lines, unemployment had practically ceased, and the country's prosperity and progress, despite persistent attacks by certain American interests, were probably greater than during any similar period of time in México's entire history, except part of Dictator Díaz's long rule.

All this was a phenomenal record in a country long of semi-colonial status, hitherto wholly dependent upon economic conditions in the larger industrial nations, particularly the United States. These constructive achievements to benefit the country, the forgotten man, the peasant, and the indigenous population indicated the powerful new impetus given the country by the most outstanding genius of the whole revolutionary epoch, Lázaro Cárdenas.

Not that Cárdenas, or any other single man, deserves all the credit. These achievements were the result of the whole trend of the period, the sweeping change from a feudal to a more democratic régime based on wider social justice. It can be said, however, that the accomplishments could hardly have been carried through without the leadership of a man of Cárdenas' caliber, a man of broad vision, clever political talents, and driving energy and determination. It can be said that under the iron hand of Calles, this progress would have been further strangled.

2

In 1931 — Ortiz Rubio was then President — I sent a New York architect friend of mine to that charming sleepy southern city of eternal spring, Oaxaca, for the 'peace and quiet' he was craving. He arrived there an hour before the terrible earthquake which shook down most of the southern half of the city, including part of his hotel. Jolted right out of his need for peace and quiet, he set to work — the best technically equipped man on the scene — to help clean up the débris.

General Cárdenas was rushed down from México City to take charge. Though my friend, Tom, could speak no Spanish and Cárdenas no English, they got on famously, and Tom eventually returned to México City in Cárdenas' private car.

The choice of Cárdenas to take charge at a time of catastrophe was based on his record for quick action and his personal integrity. For years Cárdenas had turned back part of his army expense money to the public treasury, in contrast to most other generals who devoured it all, grafted with supplies, and clamored for more funds.

In Oaxaca he cleaned up the city in record time, scourged grafting politicians, provided housing and food, took sanitary precautions, and even got provisional schools going by rapidly constructing frame buildings in the various parks. He was at that time only thirty-six years of age.

Cárdenas was born in the small Michoacán village of Jijuilpan. After the customary six years of primary education, he went to work in his early teens as a railroad handy boy. Later he became a printer and was appointed village jail-keeper. He was fifteen when Madero initiated the 1910 revolution. At eighteen he threw up his jobs and joined with the forces which had taken the field against Madero's assassin, Victoriano Huerta.

He saw service mostly under Calles and Obregón, and distinguished himself in the critical battle of Celaya when Obregón finally broke the power of Pancho Villa. At the age of twenty-one, Cárdenas became a colonel and at the age of twenty-five, as a reward for backing Obregón in the fracas which made the latter President in 1920, a full-fledged general and provisional governor of Michoacán.

Cárdenas proved loyal to Obregón and Calles by helping suppress the 1923–24 revolt of De la Huerta and the Gómez Serrano revolt in 1927. Under Obregón and Calles and their immediate successors, he was given trusted military and civil posts where trouble might be expected to develop. All tasks he performed with loyalty and probity.

He stood high in the favor of President Ortiz Rubio — they were both from the same state of Michoacán. In 1928 Cárdenas ran for governor of that state and was elected.

He instituted a brain trust, combing the country for talent, a procedure that did not sit too well with local politicians, ever suspicious of brains not concerned with grab. Cárdenas speeded up the land program — Michoacán had been neglected — and established some of the most successful cooperative village enterprises in the country. He promoted agriculture and industry, built roads, irrigation systems, and schools. In all he probably did more for his state than any executive since the days of the great Bishop Quiroga back in colonial days.

At the outset Cárdenas's policy was violently anti-clerical in a very pro-Catholic region. Fierce opposition resulted in riots. Convinced that this was an obstacle to his other constructive efforts, he promptly modified his policy, and although insisting on the enforcement of the constitutional provisions, succeeded in conciliating his opponents.

His efforts contrasted so favorably with those in most states that while governor he was made President of the Executive Committee of the National Revolutionary Party. His activities in that post soon lifted him to the Secretariat of Interior; i.e., to the head of the cabinet of President Abelardo Rodríguez. He was not particularly in sympathy with the policies and trends of the Rodríguez administration and quietly resigned to take over the presidency of the Party. In contrast to the now reactionary trend of the régime, he actively promoted agrarian reform, rural education, and the curbing of alcoholism. The head of the PNR had become the key political post of the country, and the public soon smelled out that Cárdenas, despite his independent activities was probably slated to be the next President in accordance with the wishes of back-stage dictator Calles, who, ear to the ground, realized that if a more progressive trend were not re-established, a popular explosion might result. Through the halting of the agrarian program and the arbitrary jailing and killing of labor and peasant leaders on the one hand, and of Catholic elements on the other, Calles had been rapidly isolating himself from both radical and conservative elements, while simultaneously losing the unifying support which a previous anti-American policy had given him. The fact is, Calles had begun to fear not only the masses, but also the political ambitions of a number of his power-ful wealthy associates, particularly the Monterrey or Coahuila group. Now, sensing the popular drift — 1934 being an election year — Calles sought to re-establish his hold on the masses by swinging sharply left again, hence threw his support to the younger more radical elements in the PNR, of whom Cárdenas was the leading figure. It was necessary, if Calles hoped to re-main the power behind the throne, to get a man who had not been lampooned as a part of the get-rich-quick politician gang.

Cárdenas had always been obedient to Calles and had proved himself a dependable party man, even though sticking to his

principles. Also he was well enough liked by the army to receive
its O.K., an imperative requisite for any candidate to be successful. And so Cárdenas was duly chosen — unanimously — as
the official nominee at the 1933 Calles-bossed national convention of the PNR.

Cárdenas' strongest opponent was Adalberto Tejeda, radical
governor of the rich state of Vera Cruz. Tejeda had been in
Calles' earlier cabinets; he was a pronounced anti-clerical, a
very sincere man, with strong peasant following. Very independent, he had refused to remain part of Calles' personal and totalitarian party, the PNR. He put out a platform that appealed
wholly to the masses.

But Cárdenas, as head of the PNR, had been pushing, with the
aid of numerous experts, a study of Mexican problems, out of
which had grown a program that was now issued as 'the Six-
Year Plan.' It was a complete and detailed blueprint of action
for the ensuing six years — the presidential period — dealing
with labor, land, and governmental problems; it laid down goals
to be achieved for public works: railroad and road building, irrigation, harbor facilities, etc. It provided for the greater expansion of education and rural credits. It was thorough and broad
gauge. Cárdenas used this document as his platform, and it
made that of Tejeda look amateurish.

Calles campaigned valiantly in behalf of Cárdenas and assisted
in circumventing Tejeda. Tejeda's leading supporters were either
kicked out of federal jobs or bought off with more lucrative posts.
Tejeda's agrarians in Vera Cruz were forcibly disarmed by the
army. But Calles was by now so thoroughly unpopular, his
support did not add to Cárdenas' prestige.

So greatly was the sincerity of Calles now doubted by everybody that anything or anybody he backed left a sour taste with
the general public. As a result, even the more liberal wing of the
official party carried the taint. Its leaders were believed to be
merely restless politicians, not so close to the banquet of power
and easy wealth as the more favored Calles men, but merely
hoping to get there. The men in the leftist group were younger,
less known, but were considered to have the smell of official
standpattism. In any case they were creatures of Calles' will.

That, in fact, was the whole burden and purpose of the PNR, to embody Calles' will and monopolize all possible routes to office and prestige.

Hence few people had any faith that Cárdenas would or could develop an independent policy. When his name was mentioned, people merely shrugged, 'Just another puppet of the dictator.' Cárdenas was considered — since as yet he was not well known in the country at large — as just a dutiful member of 'the gang.' He was just 'another general,' who could be expected to continue the dictatorial acts becoming all too frequent. Not much was expected from him.

Nor was he helped by his physical appearance. A young wiry chap, he had not yet developed that avoirdupois and jowl, or the commanding arrogance, one expects in Presidents. He bore the unmistakable signs of his village origin. He might easily have been confused with any small-town official. His face was bony; he was of dark complexion, with straight black hair and black eyes. His stringy drooping mustache was typically indicative of the mestizo predominately Indian. One of his children was even named 'Cuatémoc' after the martyred Aztec Emperor. People said contemptuously — using a typical expression leveled at persons risen from humble origins — 'He smells of the *petate*.' But since over half of Mexico's population sleeps Oriental fashion on straw mats, this should have been considered high praise, proof that he was a man of the people who might perhaps be for the people.

But with the support of Calles and the bureaucracy, the governors, mayors, and the army, with the whole electoral machinery so well greased and controlled, Cárdenas had the contest in the bag. Automatically he would have been named chief executive even if he had stayed home knitting socks.

But he did not swallow the silver spoon that easily. Instead he made an unprecedented electoral tour, the most active campaign ever made by a Mexican candidate. Why — when the electoral machinery assured his election — asked the puzzled public, did he go to such great and unnecessary effort? He covered nearly thirty thousand kilometers in plane, on ship, train, and horseback. He visited every corner of the Republic, even

going to remote sierra villages requiring six days in the saddle to
reach, villages that never in their history had seen a presidential
candidate or even a gubernatorial candidate. He made speeches,
mingled with the people, ate their humble food, visited their
homes and fields, asked them what they wanted. 'A school?
Irrigations? Land? Tools? A road?'

'He can never fulfill all the big and little promises,' said the
skeptical. 'More demagoguery,' said the cynical.

Also he had a real platform, full of detailed promises, all down
in black and white. Most Mexican candidates merely shouted,
'*Soy honrado!*' ('I'm an honorable man!') and beat their chests.
But Cárdenas' platform, the Six-Year Plan, was a remarkable
document calling for concrete material, moral, and social accomplishments.

Before the elections, there were rumors of cooling feelings between Calles and his protégé. People noted that the speeches of
Calles and Cárdenas did not jibe; there were differences in what
each proposed for the future administration. In several speeches
Cárdenas seemed actually to be rebutting Calles rather than his
opponent, Tejeda, and the other minor candidate, a Communist.
People also noted that considerably before election day, Calles
dropped his speaking tour and retired to Cuernavaca, where he
maintained hermetic silence.

He emerged again, before Cárdenas took office, to precipitate
a new quite unnecessary anti-clerical fight. Also, coming from a
visit to his big sugar estates in El Mante (where rebels had just
driven off his cattle), Calles stopped long enough in Monterrey
(where the socialites snubbed him publicly) to fulminate against
the 'greedy' capitalists of that city (many had been his close
political associates) for their unjust treatment of their workers —
although Monterrey was then paying the highest wages in the
Republic, far higher than on Calles' own sugar estate. It was a
firebrand provocative speech, a further demagogic bid for the
support of labor and peasant elements growing restless. Both
attitudes threatened to set new fires going in the country. Other
trouble was now stirred up in Sonora by Rodolfo Calles (son of
the dictator), who drove the Chinese out of that state by violence,
theft of property, and murder, with shouts of Mexican national-

ism. In other places the Jews were now molested in every way possible.

What was behind this? Was it to terrorize the opposition? But the conservative opposition was already pretty well cowed. Calles himself had become the only effective conservative, he and his millionaire Socialists. Most people saw these efforts of Calles, to which Cárdenas lent no support, as an attempt to stir up trouble for the new President; either so Calles could himself seize power or else to make Cárdenas wholly dependent upon him for solving the ticklish problems created, and perhaps, in a few years before he became too entrenched in his new post, to oust him as had been done with Ortiz Rubio.

What would Cárdenas do? Cárdenas, having won the election, was now the quiet one, saying little for publication.

3

After the ballots had been counted, the Calles politicians suddenly became acutely anxious, for they simply could not get near Cárdenas to talk over jobs and patronage. He would discuss none of the things dear to a politician's heart. He kept on traveling far off among the peasants, too far for men of avoirdupois to ride after him. New rumors of quarrels between Calles and Cárdenas circulated.

But when Cárdenas' first cabinet was announced, the old crowd was happy. All the forlorn predictions that Cárdenas would be merely a thumbnail sketch of Calles seemed true. Only two of Cárdenas' own known personal followers figured in relatively unimportant bureaus; all the rest were one hundred per cent Calles yes-men. Even two of Calles' own relatives, a son and an uncle, were pushed into the cabinet; a half-brother, Arturo Elías, was made Postmaster General (later he would be ousted and prosecuted for embezzlement). Furthermore, the Secretary of Public Health was none other than the new husband of 'Cholita' González, Calles' campaign *compañera* and private secretary, now not quite so slender a lady as in previous years. It was a wholly hand-picked group, and a group hand-picked by Calles. Thus Cárdenas' cabinet represented neither his own personal political connections nor any member of the group within the official party which had so ardently backed him. 'Just a Calles stooge,' was the current verdict of the new President.

And yet despite this unfavorable set-up, Cárdenas somehow managed to keep all his pre-election promises. He remembered the little schools, the dams, the roads, and even went out in person to the humblest towns to inaugurate them. Any citizen of the Republic was privileged to send a telegram free to the President, voicing complaints or making requests. And such appeals were always attended to, however trivial. As a result, the executive offices in the National Palace remained mostly vacant. Cárdenas kept moving about carrying on with his personal whims. The critical said he had no true qualifications for the presidency. Instead of looking after great national policies he was off at every beck and call to the villages. Certainly the group in power was content. They smiled condescendingly, but were glad enough to have a free hand to carry on their own little grafts and intrigues. 'Let Cárdenas look after his dear Indians, we'll look after the country,' they said almost openly.

But even before election, his trip had made him one of the best-known presidents in the history of his country. If the generals still put long fingers in the honey jar, and his indifference made him ideal for the millionaire Socialists, he was becoming even more popular among the masses. He was building up a rural political machine of his own, cell by cell, district by district, state by state — from the bottom up — a work he had already begun as president of the PNR. And when the time came, it would not fail him. He paid little attention to the big and glittering affairs of state. He let the Calles gang tend to all that. But he was building up a nation-wide following, one more real and tangible than if he had attended all the diplomatic shindigs. There is a faint echo in all this of Stalin and the Politbureau, although Calles was no Trotsky, and Cárdenas was never to be forced to carry out any bloody purges, beyond downing the brief open revolt of General Cedillo.

One immediate act of Cárdenas did strike anger and a bit of fear into the hearts of the Calles gang; he promptly shut up the notorious Foreign Club and seized it for a public building. But

Cárdenas was supposed to have a particular complex against alcohol and gambling, and since this was not followed immediately by other blows, the bitter pill was accepted as merely a pet whim.

Then, as Cárdenas continued to pile up more and more popular support in the outlying regions, Calles himself grew uneasy. His device previously had been to create trouble for each president, trouble that he alone could settle. Now once more, he stirred up the Catholics, made baiting speeches. A new drive on the Church was begun. The Calles-controlled governors suddenly enacted still more punitive laws than any yet devised. The meager political rights of Catholics were once more wholly flouted. New revolts of Cristeros sprang up. Once more uneasiness grew in the country. Open revolution was feared.

Calles, with the aid of his man Friday, Morones, also busily stirred up labor trouble. An epidemic of strikes broke out everywhere — but chiefly against English companies. This would give Cárdenas a headache in international matters.

Cárdenas accepted the challenge boldly. He showed his hand twice, and in a very simple manner crumpled the dictator's power into a piece of waste paper.

One of Calles' handy men, Garrido Canabal, ex-governor of Tabasco, now Minister of Agriculture, was utilized to precipitate the Church crisis. He sent his personal 'Red Shirts' out to Coyoacán, where on a Sunday, in front of the second oldest church on the mainland of America, they wantonly provoked a riot, then brutally shot down half a dozen unarmed men, women, and girls, emerging from Mass. I arrived on the scene in time to see the bodies carried away.

Cárdenas did not hesitate. The assailants were swiftly arrested, and the President declared they would be punished, that the laws would be enforced, that the Catholics were to be secure in all their legal rights.

Garrido sought in every way to free his hirelings. He rushed to Calles. He tried suborning under-officials, but despite Calles' backing, he found it highly expedient to take a plane back to his native state of Tabasco, where he had ruled like an Oriental despot for more than a decade. He resigned from the cabinet and left his luckless followers to their fate in jail in Mexico City. Shortly afterward he found it still more expedient to take a plane to Costa Rica, never to return until shortly before his death. But more significant than Garrido's flight was the fact that Calles' support had not saved him. Cárdenas, in spite of Calles, had acted sternly, independently, and with strict respect for the law. In the United States, where we have just begun to learn what paternalism, personal rule, and government by bureaucratic whim rather than by established law can mean, it is hard to appreciate what a terrific blow such a single act can give to a ruler's prestige. Where each public act is weighed in the scales of personal power, the balance can tip abruptly. It was proof, in the eyes of the public, that Cárdenas could and would act independently; that Calles in this instance was unable to sway him, was unable to enforce his will, that other members of the Calles machine, if they transgressed, would enjoy no security.

Cárdenas soon had his second opportunity in the strike situation. Although Calles had stirred most of them up, now, from his Cuernavaca retreat, the dictator denounced 'the marathon of strikes.'

Once more Cárdenas merely put himself on firm legal ground. Thereby the dictator's own weapon was turned against himself. The President issued a nation-wide reprimand to Calles, declaring that the constitution and the laws fully guaranteed the right to strike. That right would not be abridged during his administration. Anyway the strikes were a symptom of prosperity and rising living standards, not of social disorder. The legal instruments of settling strikes expeditiously had been set up, and all controversies would be handled in a legal manner.

All México buzzed with excitement. This was an open challenge to the dictator. Such bold defiance would likely be the signal for an immediate armed struggle.

But Calles found himself suddenly and unexpectedly quite isolated. Popular demonstrations were now staged against him. Mobs attacked Anzares, his México City residence. Soldiery held them off. Cárdenas nobly took the rôle of protecting the unfortunate ex-president against the popular wrath. Calles should also have every legal protection. Thereby Calles was suddenly beholden to the generosity of the man he was seeking to under-mine.

Peasants moved *en masse* to take over Calles' big Santa Bár-bara estate on the Puebla road, which originally had come into his hands by a dubious tax-delinquency sale. The manner by which he had obtained it was now bruited abroad. The public was now told how he had had it tilled by soldiers on the public payroll. His hypocrisy in being a large landlord — this was only one of his vast estates — while confiscating the estates of others, was heralded to the world.

Now, also, Calles' supposed control of the army was suddenly seen to be another myth. The only generals backing him were those who had shown a flair for business enterprise — the mil-lionaire Socialist gang — not those tough hombres with mass followings and a record of many battles. Only a few generals now dared express sympathy for Calles, and these were the most notoriously corrupt ones, hence the most open to personal inves-tigation. Their declarations of fealty to Calles were considered acts of disloyalty and violations of their oaths of allegiance and the military code, and they were peremptorily removed from their commands.

Nor could the pro-Calles governors lend much of a hand to their patron. Already Cárdenas had been deftly piling up their local political difficulties, and they were faced with too many urgent problems at home to come now to the aid of their chief. Several hurriedly resigned. Others were faced with petty revolts; all, in one way or another, were cleaned out.

Cárdenas, it now transpired, had already offered high posts to those of the Calles followers who had political power and popular following and were willing to sever the old tie. Mostly they de-cided in favor of the bird in the hand. Certainly Calles could expect no help from the Church, which had suffered more at his hands than from any other executive since the days of the Mexi-can Reformation. The Church, although it had no special love for Cárdenas, or for any man who had come out of the revolution-ary period, had discovered that he had a sense of fair play, that he insisted on impartial legality. Certainly the Church was not inclined to back a worse Jacobin (Calles) instead of a lesser one

(Cárdenas), one who had as governor of Michoacán refused to raise religious controversy once he discovered it interfered with the carrying out of administrative reforms, who had come to believe that religious conflict merely served to blind the people to the real problems of the country.

And finally that creature of Calles' imagination and will, the National Revolutionary Party, was now wholly under Cárdenas' thumb.

Calles after ten years of absolute domination, almost with the flick of a wrist, was done up in a day. Since under his rule so many of his opponents had been brutally assassinated, it was natural for him now to fear acutely for his own life. Hurriedly he fled in a plane for the United States, a King Lear bewailing the base ingratitude of his numerous political progeny.

Pro-Calles office-holders were now cleaned out of the government, out of the army, and out of the official party. The broom swept clean.

After a leisurely trip to Hawaii, Calles recovered his courage and came back to México in company with the discredited labor leader Morones (who had also fled). For a short time the ex-dictator tried to build up his political fences again. For a while he became a focus of opposition. In fact a revolutionary plot, centering in Monterrey, the iron and steel center, was uncovered.

Calles, Morones, and two of their followers were seized, put on a plane, and dumped into the United States, where Calles landed with a copy of Hitler's *Mein Kampf* under his arm, and frothing with false denunciations of Cárdenas' rampant Bolshevism, all phrased in the best Al Smith manner. Cárdenas was at last President in his own right; Calles was a humiliated nobody.

The power of a dictator was never broken so smoothly — at least not in México. Such a shift had always occasioned armed conflict and the spilling of much blood. Cárdenas' handling of the situation verged on genius.

4

Much of the immediate pressure which broke Calles's hold on the country was from militant demonstrations by the left. But

the cabinet which Cárdenas now installed was a wide coalition
cabinet, chosen with a canny eye to the real political forces rather
than to ideology. It ranged from the radical General Múgica,
pro-labor, dreaming of a proletarian state, to the conservative
General Cedillo, known to be friendly with the large landowners
and the Church. Both Múgica and Cedillo had popular followings and many armed retainers. The same was true of the Radical
anti-Church governor of Vera Cruz; and of the wily middle-of-
the-road politician, Portes Gil, the former President; and of
Marte Gómez, the former Minister of the Treasury. These and
other similar figures were each given cabinet positions or were
represented in the cabinet by intimate followers. It was, in short,
an opportunistic cabinet, a cabinet of checks and balances. It
could scarcely be called a Popular Front cabinet as the term is
now used. It was a strangely hybrid cabinet.

Calles had ruled by a narrow clique through a totalitarian
party. Cárdenas greatly widened out the bases of governmental
support. And now — except for the ousted Calles group — full
liberty of the press and of political expression was restored. New
little newspapers sprang up overnight. A pluralistic, more democratic process was set in motion. The National Revolutionary
Party, despite the fact that Cárdenas now controlled it, was no
longer given a monopoly of all the political activities and governmental offices of the nation; its arbitrary assessments on the
salaries of government employees were stopped, and it now had
to stand on its own bottom.

His hand full on the helm, Cárdenas drove ahead full speed
to carry out the Six-Year program. He got things down in record
time in spite of customary political intrigue and the seesaw in his
own cabinet.

But by March, 1936, differences among his own followers
reached a fairly acute stage. With the personality of Calles
eliminated, the need of common unity diminished and divergent
views re-emerged. Various secret plans began coming to light
for possible *coup d'états* by any one of three generals, Múgica,
Cedillo, or Sánchez Tapia. The first wanted to institute a definite
agrarian-proletarian revolution (although the pace of Cárdenas'
land-distribution could not have been faster); the second, Cedillo,

desired a reactionary military dictatorship, along Fascist-Catholic lines; Sánchez Tapia was out for a middle-of-the-road dictatorship.

Plenty of pressure came from without the government. Lombardo Toledano, successor of Morones as national labor leader, head of the new Confederation of Workers and Peasants, now the most powerful organization in the country, uncovered another incipient plot of the steel and iron interests of Monterrey to foment a revolt, assassinate Cárdenas, and take the reins. Involved in this — so it was charged — was the wealthy millionaire Socialist, Aarón Saenz, brother-in-law of Calles. But Toledano himself was an aspirant for power and was demanding the establishment of Mexican soviets.

The army was also getting discontented, owing to the removal of leading generals with much influence, the curtailment of the army budget, and stricter supervision of accounts and conduct.

At this critical juncture the oil controversy sprang into new life. The companies refused to meet strike demands. These were carried before the National Labor Board, which ruled in favor of the strikers. The matter was carried to the Supreme Court, which also ruled in favor of the workers. The oil companies flatly refused to abide by the Supreme Court decision. Declaring a national emergency, Cárdenas expropriated the oil properties.

Shortly after this the armed revolt of Cedillo was staged in San Luis Potosí.

CHAPTER IX

Last of the Bad Men

GENERAL Cedillo was the last of the powerful self-made, roughneck barons of the revolution. He did not belong to the golf-swinging set of the Cuernavaca Country Club, although many of its members had origins even more humble. He did not belong to the inner clique of the Monterrey industrial crowd. He had never been able to make his stiff Indian hair lie down straight as had the whiter General Almazán, also a millionaire, but now fully 'civilized,' who knew the language of big-business democracy, and was long considered by elements in our State Department as the white hope to save México from the grip of those who still took the revolution seriously. Cedillo was very definitely the product of twenty years of upheaval. He was a product of many battles and of the long clash against foreign control, in which petroleum, with proper melodramatic battle, banditry, murder, and often threatened war, had held the stage.

Like so many others, he had ridden on the crest of disorder, matching his violent spirit with the violence of the times. Having ability, greed, courage, and cruelty, he stamped his will on the lonely deserts, rugged mountains, and fertile valleys of his native state. He was the soil of its soil, a stocky, almost full-blooded Indian, with the cold cunning of a race defeated and long oppressed, one who had also acquired the ruthless personal ambition of the oppressors.

Before the Madero revolution even started, Cedillo had climbed out of serfdom of his own people to become a petty rancher, and the rancher in México, for centuries caught between the cultural thrust of the native folk and the competition of the large Spanish landholders, has survived only by fierce daring individualism. When revolution swept the land, such men had no alternative but to fight. Cedillo rode with the revolution. He rode with Villa. He helped Carranza down Victoriano Huerta. He betrayed Carranza in behalf of Obregón, and became the dictator of his state and presently loomed as a national figure.

The center of Cedillo's revolt was San Luis Potosí, where twenty-eight years earlier Francisco Madero was jailed just before the revolution started. But in all his years of struggle Cedillo had learned little of the social aims of the revolution, except to use them occasionally to feather his own nest. What he did learn he soon sloughed off when he became powerful and rich.

Certainly conditions in his own state well explained the why of the Madero revolution; few places still cried out more for an elimination of old injustices. According to McBride, before the revolution, 98.2 per cent of the heads of rural families in San Luis Potosí were propertyless, paupers, serfs, sans rights. But the cause of land reform never got much help from Cedillo. He had been an individualistic rancher too long to sympathize overly much with the hopes of Indian collectivism. By 1920, after ten years of fighting, only four villages in his state had received lands.

But as soon as his star rose, he began to add rapidly to his own personal landownership, enriching himself at the expense of the cause he was supposedly furthering. Absolute master of San Luis Potosí, for eighteen years his word was the real law there.

Some years before he revolted, he was so busy raking in land, wealth, and new concubines that he forgot to pay the schoolteachers for a whole year. When they went on strike, he branded them as 'Communists,' threw some into jail and made others work in the sun on his vast estates at the point of the bayonet. Federal pressure forced their release after many days. Some had to walk barefoot over the stones back to the capital. Some were never heard of again.

To his own followers, Cedillo did give some lands, and kept them armed like feudal retainers. They were organized into a fake agrarian league, the main purpose of which was to kill off any *bona fide* peasant leaders. Although the rights of labor unions are defined in the national constitution, Cedillo never permitted workers' organizations to exist in his mining state, where foreign capital gouges out the wealth of the hills, and where wages in the mines were lower than in most places in the country. Any attempts to hold labor meetings were promptly broken up by armed thugs and bloodshed.

When Cárdenas finally disarmed Cedillo's private militia, and sent in an agrarian commission to enforce the land laws, to provide the villages with land, with orders not to exempt even Cedillo, an undeclared war was on. The local feudal barons decided to fight, and Cedillo decided to lead them.

2

For some years he had become the white hope of more reactionary elements. Many Catholics, who, a few years before had denounced him as a bandit, came to look upon him as a savior, for he steadfastly refused to enforce the drastic religious laws in his domain. This short-sighted attitude, however, was not shared by the Catholic hierarchy. When the situation with Cedillo approached a crisis, the hierarchy made it very plain that it had no intention of backing any military adventure. It was not in sympathy with certain local Catholic elements tied up with Cedillo, and in fact the Church relations with Cárdenas, which had steadily improved ever since he took office, were apparently, if not ideal from the Catholic viewpoint, on a footing of mutual understanding. By one of those accidents of history, this relationship was probably enhanced by the fact that Cárdenas and the actual archbishop of the country had been close personal friends long before either occupied high office. The Church saw no chance of betterment by opposing Cárdenas and was willing to bide its time in the hope that certain features of previous revolutionary legislation might later on be abandoned or changed. In fact, when Cárdenas took over the British and American oil fields, the hierarchy, along with most of México, was so stirred by crusading pride that it swung in behind him and agreed to raise several million pesos to help pay — a remarkable change of attitude. The Church obviously did not want its reputation besmirched by the activities of any outlaw in the hills at a time when its legal and spiritual position in México was better than at any time since the downfall of Díaz.

A few ill-informed American business men, as well as even certain of our diplomats, also looked to Cedillo for consolation and hoped he would eventually be able to take over the country. Cedillo was also beloved by the Nazis. Increasingly he became an ardent admirer of Hitler and Nazi doctrines. One of his right-hand men was Baron von Merk, a Nazi colonel and Gestapo agent, until several years ago an active fifth-columnist in Central America, México, and the United States. Von Merk, long resident of Guatemala, at one time also stood high with the government there, which, prior to the declaration of war, was flagrantly pro-Nazi and pro-Fascist.

Even before he revolted, Cedillo was charged by the National Labor Federation of México with having smuggled in German and Italian arms, via Guatemala, and to have got other shipments from the United States. He acquired a whole fleet of airplanes. Although Cárdenas obliged him to sell these to the Federal Government, he secretly secured other planes, another Nazi agent being the intermediary.

It was also asserted that American and British oil interests were also jointly backing Cedillo's fling for power. But no documentary evidence for such charges has ever been disclosed, although Rodríguez, head of the Gold Shirts, in exile in the United States, in close contact with Cedillo and the Nazis, was receiving strange American agents and seemed to have no lack of funds. And certainly Cedillo's revolt broke soon after President Cárdenas openly charged that the oil companies were plotting armed trouble, a charge they hotly denied, although in the past they and certain mining interests had subsidized similar revolts. San Luis Potosí bordered on the rich oil state of Tamaulipas, said to be the main goal of Cedillo's planned campaign of rebellion, a state where shortly before the Gold Shirts had attempted to stage an invasion from the United States. A few days after the Cedillo revolt broke out, the oil companies spread full-page ads over the México City dailies, declaring they were entitled to fight for their rights. To put it mildly, to place such ads at such a ticklish moment of armed revolt was certainly far from loyal to the government of Cárdenas. In fact a less tolerant government would have seized the officials for sedition and treason. The fact that Cedillo had a Nazi tie-up certainly did not preclude also an American oil tie-up. Nazi activities in Latin America, prior to our entry into the war, often had close tie-ups with American business agents, much to the perplexity of our State Department, which on at least one occasion publicly denounced such an unholy relation.

In any case, Cedillo and his revolt, and similarly the psychology and practices of the oil companies, had been products of the same wildcat era of lawless violence. Just as Cedillo long felt himself above all law except his own will, so had the oil companies long considered themselves wholly above the Mexican law, and in fact in defying the Supreme Court, so acted right down to the moment of expropriation. It was symptomatic that the Cedillo revolt was crushed at the same time that the Mexican people, who for twenty years had fought persistently to win back the right to control their own resources, finally won out, with a tolerant smile from the New Deal.

In short, the broader good-neighbor policy won out over the old policy of coercing this or that Latin-American country. Certainly to have taken sharp issue with Cárdenas on the oil question would have tilted the balance away from continental solidarity. In the last war, the Carranza government was definitely and openly pro-German; today México has cast its lot in with the United States, and the whole picture of continental cooperation has been brightened over what it had been a few years before. If a drastic policy had been followed toward México over the oil issue, the whole continent would have pulled away from us, and now, in our hour of trial, the Nazis might be at our back door.

There is little doubt that Cedillo expected a different attitude toward Mexico and his own revolt by the United States; in fact, he expected full backing. But unfriendliness from us toward Cárdenas at this juncture might have so weakened the Mexican administration that Cedillo's movement would have quickly spread and led to a military turnover. Washington, by refusing to interfere, wisely discouraged the spread of his movement, and he was swiftly isolated and cornered and paid the inevitable price

— 'shot in the hills.' So passed away the last of 'the Mexican bad men.'

Today, looking back on the scene, one can better appreciate what a pretty kettle of fish we should have in our neighboring country had Cedillo, with his Nazi connections and his ignorant brutality, come into power.

Long ago Senator William Borah said of México in the days of dollar diplomacy and armed aggression: 'God made us neighbors. Let us be friends.' That this came about is in part due to those Americans who for so many years, despite abuse heaped upon them, so steadfastly sought to arouse the American public against an imperialistic policy and the use of military aggression for which we now condemn Hitler.

That the more liberal policy of friendship did not falter later on is due in great measure to the unusually able diplomatic endeavors of Ambassador Josephus Daniels.

The crushing of Cedillo helped strengthen the more orderly process in México which had been taking root ever since 1920. Instead of an illegal armed *coup*, peaceful and free elections could be celebrated in 1940. General Avila Camacho, Cárdenas' Secretary of War, was elected. He was dubbed 'the Unknown Soldier' because of the meagerness of his political utterances. In general he announced a somewhat more conservative program, and such a program has been followed. His administration has not been featured by either the brilliant achievements of Cárdenas or his radical innovations. But the country has steadily progressed, industry has expanded, and living standards have improved.

Today México is a war ally. Much of the increasing friendliness toward the United States in official quarters has been due to the efforts of Foreign Minister Ezequiel Padilla, a consistent anti-Fascist, who led the strongest pro-American bloc at the Rio de Janeiro Pan-American conference and who later was the spearhead of governmental elements favoring the declaration of war by México. His recently published book, *Free Men of America*, is a brilliant analysis of the problems, policies, needs, and aspirations of the New World nations: the best statement by a Latin American, or anyone else, that I know of.

With the advent of war, President Avila Camacho brought Cárdenas into the cabinet as Minister of Defense, thus guaranteeing, we hope, the most capable effort and a continuation of progressive policies.

PART THREE

Tropic Sea

CHAPTER X

The American Mediterranean

W ITH reason the Caribbean has been called the American Mediterranean. In spirit it is largely an inland sea, a great lake meant for the easy use of mankind. Like the Old World Mediterranean, it is the meeting point of many diversified cultures and races — more so than any other part of Latin America. As in the sea between Europe and Africa, the sailors of the small island trading craft have developed their own patois: a curious combination of Spanish, English, Portuguese, French, Dutch, Danish, and many Indian and negro dialects, with here and there the words of other far-flung peoples thrown in.

Although the imperialistic pressures on the Caribbean have never been so constant as in the case of the Mediterranean — where the urge for domination, not only by conflicting European powers, but by Turk and Mohammedan, by Arab and Jew and Egyptian, has been an everlasting menace to the peace of the area — the struggle for power in the sea to the south of us has not been absent, and in times past, before those waters became truly Mare Nostrum, the conflict of races and nations played an epic rôle. There Spain and Portugal and France and England strove for supremacy. The British sought to wreck Spain's overseas empire; her buccaneers preyed on Spanish commerce; revolts were staged in Belize and Nicaragua; and colonies were seized by the French, the English, the Danes, and the Dutch. And so the Caribbean is one of the key points of the earth. It is the China Sea of the Western Hemisphere, where the tide of peoples and cultures meet, clash, intermingle, or repulse each other.

Like the Mediterranean, the Caribbean is also held in the close embrace of two continents, and mastery of it determines the control of a large part of both, a fact even more strikingly true after the Panama Canal was dug. Even earlier the Isthmus was a focus of travel and transshipment. There the Spanish trading vessels unloaded and reloaded; there passed the China trade; there both the French and English sought to win a permanent foothold. And there finally the American flag landed and waved, and the sea was won, at least for our time, by the dominant power of North America.

The Caribbean proper extends for about 1800 miles from Serpent's Mouth Strait, between South America and the British island of Trinidad, to the Strait of Yucatán between México and Cuba. If the Gulf of México — of which in a sense the Caribbean is merely an extension — be included, the total length is 2700 miles. In width the Caribbean is from 400 to 700 miles. On the south it washes the shores of Central America, the Isthmus of Panamá, Colombia, and part of Venezuela. North and northeastward, it is enclosed by a great arc of islands: the Lesser Antilles, the Greater Antilles, and, somewhat outside the arc, to the north and off Florida, the Bahamas.

The arc closes in at the Straits of Florida, a hundred miles wide, and the most westerly tip of Cuba, the Cape of San Antonio, bows down toward Yucatán, about a hundred and fifty miles distant. The Antilles are apparently the broken segments of an ancient mountain ridge that runs down their middle regions, so that they stand embattled, like a vast protective arm thrown about the flat lowlands of Yucatán, the level tropical coast of the mainland, and the Panamá Canal.

Magnificent rivers flow into this sea. The Mississippi, which of course discharges into the Gulf, is one of the world's great rivers, rivaling the Amazón in length, though inferior in the area drained and the volume of water. The main river in Colombia is the Magdalena, over eight hundred miles long. Fed by four great tributaries flowing down from the Andean snows, and draining an area of over two hundred thousand square miles, it carries a large volume of water and is navigable to within two hundred miles of its sources.

The Orinoco, the principal river of Venezuela, which empties below the island of Trinidad, or just outside the Caribbean proper, is even more impressive. Its vast arms reach out over four hundred thousand square miles of territory. It springs from the Sierra Madre de Mérida, in western Venezuela, the northernmost range of the Andes, and flows through great plains, interspersed with narrow bands of forest. From lower down in the Andes, other tributaries drain across half the interior of Colombia, and still others strike north from the Sierra Pacaraima, the lofty barrier that is the northern boundary of Brazil. In all, four thousand miles of the system are navigable.

Not the least important of the Caribbean rivers is the short San Juan, which drains out of Lake Managua and Lake Nicaragua (one of the great inland seas of the Americas) and flows east, clear across Nicaragua. Two thirds of its length forms the northern boundary of Costa Rica. Here, too, is another short transcontinental route, long the scene of international rivalry and marine intervention. The San Juan, today a half-forgotten stream, flows through great walls of jungle, dotted with a number of frowsy river towns, and flanked by cattle ranches and plantations.

Quite as important as are these and other rivers to the New World is the Gulf Stream, which starts from the Caribbean and carries its everlasting warmth far across the sea to provide a livable climate for the Old World. For Europe the Gulf Stream is life or death. Without its geniality, the Old World would be as bleak as Labrador and as sparsely settled. If some freak of Nature were to cut off that submarine river, most of Europe's population would have to emigrate or perish; its culture would largely disappear. In a mighty war of continents, if some master mind found a way to choke off the Gulf Stream, it would wreak worse havoc on the Old World than all the armies of Hitler, and tumble a whole civilization into ruins. Some Irishman wrote a little fable about such a master mind, who sought to peddle his alarming discovery in England for a vast sum. He found no one really interested in saving their world. Gradually he had to reduce his demand, and in the end disposed of his dangerous invention to a peasant woman who paid him a few shillings, out of pity rather than apprehension or patriotism.

The Caribbean is a region of natural violence. It is frequently rocked by earthquakes, and over it sweep terrible tropical hurricanes visited upon it by the great god Huracán of the original Carib Indians. More than a dozen such storms ravage the islands every year, often disastrously. Some years ago a hurricane wrecked the capital of the Dominican Republic; frequently tempests sweep across Cuba, leveling buildings and beating down the sugar-cane and the forests. Low beaches at times have been swept bare, if not by the wind, by the driven sea on a rising tide. Smaller vessels, ignorant of storm warnings, are little likely to survive.

And yet when the weather is calm, which is most of the time, nothing is quite so peaceful as the Gulf and the Caribbean. I have traveled for days on end through seas as smooth as the water in a teacup and stretched out like purple satin. The vessel moves without a roll under the burnished sun, along white shores, darkened by palm trunks and the dense black-green of semi-jungles. The air is a balmy caress; and even if distant from the land, one can catch the citron-like perfume from flower and forest. Here and there one skirts long stretches of swamp, thick with the uplifted roots of the salt-water mangroves; or long waving fields of bright green cane, or mighty expanses of bananas or palms, feathery against the copper sky. Many of these islands are among the most densely populated spots in the world, and one can go no great distance without seeing thatched huts or little tile-roofed towns, white and shining as the sands about; and yet, despite the pressure of people, one has always the impression of Nature's being predominate over man, of an area of everlasting wilderness, of great virgin forests and lonely cliffs; a sense of great solitude and isolation. But the sea and the air and the land are teeming always, not only with human life, but animal and bird and piscatorial life in superabundance.

When our little vessel plunged and jolted over the rough bar of the San Juan River, we could see the flash and swarm of a great school of sharks; along the rivers loll alligators and crocodiles; scarlet wading birds stand poised in the marshes; and over the sea float giant turtles, looking like tiny atolls. And I could always tell when we were approaching a settlement by the swarms of scrawny-necked buzzards, in some places the only scavengers — but effective ones.

2

Sooner or later one swings into a beautiful harbor. Some harbors are flanked by great cities; some are landlocked in the arms of stout cliffs and mountains; some lie flat inside coral reefs. Magnificent is Havana, with its gray old fortresses, its round Morro Castle, its white tall buildings, and the narrow streets poking up from the wharves like little canyons. Magnificent also is Santiago Harbor, with its tight bottleneck, the scene of the heroic exploit of Hobson 'of the *Merrymack* and the merry smack.' San Juan, Puerto Rico, is a miniature Havana, and little less imposing. Kingston, Jamaica, on its palm-studded shore; Mole St. Nicholas, and Samaná Bay, onetime site of a colony of American negroes, Castries in Santa Lucia, are all excellent ports.

I have often wondered at the ineptitude of man's choice of some entry points. Just south of unprotected Vera Cruz, main Atlantic port of México, is the magnificent harbor of Puerto Alvarado at the mouth of the broad Papaloapan — River of Butterflies — a great stretch of sun-glinting blue, lying behind low scrub-pine sand-hills and stretching on to the far haze of blue mountains. There the ships of the world could ride at anchor in safety; yet historical accident, the result of Cortés' first landing on an open coast, dictated the establishment of the City of the True Cross at a point where larger vessels must lie out in the open roadstead, subject to the violent drive of the northers. La Guaira in Venezuela and Puerto Progreso in Yucatán also lack harbors. Seagoing vessels can enter Cartagena Harbor in Colombia, but only through narrow Boca Chica and a tortuous passage beside which stand the same old forts that were once stormed by Drake in the days of the Spanish Main. After a difficult run of six or seven miles along the mangrove shores of Tierra Bomba, the incoming steamers anchor at Drake's Spit, below a white town of many balconies that seems to rise directly out of the water. Baranquilla, Colombia, lies seven miles from the river mouth, and passengers and goods formerly had to be dumped ashore on a sandy beach among a discouraging assemblage of huts that reminds one of Conrad's most dismal pictures of forlorn tropical ports. Today, with the deepening of the river channel, vessels can come directly to the city.

The Central American republics have fair Atlantic harbors, although that at Colón, the entrance to the Canal, is little more than a narrow body of water behind the curving arm of a break-water. Puerto Limón in Costa Rica, where so many million tons of bananas have been loaded, is a sturdily built stone-lined port, cool gray in the early morning, topped with yellow and white buildings and a tangle of vines and trees. Neat streets lead into a trim but uneventful city, peopled mostly by British West Indians.

Baron Banana and Baron Mahogany have dictated Nicaragua's shipping centers: Bluefields and Puerto Cabeza (or as the blond gringos call it, Bragmans Bluff). The first, which takes its name from the Dutch pirate Blewfeldt, lies in a wide harbor near the mouth of the Bluefields River, down which float supplies of hard-woods, bananas, sugar, coffee, coconuts, and gold from all over the Prinzapolka.

Honduras has a number of developed banana harbors. The leading one is Puerto Cortés at the mouth of the Ulúa River on a narrow spit of sand drenched by violent tropic rains, baked by fiery tropic suns. Puerto Barrios of Guatemala, in the large land-locked Amatique Gulf, is one of the world's finest harbors, sus-ceptible of almost unlimited development. It could easily min-ister to the largest city in the world. Actually it is chiefly a petty banana-exporting point, dominated by the yellow buildings of the United Fruit Company, served by a ramshackle wooden hotel. Its streets of ankle-deep sand slither off into thatched huts, with privies on stilts adorning the beach.

Besides the flourishing ports in the Caribbean, there are many lost harbors. The importance of Porto Bello and Nombre de Dios, names to conjure with in the story of the Spanish conquest, has passed to nothingness. Now, mere collections of huts, swamped by jungle deluges, they hold little interest save for stu-dents of terrible tropical diseases or of their ruins of olden days. There Drake was buried in the placid waters of the bay that now only natives, banana traders, and the supercurious ever see.

Greytown (San Juan del Norte), at the mouth of the San Juan River in Nicaragua (once the busy center of preparations for canal-building, where huge iron dredges rust in the marshes under canopies of honeysuckle, calabashes, and gourds), is today a dying jungle village. Had it not been for the active lobbying in Washington of the holders of the worthless French Panamá canal and railroad shares, Greytown might now be as important as Colón or Port Said — one of the important key harbors of the world. But today, the San Carlos mouth of the river is almost impassable; the other is so silted up that boats drawing only four feet of water jolt head on and scrape bottom on the sandy bar among swarms of sharks. The inner channels of the delta, where once passed large ocean vessels, are now half-choked with dense jungle.

3

The Caribbean area was densely inhabited long before the Spaniard came. Bartolomé de las Casas, the great ecclesiastic, estimated that some six million natives inhabited the islands, and said that Jamaica 'abounded' with Arawaks 'as an ant hill with ants.' Today some of the countries are among the most densely populated spots on earth. The little British island of Barbados has 1138 persons per square mile. New York State has a density of only 264; and Belgium, with its complex industrial life, only a little over 700. On the mainland, however, the population becomes sparser. Salvador has 130 persons per square mile, about the same as Illinois; but Nicaragua, considerable larger than England, has only 19 persons per square mile, slightly more than Nebraska.

Even before European conquest the Caribbean was already a tangle of peoples; the tangle grew more snarled after the conquest, when folk from every corner of the earth were funneled into the region. But despite the onrush of new peoples, the pre-conquest folk have left a permanent impress on Antillean life, on customs, thought, and language. The *bohío*, or hut, of the Cuban *guajiro*, or farmer, is not unlike that of his Arawak predecessors: palm-thatch, sometimes coated with mud. Many of the descendants of the old peoples, either pure-blood or mixed, still dwell within the confines of these tropic lands. Some have risen to eminence in the professions, in literature, in the leadership of their countries; but probably the mode of life of the vast majority is little different from the time when Columbus crossed the ocean.

Five major peoples fringed that southern sea — all the way from the highlands of México through Central America, along the northern shores of South America, and through the Antilles.

On the high Méxican ramparts stood the mighty empire of the Aztecs, who under Ahuizotl gleaned tribute from realms as far south as Nicaragua and north into the present United States.

In Yucatán and northern Central America stretched the Maya-Quiché culture. The Mayas, in many respects the most remarkable of the New World peoples, had already started to decline when Cortés arrived. At one time, they evidently pushed their settlements overseas as far as Cuba and Florida. In subsequent colonial days, and even after independence, they were scattered through the islands as slaves, especially in Cuba. After the so-called War of Castes in Mexico, the defeated Mayas were sold into slavery for the sugar plantations of Cuba (mostly in Oriente) at sixteen pesos a head. Batista, the present dictator of Cuba, born in Oriente, has various physical traits resembling those of the Mayas.

Central America was a tangled skein of native peoples. Into that narrow strip of mainland were wedged folk from the north and counter-migrations from the south. The region then, as today, was as complicated in its population pattern as the Balkans.

From Panamá into Colombia stretched the Chibcha Indians, workers in gold, weavers of beautiful garments. It was on the plateaus of Colombia that corn was probably domesticated. Although the Chibchas had not made the material and social advances of the Aztecs, the Mayas, or the Incas, modern investigations place an ever-increasing valuation on their cultural achievements. Since they constructed their edifices of wood, they left fewer of the enduring monuments than did the great stone carvers of the other three major cultures; but Chibcha knowledge of many of the arts and crafts and of aesthetics was probably quite as advanced.

The island dwellers of the Caribbean were far more primitive. The main group originally was that of the mild and timorous Arawaks, who so easily fell a prey to the conqueror. They lived in round high-pitched huts, wove cotton from the ceiba tree but went mostly naked; made gold ornaments, baskets, used darts and clubs and slept on hammocks, which they invented and named. Bernáldez gives an account of an Arawak chieftain, or *cacique*, who came aboard Columbus' vessel in Jamaica, traveling out in a large lateen-rigged boat, brightly painted, with his wife, two daughters, two sons, five brothers, dependents, and vassals. One of the daughters was 'a very lovely girl of about eighteen, completely nude, as is their wont here, and very modest.'

Around his neck on a string of marble or onyx stones, the *cacique* wore a gold [or copper?] adornment, shaped like a fleur-de-lis and large as a plate; on his head a wreath of small green and red stones; over his forehead another large ornament; and in his ears golden pendants, suspended by strings of tiny green stones. Otherwise, save for a girdle worked with green and red stones, he also was naked.

His wife was 'similarly adorned, naked and exposed, except that she had one single part of her person covered with a little piece of cotton no bigger than an orange leaf.' About her armpits she wore a cotton roll, 'made like the upper portion of the sleeves of old-fashioned doublets.' Similar cotton sleevelets were worn on each leg below the knee.

The kind friendliness of these people availed them little with the Spaniards, who were eager for gold and converts, and who soon drove them under the lash in mine and on plantations. Pedro Martyr gave the population of Hispaniola as 1,200,000. Within twenty years it had been reduced to 30,000. Too late, the Arawaks turned and fought. Their greatest leader was Hatüey, who battled desperately against the invaders in Santo Domingo, then fled to Cuba to continue the struggle.

In 1513 he was defeated and seized. After torture he was offered baptism and absolution — so he might go to heaven.

'Are there many white men in heaven?' he asked. . . . 'Then I do not want to become a Christian, for I would not want to go to a place where I must find men so cruel.' So they tied him to the stake.

The Cuban natives were evidently a mixture of the Arawaks and Yucayos (found in the Bahamas). They called themselves Siboneyes ('stone men') and Tainos ('good men').

The Caribbean derives its name from the Caribs or Cannibals — so called by Columbus — a fierce brave folk, related to the warlike Guaraníes of inland Paraguay. When the Spaniards arrived, the Caribs were in the process of expanding over the whole island area, had planted themselves on the Lesser Antilles, and were warring against the other islands. They left at least some skulls and spearheads as far north as Cuba.

4

All these people have put some sort of mark on present-day life. In 1492 the men of Columbus saw the natives smoking 'tobacco,' and the weed still is called by the ancient Siboney word. The *bateyes*, or sugar granges, derive their name from the ancient folk. Various country foods, such as *gacha* (porridge) and *puche*, made of maize, yuca, and wild cassava, were originally concocted by the Siboneyes, who also provided the nomenclature. Folk of the humble classes still eat *hutias* (barkless rodent dogs) and *majas* (snakes). And the ancient *huracana* (a Carib word) still tumbles Cubans out of their *hamacas*, which often are made from the fibers of a plant still called *magüey*. Even the rattletrap omnibuses of Havana are called *guaguas*, the original Siboney meaning of which appears to be lost.

Elsewhere the natives left far more impress on later culture. Mayan and Aztec architecture provides motifs for the modernistic buildings of México City. The old terra-cotta ware still simmers over the charcoal fire. The flat-cake tortilla is still the basic foodstuff of all México. The Aztec *cacique* is today the unscrupulous political boss of all Spanish politics in four continents. The world uses tomatoes and chocolate and calls them by their Aztec names, slightly modified.

At Panamá, within stone's throw of the scientific wonder known as the Canal and the smoothly functioning machinery, in the huts of the natives are still found the carved grinding stone and the carved gourd *tula* alongside of five-and-ten utensils and mail-order crockery. Against a steep bank will be found the *jorón*, a long timber notched for footholds; near the lakes and on the coast, fishing arrows hang on the walls, alongside a cane flute or horns made from the shells of marine snails from Bocas del Toro. Many Panamanians still go to the *suguía*, or magic-maker and medicine-man, rather than to the modern physician; they still fear the evil spirit *tulivieja* (a combination native-Spanish word) rather than the Christian Devil, of whom they frequently have never heard.

Many other habits and words have entered into the life and vocabulary of even the urban Panamanian. Probably from the Quechua comes the common word *chachay*, used to describe a well-dressed child. *Chichimé*, the Panamanian expression for cooked corn, is derived from the Guaymí language; and until recently Panama City had a Chichimé Street, later baptized Fourth Street.

Many a modern Panamanian fisherman goes out in a *chingo*, which is a dugout; and for dances, the tiled floor is covered with mashed *chancaco*, a species of conifer, to make it slippery; housewives use the leaves of the *chumico* in their seasoning, perhaps on an *icotea*, a species of turtle. Children love to sing the old song:

> — *Icotea-Concha, veni a barré!*
> — *No tengo mano, no tengo pie.*
> — *Icotea-Concha, veni a apprendé!*
> — *No tengo mano, no tengo pie.*
> — *Icotea-Concha, veni a comé!*
> — *Aqui tan la mano, aqui tan lo pie!*

> 'Shell-turtle, come and sweep!'
> 'I have no hand; I have no foot.'
> 'Shell-turtle, come and learn!'
> 'I have no hand; I have no foot.'
> 'Shell-turtle, come and eat!'
> 'Here is my hand; here is my foot!'

And so Indian-America is a reality, a living reality of the nations to the south. If the earlier races in the islands of the Caribbean have been largely exterminated, pockets of them still survive. In parts of the islands, the folk are very definitely mixed with the earliest inhabitants. And quite apart from any mixing, the earlier customs, languages, music, many foods, the dwellings, numerous modes of life, are part of the modern world.

On the mainland the Indian percentage in the population runs higher. México is definitely a mestizo-Indian country; Guatemala is predominantly Indian; Salvador is Indian-mestizo. Honduras is a very thorough mixing of Indian, Spaniard, and negro. The northern highlands of Nicaragua, the center of Sandino's resistance to the invasion by American Marines, are in parts wholly Indian. Costa Rica prides itself on its pure white European blood, yet few of the inhabitants are without a trace of Indian blood, and the interior has many full-blooded Indian settlements. Panamá, Colombia, and Venezuela have both fully assimilated Indians and those of the wild variety, still in a primitive state. The women of the San Blas Indians of Panamá, a remarkable people, with beautiful textiles and interesting handicrafts, still use a ring through the septum of their noses.

The native dwellers at the time of the Conquest were in many stages of culture, but both primitive and more advanced peoples have made their definite contribution to the world of today; and in fact they are an integral part of the Caribbean realm as well as of most of the interior highland countries.

5

With the arrival of the Spaniards, the process of mestization, or the mixing of the races, began — the first European contribution to the melting-pot of the complicated modern racial stew that is now to be found around the shores of the Middle Americas.

Cortés promptly found a native woman for a mistress, interpreter, and political adviser. Many of the conquerors married the women of the native upper classes, better to secure title to their property. Concubinage became a recognized institution.

The mestizos, the offspring, belonging to neither culture and denied all the privileges enjoyed by the conqueror, yet having more rights than the natives, shouldered their way into the new nations, growing toward independence. Some mestizos, despite their submerged status, promptly attained to distinguished literary or other careers. Most, however, for centuries to come, remained in a twilight zone, living chiefly by their wits, serving mainly as go-betweens for the two races, conquerors and conquered. But in time the mestizo was to become the dominant racial and political element in the highland cultures of North and South America. His rôle diminishes in the Caribbean and the lowland areas of Central America. For there occurred more extermination and less blood-mixing, and furthermore the mestizos in those locales were soon tossed into a wider melting-pot.

The Conquest was not yet cold when the Spaniards brought in negro slaves, further complicating the racial picture.[1] Later the current became more powerful as the slave trade with the American colonies and the United States became so remunerative. The Caribbean climate made that region a favorable one for the black man in which to work and reproduce. Since he first came there, his numbers have steadily increased, his race has become widely disseminated, and his culture has expanded. The sugar industry, which arose in due time, provided a great incentive to the bringing in of more and more blacks, and down to our times it has operated to promote black immigration into new centers about the southern seas.

For a great and comprehensive story of the African slave trade and slavery, especially in Hispanic America, one should turn to the four volumes of José Antonio Saco. As early as 1517, Charles V granted a patent to favorites to export four thousand slaves to the Antilles. By 1540 the Spaniards had broken the Portuguese monopoly on slave-trading and were busy rounding them up in the African jungles themselves. The English were not far behind, and from 1700 to 1786 brought more than 600,000 slaves to Jamaica. As early as 1713, by the Treaty of Utrecht, the English took over the Spanish monopoly, the Asiento. After 1750 all the leading nations plunged into the profitable game.

The French had had a finger in the pie as early as 1763, when Louis XIV issued the necessary edict, and during the next century, according to Boyer-Peyreleau, shipped overseas three million blacks. The Dutch were also active. And various respectable New England Puritan families owe the foundations of their fortunes to the slave trade.

The negroes brought in were from nearly all parts of the African continent, and ranged from those of a high cultural level,

---

[1] Some Latin-American authorities claim that there was some pre-Colombian emigration of negroes to the Americas.

whose leaders were trained in Mohammedan universities, to the most primitive types. Remnants of the Mohammedan faith are still found among certain negro settlements. The most widely dispersed were the Eboes, many of whom had already been enslaved in Africa by other blacks. They were a low type, had to be flogged to their work, were sold cheaply and driven hard. Many committed suicide. To Cuba went many Mandingás, probably with quite as high cultural attainments as most of those who enslaved them; the squat coal-black Congos; the thin-nosed, proud, melancholic Lucumíes, who went into the eastern part of the island; the lighter-skinned Carabalí, industrious, faithful, but of independent spirit. The Carabalí language provided the basis for the universal lower-class language of modern Cuba — *ñáñigo* — as well as the general underground religious system of all black Cubans, plus some converted whites. Originally the Lucumíes were worshipers of the shark, and their sacred fiber dolls, still used today in secret *ñáñigo* rites, are adorned with the teeth of that fish. The rites are a noble pledge of faithful comradeship plus elements of voodooism. *Ñáñigo* lodges played an important part in the independence movement, and still have great, if secret, political influence.

To Santo Domingo went the majority of the Dahomeans, a warlike stubborn clan, immersed in sacrificial voodoo, who fought fiercely when the hour of independence struck. Another warlike tribe, the Coromantees, and the allied Fantees and Ashantees mostly went to Jamaica and several other British islands. Proverbially the Jamaican negro is harder to manage than almost any other negro of the Caribbean; he has struck out more often for his rights.

And so, soon after the Conquest, the blood of three races intermingled. Indian mated with negro; the Spaniards had concubines among both races; and presently a complicated nomenclature arose to designate the different types of mixture, each term indicating the amount of blood contributed by each race. By the fourth generation, merely from these three races, twelve hundred and sixty different blood mixtures were possible. I have come upon more than thirty early Spanish expressions to designate the more prevalent types of mixture.

6

With the rise of the colonial ambitions of England, France, and the Netherlands, the number of pirates, smugglers, and fifth-columnists increased in the Spanish colonial regions. Great English and Dutch buccaneers raided the colonies, looted, killed, raped or carried off the women of all the races, from the black negress in slavery to the high-born Spanish girl. In 1537 a whole swarm of French pirates descended upon the Caribbean, attacking Santiago de Cuba, the mouth of the Chagres, and the Honduras coast; other French raids soon followed. As early as 1543 Spain had to convoy all her merchant vessels across the ocean. The following year the French king commissioned private corsairs under the direction of the daring François le Clerc, to raid the Spanish Main. Le Clerc looted Santiago of eighty thousand peses' worth of treasure. He stormed Havana in half an hour, looted and burned it, and kidnapped the wealthiest citizens for ransom.

The French buccaneers laid the basis for empire, and Tortuga Island, to the north of Hispaniola or modern Santo Domingo, was known as the pirates' hide out. In due time the French arms merchants and others were able to occupy the northern peninsula of what is now Haiti.

The French also moved into Martinique and Guadeloupe as early as 1635.

The English soon learned the same tricks, and the Caribbean quickly resounded with the name of that daring Lutheran, John Hawkins; of Drake and Morgan, and many others. In 1654 Cromwell, in order to strike a blow at hated Romanism — and of course caring not a fig about empire or gain — sent a fleet to attempt to seize the leading Antillean islands. The members of the fleet, however, seemed far more concerned over loot and gold than the controversy over religion. After a number of fiascos, Jamaica was seized, by a curious conglomeration of adventurers, mostly recruited in Barbados: bankrupts, escaping bonded servants, deported criminals, Royalist refugees, and 'Puritan riffraff from London.'

The early buccaneers found the Mosquito Coast of Nicaragua,

with its numerous creeks and harbors shrouded in tropical growth, excellent hide-outs. Belize was another hang-out, and for a time, the corsair crews held Ruatán, a bay island, quite openly. These sea-marauders laid the basis of subsequent British claims to both Belize and Honduras. Later, Britishers engaged in illicit lumbering in both areas, chiefly for mahogany and dyewood. For a time the Spaniards drove the lumbering men out, but eventually England, by using runaway slaves — *cimarrones* — and Mosquito Indians as fifth-columnists, was able to convert Belize into a permanent colony and to lay hold of part of the Honduras coast. There for a period the English, before moving in themselves, sustained an independent negro kingdom. British claims were not fully relinquished until late in the nineteenth century.

Both England and France claimed all the Windward Islands, which, depending upon the tides of European battle-fronts, passed back and forth between the two countries.

Both France and England had a greedy eye on the Panamá canal route. The French, gaining a concession from Colombia, attempted, till yellow fever drove them out, to construct a canal. Workmen were brought from all over the world — Hindus, East Indians, Chinese, negroes from Haiti and Jamaica — further adding to the Caribbean racial hodgepodge.

Other of the smaller European countries tried their hands at settlement and imperialism, and added their blood to the general blood stream of the region. Sweden held St. Bartholomew for ninety-three years, and Guadeloupe for four years. The Danes bought the Virgin Islands from the Knights of Malta in 1733. Sugar and rum were produced there profitably with negro labor, until the possession was finally sold to the United States — without plebiscite — and temporarily ruined by our Prohibition Law.

The Dutch for a time had six islands: Curaçao, Oruba, and Buen Aire off Venezuela, and St. Eustacius, Saba, and part of San Martín off the Virgin Islands. Those off Venezuela were retained. The present colony of Curaçao consists of six islands, and in modern times has become important as a center for refining oil from extensive Dutch-English properties in Venezuela.

Such is part of the tangled racial and political skein of the Caribbean. It is a region of tropical and mineral wealth. It grows sugar and coffee in vast excess of the needs of the market. It exports henequén and cacao and rum. Around its shores are some of the finest and richest oil deposits in the world. From Central America come hardwoods, some rubber and quinine, copper and gold. Mercury is found in México, Honduras, and Salvador. Colombia is a great source of platinum. Under the soil of Cuba lie great unexploited iron deposits; her manganese resources, especially in time of war, are all-important; other strategic metals are available. From Belize, Guatemala, and Quintana Roo comes the world's supply of chicle.

And so here on the crossroads of the Americas, new nations and new cultures are being born. They range from white Costa Rica and the nearly white Dominican Republic to the black lands of Haiti and Jamaica and Barbados. In general, throughout the islands and in the coastal areas, Hispanic culture is giving ground constantly to negro culture, and both are decisively influenced by the United States. Negro culture in turn is distinctly modified by French, British, Dutch, and Danish backgrounds. The final result will be modes of life showing wide variations according to locale; but apparently eventually a more or less consistent racial and cultural norm will emerge for the whole Caribbean area. The coasts of Central America are likely to be drawn more into the orbit of the highland-tropic cultures, but in the islands quite another process is occurring.

The most representative synthesis, dependent upon an amalgamation of races and traditions, has taken place in Cuba, although even there it has not yet fully asserted its integrated mulatto form. But already, despite American overlordship and a curious political bastardy, Cuba has a great and unique personality.

CHAPTER XI

Life in Cuba

To MOST Americans, Cuba is Havana, a large beautiful white city beside the sea. From the sea, the city's long curving Malecón Boulevard, flanked by glistening buildings, presents an aspect of spaciousness, of amplitude and magic. If the spectacle is unique, nevertheless the city seems wholly modern and understandable.

This impression vanishes as soon as one enters the harbor. The magic deepens, but modernity momentarily recedes. Old Spain comes back to life. There at the gates stand the grim brown walls of Morro Castle. Other old fortresses dominate the hills. To the left, rising along the sides of the Guanabacoa hills, streets climb up amid a tangle of flat roofs, palm trees, and purple bougainvillea. Out of the green-gold hillside pokes a large white dome, an observatory, and the traveler feels reassured again that he has not wholly lost the modern world he knows. Black boys, diving beside the boat for coins, provide the proper romantic touch.

The landing is conventional, and the customs and immigration officials, if dark-complexioned, mostly speak some English. But as the traveler emerges through the gates, he is assailed by a wild din of importuning taxi-drivers, hotel runners, and porters. They engulf the timid and the unwary confusingly, even though all of them seem to shout a language that bears some faint resemblance to an Anglo-Saxon tongue. They grow instantly calm, but slightly grieved, if they discover you speak Spanish. Any man would, on learning that his profits thereby would be curtailed.

As you plunge into the labyrinth of narrow streets that angle up from the port between time-stained flat-roofed buildings, with their tall medieval portals and barred windows, the alien and Oriental character of Havana again reasserts itself. Here are the walls of old churches, the archways of ancient Spanish days, the battlements of another age. Why, you instinctively ask, is there so much bustle and haste in a city so ancient, and time-worn? Everybody darts about; the cars dash and career through the narrow alleys, with madly honking horns. The sense of great speed is heightened by the tightness of the space in which these vehicles of near-death maneuver. It takes time for the outsider to discover that despite this rush, he is in a siesta land. But after a bit, he does observe that in the midst of all this hurry, plenty of people are just standing about, leisurely chatting on the corners, lounging in sidewalk cafés, making their purchases without haste.

New odors assail the nostrils: coffee and burnt sugar; strong cooking fats and pungent fruit smells. One can almost taste the stink of damp hemp mingled with the sharp tang of fish and salt water. Great bags are piled high on sidewalk and warehouse; golden pineapples and papayas and red guayavas tumble out of crates.

It is a city of dark-skinned folk in white, with flippantly tilted straw hats, big cigars stuck in their mouths, and all of them excessively voluble, and voluble in shrill high-pitched voices, parrot-like voices full of nervous urge, restlessness, and combativeness. They are the voices of folk close to a peasant and trademan's world, not toned down to the suavity of salon and British tea-time. They are voices that must compete with the cry of the fowls and the shrill appeals of the market place. A tide of white-clad folk surges down the narrow sidewalks, dodging the splashes of mud from whirling wheels. Women shuffle along in rope-soled slippers, with black shawls over their heads, and market baskets on their arms.

Out of this mélange of color and sound, suddenly the taxi bursts upon the spacious central plaza, lying peaceful in the sun, gracefully dominated by tall palm trees. Compared to that of the narrow busy streets, this is a quiet world. The sidewalk arcades are given over to open cafés, where time flows by unhurtful on the balmy perfumed air. The world of the petty shopkeeper, the commission merchant, the harbor trader, has been left behind. And before one, greatly reassuring to the timid American tourist, if there be any such, is the American capitol itself — in miniature — nothing alien about it at all, except for Cubans.

A few more narrow streets, crowded with department stores and big dry-goods shops, and you emerge into the broad avenues of the better residential districts. Neither the vegetation nor the architecture nor the climate is American, but the area wears the garb of newness, modernity, hence is comforting to the visiting 'Yankee,' for as most Americans have no sense of history, they are quickly depressed by the ancient and the historical, except as temporary objects of curiosity. Dominated at home by the comfort of the latest style, living in a world constantly in the making where the old is shoved contemptuously aside to make things bigger and better, they have little sense of the continuity of time and effort over long periods. Their easily won prosperity of yesteryear — before depression and war — had given them a comforting sense of superiority and a vast supreme contempt not easily laid aside in reverence for the past or even the lessons of history.

But even if Americans stay at the National Hotel, a skyscraper edifice of great luxury erected by a New York bank, and see but little of the real Cuba, something of the magic of the island's history and its ancient life seeps into them. They will probably eat American meals with American service, and never venture — except perhaps to a few of the harbor-front dives under proper guidance — into the little untidy restaurants that serve *amarillo* and squids in their ink, and singularly savory foods of the Spanish-negro cuisine that are really typical of Havana. They will not learn to smoke the biting black native cigarettes or to drink the native black coffee, which Cubans guzzle piping hot to help them ward off the heat of the middle hours. They will even be slightly disdainful of many of the native habits, perhaps put out that the city is not quite so clean as its shining whiteness from afar had indicated, but something of the indelible beauty of this near-tropic land will be imprinted on their souls for all time.

To those more at home in other Latin-American lands, Cuba

seems shallow, really modern, compared to the ancient texture of the towns and cities of México or Perú. In Cuba one misses certain things he has learned to listen for in the highland-mestizo world. He misses the soft drawl of Indian speech and the soft shuffle of Indian sandals. Cuban speech is clipped and swift; for the first few hours, difficult even for one well versed in the Spanish language; here, too, is heard the jerky staccato of the Spanish immigrant, uncouth, aggressive, sharp in his deals. There is less grace and ease, even less politeness, than one finds in the mestizo lands of the Americas.

Here, instead of the Indians, are the swarms of black folk. They are poorer than the whites, but they are Cubans and suffer from no race discrimination. Unless they are cabinet officials or high military officers, they keep out of places frequented by Americans — not because they have to, but in order not to spoil business. Aside from that, they go and come where and when they please. And in the lower *barrios* of the city, Spanish disappears and the folk speak *ñáñigo*, the common language of the negroes of all Cuba. White folk are in the majority in Havana, but as one goes eastward along the narrow island, the number of blacks increases, and in far Oriente Province they are in the majority, even if mulattoes are not counted

2

Above all, Havana is a city of small venders, of folk hawking newspapers, shining shoes, selling candied yams from little glass cases or fruit in baskets or *refrescos* or cold drinks of unusually vivid hues. The vender is always a symptom of uprooted folk clinging precariously to life. In all lands the new immigrant is often a vender; and so one knows that the black folk and many of the white Cubans — though their ancestors may have been here on the island long before the United States was first settled — are, in a sense, still immigrants, still trying to find a rooted life, still trying to belong to a land they have not been able to claim and call their own. One must delve into history and statistics to find the reason for this.

The fact is that the Cuban has never been a free man in the

American sense. Until nearly this century, he lived under Spanish rule, often brutal. He then had slightly less political freedom than today, but perhaps enjoyed more economic freedom. Today, the statistics tell us that ninety per cent of the arable land of Cuba is owned or controlled, directly or indirectly, by absentee American capital. This means that Cuba, essentially a rural country, despite its one great metropolis, is cut off from economic independence; that the profits from its enterprises largely go northward instead of finding reinvestment in Cuba to fructify the life of the land.

The explanation is found in the prevailing system of tropical plantation agriculture, which holds the island largely to a one-crop system. A one-crop system means one-crop morals, one-crop mentality, and one-crop government. One-crop government means dictatorship, open or disguised; and no amount of wishful thinking can conjure up any more democratic system. Nor have the Cubans much more to say about the price of their crop, which is life or death to the island, than they have to say about the rising or the setting of the sun.

Cuba has but four million inhabitants. Java in the Orient, also a sugar country with much the same climate, and with similar products, supports forty million people. And yet, if anything, there is more basic poverty in Cuba than in Java. Here is a land, under the protectorate of the United States, rich in natural resources, capable of growing almost any crop except some of the cereals, which must import the bulk of its foodstuffs from the United States. For its folk are largely cut off from the soil. Most contracts with native owners for growing sugar-cane carry the proviso forbidding the planting of anything but cane. The island has been converted into a vast sugar factory with underpaid workers, with professionals hanging on to the fringe of American enterprise, with commission agents and speculators, bureaucrats and militarists, and a chronic supply of seasonal and permanent unemployed, and great swarms of petty peddlers.

However, the Cubans mostly take their lot more cheerfully than does the pessimistic observer. They are a happy-go-lucky people, not too concerned over their difficulties. Each and all, they are imbued with the speculative fever that repeatedly sweeps the island. They are essentially gamblers, and like all gamblers optimistically believe that the wheel will whirl to the lucky number on the next turn. One of the local sayings is, 'Cuba is a cork. It always floats.' You can push it down, but it will bob up again. For Cuba once had its 'dance of the millions,' when sugar for a while after World War I became like the proverbial hens' teeth for scarcity; not that it was scarce, it was merely cornered, in a private speculators' struggle with a hold-over war board scarcely famed for its probity. In Cuba wages soared. Millionaires were made. The fine new residential districts of Havana were built. New hotels sprang up. Life was gay, and Havana was ruled by the spirit of continual carnival and carousal.

Cuba has also known years of abject misery, of political disorder and revolution. Since Cuba is a one-crop country, and that one crop is sugar, the land has been preyed upon by one of the most disorderly industries of the modern world. In the international commercial chaos of our times, there has been little assurance of stability of production or of price. Sugar has ever been the paradise of the speculator. The lives of ordinary human beings, millions of them, have hung for long years on the narrow thread of violent price fluctuations and continuous uncertainty, this despite the fact that in the United States, sugar is one of the most monopolized products consumed by the public.

But Cubans have remained optimistic in spite of the warning of such able students as Doctor Fernando Ortiz and Ramiro Guerra. After all, the Cubans are next door to the land that consumes more sugar than any other in the world. Whatever the conditions of production, the American demand cannot disappear, not even with rationing. Cuba is dependent upon the American prices; it is dependent upon the generosity of an American Congress, which gives Cuba a tariff preferential; it is dependent upon an American quota, but thereby an outlet of sorts is guaranteed to them. At the present moment its prosperity is wholly conditioned by the price the United States Government is willing to pay, the amount it is willing to buy — slim pickings compared to the freer days of World War I.

If the wholesale price paid in Cuba drops below two cents,

wages go down, unemployment is accentuated, schools are closed
for lack of tax money. Sugar in Cuba, at a wage of not over
fifty cents a day, can be produced with a meager profit — if
watered-stock payments do not have to be figured — at one cent
a pound. But when the price gets above two cents, wages can
shift up slightly (there is now a minimum wage of a dollar and a
half); the payments on watered stock can then be met. When
it gets above three cents wholesale, the island has a feeling of
prosperity, or did have before it lost its European markets and
before the United States government started its war policy of
buying the Cubans' sugar crop *en bloc* at low prices, turning it
over to private monopoly, and rationing consumption, despite
vast surpluses, at high prices.

Of late, however, dire reality has struck the Cubans full in
the face. The cork may never bob up again. The price of sugar
has stayed down longer, and the market has grown ever smaller.
This year the United States, with excess stocks in hand due to
rationing, is buying close to a million tons less, not to be imported,
but merely as a charity gesture. At the same time, of late years,
sugar has been grown in more and more places about the world,
so that the supply exceeds the demand everywhere. Next to the
United States, England was long the largest market. But at the
very time when Cuba was in the doldrums of depression, the empire policy of self-sufficiency led to a concerted effort to raise
and buy sugar only within the empire. Sugar-beet growing was
started, with a subsidy, even in England itself. All Europe went
in for autarchy and sugar self-sufficiency because of the threat
of war.

As a result, unlike World War I, this conflict has brought Cuba
little advantage; in fact, it has aggravated an old situation.
During World War I, Cuba really prospered, the price sky-
rocketed, new forest lands were cut down and sowed to cane, and
the demand increased — if in good part because of scandalous
speculation in the United States — beyond all previous records.
During World War I, Cuba and the United States were really
providing most of Europe with sugar, and continued to do so
long after the war was over. In this war, except for England,
which now has its own African and Oriental sources of sugar,

Europe is cut off from the Americas; the United States is on rations and has no bottoms to devote to the importation of sugar; on top of all this, there is rigid price control and mass-buying by the American Government. Even if bottoms were available and other markets were available, Cuba, like other raw-products countries, could do little exporting, for the lend-lease system is rapidly destroying private business the world over.

The only solution for Cuba — and it is becoming a *must* solution — is for the island to diversify its crops. Otherwise it will suffer increasing misery and more disorder. It has a promising tobacco industry, although most of the processing shops have had to move to the United States because of the American tariff. It has a considerable citrus-fruit and vegetable industry, but must fight the constant efforts of Florida and Texas and California to exclude such products from the American market. The Floridans, Texans, and Californians have American votes, the Cubans do not. But in addition to other cash crops, Cuba must settle its people on the land, which it cannot now do, because the land is largely monopolized by outsiders. But sooner or later, if Cuba is to have a settled and prosperous people, capable of democratic processes, it will have to institute some sort of land program on the Mexican style.

3

Cuba, today, with no automobiles imported, with gasolene scarce, with its sugar industry dawdling along, seems more dilapidated than in a good many years. And yet Havana, somehow, manages to retain its glitter, its carefree spirit, its aspect of opulence, its devotion to enjoyable wasteful living.

The women of Havana, smart, snappy, and beautiful for the most part, add grace and attractiveness, and for the outsider, give the true touch of the exotic to the life of the city. One is always conscious of them, even though customs of old Moorish Spain still prevail, and females belonging to the better classes are cloistered. But whether they are in the shopping district or in their homes, they manage to make themselves noticeable, and doubly so, not merely for their looks, but because coquettishness is an ancient Spanish tradition not lost in Cuba. They manage, perhaps because servants are cheap and plentiful even though modern kitchen appliances are expensive and largely non-existent, to spend much time in the balconies behind the iron bars, vague but attractive and mysterious spectators of the maleness that predominates in the busy outside world.

In time, Havana takes on a certain brittle unreal quality. It is not the alien quality of it to an American which provides this unreal note. It is that ever-pressing fact that its people are not rooted in their own soil. They are not integrated with their land, and they are not integrated as a type. The race contrasts are still too violent. Eventually the norm of Cuban population will probably be the mulatto, but as yet Cuban culture is far from being one texture. There is an enormous gulf between the *ñáñigo* (white or black) and the aristocratic salons of the Vedado suburbs. There is a vast difference between the country *bohío*, the thatched hut of the *guajiro*, the peasant, and the palatial marble residence of Señor José Manuel Cortina, minister of the cabinet, with its gilded private elevator. This is more than a difference of wealth and poverty common to all lands; it is a difference in the basic pattern of life, the sources of culture, the race content.

The architecture of Havana, despite the picturesqueness of the older buildings, also contributes to the brittle note. Except for a few negro poets and writers, there is little sure stirring of Cuban art forms in architecture or anything else. Neither the spirit of Cuba nor the true spirit of the modern age pervades the city. In a mestizo culture, like that of México these past few decades, new experimental architecture has been a deep creative urge in the land. Whereas in the United States, architectural experimentation largely died with the Depression and has been choked off since then by war, in México, with an expanding economy, architectural progress was noteworthy. The modern experiments of Germany and Russia were mingled with the utilization of indigenous motifs, derived from the national life and from the architecture of the Aztecs and Mayas, motifs which still have vitality because the ancient builders still utilize many of them in their daily life. But in Cuba, one meets with but two slavish imitations: the colonial Spanish (with French notes) or the modern American business edifice. Neither breathes with the throbbing life that exists in Cuba. The people, one concludes, have not yet discovered how to convert that throb of their life and its ways into art forms. The results are merely imitative or hybrid.

This lack of creative originality plus lack of an integrated culture, plus alien economic domination, plus the universal speculative spirit, plus the splurging of *nouveaux riches* and of fly-by-night tourists, plus the fact that Havana is on the crossroads of the world, visited by uprooted people mingling with its own uprooted people, has helped make Havana one of the most corrupt cities of the world. Its brothels extend for endless blocks. Street walkers ply their trade in every nook and corner of the downtown district, morning, noon, and night. Runners tag about offering to lead the tourist to perverted spectacles. Such colossal prostitution is the obverse of the petty-peddler medal. Both bespeak an uprooted people.

Pornographic movies and exhibitions flourish, sometimes semi-clandestinely, at other times with wide-open box-office. Such a place was the Red Mill with vile wall-paintings such as those in public outhouses; on the stage burlesque tableaus without even the customary G-strings, nude rumbas with their usual contortions and belly-shaking, and movies showing the physical naked details of every conceivable sexual perversion, plus homosexuality, lesbianism, and onanism. This is a long, long way from the élite Havana of the novelists and the languid grace of Hergesheimer's tales. At present, such spectacles are not so open as in Dictator Machado's day, and a show of surreptitiousness surrounds them. But in any case they are the product of dictatorship, intellectual decay, reckless speculation, tourist-ism, the shattering effect of new commercialism and absentee ownership on the decaying upper classes that long stood for dignity and grace.

It would, however, be highly unfair to paint Cuba as a land of moral decay. In spite of alien economic slavery — or perhaps because of it — new and vital forces have been growing up. Slowly the country is growing aware of its economic necessities, the need to liberate itself from a one-crop economy. The measures taken have been faltering. Powerful vested interests oppose any change. But eventually Cuba must and will recover her lands for her own people and force profits, and interest on bonded indebtedness and alien ownership, to remain mostly in the country for reinvestment and as a proper basis for education and sanitation.

It would be unfair to Cuba not to note that, though she has few really creative writers, several artists and sculptors are at least trying to reach down into the realities of Cuban life rather than merely imitate the passing art-fashions of Europe and the United States; and that, above all, she has a few vigorous thinkers and scholars. No record of contemporary Cuba is complete without mentioning that great independence fighter, scholar, and writer, recently passed away, Enrique José Varona. Today the dean of Cuban letters is Fernando Ortiz, whose remarkable studies of the negroes of Cuba deserve translation into English, if for no other reason than that they would throw a great amount of light on our race question and the origins of the American negro and his culture. Ortiz is the author of numerous vital works on economics and sociology and has recently brought out one of the best studies on the sugar question with reference to Cuba yet published, a classic along with that of Ramiro Guerra. Jorge Mañach, a good poet turned mediocre politician, at one time gave us a penetrating essay on Cuban character and psychology, a study of *choteo*, or the deep significance of Cuban persiflage as an escape mechanism, and an excellent, if overstylized, biography of Martí. There are fine historical studies by the Guggenheim scholar Portel-Vilá; the penetrating scholarship of young Elías Entraalgo; the ringing negro poetry of Nicolás Guillén.

Cuba is known for its sugar wealth; it is known for its old castles; it is known for the beauty of its modern capital; but the island also has a great cultural heritage, a singularly rich folklore, both black and white, a record of many great and heroic deeds, a fine reservoir of popular music, song and dance (which thus far Hollywood has learned only to falsify), a sturdy peasantry, despite much disease and exploitation, and a fine intellectual life. In these things are to be found the real wealth of the island and its real future once it gains proper control of its own agricultural and mineral resources.

CHAPTER XII

Black Belt of the Caribbean

IN THE alley mire of Puerto Barrios, banana port of Guatemala, black Jim was squatting under a mango tree and weaving a double-rhomboid fish trap out of river cane.

'Don' be so good this heah, sah, as the bamboo we alls got back home, but c'n catch ebery fish mahn a pound. Some weeks Ah profits goin' on fifteen quid, sah.'

Jim, a young Belizan negro, subject of His Majesty, the King of England, is part of the great tide of dislocated black folk about the Caribbean from Havana to Barbados and Trinidad, from Belize to Venezuela and the Guianas.

The islands and mainland of the Caribbean, a more violent melting-pot than the United States, swarm with races of every hue, living in every epoch of society from that of the primitive jungle to the effete degeneracy of Havana-Creole aristocracy.

Habitants, originally thousands of miles apart, have been lifted up and set down side by side in the countries of the southeast. The Caribbean is a vast ethnological laboratory. Spanish and Portuguese meet French and Dutch, English and Americans. Jews fled there from the Spanish Inquisition; today, still more flood in from the Hitlerian inquisition. Full-blooded negroes practice the fearsome obeah. East Indian coolies and Hindus tread new tropics. Chinese have flowed in by tens of thousands. The descendants of native Indians who greeted Columbus still lounge under royal palms. Interbreeding has created many mixed types — mestizos, zamboes, *chinos del pais*, mulattoes — all along the chromatic scale from black to white — ash-gray, yellow, red, golden, brown, bronze.

But the most intense, most vital of all, are the negroes who swarm out of overpopulated Haiti, Jamaica, and Trinidad. In the making is a new breed of mixed blood from all the elements mentioned, but it appears that Africa will rule racially, however submerged politically and economically. The negro is the prolific, the virile, the most numerous and dominant type, and his culture assumes increasing importance.

Today from all the more densely populated countries, the crowded sons of the African jungles are outward bound for the frontiers of this wave-washed empire. The fruitful race sweeps over all the adjacent shores. The emigrants take with them their songs, their dances, their magic, their bright-colored clothes, their shining gold necklaces, their polite dignity and carefree joy. From Havana down to Magdalena, the break and sob of the rumba, rattled on gourds, blown on native earth pottery, sets black folk jiggling primitive joy in contortions to us lascivious, to them but expressions of a normal love-desire — their boundless procreative urge, exuberant as the jungle, simmering as the humid sun lands.

For these are the breeders in this vast circle of ocean, island, and sky. Spaniard, Frenchman, Englishman, Dutchman — they came, they conquered, they faded away in the poisonous sweet arms of the Cariba and Chibcha girl. But the negro brought even greater love and lust than the natives. The super jungle man, he had jungle wisdom with which to defy the fever, so his kind have multiplied with lore, scientific but unrecognized by science, and have continued to multiply in a frenzy of fertility and magic which has matched the lavish reproductive powers of steaming earth, hot sun, and warm syrupy water of rain, river, and sea. The white man's sanitation gives him still greater chance to survive, despite the exacting toil laid upon his shoulders. The Caribbean is a black empire going increasingly black.

From the southern negro states, Florida, Alabama, Georgia, Mississippi, Louisiana, Texas, a vast arc swings out along the mainland continent to Venezuela and the Guianas in which — except for México, where there are only coastal clots of negroes — the colored man plays an ever more important rôle. Another vast arc curves from Key West through Cuba, Puerto Rico, Santo Domingo, the Virgin Islands, and the Lesser Antilles to the same south region; and in the embrace of these two arcs are seas, dotted with other islands, also the home of black folk. It is their empire.

The Spaniards killed off both Caribs and Arawaks, and to replace them, negro slaves were imported from Africa. Ironically enough, this influx was stimulated by both necessity and humanitarianism. Las Casas, who crossed the ocean fourteen times to plead for better treatment of the aborigines, was instrumental in promoting the slave trade to protect the native Indians from extermination by unwonted excessive toil on plantations and in mines. God had gone brown but not black.

Before long, the Caribbean became the slave clearing-house for the United States. The great marts were Jamaica and Haiti, which even today remain the largest of the most densely inhabited negro centers. Even in this year 1943, the contract-labor system, which now takes Haitians and Jamaicans to alien shores, is still called 'the slave trade.' But in spite of adverse economic conditions, the negro flourishes. From his fertile loins come forth numerous progeny. Islands grow crowded. Families emigrate. They jostle each other anew on far shores.

The rise of population in this region during the past century has been phenomenal, and in general, however tampered with are some census figures, as in Cuba, it has been a black and mulatto increase more than a white increase. Even in the sparsely settled, more predominantly white Dominican Republic, the population has been rapidly expanding. By 1757 this Spanish third of the island of Santo Domingo still had only 6000 whites and blacks. By 1785, the reviving slave trade increased this five times to 30,000. By 1819, the population was 63,000; by 1908, 605,000; by 1920, 894,665; and by 1927 over a million — an increase of nearly sixteenfold in a little over a century. This was greater than the rate of increase in the much vaster area of the United States. Elsewhere in the Caribbean, the population increase has been for the most part even greater.

In the black islands, population density now varies from 165 a square mile in the Virgin Islands (with their relatively small habitable area) to 1095 a square mile in Barbados. New York State has a density of only 265. But New York, the greatest mart of the world, is highly industrialized, highly productive, and caters to the needs of a vast nation. Although the soil cannot produce so copiously as in the Antilles, a larger part of the state's surface is arable than on most of the islands, and that part more scientifically cultivated. Many square miles in the islands are mountainous or barren volcanic outcroppings. Thus the population density is really greater in much of the Caribbean area than the statistics indicate.

Perforce most of the island folks live in abysmal poverty, and doubly so since in many of them the land is owned by outsiders or concentrated in large holdings. Many are still little removed from the African jungles. People so crowded, and with such slender grip upon elementary food and shelter necessities, are eager to emigrate to new regions where labor shortage or sparser population permits new opportunities. Already the overflow from the Haitian and Jamaican breeding grounds has swept all around the Caribbean and has increased by many thousands the black population of the United States itself. The Caribbean is an enormous black incubator.

2

Along with this negro dissemination has gone a quite different process. Still another history-making force is driving with relentless impact upon this seagirt world, breaking down old barriers, destroying traditional cultural patterns, creating a new political and economic life.

The insatiable greed of the United States for raw materials has flung our traders, our business men, our capital, and now our federal tax money and our bureaucrats south over the Caribbean. With them, at various times, have gone missionaries, Marines, treaties, governors, roads, autos, Orange-Crush, loans, schoolteachers, Rockefeller fever experts, Mr. Platt, both Roosevelts, General McCoy, Pan-American Congresses, and tourists. Diluted jazz, imported from there, has been re-exported, thus returning a step nearer to its ancestral home.

Today Americans own most of Cuba's wealth, the land we freed from Spain, most of Puerto Rico, most of the Atlantic coast of Central America that is under cultivation, much of Colombia, and a big share of Venezuela. Our investments in Haiti, the Dominican Republic, Jamaica, Trinidad, and elsewhere have increased rapidly. New tools, new methods, new ways of life, have intruded, have shaken the whole region, will shake it more during the years to come.

The shock of this new industrial technique is one of the major causes, along with overpopulation, which have uprooted black folk from their old homes and habits to set them in motion for far parts. At times the force has been more inexorable than a platoon of Hitler bayonets. Negro emigration has gone hand in hand with our economic expansion, our mastery over new products and new regions. America provides the capital and the methods; Africa provides the labor.

The whole pattern of American economic invasion has been set by the plantation system. Most of our activities, the railroads, banking system, business, have been ancillary to the raw-product plantation for producing sugar, coffee, tobacco, or bananas on a large scale. The revival of the earlier colonial plantation by American entrepreneurs along modern lines with modern machinery has necessitated a new cheap mobile labor supply. The negro has filled the bill. He is shunted from crowded areas to less crowded areas. American enterprise and negro labor have been shaping a new era in the whole Antillean region — not a particularly happy era, but one with far-reaching economic, social, and political significance.

The Caribbean has witnessed various cycles of the large plantation. In the past, as in the present, it has been closely linked with black labor. Spaniards and the English — after the native Indian had been stricken down — turned to Africa for their cheap labor supply to exploit. Early Crown grants and English patents partitioned the islands into large *repartimientos* and huge estates. Semi-slave conditions and brutalities, new diseases and rum, led to a rapid decline in the native population, the souls of which the early Spaniards were valiantly saving for Catholicism, apparently desirous of passing the Indians on to Paradise as soon after baptism as possible. Negro slaves replaced the vanishing natives, until Jamaica, Haiti, the Virgin Islands, Barbados, Guadeloupe, Martinique, etc., became completely black. The rise of the slave-plantation system in the United States later made the African slave traffic important in its own right.

With the emancipation of the negro slaves in the Caribbean, the old plantation system broke down completely in many places. Gradually there was a greater or lesser reversion to small holdings, more diversified crops, more individual self-sufficient agriculture.

Twentieth-century developments show two tendencies. In some of the British and French possessions, notably Jamaica (but not in Barbados, which is quite strangled by large estates), the late nineteenth-century shift to small holdings has been buttressed up by state assistance, education, the dissemination of knowledge of proper farm methods, rural credits, and other salutary measures. But in the islands dominated or owned by the United States there has been, rather, a reassembling of the large plantation with modern machinery, as in Puerto Rico and Cuba.

But while the plantation is now run along new lines, it still represents, perhaps more than under Spanish rule, an absentee landlordism, and its labor remains largely in semi-serfdom, controlled feudally. Thus the plantation, plus negro dissemination, while creating a new era in the Caribbean, has also created new and serious problems. Not only do they portend a future clash between the negro worker and the system, but they have turned whole islands over into one-crop countries, a pernicious development with far-reaching implications. Old cultures are being smashed. A new integrated culture has yet to be born, and in the chaos of this transitional period, capital, with the aid of Marines, diplomatic pressure, alien labor, and corrupt officialdom, has been seizing the raw products necessary to the United States. It has been precisely the system and relationship which Hitler has been accused of trying to implant in Europe in the relations of German industry to the other countries.

3

Cuba's white gold (sugar) depends upon black ivory (the negro). The post-Spanish War plantation system, introduced by American capital, and which for some decades made the island the world's greatest sugar-bowl, rests upon cheap imported negro labor. In spite of immigration restrictions, new swarms of blacks are annually attracted to the sweet rim and fall into bitter toil akin to servitude. According to census figures, the black population has steadily declined since 1841, but this is largely a juggling of figures and classifications and bears little relation to the actual picture. Negro and dark mulattoes are said to number but one third of the population; actually, few Cubans are without some African blood. Humboldt claimed that 60,000 negro slaves had been imported by 1763. By 1790 they totaled 90,875. From 1790 to 1820, 225,575 were officially recorded, and probably 60,000 more were smuggled in. The 1827 census showed more negroes than whites, a proportion that has since been reduced through intermarriage and white pride in whitewash figures. In 1820 the negro trade became illicit until 1833, but during this interlude it continued clandestinely. By 1880, a million black slaves were estimated. As early as 1835, José Antonio Saco, the great authority on New World slavery, declared that Cuba must have white immigrants or go black.

Negroes no longer come from Africa — they are imported from Haiti and Jamaica. After Cuban independence they were for a time excluded, though many wriggled in on lonely shores on dark nights. The 1912 decrees of President José Míguel Gómez, who owed much of his political strength to the negro *ñáñigo* lodges, lifted the ban against the black outsider. Only 709 Jamaicans and 233 Haitians entered officially in that year, in addition to the incalculable number of untagged bootleg immigrants, but the *enganchadores*, or contract-labor scouts, soon got busy, and in 1912 the officially tabulated influx had increased to 27,088 Jamaicans, 35,971 Haitians, and a few other black Antilleans — about eighty per cent of the total recorded immigration. In 1927, the annual figure dropped to 17,000, but this was still more than half the total. By 1928, because of the general collapse of the sugar industry, new restrictions were imposed, but 'emergencies' (provided for by law or decree) prevented enforcement of the exclusion provisions. The United Fruit Company, which is not one of the largest plantation-owners in Cuba, was alone given a permit to import 9600 negroes.

The *guajiro*, the traditional independent Cuban peasant, is vanishing. He becomes a plantation peón, uprooted from the soil. When he can no longer compete with the low negro standards, he drifts into the cities to carry burdens, peddle, or work on the docks. He does not submit so easily to the large-scale labor system. Hence alien negroes must be brought in to cut the *zafra* and work the mills. These needed laborers are delivered by contractors at from fifteen dollars to twenty-five dollars a head. They are customarily lodged in *barracones*, long thatched barracks often without walls and having an open pit in one end for toilet facilities. They sleep on hammocks, which are rolled up in the daytime to hold the workers' worldly possessions. In certain instances these contracted workmen are kept under armed guards and driven with rubber whips until their debts are liquidated. The native Cuban workers speak Spanish or negro *ñáñigo*; the Haitians, a French patois; the Jamaicans, English. These language barriers prevent mutual understanding and hence checkmate labor troubles. On the other hand, the negroes, like the white *guajiros*, escape as soon as possible and drift to the cities, where they both eat and work less. As many such contracted negroes are brought in with the proviso that they be returned to their point of origin after a period of two years, as the time approaches for the end of their stay the companies even encourage desertion in order to be spared the cost of transportation. Such negroes then remain domiciled on the island. At times feeble attempts have been made to round a few of them up and ship them back.

Helmeted, sword-girt Ponce de León of the sixteenth century came early to Puerto Rico to find his sought-for Fountain of Youth. Today Doctor Gregory Washington X, a negro practitioner, offers a worthy substitute. Expansive letterings on one of San Juan's busy streets proclaim glandular injections to restore youth and virility. Being in the professional class, Doctor X is more fortunate than most of his fellow citizens, black or white, for native Puerto Ricans, one third of whom are recognized as black, and few of whom are without trace of darker origin, own only about fifteen per cent of the island's wealth. San Juan seems a prosperous little town, with its modern buildings, paved streets, American-style policemen, and darting American autos (differing only in temperamental behavior), but the large-plantation system has displaced the former diversified cultivation on small holdings. This is one of the notable blessings of American citizenship to Puerto Rico. Most of the population of the island is in the bare-foot pauper class, and the farther one penetrates from San Juan the less tangible becomes the direct evidence of famed American prosperity.

As in Cuba, the post-annexation plantation régime tends to turn the island black. The older Spanish culture is being defeated by American rule on the one hand and the negro invasion on the other. This tendency is even greater than in Cuba. For our new immigration laws cut off the normal Spanish immigration which throughout past centuries flowed and still flows into Latin America to leaven the population and provide new blood for the ruling white castes, constantly menaced by racial submergence either by the Indian or the black. The Spanish immigrant fortified the existing ruling-class culture and the old-time feudalism, and felt wholly at ease in the New World environment with its Hispanic traditions, so that he built his family life and his fortune in the country of his choice. This was formerly true also in Puerto Rico. Usually the Hispanic immigrant remained on his hard-won estate to manage it in person, took a native woman to wife, and became a resident citizen.

The American streamlined plantation system brought no comparable permanent American immigration. American immigration into the Caribbean is small and unstable. American school-teachers go down for a temporary lark. The administrators of the large foreign-corporation properties come and go, and this form of absenteeism dominates the entire island now that the Spanish influx has been cut off, but not the negro immigration from adjacent islands. Living standards are constantly lowered, and as Puerto Rico is so overpopulated — more than four hundred to the square mile — the lighter-skinned people emigrate to the United States for better opportunities. Several hundred thousand are in New York alone.

4

Pass from British Honduras along the Atlantic coast of Central America, and the story of black Jim weaving rhomboid traps is repeated in a hundred elementary work patterns. The interior of British Honduras is Indian, but the city and coast dwellers are black descendants of slaves, brought in during past centuries to work in the lumber camps, in chicle gangs, to collect chinchona bark. For centuries negroes have percolated into this whole region. The modern banana, sugar, hardwood, and rubber plantations have again accelerated the process.

In British Honduras the king of the chicle industry for many years was of negro origin. A powerful figure, the invisible ruler of an enormous tropical empire, his scepter was wielded over one of the wealthiest raw-product industries in the world.

Not all his compatriots have been so fortunate; many are driftwood, international Okies, caught up in the lost back-flow of the low *boca costa* region from there south to Panamá and beyond. Go into any Central American Atlantic coast town. Africa predominates. In bedraggled Greytown, Nicaragua, dead dream of a never-built canal, old Ma'tha, hotelkeeper, Jamaican one generation removed, calls the tropic dawn shower 'the pwide of the mahnin', sah,' and under her enormous green teamster's umbrella conducts you, with a swish of the long skirts of her Mother Hubbard calico gown, through the grass-grown streets, swarming with kinky-haired children, naked, mud-smeared, skins coal black, ash gray, yellowish. Only 7 per cent of Nicaragua's population is negro, but this 7 per cent is concentrated along the Atlantic coast, where it dominates, and where English and Spanish are spoken interchangeably. A large proportion of the officials are negroes, originally from Jamaica or Belize. In Greytown, a negro customs official directed the inspection of my baggage. In Bluefields, a negro youth filed my cables; another accepted my registered letters. I rode to Puerto Limón in Costa Rica in a steamer owned and run by an attractive mulatto captain.

In Puerto Cortés, another banana port, half-naked pickaninnies fight to handle your baggage. Along the rows of breadfruit trees tall ragged Haitians approach you, never looking for a job but a 'posishun, sah,' or 'emplawment, sah.' All up and down the coast (as in Nicaragua) the negroes through the seventeenth and eighteenth centuries were largely assimilated by the Mosquito Indians and other native tribes. In Honduras this inter-racial mixing has been very thorough. The modern population of all Honduras is about equally mixed of Indian, negro, and Spanish. On this is now being overlaid the new negro influx into Puerto Cortés, Tela, Trujillo, and the banana hinterland.

Climb up through the Costa Rican banana region. Everywhere the negro. Black faces peer from clapboard shanties. Mr. Brown and his wife, both ebony black, both enormously bepaunched, stroll through the jungle mud. A United Fruit clerk, he heralds his importance in patent-leather shoes, white spats, white waist-coat, and brown derby; she with white satin dress, wide white lace hat, and pink sunshade.

Some of the Central American countries, most of them ruled by mestizos, have attempted, rather futilely, to set up barriers. In Guatemala, negroes at present can be brought in on contract for only two years, subject to return to their native countries. But extensions are granted, or, as elsewhere, the negroes drift into other pursuits, disappear and cannot be discovered, so the coast parts of the Isthmus grow increasingly black.

Like Jamaica and Haiti in the old days, Panamá has become a labor clearing-house for the region. The influx there began with the building of the canal. Native labor was scarce, hence expensive. No other race could stand up under the climate or work so cheaply as the black man. So if Jamaica and Haiti are the major breeding centers, Panamá is the new center of convergence and dispersion. Blacks from Jamaica predominate. Thus in the Canal Zone British citizens outnumber American civilian citizens. Steamers from the whole world pass here, and strike out all around the Caribbean, with negroes being shipped to Central America, Colombia, Venezuela.

In Colombia one third of the four million coastal population is black. They are found concentrated in various coast areas, in the lowlands of Magdalena and in Baranquilla, the chief port. Following various bloody labor conflicts, at one time the banana companies were allowed to import ten thousand alien negro workers. They were, in short, strike-breakers. For quite a period, black labor rapidly displaced the native white and Indian labor, until along in the thirties a more nationalistic policy was followed.

Thus all these regions have been tending toward large-scale agricultural production, controlled chiefly by large American companies, although in more recent years in certain countries here and there the brakes have been put upon such alien ownership. Our long depression, of course, saw the magic of capitalist prosperity collapse in the minds of the southern folk and brought about the imposition in Central America by the highland mestizo and Creole rulers of new doctrines of economic and political nationalism — the general Fascist trend — so that in Colombia particularly, to a considerable degree in Jamaica, and to some extent in all the countries, the foreign-owned plantations have found themselves ridden with extensive new restrictions, labor controls, and heavy taxation, plus taxes on the export of capital.

Today a new page is being written. Now that the traditional American system of private capital investment abroad is going to the dogs, and is being replaced by socialistic lease-lend — a colossal hand-out to the whole world that is rapidly wrecking private enterprise all over the globe, where it has not already been destroyed by the Russian and Axis systems — a further change in the tropical plantation system is in sight. Whether the American official hand-out system will merely temporarily continue to subsidize the political *status quo* to the south to the benefit of convenient dictators, or whether increasingly it will enter the production field and remain there, it is too soon to see. Whether this will tend to restore the land to native ownership or create a sort of super-government holding concern on an international scale, it is too soon to prophesy. But so long as sugar, coffee, bananas, rubber, cacao, and similar products are produced, the labor supply will be all-important, and a considerable labor surplus can be found only by bringing in black folk to new development areas. As in Spanish days, the modern entrepreneur discovers that the Indian, now mostly in the colder highlands, is ill adapted to low-land agriculture on a semi-serf basis.

5

Turn now to the main incubators of the black labor supply: Jamaica and Haiti. Why does Jamaica, in many ways one of the happiest spots in the Caribbean, supply such a constant tide of black emigrants? Largely because of overpopulation and primitive cultivation. Lord Olivier, a former governor, wrote in the *Edinburgh Review*, in January, 1929:

'Towards the close of the day when the rainy season is promised and forgetful deities are being importuned with incantations and drummings, or petitions, salvaged from the not yet Revised Anglican Prayer Book, red stars of fire by night and feathers of smoke by day spangle and blur the fringes of American woodlands ... and the long blue escarpments of Antillean mountainsides.'

Fire-stick cultivation has returned to Jamaica, where 'bread-kind' crops (i.e., starch-producing tubers such as cassava and yams), which provide the preferred negro diet, have largely replaced the traditional plantation crops.

Originally Jamaica was settled as a white man's country. Under Spanish rule, the entire island was parceled out to eight noble families. Under English rule all desirable lands were granted in tracts of two thousand acres or more to English gentlemen, who built luxuriously furnished homes. At the time of Great Britain's acquisition of the island in 1658, the white and slave population did not exceed three thousand; today it runs over a million, almost entirely black.

For several centuries the island lived in paternal prosperity — for the landed proprietors. Then rebellion broke out. The slaves escaped to the mountains, where they grew 'bread-kind' and carried on constant warfare against the authorities. Finally they were legally emancipated. New towns grew up. Labor for plantations became scarce, more costly. The estates suffered. The negro quarters on them remained a wretched collection of semi-abandoned hovels. The weeds grew among the British gentlemen's crops. As in the British and Dutch Guianas, Trinidad, and elsewhere, Hindus and East Indian coolies were hurriedly imported. Also the authorities tried to drive negro labor back on the declining estates by heavy taxation — the smaller the free-hold, the greater the proportionate tax — a method similar, in part, to that of the Bolsheviks in attempting to drive the free Russian mujiks into collectives, and to that of México in Díaz' time.

A serious armed outbreak occurred in 1865 under Governor Eyre. As a result, a resurvey of available lands was made. Governor Sir Henry Blake threw overboard the estate theory entirely and started an orderly settlement of the peasants on the lands recovered through the survey acts. Also he founded the Jamaican Agricultural Society to promote improved methods. After 1897, following the West Indian Royal Commission report of that year, the Department of Agriculture was established, which soon resulted in the Imperial West Indian Department of Agriculture and the Tropical College of Agriculture in Trinidad. Through these commendable institutions, numerous traveling instructors, and a system of agricultural loan banks, the British Government, recognizing the advisability of small holdings, has attempted to build up agricultural knowledge and diversity of crops. Among other new products, chinchona and tea, oranges, grapefruit, and bananas have been introduced. The greater share of Jamaican exports now come from small holdings. Gradually, although the more ignorant negroes looked upon official scientific efforts as 'buckra' or white 'foolishness,' the level of knowledge and methods has risen, and the traditional primitive African practices have been increasingly supplanted.

For a time the cultivation of bananas, which, until the present war, became every day more important, threatened to reinstate the large plantation. Various alternative methods were tried. The United Fruit Company donated considerable sums to promote cooperatives, provided technical advice and assistance to small growers. The final solution has not yet been found. If only scientific control through the large plantations will fill the bill, this will likely, whatever the greater efficiency, drive still more Jamaican negroes abroad, while drawing in alien contract negroes from other islands less imbued with a spirit of independence. This has occurred in the past and may occur again.

But as yet, although poverty drives many of the islanders to emigrate to escape overpopulation, by and large Jamaica, thanks to various black revolts, is today far happier than those islands and regions where the American dollar has made its sway supreme. In the American-controlled regions flourishes the inhuman system that the British partly abandoned in Jamaica more than four decades ago, before the United States even began its colonial acquisitions.

Haiti, another breeding spot, occupies a third of the island of Santo Domingo. The other two thirds is occupied by the Dominican Republic. This latter country, long cherishing its Spanish traditions, is whiter than most of the Caribbean, except Costa Rica and the Colombian highlands. Only one fourth of the Dominican population is negro, mostly overflow from Haiti. Perhaps partly as a result of this whiteness, it is less densely populated — there are but fifty-four inhabitants to the square mile; hence living conditions are better and property more equitably distributed — though the murderous Trujillo clique, now in power, has been seizing properties right and left and welding them into large patrimonies, thus destroying an old tradition.

The Republic, because of its sparser population, fears the pressure of densely populated black Haiti, squeezed in the narrower section of the island, and has long excluded black emigration, though this is a losing fight. For just over its borders Haiti swarms with folk, nearly three hundred of them to each square mile, and (compared to the Dominican Republic) with scant arable land because of the vast stretches of mountains. Of Haiti's three million inhabitants, only three thousand are listed 'whites,' and one puts a question mark even on this small tincture.

Nearly a century ago, black troops from beyond the Massacre River overran the entire island, and the Haitian ruler of the day made efforts to bring in more blacks, especially on the Dominican end. He even invited freed negroes from the United States to settle there. Several shiploads went to found Samaná, where their descendants live to this day.

After the Dominican Republic had asserted its independence from Haiti, a negro exclusion policy was established, to be broken only during the 1916 American military occupation, when many blacks were admitted to work the American sugar plantations in

the southern part of the country. This has been one of the outstanding native criticisms of our Marine rule, and the fact still
rankles. But if barriers were knocked down temporarily, actually
Dominican officials, before and after, have themselves been lax.
At harvest times, the dollar has always talked, and the blacks
were allowed to slip through the gates. Also by utilizing exception
provisos or openly flouting the law, the politicos, over the years,
have let in many more Haitians than the Marines ever did. The
exclusion law has a wedge clause, 'except in cases of emergency.'
'Emergency' has gradually led to the introduction of many
Antillean negroes. As the plantation system grows, this immigration, in spite of all restrictions, is bound to increase. The vast
quarter-million Romana plantation is manned by negroes from
Haiti, Puerto Rico, and elsewhere. Native Dominicans, for the
most part (till recently) fairly well-to-do peasants and petty
landowners, refuse to work for plantation pittances, and, as officialdom can be induced by means readily imaginable to let down
the bars, negroes are brought in and pass on into the population.
Also negroes constantly slip over the line and squat on the wilder
western portion of the Republic. The land is there, unused; their
hunger is great.

All this causes flare-ups when economic interests come into
conflict with white Dominicans. Particularly feared are these
small Haitian squatters who take up hill lands and are not under
contract or plantation control. Such a blind flare-up occurred a
few years ago when Dictator Trujillo, in a high-spirited state
after a party, personally directed the slaughter of thousands of
these innocent and peaceful intruders, men, women, and children.
Latin America constantly accuses the United States of narrow
race prejudice and points a finger of scorn at the brutishness of
American lynchings, but in a single night the strutting little
Trujillo of the Dominican Republic wiped out more black folk
illegally than has ever occurred within the borders of the United
States in its whole history.

Even into overpopulated Haiti come negroes from elsewhere,
part of the process of shuttling the black folk around, shuffling
their languages, preventing labor trouble, seeking docile low-paid
hands. Into crowded Haiti come Jamaican negroes because of the

greater ease with which they can be handled by American fore-
men, speaking no French, and because as aliens they can be
contracted for at lower rates than the Haitian wage, miserable
though it is.

Nine tenths of Haiti's population is made up of full-blooded
illiterate negroes, practicing voodooism, living in semi-patriarchal
communism of African derivation. The per capita ownership of
land is less than one acre; and half the acreage of the island is
government-owned. The squatter system which grew up during
the past hundred years or more ignores titles. The American intervention administration, while it lasted, was very insistent
upon cleaning up the tenure tangle. This definitely endangered
squatter possession, for even generations of actual residence
counted for nought in the face of yellowed ancient deeds. The
State is now charging a six per cent rental on sale values. As
agriculture is primitive and barter largely in kind, even this small
rental is often beyond the capacity of the peasant to pay. Someone has but to offer a higher price for the land to dispossess the
occupant.

This dispossession in Haiti has also been the prelude to a growing system of large estates under American absentee management. Numerous 'Yankee' syndicates have got in on the ground
floor to revive the sugar industry, which declined at the time of
the expulsion of the French. This will change the Haitian from a
peasant into a casual laborer who finds work during the harvest
but is apt to starve in the cities the rest of the time.

Today lease-lend has provided a new twist. In buying up *en
masse* the large cash crops of Haiti, and simultaneously limiting
production, the push is not in the direction of the smaller independent proprietor, but to strengthen the large plantation with
subsidies while increasing unemployment also. The new American Government promotion of rubber and fiber production also
threatens to implant a system of large holding and to undermine
the small producer still more. Doctor Price-Mars, senator, historian, president of the Institute of Ethnology, and one of the
staunchest supporters of wartime cooperation with the United
States, in a recent communication to me for publication declares
that 'the large-scale production to be started demands the ex-

ploitation of vast estates which never have existed in the country or only to a very slight degree.' This will have 'a tendency to extend pressure on small owners to force them to give up their land. ... It is impossible to exaggerate the terrible repercussion on the future of the peasant masses,' for Haiti is almost wholly agriculture and has 'a density of 294 inhabitants to the square mile' — more than New York.

Thus, the new 'American' system has caused wholesale dislocation, emigration, and even misery. It has helped keep up an ever-ready surplus of labor, and this has forced wages down to about twenty cents a day without rations. The alternative for the inhabitants is to abandon the island, although this is often merely jumping from the frying-pan into the fire.

6

Just as the Adriatic and Mediterranean have been battlegrounds for many races, and still are, so the Caribbean is another imperial sea where the story of clashing peoples is being worked out in our times. For the present, and perhaps for a long period to come, European and Asiatic penetrations have been shut out. But American imperialism, based on dollar diplomacy — formerly private, now New Deal, state-managed, pseudo-collective, and far more powerful — makes advances. Private dollar diplomacy made advances economically, which have not held firmly in México, Jamaica, or Colombia, and which have been resisted to some extent in all the countries — but not so the New Deal advance. Politically all the countries are now acting in full accord with New Deal desires, and the Roosevelt policy has shown a commendable pliant opportunism in dealing with local systems as compared to previous big-stickism. For the time being, military and Marine intervention is a thing of the past, but the most far-reaching military expansion, through the acquisition of new bases and the occupation of Dutch possessions, the most extensive push southward since the Spanish-American War, has been occurring since the start of the new world-struggle.

But racially the picture is very different. We have sent few American colonists to the Caribbean areas. The old 'go west' slogan has never become a 'go south' imperative, nor is this likely ever to happen. After all, there we stand face to face with, for the most part, the most densely inhabited portions of the New World. Inevitably the process has been, not to colonize, but to buy up land and resources, to wield political, financial, and military power. Partly this has been possible through the economic rivalries of the various petty nationalisms, the acute competition of the various countries in the same raw products, all of which are controlled directly or through prices fixed in New York, and now more than ever by the New Deal 'plow-under plus hoard-and-subsidize' policy of artificial scarcity, plus lend-lease, plus economic planning. Such external control over the Caribbean countries has been possible in good part also through the failure of a regional culture to become integrated or a single race to become politically dominant. It may be many decades, even a century or more, before American rule is challenged definitely by the people themselves, although the leadership of México, thus far partly successful in asserting national sovereignty over some of her resources, may speed the process on the economic front.

And so, just as the Slavs, the Teutons, the Italians, and the Greeks have fought for foothold on the Adriatic waterway and for mastery, so today the American negro, the Indian, the mestizo, and the remnants of the conquerors, the Creoles, struggle for life and mastery.

Racially it means that on the islands, and possibly along the mainland coasts, the negro is likely to win. But politically and economically, the American, backed by his industrialism, his super-officialism, and his growing system of national socialism, drives down relentlessly upon the island-girt world to assert overlordship. And curiously enough, to the extent that his activities are successful, he promotes, not the winning of the southlands for American settlers, but the ever-wider dissemination of the negro.

For the time being this has resulted in growing denationalization and cultural chaos. Undoubtedly this in turn facilitates American control, direct or indirect. As the cultural patterns of these countries are broken up, so social organization is disrupted and political homogeneity is lost. The answer is dictatorship, and the dictators are for whoever keeps them in power. American money effectively maintains such a *status quo* (although if we do not soon produce goods to export to give the loan money some real value, that control may crumble). Dictatorial control sooner or later is weak control, but for the time being it makes it easier for American economic penetration to proceed smoothly on its way. Fear of popular revolt causes actual rulers to fawn upon us, to hand over bonanza concessions, and to pass laws favoring the United States, however disregardful of native requirements.

We insist on stable governments down there. Marine intervention or the threat of it provided a makeshift way of securing this. Then during the twilight period of our depression, revolutions hit all the countries, and Marine coercion had to give way to the good-neighbor policy; thereupon government loans (minus Marine intervention) took the place of private loans. This has worked because it froze in office the existing self-perpetuating tyrants. If new ones arise, they will be similarly frozen fast in their power. In the long run this may prove as pernicious a system as the previous private-loan system and an even more powerful weapon of coercion. While there was direct intervention, there was at least the faint possibility that it might eventually be liberalized in the direction of intervention toward freedom and democracy, although this never occurred despite the solemn holding of Marine-controlled elections. Upon the rock of this vast investment of American Government funds, the good-neighbor policy — unless proper wisdom arises — may eventually founder; for in case of controversy, the dispute will no longer be with a private company but with the United States Government itself. . . .

And so, the large-plantation system, the one-crop system, the importation of blacks, all promote the dictatorial processes in the Caribbean. The plantation system, as now organized, blocks and weakens public education, prevents individual independence, creates economic and race conflicts, and postpones cultural amalgamation and effective democracy.

Probably we shall remain masters of the Caribbean for a long time to come, for powerful nations, especially when contendants are distant, have always dominated near-by seas for considerable periods, as the Saracens long dominated the Mediterranean, as Japan has come to dominate the China Sea. But there is little doubt, however much the apologists for colonial expansion may prate about good roads and sanitation, that the system now in force in Cuba, Puerto Rico, and rapidly being extended elsewhere means an unhappy, poverty-stricken, sickly population, chained to an absentee landlord system, ever driven under the lash of the need of the Colossus of the north for raw materials at cheap prices. The New Deal and the good-neighbor policy have done little to remedy this basic situation; they have merely turned it into a Roman super-state policy.

There have been reactions, just as there have been slave revolts in Jamaica. There will be more. Fortunately, certain leaders in the United States are rapidly coming to realize that in the long run it is foolish to wrench away raw materials from people under such slave conditions, for they cannot buy back our manufactured products. This helps create recurrent depression at home, unemployment, and the further curtailment of the market, which endangers our own economic stability. The need for foreign markets, which as usual is one of the things close to the roots of the present war and the chronic depression resulting from the lack of them, has already forced some of our brilliant statesmen to recognize the necessity that the living standard of people now backward and too primitive and too poor to consume civilized goods must be raised.

Also, the negro and the native populations have shown a spirit of rebellion of late years, which, in spite of our powerful financial controls, in spite of the constant menace of our close and overwhelming force, will inevitably reappear. This was revealed in the long Mexican revolution. Elsewhere, as in Colombia and Jamaica, private companies were forced to revise their methods. They have been greatly revised by our own National Government as well. The great fear to the south is that the more benign features of the good-neighbor policy will not continue under future administrations, that it will not follow through to logical or, at least, hoped-for results, that it will not proceed from the political to the economic field. This seems unwarranted. It already has one heavy boot full in the economic field. In some directions, particularly along industrial lines, the efforts seem highly commendable; in others, especially with reference to agriculture and raw materials, a grand crash seems to loom around the curve.

History teaches lessons for both the strong and the weak, aggressors and non-aggressors, the efficient and the inefficient. The negroes of Haiti rose against the French and drove back the greatest overseas expedition France had ever attempted. Haiti was the first Latin country in the New World to achieve independence and not the first to lose it. The successful war for freedom created a tradition not likely to perish soon. The Jamaicans rose against both the Spanish and the British time and again, and in the end gained many new rights and economic benefits from their rulers. Sandino cost more than three years of war and was never subdued. Not so long ago Marcus Garvey with a message of Pan-Africanism stirred the black hordes from Harlem to the Antilles. Other prophets are bound to arise.

Already the racial and cultural struggle in the Caribbean is a long, long chapter. Likely it will never be closed, least of all in our day. But the reading of the trials and tribulations of the rulers of past centuries, in that area, as well as others, should remind us that even the greatest empires of man have been relatively short-lived. It should also remind us that the Caribbean problems, now so neatly pigeonholed in a mouth-filling political philosophy, are bound to grow increasingly complex as the years pass, and that none of us yet have enough knowledge at hand — even if the good-will and tolerance are available — to solve them decently or intelligently. The people of a large section of our country, and many in other parts of our land, are quite psychologically incapacitated for acquiring that knowledge, for their doctrine is that of white supremacy. Such a doctrine will fail us, just as it will fail us in the Orient if it is allowed to interfere with the four freedoms, just as it is already failing the British in India, just as eventually it will also fail Herr Hitler.

CHAPTER XIII

Colombia Returns to the Fold

IN 1938, Colombia, after quite some years of radical experimentation and flirtations with the totalitarian powers, came back happily into the fold of American State Department influence, Pan-Americanism, democracy, and safe investments. On November 26 of that year Bogotá and Washington simultaneously announced the signing of a pact (November 23) to provide Colombia with air and naval missions from the United States.

Perhaps it was something more than coincidence that, following the treaty, Colombia, for all practical purposes, broke off diplomatic relations with Germany — that was before war had begun — because of the arrest of a Colombian Legation secretary for photographing atrocities against the Jews. Minister Rafael Jaramillo left the Reich in a great rage.

Already Colombia was backing Roosevelt's protest against Jewish and Catholic persecutions. Subsequently at the Lima conference, Colombia pumped ardently for a Latin-American league and continental armed defenses under United States leadership. It backed all Hull's proposals and set a stony face against the numerous projects that annoyed him, particularly those of Argentina.

From 1938 on the United States enjoyed a more excellent press in Colombia than anywhere south. Most newspapers and magazines controlled by the official Liberal Party in power — *El Tiempo, El Liberal, El Espectador, Cosmos, La Razón*, etc. — whatever their previous attitude, immediately joined in chorus, praising the government for having contracted for an American military mission.

Only a few papers still had off-color notes. The semi-independent *El Gráfico* recalled the disagreeable alienation of Panamá, warned the republics to the south that they were but 'twenty Ibero-America horses that Uncle Sam may ride'; that 'beside the [American] apostles stand the business men'; that Roosevelt was 'not eternal' and that American officeholders 'of another type' likely would bring 'unpleasant surprises.' But despite this acidity, even *El Gráfico* urged that as long as the good-neighbor policy should prevail Colombia ought to go along wholeheartedly — with deeds, not merely with worthless speeches in international congresses — by the side of the United States.

The only extremely sour comments on the new American military tutelage came from the Conservative Party press, largely under the thumb of large feudalistic landholders and the Catholic hierarchy. *El Siglo* was most outspoken. It admitted the need for technical assistance, but such missions should be brought in from countries with which Colombia has 'more affinity of spirit.' Italy and Germany, it declared, had far superior technicians. Nor is the United States 'first in the domination of the sea.' Even worse was the danger from American culture, which only consists of teaching people 'to shave, bathe, and use sanitary toilets.' It provides automobiles, elevators, 'senseless movies,' but with respect to 'universal ideas,' only 'insufferable mediocrity.' We are, it seems, enemies of the 'Christianity that radiates from Rome'; we represent 'Luther against Christ.' Our amorous and literary attitudes are compassed by *Gentlemen Prefer Blondes*.

Such divergence of opinion indicates the reality of Colombia's freedom of press and expression. In fact, compared to most of her sister republics, Colombia is a shining light of civil liberties and free suffrage.

Perhaps, however, good-neighborliness should rest as much upon knowledge and understanding as upon military missions. But, though in area and population Colombia is the fourth country in South America, and, next to Uruguay, the most densely populated, few Americans know much about it. For centuries Colombia — the first mainland region settled in the New World, and with Venezuela the cradle of Latin-American liberty under the leadership of the great Bolívar — was the outstanding cultural leader of all Latin America. Numbers of its institutions of learning were founded before the Pilgrim Fathers landed at Plymouth. It has produced more than its share of the notable literature and scholarship of the Spanish-speaking New World; but it is doubtful whether the important names of Mutis, Caldas, Isaacs, Silva, Rivera, Vargas Vila, Marroquín, mean much to us North Americans. For the twenty-two months prior to November, 1938, the *New York Times Index* records — aside from accounts of efforts to collect the Colombian debt — only twelve meager items about the country. Yet Colombia is one of the most strategic countries for continental defense and for the security of the United States.

At a time when the safety of the United States was being increasingly endangered, it seems inconceivable that the greatest paper on earth should so ignore the important cultural and political events of such a key nation. Adequate reporting should have given a democracy the news vital for good-neighborliness, for national security, for an intelligent appraisal of the hemisphere situation. This is in no sense a criticism of the *New York Times*, which beyond a certain point cannot race ahead of popular interest. It is merely a sad commentary on the intellectual level of the most enlightened group of newspaper readers in our country.

2

But if interest in the United States is scant, the press of Colombia bubbles constantly about all things American. The leading daily, *El Tiempo* (owned and formerly edited by ex-President Eduardo Santos), except for being in Spanish and conserving a somewhat rancid English format, is largely an American newspaper — page on page of United Press news and American feature articles. There are to be found Walter Lippmann's profound comments, Ripley's 'Believe It or Not,' a whole page of American 'funnies,' a page and a half of ads of American movies (a few Mexican movies), many advertisements of American products.

The only persistent German advertising prior to the war was
that of the Hamburg-American Line, which in 1937 put into
service a new crack electric-motor, air-conditioned liner (a Bren-
ner Vulkan Werft product), and several small ads of typewriters,
office equipment, paper, and cement-mixers. On very rare occasions there were page write-ups of the wonders of Mussolini
or the Third Reich — accounts that smacked of subsidized
propaganda.

Formerly *El Tiempo* was sharply critical of American policies,
very doubtful of the Hull reciprocity treaty. It berated us for
our failure to satisfy recent demands of Panamá. But by 1938
El Tiempo had become as pro-American as a D.A.R. publication.

Colombia's gradual change of attitude toward the United
States, since the days of the so-called 'rape of Panamá,' when
Teddy was hurling so many invectives, has been remarkable.
This change has been due chiefly to diplomacy, commerce, and
loans. Although a recent Colombia orator averred that nine
tenths of Colombia's population are poets, and though her in-
telligentsia affect to be interested only in culture and spirituality,
over the past few decades it has not been American culture, but
trade, money, and power that have so completely transformated
the southern country's opinion of us.

Colombia, despite its great cultural contributions and progress,
undoubtedly was a very backward country economically, and
greatly lacking in political stability. Repeated revolution was its
meat.

But when in 1914 the Canal was opened, change was swift to
come. As Colombia lies athwart the Canal at the top of South
America, with ports on both the Pacific and the Atlantic, its long
economic isolation was soon broken down. Overnight the country was plunged into the hurly-burly of the modern world. The
First World War speeded up its economic transformation; the
present war has speeded it up still faster.

By Bryan's day Colombia was no longer a pithecoid community
in American eyes. Not because we bothered much about her
culture; rather, to make it possible for American capital to exploit
her soil, gold, platinum, emeralds, and other raw products, to
grow bananas and run her public utilities, the United States

Government belatedly admitted previous wrongdoing and proffered her a $25,000,000 olive-branch — a sort of heart balm. After proper concessions had been made to American capitalists, the first installment of this gift-money finally became available four or five years after the First World War.

Following 1914, American trade and capital expanded rapidly south from the Caribbean. In 1912 there was only $2,000,000 of American capital invested in Colombia; by 1930, $272,000,000. British investments then totaled only a quarter of a million. By that year the United States was taking 61.4 per cent of Colombia's exports and providing 41.4 per cent of her imports; by 1938, 53.7 and 50.2 per cent, respectively.

The Tropical Oil Company and the Andean Corporation, subsidiaries of the Standard Oil Company of New Jersey, and other powerful American oil and steamship companies acquired vast tracts of petroleum acreage, still scarcely tapped, although in 1932 production totaled nearly nineteen million barrels. The United Fruit Company gathered in large plantations and contracted for nearly all banana exports. In 1936, more than eight million bunches were shipped out of Santa María. Concessions of iron, coal, lumber, limestone, and platinum were secured. Railroads passed into American hands. The Electric Bond and Share Company became powerful. Loans multiplied. Lindbergh made a good-will flight. The Pan-American Airways became a leading international carrier. The Great White Fleet, the Grace Line, and other steamship enterprises built up a lucrative freight and passenger trade. Colombia was tied into the American orbit with strong economic bonds.

The usual dreary scandals came to light. The Barco concession, Mr. Mellon, and several leading New York financial institutions stood in the glare of the lineup. Improper loan manipulations, secret diplomatic coercions in behalf of concessionaires, filth in the sales of armaments, were unearthed in various Senate investigations. Thanks to discreet pressure from our State Department, which refused to permit Minister Jefferson Caffery to tell of his activities, the public never learned the full truth about any of these things, even after months of congressional investigation.

And then, after 1929 — so dependent had Colombia become upon the American market — the country went into an economic tailspin, hitting bottom with our own depression. But unlike most of the Latin-American countries during that trying period, the traditionally unstable Colombia miraculously weathered the storm without serious political upheaval. The country's growing tradition of peace was successfully maintained, and in 1930, political power was passed on, in fairly democratic fashion, to the Liberal Party, thus terminating fifty years of Conservative Party rule without the usual bloodshed.

3

The new Liberal Party administrations followed a New Deal pattern, with heavy stress on economic nationalism. Having no more foreign credits, Colombia was obliged to set up rigid exchange and trade controls. Severe restrictions were put upon capital outflow. American loans went unpaid. American investors could not get full profits out. All financial arrangements had to pass through the government Instituto de Coordinación de los Cambios.

The situation was ideal for the totalitarian powers, for barter and bilateral trade. In 1933, Japan, for the first time in history, established a legation in Bogotá. Germany flooded the country with Aski marks, and Colombia's surpluses of coffee, cotton, vegetable ivory, and rubber began to move. For a time Colombia coffee was even shipped from Hamburg to New York.

Heavy German investments were made in oil, banana lands, and other enterprises. New German immigrants arrived. Aviation particularly caught the eye of the Germans. SCADTA (Colombia-German Aerial Transport Company) is the oldest commercial aviation line in existence. With new Nazi impetus behind it, the line was expanded. It flew the greater share of the country's more than four thousand miles of routes. The remotest *pueblos* were tapped. As a result, in proportion to population, Colombia probably had more miles of commercial aviation than any other country in the World.

Besides economic nationalism and these new relations with the totalitarian states, the depression crisis resulted in increasing labor militancy and punitive action against United States companies. 'Anti-imperialism' became the new slogan. Labor leaders were sent in droves to México to study the labor movement there. Severe and bloody strikes occurred in banana and oil fields and in mines. American overseers had to flee the country. Student riots occurred. President Alfonzo López (1934–36) was faced with startling peasant revolts, particularly the sanguinary uprising of Santander.

Even under Conservative rule, Colombia had been one of the first countries in the world to provide old-age pensions, workers' compensation, the eight-hour day, and had been one of the first to ratify the Geneva labor codes. Even so, economic distress now forced new and more radical land and labor reforms.

After consultation with the peasants and the Conservative leader, Laureano Gómez, President López put into effect a moderate land-distribution system. He took steps to placate labor. Reforms culminated in the 1936 constitutional revisions, which placed social needs over and above private interest and made possible government ownership of or participation in all industrial and agricultural activities for the purpose of rationalizing output, establishing quotas, prices, and wage levels. Education was taken entirely out of the hands of the Catholic Church, which ceased to be the official state religion. For the first time in the country's history, education for women was provided in secondary schools and in universities. Vocational education was expanded. These and other religious and educational regulations and innovations aroused Catholic fears. Considerable property was hurriedly transferred to American Catholic corporations; for instance, the Candelaria Church to the American Educational Endowment Fund, Inc.

The banana industry was sternly regulated, and a representative of a fruit company was arrested for wholesale bribery and stealing of judicial documents, and was deported. The American public utilities found themselves hedged about by new tax, rate, and wage regulations. The President declared that Colombia was taking steps to acquire all railroads. The goal was economic control over the national resources. In other words, nationalistic socialism, as in México, was in full march.

July 18, 1938, a further program was worked out for promotion of self-sufficiency in foodstuffs (i.e., expansion of rice, wheat, corn, vegetable, and similar cultivation); conservation of forests (Colombia has more acreage than the United States); scientific exploitation of tropical resources (rubber, coffee, cacao, copra, bananas, medicinal herbs, etc.).

The United States, as in the case of México (but this time the New Deal), worked increasingly to break down this new-found Colombian independence. American business fought to get loan payments resumed, to unfreeze exchange, to get profits out, to set aside labor legislation and social controls. The State Department worked diligently and efficiently. A new trade treaty was negotiated, and little by little exchange controls were partly broken down in our favor.

4

The real chance to reassert American influence came with the election of Eduardo Santos, who became President in August, 1938. Before taking office he journeyed to this country and was royally entertained by Washington officials and the business interests affected. A new friendliness, based on better business and American governmental assistance, flowered forth rapidly. A love fest began. Exchange restrictions were further modified. New steps were taken looking toward debt payment. Colombia backed off from 'controlled' to 'stabilized' currency — a step toward the restoration of the work done by the Kemmerer financial mission at the time of our payment of Bryan's $25,000,000. Labor and the peasants were more sternly dealt with.

American army planes flew south to participate in Santos' inauguration ceremonies. American diplomatic representation was raised to ambassadorial rank, and Spruille Braden, long interested in mining activities and other business in Latin America, was appointed. SCADTA became a Pan-American Airway subsidiary.

And so American diplomacy and American business worsted all competitors, including England, which had seen trade difficulties with Colombia multiply as her imports dropped below one half of one per cent by 1937. New North American air and naval missions told the tale, and thus was laid another triumphant stone in the State Department's new structure of continental defenses under American leadership. This was further rounded out by sending in an American police mission to help Colombia run her secret service, control smuggling, check up on foreigners and so-called subversive elements.

Colombia, after her short Odyssey of political and economic independence, came safely — and quite happily — back into the Caribbean orbit of American influence. With the country now sowed down with American agents, undoubtedly if we can continue to provide enough credit and buy enough goods, both political and economic cooperation will become truly rosy, and after the war a new dawn of American financial penetration — this time by our government rather than by private capital — will be at hand.

Certainly Colombia has become one of the most active of the Latin-American countries in suppressing fifth-columnists and aiding in continental defense. All irony aside, the successful wooing of Colombia, since the bitter Panamá episode, has been — in the face of early Marine interventions, the corruptness of the earlier loan rackets, the depression of 1929, which shifted the country toward European ties — one of the marvels of modern diplomacy and statesmanship.

Alfonzo López has now been returned to the presidency. He, too, has now seen the light and like his predecessor has been fêted and dined in Washington. Colombia is a democracy on the side of democracies, and we even hear these days more than we used to of the great cultural traditions of our good neighbor. And so Colombia, long quite unknown to her great neighbor democracy, is safely back on the old prosperity roost, although, owing to the war, she gets few needed supplies.

The rapid opening of new mines, the expansion of petroleum production, the revival of rubber projects, the rise of new factories — these and other activities, due to World War II, today are helping to round out Colombia's economy, long a one-crop country. Heretofore coffee a glut on the market, constituted two thirds of her exports. The diversification will give the country greater stability and a wider basis for general prosperity. So long as Colombia was largely a single-crop country, her whole economic prosperity dependent upon prices fixed in a foreign market, her efforts at economic independence could have little validity and were merely prompted by desperation. With more varied development a real economic independence and interdependence can arise, and Colombia can take her place as a mature member of the concert of Western Hemisphere nations.

CHAPTER XIV

Venezuela: Oil Kingdom

MY FIRST close contact with things Venezuelan came many years ago when I met Doctor Carlos León, in exile in México. Stocky, genial, freckle-faced Doctor León had once been Minister of Education. When the now-defunct satrap of Venezuela, Vicente Gómez, illegally seized power, Doctor León declined an invitation to serve in his cabinet. A few days later, a policeman tapped León on the shoulder and he was led off to the horrible Rotunda prison, where for seven years he was held with seventy-pound iron rods and chains on his legs. For decades the cruel and bloody Vicente Gómez held his people under the lash of terrorism, while the subsoil of Maracaibo spouted out billions of dollars of oil for foreign lands. When Gómez died, he personally owned nearly half the potential oil land of the country, the richest estates, most of the cattle industry, and was close to being the richest man on earth. More than a hundred illegitimate children, plus many common-law wives, leaped forward to claim part of this vast wealth.

Since then, Venezuela has been licking her wounds, dazedly trying to shake off the black nightmare of the Gómez dictatorship.

Although the dictator shuttled, as the whim struck him, among dozens of country mansions and city palaces, mostly he lived at his Las Delicias estate, beside a small wooded stream, near Maracay. A busy man, he felt all should be busy, and every morning at daybreak the military bands had to march playing loudly through the streets of Maracay to help everybody else to get up and bustle about. But should not the people have been grateful? Did he not build in the little jungle highland town of Maracay the finest opera house in the country?

As in the days of the benign monarchs of old, artists and performers, the finest in the world, were imported. First they had to give private performances at Las Delicias, the women patted and kissed by the dictator, before appearing at the nearly empty theater, which the bulk of the population could not attend for the lack of the price of admission. To his estates, and those of his friends, not to benefit the economic life of the country, he had fine concrete highways built. He also built at government expense four sumptuous hotels in remote places where he and his friends could celebrate. He put up a large private zoo at Las Delicias; and he also built a bronze fence around a tree where once sat Simón Bolívar, the great liberator of Americans, who dreamed of human freedom and fought for it. Gómez had even falsified the day of his birth in order to make it coincide with Bolívar's. On Sundays Gómez and his cronies devoted themselves to cockfights, matching their prize birds, with colossal bets. In the afternoon he entertained his guests with his private orchestra.

This paternalism and peace of the sword cost all Venezuelans their liberties, their freedom of speech and of press, their political rights. Gómez eliminated the national debt, thanks to the discovery and exploitation of oil and the mounting price of raw materials due to the First World War and to the post-war economic extravaganza; but the people were ground into misery; wages were a pittance compared to the cost of living, and membership in a labor union meant jail or death. The peons on the estates were treated like cattle and mostly held in serfdom. Under his benign rule, petty local tyrants, abusive and bloodthirsty, oppressed the people, and for their own selfish ends, since Gómez had looted the major part of the country's wealth not in the control of foreign enterprise, squeezed the last penny out of the already exploited people. The masses, even the better-paid oil workers (for the cost of living in Maracaibo is fantastically high), lived, and for the most part still live, in mud huts, with only a hammock and a homemade table for furnishings, old tin cans for utensils. Work clothing was ragged, Sunday clothing almost unknown; the streets swarmed with beggars.

The interior of the country got no roads and was left to decay in ignorance, to sink back into the jungle, the swamps, and the desert. At the highest, only 10,000,000 *bolivares* a year were spent on education out of a budget of nearly 300,000,000, whereas 25,000,000 were spent on the spy system.

Gómez personally monopolized most retail businesses — food, butter (over a dollar a pound), milk, building materials, cotton wear (by destroying all competing factories). In the United States he maintained high-priced American propaganda agents, who molded American ideas of Venezuela and pictured it as an enlightened paradise rather than the vast concentration camp it really was. In this effort, the agents were assisted by powerful American interests extracting vast wealth from the country. Gómez controlled every publicly uttered word in Venezuela. He came close to doing the same in the United States, and few of the thousands of exiles in this or other countries could find any important platform from which to tell of the injustices being wrought in their fair land.

2

For two days Venezuela lay dazed by the news of Vicente's death — which had occurred December 17, 1935. On the afternoon of the nineteenth the people poured into the public plazas all over the country, shouting, laughing, crying, dancing. Police-forces swept fire over them everywhere, but they quietly gathered up their dead, and presently the same people, so long cowed and silent, laughed and shouted, and again marched on fearlessly, unconcerned with the menace of death, carrying placards about liberty. They tore down the palatial clubs of the governing clique; they ripped away every picture and statue of the dictator, in itself quite a titanic undertaking; and in Caracas they tore apart the homes of every single member of the big Gómez family tribe; brick by brick and stone by stone, they took them apart. At Puerto Cabello they threw fourteen tons of massive leg-irons into the sea.

The new provisional president was Eleazar López Contreras, a tall thin old man, part and parcel of the Gómez system. As Minister of War under Gómez, he had once arrested his own son for leading a student protest and had had him beaten into bloody pulp in the Rotunda. Now he surprised the same Gómez clique and the people by severely punishing those who had fired on the crowds.

He opened the prisons, shipped the whole Gómez family tribe and many petty tyrants out of the country on a gunboat, allowed liberty of speech, press, and assemblage. The exiles came back like heroes, some to high posts. Labor unions sprouted like mushrooms.

This almost unprecedented liberalism lasted two months, then the press was again censored. In protest the newspapers stopped publishing entirely. A general strike developed. Once more the people were machine-gunned on the plazas. They soaked their handkerchiefs in the blood of their dying ones and wrote their resentment on the public walls in huge letters.

After several days of rioting, President López promised to a delegation from a monster manifestation that he would grant all popular demands and permit full freedom of the press, radio, and speech. He arrested the officer responsible for firing on the people in Caracas and had him put on trial for murder. He made all the Gómez wealth the property of the nation, cleaned out more of the worst Gómez political holdovers, and in their places put exiled liberals, younger men of the people. New elements were taken into the cabinet on a coalition basis. López apparently really wished to get nearer to the people, and tried to do so. The government feverishly began building schools and hospitals.

Elections renovated Congress. New labor and farm regulations blossomed out. New blood and new ideas constantly wedged into public life. Venezuela ever since has been moving, by a somewhat tortuous zigzag, toward more freedom and more orderly popular government.

If the violence, inevitable after a régime such as that of Gómez, was singularly brief and limited, this was due in good part to the unexpected ability and tolerance of López, who quickly sensed that if the old iron-handed methods were continued there would be a really frightful bloody upheaval. At the same time the people themselves seemed to realize that, if possible, extremes should be avoided, for out of violence would merely spring some new form of dictatorship. It cannot be said that the old abusive practices of Venezuelan officialdom have by any means been put in limbo, but in the public declarations of both government and opposition elements there is today a high tone of reason, tolerance, and patriotism, a patience on both sides all the more remarkable among a people and in a land so long and terribly abused.

3

It is difficult to classify Venezuela according to our regional scheme. It is distinctly a Caribbean country, although the mouth of the great Orinoco lies outside that inland sea. At the same time, Venezuela's dominant topographic feature is an arm of the great Andean range that arches away from Colombia northeastward as a coast range that dies away at La Guayra. The lower coastal mountains on the east are a logical continuation of the same formation. Thus, if Venezuela is a Caribbean country, it is also in good part a highland mestizo country. In the highlands are found the most flourishing life and culture of the country, the healthiest cities, the bulk of the population.

But Venezuela also belongs to the Green Hell region of hot jungle lands. The Maracaibo lake area on the coast, in a big 'V' made by the Andes Cordilleras of Venezuela and Colombia, is simmering tropical country; its banana plantations are tropical; many of its products are from the steaming lowlands. Also, beyond the coast range, to the south, lies the great Orinoco-Apure river basin, comprising two thirds of the country, and this, too, is hot, rank jungle, reaching clear to the borders of Guiana and Brazil, where the terrain gradually rises toward the great wild Sierra Pacaraima and the Sierra Curupira, in places over nine thousand feet high. There are found the headwaters of many Orinoco tributaries and of the mighty Ríos Branco and Negro of Brazil, the largest northern Amazón tributaries. In the lower hot country, as in the Amazón, are also found great rolling llanos. Once Venezuela was one of the greatest cattle countries on earth.

Thus Venezuela is a meeting ground of three of the major regionalisms of Latin America, and presents many of the characteristics of each, natural and human. All three help shape the national culture, the racial mixing, and the psychology of the land.

The population of Venezuela, like that of Honduras and Brazil, is a blend of white Indian and negro — according to one authority (one cannot depend on official statistics) 45 per cent white, 45 per cent Indian, and 10 per cent negro.

The original Venezuelans belonged to the aggressive Carib group that overflowed through the greater part of the West Indies. The highest-developed aborigines lived in the highlands, where they enjoyed a more invigorating climate and suffered from fewer insect-propagated diseases. The Oracas, Tachiras, Mombunes, and Jirajaras of the highlands were much hardier than the Maracaibo Indians or those of the inner jungle areas. The Maracaibo Indians, to this day, live languidly in grass huts and paddle about in dugouts. These pre-conquest differences entered into the make-up of the modern population, determined the modern mestizo types of Venezuela. The more vigorous and independent mestizo is usually the product of the mixing of Spaniard and highland Indian.

Venezuela was the first mainland sighted by Columbus — in 1498. The following year, the Ojeda and Amerigo Vespucci expeditions put in at Lake Maracaibo; and it was Ojeda who called it 'little Venice,' not yet knowing that the handsome tropical inland sea would be coated over four centuries later with the constant scum of petroleum.

Colonization proceeded apace, and *conquistadores* and *adelantados*, such as Juan de Villegas, Rodríguez Suares, and Maldonado, thrust boldly on into the high cordillera. They were a wild breed. Lope de Aguirre ran amuck, looting, raping, and killing both natives and his fellow countrymen, till tracked to earth by Pedro de Molina. By 1550, Diego de Losado had founded Caracas, and in less than a decade four of the present day cities, Valencia, Barquisimeto, Mérida, and San Cristóbal — the latter far inland and more than five thousand feet above sea level — had grown from straw-hut settlements to handsome proportions, laid out according to Spanish plan about fine plazas, faced by cathedrals, municipal palaces, massive barracks, schools, and mansions.

As the Indians of the lowlands, where much of Venezuela's wealth was to be found, were shiftless, and as highland Indians, transported there to labor, died off rapidly in those less healthful regions, many negro slaves were soon brought in to work the hot plantations. The highland Indians, if reduced to temporary serfdom, were better treated than the natives of many other colonies, and the Spaniards intermingled with them more freely and with less concern for royal edicts against miscegenation than in many other places.

The upper-level natives soon became freedmen because plantation agriculture did not flourish in the narrow high valleys, and because few rich mines were discovered. In fact the highland Indians were soon used as armed retainers, whereas elsewhere natives were forbidden to ride horseback or bear arms. The lowland Indians were also less molested, for, in spite of lashings, they did not prove productive enough.

Yet caste and race lines were sharp enough, the sphere of each racial bloc pretty distinctly defined. This was especially true for the blacks, who were classified as mulattoes, zamboes, and pure blacks, and in the order named increasingly restricted. The privileges and duties of each group were established by precise regulations. Thus as one descended the chromatic scale, the offense for the guilty person of one group might be merely to be branded; in the next, the same offense might call for the cutting off of a hand or the tearing out of a tongue.

As a result, plenty of class and race hates were released when independence came. There was then no basis of cultural homogeneity, economic security, or popular education for the democratic republic that was theoretically established.

Out of the new Andean race and culture, largely mestizan, came the leaders of independence — Francisco Miranda, the early apostle of colonial freedom, and the great liberator of the continent, Simón Bolívar, and thereafter, also, a series of generals and tyrants to curse the land with their wild lusts and greed for untasted power. José Antonio Paez, 'the murdering tiger from the hills of Guayra,' José Tadeo Monagas, of Spanish, negro, and Jewish blood, who carried murdered heads in sacks: Guzmán Blanco, who filled the land with his own statues and French theaters; Francisco Linares Alcántara, the mulatto whose only recognizable political policy was 'to toss gold pieces from the cathedral'; Joaquín Crespo, who flaunted an Italian opera singer as his mistress, thus showing that he was at least a brave man.

4

Among new elements who had the chance to function once more when more liberal and honest government came into being after Dictator Gómez' downfall was that remarkable leader of Venezuelan letters, Rufino Blanco Fombona, the author of thirty-odd books, who became governor of one of the provinces.

An adventurous soul, a creative mind, one-time diplomat, a rebel spirit who had faced mobs and jails, he is in the epic tradition. Previously also a governor and a plenipotentiary, he was among the very first to fight the Gómez tyranny. He spent two years in prison and was in exile as early as 1910, mostly in Spain, where he founded the publishing house 'America.' His classic, bitterly anti-Spanish volume, *The Conquistadores of the Sixteenth Century*, despite its polemical attitude, is one of the most accurate and brilliant accounts of the Spanish invasion and is widely used in American universities.

He has published a two-volume biography of Bolívar and three volumes of the Liberator's correspondence. His *El Hombre de Hierro (Iron Man)* is a tremendous indictment of the Castro bureaucracy; and he follows through his smashing blows in *El Hombre de Oro (Gold Man)*. In general he is most moving in his descriptions of intimate Venezuelan life. His *Cuentos Americanos (American Tales)* are racy short stories of customs and types, stories charged with pessimism and joy, mockery and simple pity, and through them smoulders the relentless passion of a wholly honest man.

Another figure who resumed importance, a glory to the cultural life of any country, was José Rafael Pocaterra, who was jailed in 1919 and held incommunicado in heavy leg-irons for three years. Escaping, he fled for his life in 1922, to become a professor in Montreal. By 1939 he could come back to his homeland, and became President of the Venezuelan Senate and shortly a member of the cabinet. Before being driven abroad, he had published four notable works of fiction. Then his liberal and literary career was cut off. After five years of exile he produced his four-volume work, *Memorias de un Venezolano de la Decadencia (Memories of a Venezuelan of the Decadence)*. It is perhaps our most complete

and therefore horrifying record of the first two decades of Gómez'
rule — a fine example of pamphleteering on the plane of literature
and truth.

The greatest contemporary novelist of Venezuela, Rómulo
Gallegos, had to go into exile in 1931. In 1936 he was called back
as Minister of Education, in which post he was bitterly attacked
by the clericals. He is now President of the powerful opposition
party — Acción Democrática — which is doing more than any
other organized group to lay the basic problems of Venezuela
before the people. But his true greatness is as a novelist. His
Doña Barbara, published in 1929, is one of the few really noteworthy novels of Latin America, known wherever the Spanish
language is spoken. It is a powerful picture of the Venezuelan
cattle country, a portrait of a beautiful ruthless female cattle
baroness, and goes to the roots of Venezuelan rural life, in striking
contrast to the more urbanized literature of other writers of his
country.

Mariano Picón Salas, a Venezuelan writer educated in Chile,
was also called back to a high educational post in Venezuela in
1936. He has written a fine book on Chile and its problems, and
two strong fictional works, *Odisea de Tierra Firme (Mainland
Odyssey)* and *Registro de Huespedes (Guest Register)*.

Another Venezuelan notable, Santos Anibal Dominici, one of
its leading physicians, with an international reputation, and
author of numerous medical works on fevers, leprosy, tuberculosis, typhoid, and intestinal diseases, was also restored to full
usefulness. Ambassador to the United States from 1914 to 1922,
he resigned in the latter year in protest against the Gómez tyranny. After Gómez' fall he was promptly made Minister to
France, and was later taken into the cabinet at home.

5

The great dramatic story of Venezuela of modern times is
petroleum, a story of American and British economic imperialism,
that we are not permitted to tell at this juncture of world history.
Many have blamed these great international corporations for the
Gómez dictatorship. This is hardly a just charge, for Gómez was

a continuation of a century of traditional tyranny in that country. What is perhaps true is that the foreign corporations made
hay while the sun shone; they took every advantage of the extreme favoritism shown to them by the dictatorship; they entered
into full partnership with it, and probably Gómez would never
have been able to hold on to absolute power for so long against
the will of his harassed and terrorized people had it not been for
the financial prosperity created by petroleum exploitation.

Today the Venezuelans recognize more clearly that the industry must be organized differently from in the earlier wildcat
period, so that the country derives more benefits from the rapid
withdrawal of its subsoil wealth.

The one hundred and twenty million *bolivares*, or less than
forty million dollars, paid annually by the companies in taxes and
wages (and this is offset by all company imports coming in duty
free) at present constitute the only return for the country from
the vast industry. On the other hand, gasoline, in the greatest
petroleum country of America next to the United States, has aver-
aged, during the past ten years, many times the price in Texas.

Some efforts have been made to provide better wages for the
workers in industry in accordance with the new labor code —
Article 27 of the constitution, put into effect after the downfall of
Gómez.

The new labor law of July 16, 1936, provided for an eight-hour
day, holidays with pay, compulsory profit-sharing, and that at
least 25 per cent of the employees had to be Venezuelans. The
profit-sharing provision, however, was not put into effect until
December 17, 1938. It provided for an increase in wages of from
2 to 12½ per cent. Unfortunately, right afterward, the Supreme
Court annulled Article 27, and wages were thereby reduced for
the oil companies a total of ten million *bolivares* annually. The
leading financial editor of the country, Romulo Betancourt, com-
mented in *Ahora*, March 23, 1939, that the cost of living in the
cities, especially in Caracas, probably the highest in the world,
was in good part due to the meagerness of Venezuelan agriculture,
its scant industrial development, its reduction to the rôle of a
mere raw-product purveyor.

Expert Hedderich Assmendi declared that 85 per cent of the

children of working-class parents in Caracas get so little to eat and
such improper food that 'they are on the road to perishing.' The
housing for the working classes of Caracas is abominable; 26 per
cent of the houses are without toilets; in 18 per cent more, the
toilets are almost unusable.

Elsewhere Betancourt has pointed out that in 1938, for example, wages and taxes from the petroleum industry provided
110,000,000 *bolivares*, but that under concession terms the oil
companies may import machinery, food supplies, etc. free of
duty, so that they were thereby exempted from 95,000,000
bolivares, which other companies or industries importing a similar
amount of goods had to pay. Thus in reality the effective return
to Venezuela for her fabulous production of oil was only 15,000,-
000 *bolivares*, or less than $5,000,000. In contrast to this the total
value of oil exports (1937) was 828,264,580 *bolivares* on 187,000,-
000 barrels.

These data, though important for Venezuela, are less important
than the fact that we are still a long way from a coordinated
economic pattern for the American continent and a proper joint
utilization of all possible production in wartime. Thus, many of
the boats of the British and American oil companies in Venezuela
fly under foreign flags; as a result, instead of Venezuelan production's being organized on the basis of fair and necessary continental distribution, much oil is sent to the points where the
largest profits can be obtained, to countries where prices are not
controlled as in the United States. Thus it is that many countries, particularly in Central America and South America, as
openly related recently by high American officials reporting to
the American Congress, have priority over the needs of the American public, who are at present rationed on heat to below the
minimum of health and efficiency in the war effort.

A large group of Venezuelans are urging that the government
utilize the rich oil lands of the recent dictator to drill wells and
that it establish a refinery of sufficient capacity so that the country, which produces oil as its main source of wealth, may have
petroleum products and derivatives as cheaply as most other
countries, and point out that this would also serve as a yardstick
for the just regulation of the foreign companies.

The Venezuelan budget in 1937 was around 250,000,000 *bolivares*, or less than a third of the gross sales of oil from the country. Thus the Venezuelan Government and the millions of inhabitants represent a small business indeed in proportion to that of the foreign oil companies. It is little wonder that they can shape legislation almost entirely according to their own desires.

This overwhelming superiority of the oil industry over all other activities is reflected in the export figures. Oil accounts for 90 per cent of all exports, certainly a most unhealthy condition for any country. Out of an export total of 888,000,000 *bolivares* in 1938, oil minerals and re-exported merchandise accounted for 845,000,000. Exports of coffee, cacao, hides, etc., products of which the wealth largely remains in the country, totaled only 42,000,000 *bolivares*, scarcely 5 per cent of the total. And since Venezuela does not get proper fiscal returns on oil exported, she must resort to excessive import duties on merchandise imported and heavy taxation that make the cost of living intolerable. Thus, since Venezuela produces but 15 per cent of her own wheat, in 1938, 6,000,000 *bolivares* were imported, on which the duty amounted to over 10,000,000. Such taxes on the vital necessities of life represent a crushing burden.

The backwardness of Venezuelan agriculture is in good part due to the monopolization of the land. The prevailing system of great estates was established by the Spanish conquerors. The *llaneros* joined the early independence movement in order, among other reasons, to obtain lands, as promised them by their leaders, Bolívar and Paez; but Bolívar was soon dead, and all the soldiers of liberty ever got were farm bonds, good for lands, which were never parceled out. The bonds merely went into the hands of speculators and grafting politicians. The colonial system prevails to this day and the process of land enclosures still goes on.

Only a few years ago four thousand peasants of the State of Lara, who had selected good lands, were driven off, and their properties stolen by the large adjacent landholders.

Congressman Andrés Eloy Blanco, one of Venezuela's best writers, has called land monopolization 'the social ulcer of Venezuela.' This is the chief reason her vast fertile acres are scarcely used. Official statistics show that most of the rural population is propertyless. Thus in the State of Aragua, 84.69 per cent of the taxed land is in large holdings; in Yaracuy, 77.95 per cent; in the Federal District, 84.65 per cent. Most of the farm workers are serfs, share-croppers, squatters (*pisatorios*).

6

Today Venezuela is hard hit by war-tense conditions. The tankers that take out oil bring in no goods, and scarcely a laden vessel touches her ports. When it is considered that she must import most of her foodstuffs, this means that the country is close to starvation, because even when few goods are obtained from abroad, their cost is beyond the means of all but the very well-to-do. This also means that a violent loss in import duties and excise taxes has resulted, and on these the finances of the country rest rather than on the one major industry, oil. The government therefore has less money to meet a situation of growing seriousness. This condition is aggravated by the fact that less of Venezuela's normal production of other goods than oil is leaving Venezuelan shores. This also brings further economic upset to the national economy — unemployment, dislocation, still more reduced revenue.

As in so many other Latin-American countries, the crying long-range need is for diversification of production, the need to build up independent national industries, communications, and a merchant marine, and to see to it that a fair share of the wealth extracted from the soil, as is done in México, remains in the country for the development of an adequate school system, sanitation, public works, etc. This, in short, is but an elementary synopsis of what should be a basic principle of an enlightened inter-Americanism. It is not remote from the famous four freedoms.

PART FOUR

Green Hell

CHAPTER XV

Vargas of Brazil

THE most dramatic episode in the crowded, picturesque career of Getulio Dornelles Vargas, Dictator-President of Brazil, occurred in the early morning hours of May 11, 1938, when old marble Guanabara Palace — the White House of Rio de Janeiro — was attacked by Fascist revolters bent on overthrowing the government.

Vargas, a brother, two sons, two daughters (his wife stayed in bed), and two faithful bodyguards held off the mob of attackers for more than three hours till help arrived.

The *coup* had been planned by high navy officials, politicians, and the Green Shirt Integralistas. Their followers attacked barracks and public buildings, as well as the Pan-American airport, in widely separated parts of the city, and at certain points were successful. At the palace the guard had been treacherously replaced by picked Green Shirts disguised in navy uniforms, who planned to seize and kill the President — just before dawn of that crisp autumn day of May.

A faithful guardsman gave the alarm.

'We were all in bed when the trouble started,' said Alzira Vargas, the President's dark-eyed, twenty-three-year-old daughter, now the wife of Senhor do Amaral Peixoto, governor of the State of Rio de Janeiro.

Pulling on a robe, she ran into the dark corridor. The light and telephone wires had been cut, but she found the rest of the family by following their voices. Machine-gun bullets whined around the doors and windows. Armed only with pistols, the little group held off the assaulters.

Near daybreak General Enrico Gaspar Dutra, Minister of War, arrived with help. The collar of his uniform was soaked with blood from a bullet wound in his ear. After overcoming rebels in another part of the city, he had brought forces to drive off the attackers.

A little later, Colonel Oswaldo Cordeiro, still clad in pajamas, arrived at the head of a mixed contingent of police, soldiers, and civilians, and attacked the stubborn rebels on the flank. Vargas was saved.

Perhaps no national leader, except Joseph Stalin, is more enigmatic than dynamo-dictator Vargas. His political lineup was long obscure. Consistently it was anti-Communist, although his country is now allied with the Bolsheviks; for a time he was openly Fascist. He blew hot and cold for democracy, and only when Germany lost control of the seas and the United States poured unstinted millions into the canny dictator's coffers, did he shift toward a pro-American position.

To American correspondents, Vargas always spoke glowingly of democracy and Pan-American unity; then he would dash off a telegram of congratulation to Hitler; then he curbed local Fascists and Nazis. To his own people he spoke much of the Brazilian 'New Order,' denounced all alien 'isms,' and was eloquent about the destiny of strong young nations. On the one hand, American army, naval, and air missions linked defense efforts closely; on the other, powerful German and Italian business interests retained great influence among the ruling families of the country.

His Foreign Minister, Oswaldo Aranha, was consistently pro-American. But other members of the cabinet were very pro-Nazi.

Vargas' vacillating position for so long a period is understandable. Underlying it were basic considerations:

1. Brazil, being for Brazil, was also for hemisphere defense without loss of sovereignty.

2. But Brazil felt it could not jump either way, even should Germany be successful in Europe, because (*a*) the United States would still remain powerful and (*b*) Brazil, at her present stage of development, *must* have the markets of both Europe and the

United States. On the other hand, for Brazil, the British Empire is a serious competitor in tropical products.

3. The growing volume of commercial interchange with Argentina, which, even before the war, was a larger trade factor than England. This led to one of the world's greatest free-trade covenants — among the nations of Argentina, Brazil, Uruguay, Paraguay, and Bolivia — in an attempt to bridge the present economic crisis. This resulted in the burial of long-standing antagonisms.

4. The growing possibility of greater self-sufficiency through industrialization.

In all these respects, whatever his international flirtations, Vargas stated his position clearly. Repeatedly he declared for 'continental safety and peace' without 'aggressive intentions against other peoples.' He declared: 'We will not tolerate any act which attempts to lessen our sovereignty. Whoever tries by any means to put us in an inferior position of protection must suffer our complete repulse.' With regard to trade and diplomacy, he declared: 'We try to maintain good relations with civilized peoples [among which Russians are not included] without preference of ideological or political systems, but if we are forced to adopt rigid reciprocity — to buy from those who buy from us — we cannot be blamed.'

Before the war this policy tended to aid the United States, Germany, Argentina, Japan, and Canada. It meant hard plugging for Italy. It tended definitely to injure England and France. It benefited nearly all the other continental countries except Russia.

Since then, as gradually was the United States, he was forced from a neutral position, and eventually abandoned Fascist sympathies to throw in his lot with the United Nations in war on the Axis.

2

Rio Grande do Sul is Vargas' home state. Larger than the republic of Uruguay (its next-door neighbor to the south), it has a temperate climate; but, historically, it is the most turbulent of all Brazilian provinces. Time and again it has fought the central government, and time and again it has been rent by internal struggle. For the mountains divide Rio Grande do Sul into two ways of life.

The eastern seaboard has rich agricultural lands, which have been colonized by eager individual settlers — chiefly Germans, Italians, Bessarabian Jews. Beyond the mountains lie the *campos* or open plains, and rivers that flow crystal-clear into the great Paraná. There roam great herds of cattle and horses. There, the flying *vaqueiro*, or cowboy, whirls his lariat around the legs of wild steers and ponies. There, encroaching farm settlers from the coast still battle against the cattle kings, a feud complicated by the marked Spanish-Portuguese character of the cattle country and the German-Italian character of the eastern seaboard.

In times of grave crisis in Brazil, two groups have always played a strategic rôle: the *vaqueiros* and the navy. In northern wilderness country without proper unifying communications, the war boats can ply the vast rivers. Similarly, on the southern plateaus cavalry is all-important. Cowboy and sailor have ever been symbols of 'democratic revolt' in Brazil. There is a cowboy roll to Vargas' own swift stride, for he came from cattle country and rode to power with the *vaqueiros*.

Born on April 19, 1882, in the quiet, Jesuit-governed town of São Borja, just across the border from Argentina, he has all the hard-riding, hard-fighting, indomitable passion and fury of the *vaqueiro*. But he also has the inscrutable exterior of spiritual self-sufficiency derived from long nights in the open, solitary country.

Vargas is a great orator and does justice to the poetic Portuguese language. One feels in his words the rhythm of the songs of his homeland people, sung around lonely campfires; one feels something of the cold winters of the plains, and of the hot, dry summers.

'At times,' says one commentator, 'he is a volcano; at other times, he is as frosty and undecipherable as a silk-hat British diplomat.'

In his youth he was no slouch with the guitar himself. They tell of a courtship when he was a private in the army. The girl liked his music but turned up her nose at his plebeian status.

'You will be sorry some day not to sit in Guanabara Palace,' Dom Getulio is said to have told her. 'You are scorning the future president of Brazil.'

Vargas' father, starting as a lieutenant, turned to politics to become machine boss of the state and several times mayor of São Borja, so that young Getulio early learned the tricks of office-getting.

He went to a private religious school, then was packed off to high school in Minas Geraes, the rich mineral state to the north, to prepare to enter the national military academy. Old comrades of those days say he had a thirst for knowledge that drove his teachers to distraction, and a spirit of independence that kept him in hot water. All the proper auguries of future power were there. He learned so much about the mining folk of Minas Geraes that he was able later to command the political loyalty of that important state.

But during the third year in the military academy he took part in a student uprising against the commandant and was thrown out. The career his parents had planned for him was ruined.

Getulio grimly joined the army as a private — a disgraceful step, in the eyes of an established Brazilian family, for the army is largely made up of levies of ignorant serfs and negroes. But Dom Getulio profited from this experience too. What he learned of the psychology of the common soldier later stood him in good stead.

He had already hitched his wagon to a star. He saw he could never crack his way into the upper military caste. 'The army will never make me President,' he told friends. He studied law and next emerged into the limelight as editor of his own local paper, *O Debate*. Soldier, lawyer, journalist — excellent tools for prying out the gold of his ambition. Politics promptly opened its doors.

A year after taking his law degree, he was appointed prosecuting attorney in São Borja. Two years later he was elected to the state legislature for a lone term. For the next six years or so he had to content himself with private practice while he built his political fences. After another term in the legislature, he was elected to Congress.

In Rio de Janeiro this impulsive, adroit son of the cow country found himself quite at home in the maze of bureaucratic intrigue. Within two years he became an outstanding figure, and Washington Luis, inaugurated President in 1926, made him Minister of Finance.

He resigned to become governor of his home state. Rio Grande was in typical upheaval, undergoing two years of civil war. With tact and liberal concessions Vargas pacified the opposing parties, introduced numerous reforms, organized the labor elements, and promoted public works. He toured the state constantly, coming into contact with all classes and winning the support of the *vaqueiros*.

By 1930 he was ready to rule the nation, and Brazil was ready for him. Depression had played havoc. The leading product, coffee, was a drug on the market. National revenues had fallen off. The mines were scarcely working. Unemployment was rife. Discontent boiled on every side. The faster the government bought up coffee and burned it the more coffee was grown, despite efforts at crop control. The *vaqueiros* were tired of paying government subsidies to the bankrupt São Paulo coffee barons who ran the nation's politics and got the cream of all rewards. Why salvage merely one state and industry, the *vaqueiros* argued, when the whole population was suffering? The time was ripe for a 'New Deal.'

Vargas forged the Liberal Alliance, utilizing the mining state of Minas Geraes, northern tropical Parahyba, and his own cowboy state of Rio Grande do Sul as the nucleus. His platform as candidate for President promised widespread political, economic, and administrative reforms. It promised to end coffee valorization and favoritism toward São Paulo and Rio de Janeiro.

The returns from the March elections in, President Washington Luis instructed Congress to declare Vargas' opponent elected. Vargas insisted that the outcome had been falsified and led his hard-riding *vaqueiros* into battle. Swarming north, they overwhelmed São Paulo; then, uniting with the unemployed miners of Minas Geraes, moved on into Rio and control of the nation.

3

As 'provisional President' Vargas worked fast. He organized labor unions, which he kept under his control, passed minimum-wage and maximum-hour laws, aided the peasants, halved all rural debts, reorganized the army from top to bottom, and promoted numerous other reforms.

His path was not unobstructed. The disgruntled army caste revolted and was suppressed. In spite of concessions, rich São Paulo rose in arms. Vargas put down the movement with blood and fire, and then, to the dismay of his own followers, made peace with his former enemies, giving them political preferment and continuing the heavy coffee subsidies. His rule was constantly harried. He faced six major revolts in four years, and innumerable minor revolts. Indiscriminately he branded his adversaries — radicals and conservatives alike — as Communists.

Except for very short intervals, Vargas has governed Brazil with martial law for the past thirteen years, replacing the courts with the firing squad.

Yet to American correspondents he insists he has created a superior type of democracy. Circumstances, he modestly states, made him a dictator in spite of himself. By abolishing all political parties he claims to have freed the people from the politicians. The people are now at liberty to appeal directly to him on any and all questions.

For a time one party was allowed to flourish and even received much police aid — that of the Integralistas or Green Shirts. Under the leadership of Plinio Salgado, a cadaverous, gleaming-eyed young man, it drew in more than a million members, with powerful German and Italian support. It committed the customary depredations against dissidents and supposed radicals, advocated a Catholicized version of nationalism and the corporate state, and harassed the Jews. At one time Vargas ordered six hundred Jews deported. Many were arrested, but discreet pressure from official American quarters caused him to halt his plan.

When the limited preparations for the elections of 1938 were progressing, Vargas suddenly made a *coup* against his own government — November 10, 1937 — and established what he then called openly a totalitarian régime, but which later he suavely characterized as 'democracy according to Brazilian needs.' Secretary of State Hull hastened to inform the American press of United States friendship for the new régime.

A new constitution, never voted on by the people or by the Brazilian Congress, was ready for the occasion. Under it, civil liberties were all but abolished. Newspapers were required to print everything demanded by the government and could no longer criticize the administration. All local and state self-government was abolished. Congress was made over into a hand-picked body. A new economic council, along Fascist corporate lines but entirely subordinate to the President, was created.

The constitution further provides that no laws may be enacted which are not initiated by the President himself, and Congress is allowed only two speeches to debate them. Judges and popular juries may be arrested if they return verdicts contrary to the evidence or to what is deemed the public interest. The President, without consent of Congress, may declare war. He alone can nominate his own successor — which can be himself.

Vargas celebrated the new 'democratic' order by a huge parade of the army and of Green Shirt Integralistas. Twenty Girl Scouts burned the twenty state flags — all but one of the governors of those states had been replaced by military appointees.

But once having established this pseudo-Fascist state, with the aid of the Green Shirts, Vargas quickly turned on their organization, accusing it of getting help from foreign sources. Soon the movement was outlawed. On December 3, 1937, Vargas formally dissolved all political parties. Since many high naval officers and other officials had been Integralistas, it is not surprising that in May of the following year they made the abortive attack on the presidential palace which gave Vargas and his household three bad hours.

Vargas is a hard worker. He has constructed many miles of highways, electrified the government railway, opened new mines, strengthened national defense, expanded public education, all — until recent American credits were granted — without foreign loans. Foreign banks have been all but eliminated (government banks have been set up to extend agricultural and industrial credit on easy terms); British railways and public utilities have been expropriated; the oil industry has been nationalized; rubber production and distribution have been made a national monopoly, thus wiping out the oldtime speculators; all producers must now provide proper laboring conditions; each *seringueiro*, or rubber-gatherer, must be provided free with at least an acre of good ground for his hut and vegetables — a long way indeed from the days of horror described by Eustaquio Rivera in his great rubber novel, or the miseries told of by Ciro Alegría in his *Broad and Alien Is the World*.

4

This little dictator-president who dresses so smartly is ever busy, full of projects. Standing, he is not impressive, but when he is seated one is immediately struck by his massive head and features, the large ears, the powerful jowl, the black smudge of eyebrows arching out high from a big, commanding nose, the enormous domed forehead and skull.

Everybody who meets him knows his easy charm, his persuasiveness, his force. His remarkable oratory has undoubtedly brought him a large mass following. However much criticized are his administrative methods and his destruction of all civil and political rights, in many ways he has done more for the common man of his country than any previous president.

He keeps circulating about Brazil. One day he is flying by plane far into the interior, a thousand miles or so, to see how best to develop the Amazon jungle region, where he has promoted much new colonization. The next day he is flying to inspect a new nickel mine. He is actively promoting new tea and silk industries. He has started new explorations for oil and trial drillings. With the aid of the United States he has started to develop a native steel industry that in the course of time may be the equal of any in the world.

His sons have been educated abroad — one in Germany, one in Italy, and one in the United States — the last at Johns Hopkins in Baltimore. When, several years ago, one son returned to

Brazil, Bruno Mussolini (son of the Italian dictator, now dead) personally flew him across the South Atlantic.

Such catholicity of tastes in Brazil's foreign affairs led the American State Department to redouble its efforts to please Vargas. Washington officialdom leaned over backward to play ball with him. No other southern dictator has been more smiled upon than Vargas; none has been granted larger credits — privileges he might not have enjoyed had he clarified his position completely at an earlier date.

Vargas himself is concerned only with what *he* thinks best for Brazil, and so far his power has not been successfully disputed despite so many revolts revealing the deep unrest that pervades the country. For Vargas has crushed every hint of opposition ruthlessly. His enemies have been killed. Or they are now in exile — by thousands — or in jail, some thirty thousand of them. Some have made their peace with Vargas, or have turned from political pursuits. Plinio Salgado, head of the Green Shirts, long hunted by the police from pillar to post, is now in retirement, quietly writing a life of Christ.

Some persons fear that Brazil's spiritual progress will not keep pace with Vargas' material achievements. Others claim that his good works will be swept aside by inevitable revolution when his power wanes. In the meantime Brazil is the expression of his dynamic will.

Even in war, Brazil is still a deeply divided land. But with the rapidity with which new industrialization is forging ahead, after the war the country will probably embark upon a period of economic expansion comparable to that which, in the United States after the Civil War, drove our country in a few short years to the pinnacle of world productive capacity. This achievement will depend upon the proper and rapid taming of the vast Amazón basin.

CHAPTER XVI

Brazil the Enigma

T HE cup of coffee you drink in the morning may change the fate of nations. The chances are it comes from Brazil, the greatest coffee country on earth. Normally sixty per cent of all Brazil's exports are coffee; she supplies two thirds of the world's supply and could provide all of it. Since the United States is the greatest coffee-consuming country, Brazil is bound to us by powerful economic links. In fact, in few other countries in the world, except possibly Cuba and Panamá, does the United States have such strong economic and political leverage as in Brazil. Over the years that relationship has been converted into as firm an official friendship as we have with any other Latin-American country.

The amount of American capital invested in Brazil during the past few decades has risen rapidly. Although British investments in bonds, railways, public utilities, mines, plantations, and manufacturing totaled, prior to the war, approximately $1,300,000,000, in a few short years American investments had swept up to over half a billion dollars, and were still increasing. In Brazil are found great American meat-packing concerns, heavy investments in transportation, light and power, in mines, and plantations. There on the Tapajoz River is to be found the great 3,700,000-acre Ford rubber estate. American steel companies own a good share of Brazil's vast supply of iron. Since the United States Government has largely monopolized financing abroad, vast additional sums have been extended to Brazil for steel mills, armaments, purchase and storage of many agricultural and mineral products. At Brazilian ports touch the fine reconditioned vessels of the new good-will fleet. Out of the skies swoop down the fine sky-liners of Pan-American Airways.

But in the half-dozen years before the war, new factors were arising to challenge American trade supremacy and influence. Because of shifts in Brazil's internal economy and political life and the new barter and trade methods of the German Reich, from 1935, almost to the outbreak of war, German exports to Brazil exceeded those of the United States. Whereas in 1933 we supplied 21 per cent of Brazil's imports, and in 1937 23 per cent, Germany in the first-named year provided only 12.1 per cent, but in 1937, 23.9 per cent, almost doubling her sales in five years. England was the principal sufferer, dropping down to fourth place, or a lower position than that of Argentina.

Much of the explanation for this trade shift must be found in the expansion of Brazil's cotton-growing industry, in good part fomented by the Japanese, which swelled from a meager 231,000 contos of raw cotton in 1934 to 1,512,000 contos in 1937. While the United States was restricting cotton production and progressively losing the world market, Brazil was winning what we lost, and today could put around 2,000,000 bales into the export trade if there were a market. Brazil can easily put under cotton cultivation virgin acreage equal to the no longer virginal cotton acreage of the United States. With lands far more productive, with definitely cheaper labor, Brazil will be in a strong position on any free international competitive basis.

Prior to the war the scramble for world armaments led to new activity in developing Brazil's great wealth of mineral resources, as yet scarcely tapped. Eminent geologists declare that she has the richest iron deposits on earth, about a fourth of the world's supply. Next to the Soviet Union, she has the greatest manganese resources. Bauxite, chromium, copper, gold, nickel, platinum, some tin and wolfram are but a few of the possibilities. Supplies for helium have recently been discovered, and the Brazilian Navy Department is increasingly gratified at the success of recent oil borings, especially in Bahía.

Starting from the steaming state of Bahía (just below the 'Bulge'), mountains much like our own Appalachians sweep down Brazil's east coast. They pass through the mineral storehouse of

Minas Geraes, which has most of Brazil's vast iron supply, and diamonds and emeralds, gold and platinum, manganese and nickel — most of the strategic ores for which nations go to war. Then in tropical glory, the range swings past Rio de Janeiro, the beautiful, luxurious capital of Brazil — purple seas to the east, teeming jungles to the west. But upon reaching Rio Grande do Sul, the southernmost state of Brazil, the mountain ridges curve southwest in a great basaltic elbow and fade off into level plains, the pampas.

In area Brazil is the fourth country in the world, larger than the continental United States, and with 48,000,000, mostly pauper, inhabitants is potentially the wealthiest land on earth, with the possible exception of the U.S.S.R.

The country is fifteen times the size of France, and its population is greater than that of France. A vast land of mountains and plateaus, jungles, and mighty rivers, a realm of fabulous resources.

2

Brazil is the paradise of large estates, *fazendas*. In few countries in the world is rural property so inequitably divided. Although the census in 1920 showed that 70.8 per cent of all males over twenty-one were engaged in agriculture, most of them worked and still work under a system very close to peonage and own no property whatsoever. According to the census, the régime of large landed property prevails. Thanks to foreign colonization, the land is more or less split up in the coastal region of the south, but not even a tenth part of the total privately owned area of the country belongs to small proprietors. Four hundred million acres — nine tenths of the acreage included in the census — is divided among only 164,274 large properties. In other words, two per cent of the adult male population of the country owns nine tenths of the land.

This is accompanied by an incredibly low living standard. Mostly labor is close to peonage. According to the United States Department of Commerce (May, 1938), the average Brazilian factory wage is only eleven dollars a month. Rural workers get far less. Of the western nations, Brazil is close to the bottom in per capita purchasing power. These class differences are reflected in education and public health. Seventy per cent of the population is illiterate. Of all the twenty Latin-American countries, probably only Salvador and Haiti have a smaller percentage of children in school. Brazil's public-health statistics are among the worst in the world. Tuberculosis, leprosy, syphilis, smallpox, typhus, Chagas' disease, beriberi are mostly unchecked scourges. Yellow fever still lashes large interior areas; deaths from it increased seventeen hundred per cent between 1908 and 1938.

These are some of the most tragic aspects of one of the largest and wealthiest countries on earth. The greater portion of its inhabitants are crowded in a coastal stretch of two hundred miles. Interior settlement, because of the difficulties of the terrain, the density of the jungles, and the lack of communications, not to mention inadequate health conditions, has increased but slowly. Land monopoly has blocked development, prevented diversification and the development of new industries.

Inevitably coffee will become ever less important in the total national economy. Great effort is now being made to build up new industries. This has large significance for the United States. Eventually it will profoundly affect our political rôle as supervisor of the two continents, the interpretation of the Monroe Doctrine, and our future trade.

3

Brazil is the key South American country in any system of international relationship with the Old World. For, both geographically and culturally, Brazil is far closer to Europe than to the United States. Few Americans stop to realize that the farthest coastal point of Brazil is nearly two thousand miles east of New York: that the distance from Natal in Africa is only sixteen hundred miles; that Rio is approximately five hundred miles closer to Cadiz, Spain, than to New York. Before the war Rio by air was five days from New York, but transatlantic planes from Berlin used to make it in forty hours. Air France and Lufthansa had transatlantic service to the southern continent for many years before Pan-American Airways began service to Portugal. Italy also briefly established an overseas service.

Closer to Europe than it is to us, and with increasing industrial diversification, Brazil, before the war, was becoming more and more a part of Europe's economic and political system. It was with increasing difficulty that she was held to an exclusive Pan-American rôle; later on it may prove even more difficult.

The drama of this international struggle for supremacy in Brazil was given point shortly before the war by the visit of Foreign Minister Aranha to Washington, and the simultaneous visit of Colonel Gustavo Fario to Germany to purchase German and Italy war materials. The drama was also revealed at the time of the Lima Pan-American Conference, when Brazil swore friendship with the United States but simultaneously announced the signing of a new trade agreement with the Reich, a step soon followed by new barter arrangements with Italy.

The complexity of Brazil's international relations is accentuated by certain internal population problems. The difference between the north and south of Brazil, always marked, has frequently resulted in secessionist movements. So difficult was this antagonism even in colonial times that for a while the Portuguese Government had to set up two different governments. This geographical highland-lowland, temperate zone-tropical separatism is deepened by racial differences. Southern Brazil is predominantly European: half a million German immigrants, two hundred and fifty thousand Japanese, a million and a quarter Italians; and the latter, especially, have mixed widely with the Portuguese population. Northern Brazil is more native, a mixture of Portuguese, Dutch, and French, with Indians and negroes — a violent melting-pot.

The various European elements in Brazil's population, among which, with the exception of the Portuguese, Axis subjects predominate, played a big part in bringing the country for a time into closer embrace with continental Europe. But with the outbreak of the war, the control of the seas by Britain and the United States, Brazil's trade ties with Germany were brusquely severed, and gradually, with the help of bountiful loan funds, Vargas shifted ground, presently began damping down on Axis propaganda, and is today a full-fledged partner among the United Nations.

And as for Brazil, what direction will the unfolding of a great nation take? Will it finally shake off its political totalitarianism and become a great democratic force, utilizing its limitless resources for the welfare of its people and mankind?

Some commentators believe that, in the not far future, Brazil's Spanish-speaking neighbors will combine against it under the leadership of Argentina, and dismember its hinterland. Others believe that Brazil, rapidly striding ahead in wealth and power, will turn imperialistic and dominate the continent. Others feel that Brazil will be the real pivot of a new system of friendly continental cooperation.

For a proper and balanced Pan-Americanism, eventually there will probably arise as its foundation a series of regional federations: Brazil in itself; the United States, Canada, and part of the Caribbean; México, Central America, Colombia, and Venezuela; Argentina, Chile, and Paraguay; Perú, Bolivia, and Ecuador. Certainly Brazil is a great country with a great future. Around it probably will swirl many conflicts before mankind learns better ways. But it is capable, as are few countries of the world, of sustaining a vast population in comfort and happiness. Those possibilities have not been plumbed, the surface has been scarcely scratched.

4

Undoubtedly the world is on the eve of great tropical conquests. Today we have all the technique necessary to open up the jungles. Additional techniques will develop in the process. That they are not being developed is due to infamous political conditions, slothfulness, lack of imagination and initiative. Today Brazil is rapidly becoming industrialized, and the need for further development of interior resources will increase rapidly. Brazil's westward movement is close at hand. For obvious reasons it can never be a westward movement of unbridled individualism as in the case of our own West. It will require the coordinated effort of government, society, and science.

In thirty-five years — less at the present rate of use — the principal mineral resources of the United States will have become exhausted, and we shall have to turn imperialistic or discover synthetic substitutes, as we are now doing. By then Brazil will be coming into her own as one of the great producing nations of the world. Halford J. Mackinder talks glibly about the heart-land of Eurasia as destined to dominate the world because of superior area and population. If the Brazilian jungle is tamed, the region will have far more prolific and varied productive capacities than the Eurasian heart-land.

With the new use of plastics, perhaps the basis of a great new era in civilization, Brazil will become one of the greatest sources for the necessary materials. This will provide us with another economic link.

What will the future hold? After the present war will Brazil drift back into the orbit of European nations needing her cotton and other materials of a more strategic nature? Will the new rubber industry serve as another economic tie with the United States? Or will synthetic rubber wholly replace present South American development of new sources? Much, perhaps, will depend on whether a free trading system on an international scale develops after the war or whether the present tendency toward more exclusive continental trade blocs prevails. Of such factors are the enduring relations of nations made, not alone by good-will, speeches, war expediencies.

What is needed, regardless of the economic system resulting from the war, is the creation of an integrated American economy, with planned and equitable use of resources and properly co-ordinated industrialization of Latin America in accordance with the best needs of each country, not merely the United States. We have not even begun to work toward such a goal.

Brazil, above all, exemplifies the need of a coordinated plan of economic development; and that plan would be stronger if also coordinated with the proper economic unification of the Americas. Without such a plan, if power politics and imperialisms rule the world, new developments in Brazil will obey the immediate-profit motive, which means three things: First, a development by private foreign corporations of merely easily obtainable raw products, without reference to the national needs, the internal prosperity, the defense of Brazil, the continent, the aspirations of inter-Americanism, of the United States. Second, a stiffening of Brazil's own industrialization. Third, a failure really to develop the manifold resources of the country, for the simple reason that Nature, the jungles, the tropics, must be approached with a whole general staff and attacked like a formidable enemy, with the combined intelligence of the whole nation and perhaps the whole continent, if it is to be tamed and utilized. This requires at the outset an overhead cost beyond the means of any private corporation interested merely in quick profits. It means that problems of health, communications, and community living must be simultaneously taken care of, as well as the development of vast sustaining industries, all at the same time, otherwise the labor supply will be deficient.

The loan made by the United States for Brazil to put up a steel industry, to be under joint government and private control, was a step in the right direction. Roads are also being built and other facilities provided for the British-owned iron mines. It is too bad that these mines, which will thus be so greatly benefited, should not also have been brought under the same joint control, for it would seem that American taxpayers' money should, if used in alien enterprises, safeguard in every way the prosperity and economic independence of the peoples aided.

Another great adventure of American governmental economic expansion — the new public, rather than private, dollar-diplomacy — is the effort to get the rubber out of the Amazón region.

General settlement in the Amazón basin has been slow. Two major factors in the past have operated. One was the great rubber boom prior to the maturity of the Dutch and British East Indian plantations. The demand for rubber in those days, with the sudden expansion of the automobile industry, kept racing ahead of supply. Rubber at one time went to over three dollars a pound. Fabulous fortunes were made. Manaus and Iquitos on the Amazón grew to flourishing little cities. Manaus even built a huge opera house in the heart of the jungle. It was a veritable dance of the millions.

For this, workers were needed, and they were combed from

Bolivia and coastal Brazil. Even wild Indians caught the fever when they discovered that this tree sap was exchangeable for cotton cloth, beads, knives, and sundry magical articles, and drifted down from the headwaters in huts perched on huge crude rubber rafts.

The labor supply for Brazil was in good part recruited from the northeastern state of Ceará, to some extent from Rio Grande do Norte and Parahyba. These states, but particularly Ceará, are the western Nebraska and Kansas, the Oklahoma, of Brazil, and have played a similar rôle in the dispersion of peoples. Ceará has a capricious climate. At times rain is plentiful; the land is then bountiful; for a short while, fabulous crops can be grown. But the inevitable years of drouth come. Men, as suddenly as they rushed into the magic prosperity, are thrust back into poverty. They lose their farms; they starve. They migrate in rags to the coast. Businesses collapse because loans cannot be collected and the hinterland market has suddenly vanished. Uprooted folk drift back south, to João Pessoa, to Recife, to Rio, or north to Belen at the mouth of the Amazón. From there many trickle on up the river, looking for more farms or any other means of making a living. Thus Manaus, today, in spite of the collapse of the rubber boom so many years ago, is larger if poorer than in the days of its glory.

As time went on, plantations were set at favorable points along the riverbanks, as around Santarem, and in fact along most of the rivers as far up as the fall line. Minor industries have arisen. But man's hold there is precarious, and will be until a large-scale organized attack is begun.

Today, once again, there is a rubber boom, all through the Amazón basin. The clock has been turned back. With Japanese conquest in the East, the rubber world is back where it was before the First World War, and the rubber of the Amazón reassumes some of its old importance.

There has been considerable labor stampede. Thus to the Bolivian rubber region have gone the agricultural workers of the rich Santa Cruz region, until the plantations there are stripped of labor and valuable crops are perishing. The incentive has been the chance for workers to earn forty to sixty cents a day gathering rubber, instead of the previous fifteen or twenty-five cents.

But it reveals the anarchy of labor supply; for whereas in certain adjacent areas in Perú there is great unemployment, the national boundaries impede any rational use of labor on a continental basis.

In Brazil the present rubber expansion has synchronized with one of Ceará's periods of scorching drouth. There on the coast men are idle, hungry; the boom gives them some chance to escape.

But the Amazón trip is expensive, and for a poor man dangerous and difficult. The present price of rubber, if higher than normal times, nevertheless is kept down by government-to-government contract, and this makes it impossible for Brazilian contractors to offer the transportation or the high wages of previous boom epochs. Besides, such contractors do not know when the war will end or how soon the bubble will burst and they will be left holding the bag. They are correspondingly cautious.

The matter has had to be handled by the government, with funds provided by the United States. Thus, although apparently rubber has been kept down in price, because of these enormous concealed costs it will probably be the most expensive rubber ever procured by the hand of man. Unfortunately the Brazilian worker is not going to get any appreciable share of that enormous outlay.

Since June, 1942, various Brazilian agencies have been working on the labor-supply problem: the Bureau for Economic Coordination, headed by João Alberto Lins de Barros; also the Amazón Supply Service and the Immigration Department, both headed by Doctor Henrique Doria de Vasconcellos. The initial shipment of labor, about three thousand men, with some seven thousand dependents, did not work out so well. Unaccustomed to the climate, already in weakened condition, many fell ill. Mortality was high. Not wishing to abandon their families without resources, many drifted into the towns for work or onto river plantations rather than brave the dangers of the jungle.

And so, this problem of getting at least fifty thousand additional workers from the northern dust bowl to the hot, humid Amazón Valley is far more than one of mere transportation. It involves distribution, housing, health, and assured supplies. It involves family relations, personal adjustment, new skills. All told it is a problem of formidable proportions.

Transportation is in itself a real headache. The original plan was to bring workers down to the coast and ship them to Belen and on up the river. But Axis submarines have practically put a stop to coastwise maritime traffic around the Bulge. Thousands of soup-kitchen migrants were and are crowded in Fortaleza and other places, unable to get farther. Overland travel is a trying ordeal, six hundred miles through terrible country few sane men are willing to face to reach Carolina on the Tocantins, then five hundred miles more down the river, then a thousand miles or more up the Amazón. The government has arranged to pay the families of such men a pittance while they stay behind, and has been establishing hovel-hotels and food-stations every nineteen miles through the jungles for the marchers. But they are not provided with the proper inoculations and health safeguards before starting; the food and rest stations have no proper sanitary equipment. This method is unfair in that it means breaking up homes, a big sacrifice in itself, a separation that might well prove permanent or have to be endured for many years. The wages of the rubber-gatherers are not sufficient for them ever to send for their families. Hence it would mean that they themselves would not become permanent settlers in the Amazón, except by family abandonment, and would eventually work their way back. These workers must face a wholly new environment. What wages will they receive? For how long? What permanence is there of employment? What future? Will they shortly be left stranded in an inhospitable and dangerous environment? This side of the problem merely receives the customary hush-hush. For the present brief moment they will, of necessity, probably enjoy better living conditions than rubber workers in the past, who went to a living death.

On its end, the United States is sending in supplies to the new workers — food, tools, motors, shotguns, cups, boats. These materials are being supplied by the Defense Supplies Corporation, a subsidiary of the Reconstruction Finance Corporation, and are put into the hands of Brazilian *aviadores*, fly-by-night distributing firms. What controls exist so that the rubber workers will not as in the past be charged more than all their wages for these supplies, already paid for by the American taxpayer? But medicines, doctors, and so on are being provided. Pan-American Airways has been subsidized to hack out new airports.

It is obvious that all these are emergency moves made necessary by the desperate need of the United States for rubber. Last year Brazil's output was only twenty thousand tons. If all goes well, this may be doubled in 1943. But it means a very costly emergency effort to secure what constitutes but a few day's supply for the United States. This may be unavoidable, but it would not seem so extravagant if permanent settlement and development were thereby assured.

However, if the Far Eastern plantations ever become accessible to us again, the Amazón effort will collapse overnight. For rubber can be produced in the Far East at a profit for six cents a pound, far less than gleaning wild rubber, especially from the remoter regions. New synthetic rubber can be produced, if not cheaper than the normal Brazilian supply, far cheaper than that from nearly inaccessible jungles requiring superhuman effort and risk. Besides, synthetic rubber has been heavily subsidized and its market will be duly protected. No long-range guarantee has been worked out for Amazón rubber.

The Amazón effort, therefore, sooner or later, is doomed to collapse unless coordinated with other developments. For it does not represent an orderly attempt to establish a permanent industry, let alone the sort of all-round promotion required if the Amazón is to be properly brought into a stabilized producing condition. It is just another boom, a wartime boom, the aftermath of which may in many ways prove tragic for the region and for the workers yanked away from their families. At a very high price in human wealth, health, and happiness, some beneficial by-products will result. A few new farm lands will be opened; perhaps a few new small industries may survive. The new airfields are a permanent asset and besides serving for present and future defense, can become centers for small new settlements and enterprise. But these results are minor compared to the cost involved. In short, this is far indeed from any coordinated plan for the permanent development and stability of the Amazón basin and its old and new population. Valuable lessons, of course, will be learned.

Let us consider more intimately the nature of the Amazón **basin, its** history, resources, and possibilities.

CHAPTER XVII

Future of the Amazón

THE Amazón basin of South America is the mystery, the challenge, and the hope of the New World. Alternately it is pictured as the world's hell hole or the paradise of riches beyond man's wildest dreams.

Certainly until man has made a determined and scientific assault upon this region, the New World will not have realized its full potentialities; South America cannot be said to have reached maturity or to have found its true place as one of the great active continents of the earth. Here is one of man's last great physical frontiers. To tame that great wilderness will require the most extensive application of political and economic knowledge, the latest instruments of science, and the noblest aims of human betterment.

That the development of one of Nature's wealthiest and greatest strongholds has not been undertaken is due probably to historical circumstance, to the fact that the weapons needed are far more numerous and specialized, the problem more complex, immediate returns less promising, than in previously occupied areas. It is as if some mysterious power had withheld the greatest prize of earth until human wisdom and collective intelligence should become worthy of the eventual reward.

If the difficulties of Amazón development promise to be greater than those of almost any region yet tackled by man, the ultimate rewards will be correspondingly great. Organized energies comparable to those expended by the Soviets in opening up the Arctic or those of the Australian Government in opening up the northern desert, if expended in the Brazilian jungle region, would in due time bring in ten times the material recompense.

The Amazón basin's unplumbed resources, its new vegetable products, its wealth of minerals, can provide science with new stimuli, can lead to novel attainments and unlock fresh secrets for man's mastery of earth everywhere and heighten his material and spiritual enjoyment therein.

The Amazón development cannot be accomplished in the same manner as that of the West of the United States. Only to a limited degree can its benefits be seized by individual enterprise and recklessness, however much these may play a part. Nor are the same historical forces at work today which made the great Mississippi and later La Plata basin of Argentina, Uruguay, and Paraguay such necessary food reservoirs for the toiling millions of Europe. The great staple products which provide food, clothing, and shelter can now be grown or manufactured in so many parts of the earth that, given our present deficient systems of international organization and distribution, they are ordinarily a surfeit. The Amazón basin, rather than a supplier of elementary needs, is a storehouse for a super-civilization which mankind with its present jarring nationalisms has not yet reached. The Amazón will likely be an answer to a scheme of life to which man's specialized knowledge already entitles him, but which his present incapacity for social and international organization denies him.

2

The Amazón River basin, the greatest in the world, has an area — 2,700,000 square miles — almost equal to the whole continent of Australia, and is a million square miles larger than all Europe exclusive of Russia. The basin laps over into four adjacent countries, is equivalent in its entirety to eighty per cent of the area of Brazil, the fourth largest country in the world.

A million square miles of timber have scarcely known axe or saw. Hundreds of species of trees, from the strong, light balsa wood, which provides the rafts of downstream travelers, to the heavy deep red *aitá*, one of the hardest of all woods, promise unlimited interest for science, industry, and the elaboration of synthetic products. The dominant tree nearly everywhere is the towering Brazilian nut tree, linked with our own Christmas festivities, which sometimes reaches a circumference of forty feet. Merely the medicinal potentialities of the Amazón will multiply present drug resources many times with new discoveries. There also are to be found extensive mineral deposits.

All this suggests that the future development of the Amazón is not merely a national but a continental, a world problem. Brazil itself borders on every country in South America except Chile and Ecuador, but the Amazón basin extends into Ecuador, from which flows down the great Napo River, the first gateway of exploration by the early Spanish Orellana expedition. In Ecuador also flow the swift falling Pastaza and Morona, northern branches of the mighty Marañón.

Out of southern Colombia come rushing the great Putumayo and the Japurá, with its important tributaries, the Caquetá and Caguán; and from its eastern plains flow forth the many tributaries of the mysterious Río Negro, still partly unexplored.

The Madeira branch, itself one of the world's great rivers, two thousand miles in length, which flows into the Amazon just above the historic rubber city of Manaus, reaches its long fingers far up into Bolivia and Perú. Among its mightier tributaries are the impressive Madre de Dios (Mother of God) River; the Beni, fed from the eternal snows of Sorata and Illimani, two silver giants towering nearly twenty-two thousand feet into the sky of the Southern Cross; the Guaporé, forming the border and reaching back into Matto Grosso; and Theodore Roosevelt's renowned River of Doubt.

The Amazón headwaters are customarily said to be those of the Marañón branch, which takes its start in lofty Lake Lauri Cocha near the great Peruvian mining center of Cerro de Pasco and, flowing northward half the length of mountain-ribbed Perú to the Ecuadorian border, turns east, finally bursts through the last Andean ridge in a swirling millrace at Pongo de Manseriche, and eventually, after flowing fifteen hundred leisurely miles, joins the Amazón near Iquitos, Perú's main river port, only three hundred and fifty feet above sea level but still twenty-three hundred miles from the mouth of the mighty stream. Iquitos, with its jungle clamor, busy river wharves, motley assortment of primitive and civilized races, its market of monkey meat and magic herbs, is the upper limit of ocean-going vessels, although it is possible to go in comfort hundreds of miles farther, as far up into Perú as Yurimaguas on the Huallaga. All told, the Amazón tributaries provide large or small vessels with a thousand miles of navigability merely within the borders of Perú.

Already at altitudes of twelve thousand feet above the sea, some of its branches are mightier rivers than most of those in the United States. Above Ayacucho, the Apurimac, along which I once traveled for many miles, is a vast and noble stream, cleaving its way through granite walls five thousand feet high or below mountain terraces, some built nearly a thousand years ago by Quechua agriculturists and still in use. At places it is still spanned by Inca suspension bridges, slung from ancient masonry towers, the former fiber cables now replaced with steel. In the lower reaches these streams become placid rivers. Río Negro is ten miles wide at the Boiacú channel; the Tapajoz is eight miles wide at Boem.

In Brazil itself are also mighty tributaries. Half a dozen such, flowing south from Venezuela or the Guianas, are greater than our own Hudson. The Tocantins river system strikes far south for fifteen hundred miles into the Goyaz mining region. Similar in length and majesty are the Xingú and Tapajoz, the Purús and the Jurúa, and in Perú, the Ucayali and Huallaga.

Each stream and region drained has its peculiar characteristics and resources. Río Negro and the Jutahy are literally black; the Branco is milky white, and the two streams merge at Carvoeira like 'cream being poured into black coffee.' The Tapajoz and Guaporé are usually crystal clear; but most, as the Purús, Jurúa, and Ucayali, and of course the Amazón proper, are yellow with alluvial sediment.

Today, four centuries after the Spanish conquest, over eighty per cent of South America's population lives within two hundred miles of the seacoast. Only the fringe of the continent has ever been truly brought under man's sway. Less than a fifth of the continent lies within twenty miles of a railroad, until recently the maximum distance within which agriculture could profitably develop. Brazil has forty-four million inhabitants (forty-eight million by recent estimates), or more than France, Italy, or England, but the country's development is also largely limited to a coastal strip.

South America never had a frontier in the United States sense of the word. Without pushing the statement too far, it may be said that the Spanish and Portuguese conquered man instead of Nature. Though early expeditions explored far and wide, the settlements which endured rarely went beyond the limits of pre-conquest indigenous occupation; in some places they definitely receded. The same barriers that prevented the Indians from utilizing many portions of South America also blocked the Europeans. The great exception was in Argentina and Uruguay, which, until the introduction of European livestock and new cereals, could not be utilized very much by the natives, who mostly had jungle or mountain skills, but which subsequently provided the broad acres for frontier colonization similar to that in the United States. Eventually the open pampas regions made more rapid progress than any other parts of the continent. But in general, most of South America, from early days till now, has been ruled in the spirit of the early conquest. This persistent feudal spirit has delayed the utilization of natural resources and the evolution of the continent.

Another factor has postponed the use of the continent for the more enlightened benefit of its various nations and peoples. This has been too great subordination of economic activities to the needs of Europe and Asia and more recently to the United States. Before Pizarro's day, the Incas developed a great regional culture. Their highways ran north-south through the Andes, from Colombia clear into Argentina and Chile. With excellent communications, the early peoples built up a well-knit empire along self-sufficient lines, with a maximum use of resources for their own welfare. Perhaps no group in history ever has utilized Nature's gifts so completely and intelligently, up to the limits possible with existing techniques and knowledge.

But this fine structure went to pieces with conquest, so that now it is doubtful whether as much land is cultivated in Perú as in the Inca days. The old irrigation systems fell into disuse, the old highways deteriorated, the old industries declined. The new highways ran from highlands to coast in order to ship out materials to Europe. Flourishing outlying areas were ignored. The conquest turned its attention to the extraction of minerals by negro and Indian slaves more than to agricultural pursuits. Gold and silver, which previously had been used merely to adorn temples, became the sinew of trade.

This process was paralleled in most of the continent. When new resources were tapped, new industries founded, the older self-sufficiency and humanitarianism, whatever its deficiencies and primitive characteristics by present standards, were destroyed. None of this led to the rational use of native resources primarily to benefit the peoples. It created quick wealth for the ruling feudal strata of European extraction and later for foreign capital. It produced majestic coastal cities and a glittering urban civilization quite out of proportion to the level of culture and comfort in the interior. Even in Argentina, in the pampas and Patagonia, as well as in southern Chile, where Nature has permitted considerable settlement in our own western style, the prevailing system of land-holdings and race exploitation has resulted in senseless imitation of the old feudal pattern.

Men in South America have not been able to achieve freedom on a large scale by way of the frontier as they did in the United States. The obstacles imposed by Nature, as well as those imposed by man, have prevented that fine burst of individual initiative which featured much of our national growth. Yet given South American needs and the international situation, the opening up of new regions, and particularly the Amazón basin, becomes increasingly a national and continental necessity if the Western Hemisphere is to become strong and rich enough to defend itself.

3

What are the obstacles? The possibilities? To what may men aspire in this vast Amazón region?

First it is necessary to review the manner in which man thus far has rolled back the mystery of the unknown from the Brazilian jungle and highland area since the days of Orellana's early sixteenth century voyage, and to what extent the region thus far has been settled, its resources utilized.

The earliest days saw a fever of exploration. The Spaniards — undeterred by Orellana's tale of the terrible female warriors, the Amazons who gave the river its name — pushed over the Andes from the headwaters and explored downstream. The Portuguese, like the famous Pedro de Texeira expedition, pushed upstream, and intrepid *bandeirantes* struck northwest from São Paulo, across the grassy plains of Matto Grosso and into the Madeira country. The French and Dutch struggled south from the Guianas. Later runaway slaves penetrated far into the jungle, mingling with the Indians or finding independent livelihood. Though all these races fought, they also mingled, intermarried, giving rise to what Vasconcelos calls 'the cosmic race' of the continent, a breed well adapted to grapple with a tropical region. Numerous permanent settlements resulted.

Not until the nineteenth century were more systematic surveys made. These ventures had an international aspect. The great German Humboldt, the Frenchman Castelnay, the Englishmen Bates and Wallace, the Americans Orton and Heath, provide gold-star names. Agassiz and his work are inseparably linked with the region. In the eighteen-fifties Lieutenants Herndon and Gibbon of the United States Navy, starting respectively from La Paz in Bolivia and from Perú, crossed the Andes from the Pacific side. Their report to Congress remains one of the classic works on the Amazón.

Scientific study became more specialized with the ornithologist Leo Miller; the geologists, the Brazilian Olveiras and the American Hartt; the Swiss botanists Huber and Ducke; engineers such as Colonel Church of Madeira–Mamoré railway fame. The Brazilian Barboza Rodríguez explored and wrote his monumental treatise on the palm tree. Madame Condreay explored the rivers of Pará, and the Swiss scientist, Emilia Snethlage, so praised by Theodore Roosevelt, explored from the Xingú to the Tapajoz. Roosevelt himself put the River of Doubt definitely on the map and into the columns of the *New York Times*. The fact that his enterprise was carried out as late as the second decade of this century reveals to what extent even preliminary exploration has been delayed.

Much of Roosevelt's success was due to the cooperation of Colonel Cándido Mariano Rondón, who pushed the Brazilian telegraph service into the remotest corners of Matto Grosso and opened up vast new stretches. He is probably the most important figure thus far in the whole history of the region. Fifteen years ago a commission of the United States Department of Commerce, investigating rubber, pushed far into the hinterlands. About the same time another party, by land, water, and hydroplane, explored the western affluent of the Río Branco up to the Venezuelan border.

The Amazón was not opened up to international navigation until 1867. After that date increasing knowledge of the practicability of ordinary travel far into the interior, regular steamship schedules, the discovery of new products and opportunities, made life more agreeable and profitable.

Then came the rubber boom. The output more than doubled from 1890 to 1905, rubber stations were humming in far Amazonian corners never before penetrated. Great fortunes were made. The Suárez brothers founded a veritable private empire in eastern Bolivia.

If the rubber workers encountered mostly hardships, disease, near slavery, many escaped to found homes and farms, to become permanent traders or settlers. The population of Belem, the Atlantic port, grew to over a hundred thousand. Manaus, a thousand miles upstream, became a scintillating modern city, a bonanza town, where wealth, luxury, and vice flourished.

The rubber boom collapsed, but rubber collection had led to the utilization of the river and all its tributaries as far up as the first rapids or falls, so that a vast additional area was no longer merely a terrifying unknown, and numerous other products began to be exploited, such as vegetable ivory, nuts, oils, fibers, herbs, and so forth, which though not returning the flash-pan fortunes of the rubber kings, laid the basis for permanent growth. New plantations were laid out along the Tapajoz and Mañués. New discoveries, such as the use of the poisonous timbo weed, which provides rotenone, an insecticide, that now annually saves millions of dollars of American crops without the health injury from previous concoctions, have provided new industries. The cattle business has thrived from the proximity of new markets. Although the rubber industry's boom was short-lived, Manaus suffered only brief relapse and today has ninety thousand inhabitants, nearly double what it had in the days of its splendor and splurge. Belem now·has a population of three hundred thousand and has become one of the show cities of the world. Today roads are being built up into the Río Branco, where less than two decades ago explorers perished miserably. One road is to reach clear to the British Guiana frontier, the other to the Colombian border. Over on the southwestern edge of the basin new railroads are being pushed into Bolivia and Matto Grosso. Today Pan-American Airways is flying directly across the Amazón basin from the West Indies, thus cutting down the time to Buenos Aires, by night flying, to only two days.

4

Popular imagination has pictured the Amazón as a prehistoric antediluvian swamp, infested with dangerous animals and plants, poisonous serpents, where disease stalks at every turn, an inferno where the relentless sun eats away men's reason. Although one of our common-school geographies shows a man and horse being dragged down into the morass by a huge serpent, actually snakes are no real problem. Fantastic stories of the local boa constrictor have been told, yet they are so docile they often are kept as household pets to keep off rodents. In a number of humble dwellings I have observed boas coiled about the rooftree, basking fat and contented, a beloved part of the local ménage.

Insects are, however, prevalent. Gnats are often a painful nuisance. Ants are often dangerous and destructive. In lowland regions insects are not only terribly annoying but on occasion carry dangerous diseases, especially malaria. But in many places beriberi and yellow fever have largely been eliminated, and leprosy, never of much danger to the hygienic, is being curbed. Much is being done in certain locales to prevent malaria. Much more can be done. But in many parts of the *Amazonas*, insects are less annoying than in the Louisiana bayous or in New Jersey in summer, and large areas are free of them entirely.

Through vast extensions of the Amazón basin the climate is quite endurable. The mean average temperature for the hotter parts is eighty degrees, or the same as Panamá City, where white residents live more comfortably than the people of New York or Texas in summer. Only about five per cent of the vast region is below normal flood level. Elsewhere the forest becomes open and can be traversed for the most part even without a machete to cut underbrush. Much of the region is high and healthful.

Nor is it all forest. The rainfall is good but not heavy. Brazil, in fact, has more open grass country than the whole Argentine pampas, and most of it is in the Amazón basin. Stretching east from the Río Branco to the Guianas is a vast rolling plain as large as Vermont. Boa Vista, the capital of this cattle empire, is practically free from malaria. Such *campos* are found throughout the region wherever the forest fades into grassy plains.

Despite the fact that the greater part of the Amazón empire eventually can be populated by white men, the problems remain tremendous. Difficulty of transportation heads the list of obstacles. The rivers probably will continue to provide the main arteries; but to utilize them properly and get around rapids or falls, expensive canals and locks, railroads or roads must be built. The Madeira–Mamoré line cost thirty million dollars for only two hundred and twenty-six miles. In other places the airplane will prove invaluable.

In many regions a single paying industry would not bring returns sufficient to warrant development. From the outset such an industry would have to be coordinated with other activities in order to create a stabilized economic situation and provide the basis for a sufficient permanent population.

The opening up of the Amazón basin presents a complex of problems never before faced in ordinary colonization. The rewards will be great everywhere, but in many cases returns cannot be enjoyed for years. The bonanza days — the rubber, gold, and diamond rushes — were not sustained thereafter, except to a limited degree and in a few pockets, by a continuous tide of settlers to bring about the development to any great extent of a stabilized economy and culture. Mere commercialism may wrench out a few tropical products, but this means that the white man is the manager, not a settler. The individual, with a minimum of family ties, stays a while, makes way for another.

It is true, part of the region may be developed in much the old style by purely individual enterprise, as for instance the more habitable cattle sectors. But the simple economics of 'cheap land' will never be the dominant motive of the settlement of the Amazón. The initial capital costs will be high, not low as in the case of our own West.

The rewards nearly everywhere will be large eventually, but few colonists can single-handedly become pioneers. The newcomer will have to be sustained by the rest of the community. Settlement in the Amazón is not merely a question of planting foodstuffs and waiting for the tide of later immigration to catch up.

The rubber industry, of course, especially with the development the last few years of disease-resistant strains of high yield, offers almost unlimited opportunities. This can be developed and stabilized on small holdings as in much of the Far East, but even so an inevitable seven years must elapse before the trees begin to give some return.

For the Amazón basin as a whole to reach a stabilized economy and permanent progressive settlement, there will be required government assistance, long-term, large-scale planning with proper coordination of all efforts, and the simultaneous development of a many-sided economy, something that can scarcely occur under purely laissez-faire methods depending on fairly immediate large returns.

The great pioneering movements have occurred in the past for a multiplicity of motives, but mainly because men on the border saw a chance to live life over, or begin it, without the handicaps of other men's devising. All such episodes in history, however unplanned, nevertheless have been directed consciously or unconsciously toward the purposeful creation of a better economic and social order with new freedoms. The dream never has been absent. This hope of new freedom, in the case of the Amazón, can be created only by great social and scientific planning and cooperation.

'For a long time,' remarks Isaiah Bowman, in his remarkable

study, *The Pioneer Fringe,* 'the pioneer beat science at his own game.... But the science of settlement now enters on a new phase, and that is why it is so tremendously important for governments today.' In short, today the pioneer must be science itself as much as the individual. Collective purpose and long-term planning, as well as the individual aspirant, become the frontiersmen. The effort no longer can be merely popular, it must be specialized. As Eduardo Romecín, the Bolivian statesman, has stated of the Chaco and the upper Amazón wilderness, 'Colonization of the frontier when it is undertaken must be on a large scale with provision for broad communal organization if the great physical obstacles that defeated all prior attempts are to be overcome.'

The new techniques making possible a wide-scale attack on the Amazón are rapidly maturing and converging. Air conditioning now makes dwelling comfortable in any climate, provided electric power is available, and for this the Amazón will not lack. Knowledge of tropical medicine lags, but controls are far greater than when the Panamá Canal was built. Today a much wider choice of means of communication exists.

Not a fraction of the oils and saps of the trees in the Amazón have found the industrial application they will have some day. The drugs available to medicine probably will be multiplied many times by discoveries in the Amazón. And the rich vegetable life may yet provide the world's great source of raw materials for synthetic products, plastics, and textiles. Unlike coal or petroleum, these vegetable materials always can be reproduced. The Du Pont laboratories and similar establishments are providing more and more of the basic knowledge and skills to make the forthcoming conquest of the Amazón both feasible and profitable.

When great air-cooled cities arise on the banks of the Amazón and its tributaries, their addition to the health and wealth of Brazil will greatly benefit the United States. The economies of North and South will complement each other more fully. What enriches one will enrich the other. What defends one will defend the other. Pan-Americanism can be a truly cooperative effort.

The development of the Amazón basin will be of great benefit to all South America, but particularly to Bolivia, Perú, Ecuador, and Colombia; it will make accessible some of the finest and most healthful regions of the continent which lie east of the Andes.

It, as much as anything, will make possible the economic integration of the continent.

5

This is not merely a Brazilian problem, but a problem for the whole continent. At present the effort is beyond the capacities of private capital alone. It is beyond the capacities of Brazil alone. But it is not beyond the capacities of the Western Hemisphere and its two hundred and fifty million people — even in wartime.

Here is a chance for statesmen of foresight and courage to set about a great constructive enterprise that will fire the imaginations of the world for a century, and lift us above the example of other continents. We can afford to parallel our present effort toward proper defense with a truly great enterprise. Rather than fearfully waiting for a possible blow from long degraded enemies, let us put forth our own positive challenge by a great undertaking which will bring forth the wisdom and finest constructive achievements of our age. Hitler busily creates new industries, opens new mines, tills new lands, in regions conquered, as part of his long-range plan of trying to make Europe so self-sufficient that his rule cannot be broken. We, in the Western Hemisphere, cannot hope to match the growing productive capacities of the three hundred and fifty million people controlled by Hitler plus the three hundred and fifty million now controlled by Japan, merely with the labor and resources of the United States and Canada with a hundred and forty million people. It would mean slavery, exhaustion, ruin to accomplish it. We must push ahead the development of Latin America, of the whole continent — and on a magnificent scale — even in wartime. Let us therefore marshal the New World forces for a concerted, planned, scientific assault upon the great Amazón basin. Let the enterprise have no taint of imperialism. Let it be in a new spirit of cooperation by free people to advance the welfare of mankind. Whatever the fate of the Europe and Asia, we can make a new America that we can defend forever.

PART FIVE

South American
Highlands

CHAPTER XVIII

Mornings in the Andes

DURING the nineteenth-century civil wars in Perú, an old saying was that when armed trouble descended on Lima (the capital on the coast), the inhabitants ran indoors and barred their windows; but when something happened in mountain-perched Arequipa, the men seized their guns and rushed out, crying, 'Who are we fighting for now?'

But farther up in the highlands when there was excitement, even if bullets were flying, the Quechua Indian inhabitants went about their daily tasks quite unconcerned. Jar on head or shoulder, like ancient Rebecca, they went to the well; or continued washing clothes on the stones; or kept on tilling their fields of potatoes, corn, and oca. Their fight, their problem, was ever how to survive in those harsh lofty heights of the Andes, not to engage in the periodic struggles for power.

Over beyond the highlands is another region, the inner basin of the great Amazón River, the low *selva*, a vast empire of tropical jungle; but only five per cent of Perú's population is found in that rich but poisonous area; as yet the real drama of the country is the eternal shuttle between highlands and coast lowlands.

Lima is colonial, European, more so than any other city on the continent, except possibly Buenos Aires. Yet Buenos Aires with its big meat-packing establishments, its majestic river meandering through several thousand miles of pampas, is linked by close bonds with the wheat and cattle regions at its back door. Not so, charming Lima; it is almost isolated; culturally and economically, it lives its own life apart as a seat of power, proud and indifferent, save that it does have a strange nostalgia for its great historic past and does look out upon the seven seas. Right at its back door tower the Andes, seeming alien, different, almost as if trying to push the city off entirely from the narrow sandy littoral where it dreams in eternal spring. It was founded by the Spaniards as an army camp; it grew into a great colonial mart of wealth and culture and commerce; it grew into a bureaucratic modern city, one of the finest in the New World. But because Lima, and the coast in general, are so different racially and culturally from the interior, a great cleavage exists in Peruvian life.

Arequipa stands midway between Lima and the Andes, both in population and culture. Nearly eight thousand feet above sea level, it is slightly higher than the capital of México, but far below the lofty region, from ten to fifteen thousand feet or more, where half the population of Perú lives and works. Strangely enough, the city has a certain Mexican flavor. Racially more mixed than almost any place in Perú, dominated by its mestizo population, in this also it is more like México. It is quick, mercurial, restless; its hardy, vigorous people enjoy sharp-flavored foods; they alternate easily between brooding and gaiety. They do not have the methodical patience of the people of the high sierra, nor the polished passivity and delightful frivolity of easy-going Lima. Arequipa stands midway between the two most important regional expressions of Perú. It is the gateway to the sierra. It is middle-ground in race, culture, temperament, and historical significance.

The sharply defined regional contrasts of Perú, with their corresponding distinct cultural patterns, make it a richly diversified country, and along with México, the most interesting in the New World. These regional differences have created serious problems of communication, of transportation, of economic unity; serious problems of government, and have led at times in Peruvian history, as in the days of Santa Cruz and Salaverry, to armed hostility; but without those differences, Perú would not be Perú, and when they have finally been woven into a pattern, the country will have become one of the regions of profoundest meaning for mankind. On the scroll of the future it is written that Perú will be a leader in original social organization and in culture. When the tale of the centuries is finally told, probably Perú, once more, as it was in the days of the Incas, will be essentially a mountain culture, part of the mestizo-Indian bloc.

Of the folk of the sierra, I write.

2

Mornings in the Andes are beautiful, often terrible. The chill upland air strikes to the marrow, but the spirit uplifts before some of the grandest spectacles Nature has placed in the path of man. The Andes, above all else, are a constant challenge, a challenge to the purposefulness, the patient industry, the imagination and courage of man. Only a great people, a great race, can survive there. Aside from the relatively few narrow fertile valleys, through all the ages, man's ingenuity has been taxed to wrest a living in a setting so difficult; to traverse the vast ravines, to terrace the hillsides, to build homes on mountains almost devoid of trees, to keep from freezing during the icy months in a region where fuel is scarce. The people who have done that are admirable folk. They have learned to live peacefully and wisely on the edges of majestic abysses.

Go to thatch-roofed Acobambo, with its eternally roaring river, its sharp cow-dotted fields cut against the mountain skyline; to Chanchas, on red and green hills, far vistas of other villages on every spur; to lofty Ocuviri, where vicuña herds plunge through crags in a cloud of dusty snow; to the perfumed plaza of Ixcuchaca, village of the bridge of high towers, of oleanders and white peaches and thousands of trilling birds; Cuenca, with its fences of dried thorny shrubs, its adobe and stone walls, its ramparts of gnarled cactus, a place redolent with square-stemmed wild mint, bright with yellow wildflowers and morning-glories; Huayacachi, a bower of green and gold, tangled roses smothering spiked maguey plants, and high above all, a thin church tower; Viques, red prickly-pear blossoms among rocks, a town so lofty that the false pepper trees, native to Perú, are but shrubs, the air so vibrantly clear that the maguey plants are purple against red earth; Pilchaca, a study in yellow, where compositae dot the fields and Swedish broom everywhere throws sulphur-colored glory; Incaquasi, eternal mist on crags; Pucará, of stout adobe walls and freshly tiled ochre roofs; Colquemarca, with its browsing herds of insolently indifferent llamas. From the standpoint of material equipment, these simple, delightful towns may seem primitive, but they have a richer community life, a more significant cultural and historical heritage, than places of similar size in our own country....

It is April. There is no rain this morning. The air is crisp and cruel. Since before dawn we have been jogging on our mules down from the fifteen-thousand-foot lonely heights of Tutipucro, where only the *puco-puco* bird chants its monotonous cry over and over again; down through the broken ravine of Punqui, where the nickel glistens in kidney-shaped milky quartz crystals. We come with Indians now, and herds of llamas; man and beast are loaded with goods for the market. The small feet of the llama patter; the fur-clad feet of the Indians rustle on the stones.

Below us at last gleam the red roofs of Ayacucho, bright rubies set among the thick green of fruit trees. We are arriving. It is good to arrive. We stretch and rest in the saddle and go on, slowly jolting, winding in and out among the stones. Beyond us, behind us, beside us, the crags dance in the dazzling upland light. As one swings around a bluff, the cliffs seem to rush in upon one; then as a ravine yawns and distance re-establishes itself, they turn and reel back. A condor wings slow and sure, swings black against a cloud, disappears like driftwood into a surf of white cloud against an azure-blue sky.

We reach the dilapidated plaza of a little settlement. The sun reverberates there, bright on the leaves of a camphor tree and dappling a gigantic trunk of spreading shade. We are hungry. We are directed to a large house, where an old man, with a neck and head of chocolate marble and a wide beard of white spume, greets us in the corridor. The hoofs of our mules clatter on the pave of the patio, made of innumerable tiny pebbles, raying out starlike in perfect design from larger conveniently placed flaggings. The place is peaceful, ancient. Our voices were muffled by the arcades; a cry would have been as sacrilegious here as in the small but massive church across the way, with its combination cross and lightning rod. The minute we saw the old man we realized he could belong nowhere else; he belonged in this old house, like a dried pea in a dried pod.

As we swung off our mounts, we were startled by the cry of a peacock with spread tail — the bird seemed like a crazy king in a ruined empire.

The village itself is rather forlorn — a few drowsy houses, thinning out to little stone huts, tiled or thatched, orchards, fields, corrals, a few animals. The place follows the simple routine of the seasons; it has only one ambition other than those of daily joys; mostly it vegetates. That one ambition is to celebrate the village saint. Once a year there are fireworks, a big market with vendors from hundreds of miles about, special dances, a special Mass. All year the village works on costumes, accumulating funds; it celebrates; then it goes back to its daily routine of living, to wait for next year's fiesta, which, God willing, will be bigger and better.

But in general here is a simple rural life; there are Indian vendors in the plaza, with only a scraggly array of wizened potatoes, corn, candy; there are few needs to supply. The Indian tradesmen from higher in the sierra do not stop here to trade; they trot on into Ayacucho, a large center, filled with churches and monasteries.

The roads that move in and out of this village were made for other places. It is an accident that they pass through the single cobbled thoroughfare. Those roads lead over the sierra toward Cuzco, ancient seat of Inca empire, toward Madre de Dios, a great jungle of the Amazón headwaters. Follow this other one for an anguish of weeks, and you will finally scale the Andes seventeen hundred feet up and drop down on Ica, down to the desert and the sea and its white-drenched guano islands. This other one goes on to Ayacucho, on to the plateau, on to Huancayo, market *par excellence* of the Andes, on to the flowering bower that is Tarma, down the narrow death road to Chanchamayo Valley into the deep jungle. But those roads go in vain so far as this village is concerned. This little place does not hear the cries of those who go, or those who come. Perhaps it does not need to. From here, one sees beyond the peaks — into the sky; the place

is more infinite than the sea; its spirit more peaceful than the
reaches of the green jungle, the green hell.

And yet precisely in this out-of-the-way spot, I met the man
who has traveled more of the wildernesses of South America
than perhaps any other human being. We had just sat down to
almuerzo at a table under the arcades of the silent house, when
presently Herr Hoffman appeared. He was traveling for a well-
known German drug house. He had a five-year contract to in-
troduce the firm's products to towns and settlements off the
railroad, in the wilderness, in the Andes, in the jungles, out on
the deserts, places not marked on the maps. He had covered all
of wind-torn Patagonia, had slept in a hundred *toldas* from Tierra
del Fuego to Buenos Aires; he had wandered over the Chile lake
country and the Chilean deserts; he had been through the whole
tangle of Brazilian jungle waterways, where scientific societies
promote elaborate publicized expeditions by famed explorers who
get lost. He had gone up one river where three tributaries showed
on the map. He had to cross several hundred. He had covered
that region of death known as the Chaco. He had threaded the
farthest reaches of the Argentinian pampas. He had a year
more to go — in upper Perú, Ecuador, part of Venezuela and
Colombia, perhaps the Guianas. Presently he would be peddling
his wares in Leticia, where the soldiers of Colombia and Perú
not so recently perished in swarms in the foetid jungles.

Into the smallest hamlet he would go, search out the storekeeper, sell him a stock of simple home remedies, then cover all
the houses in town with samples and printed instructions. And
so, many an Indian out in the jungle now uses commercially
prepared aspirin and quinine against malaria, clove-oil, what not,
instead of depending entirely on his herb knowledge and his
mumbo-jumbo of magic. It was amazing, this lone, jovial middle-
aged man, wandering around the wildernesses with Indian porters
to carry his trunks of supplies. Also it gave me a clue to many
things.

It seemed foolish, the petty sales that could come from a tiny
village like the one we were in. But the people in such villages are
numbered by millions. Here, in reality, was but a dot on the
map of a vast untapped market; and after his visit, so long as

his firm existed probably Indian mail-carriers would come out through the wilderness to remote points, and from there private messengers would be carrying those little flasks of health to places where no doctors live, where man is close to Nature and knows little of science. I could imagine no American salesmen doing this, scarcely even any native Peruvian. An American drug firm would merely establish an agency in Lima, and contact the drug-stores in the main centers.

But except for this accidental traveler, the highway went in and out, going somewhere, coming from somewhere, but meaning little indeed to this little community perched solitary on the crags, sufficient unto itself, forgotten by the world, knowing nought of the world, but perhaps knowing more of the universe itself than many a civilized and more comfortable place.

As we sat there chatting, somewhere an Indian began playing a reed *quena*; he played for hours, his quavering monotonous notes, without melody, repeated over and over again, like the cry of the *puco-puco* bird we had heard in the heights. Among all peoples there is a subtle relationship between man and beast; the place they live, the climate, the altitude, the very vegetation, impose certain bonds. How often I have noticed a certain asso-nance between the cry of the birds and the pitch of the voices of women of the same locality! There was something which the birds knew and the animals of the field knew in the playing of this reed *quena*. Perhaps some scientist will discover that in America, there is a sound harmony between the American voice and the screech of streetcars or the rattle of trucks or the hum of motors.

Toward nightfall the rain began falling in endless drizzle and the temperature dropped to the shivering point; but the Indian played on and on. His notes became more quavering, more mel-ancholy, till I wanted to cry out in misery of soul. I could under-stand why dogs yowl.

'My God!' I exclaimed to the aged servitor, the only living soul I had yet seen in the big house. 'Why does he play so long?'

The old man looked at me out of the deep pouches of his lizard eyes: 'People find their pleasure in different ways.'

3

Beyond Cerro de Pasco, we had traveled since early freezing dawn. I had a little white horse. Like the people, he had enormous lungs. He never seemed to tire.

Now the pale sun wheeled low against the crags where light still glistened. But shadows closed in on the growing fields and little by little mounted the flanks of the gigantic peaks. We turned a shoulder of cliff and plunged into night, save for a few lights beyond, seeming to shine suspended in the abyss. It was a village, tucked like some weatherbeaten saint in the niche on the wall of the precipice.

In a little inn, three Indians stood around the kitchen charcoal fire. They looked like strange sacerdotes in their thick ponchos and long tunics. They were chewing coca leaves and laughing softly.

I asked for food and threw myself on a bench covered with an alpaca pelt. From where I watched the three Indians, the glow of the firelight fell on their bronze faces, touching also the colors of their ponchos; but no spark came from their black eyes; their faces were just burnished metal. It was a ready-made sketch in red and black charcoal.

The evening torrent descended, shaking the hut, driving on the thatched roof, a roar out of the dark. The wind howled among the trees interminably. Over the roar of the tempest, a *tuco* cried, like a wailing echo. Tidings of death! The cry came closer. The *tuco*, a big bird, with massive parrot-like bill and pouched throat, seemed a personification of the tempest, coming to devour us, hut and all. The Indians huddled in a corner. And the woman tending the fire lifted her voice in a sudden wail: 'Taitito — Oh, Lord, Our Father, have mercy, have mercy.'

The next morning was a song of clear light. Every washed roof was glistening bright; the leaves were gleaming like enamel, like polished metal.

With my fellow-traveler, a painter friend, we climbed up to a rock, where he set his easel. Beyond stretched the broad yellow path, lined with lavender flowers, a willow tree and a eucalyptus with tiny pencil leaves. A red-tiled hut hung on the edge of the slope, a stone bridge was on the left. And mountains were behind, on all sides, everywhere, rising sheer and swift.

In front of us one mountain rose like a chunk of blue granite; one was like a volcanic upheaval, seamed and twisted, erratic in form; the third was a sweep of smooth detritus. High above, just a pale blue slit, was the sky.

My friend set out his easel. To myself, I said: 'No man should paint this. Three giants in one tiny frame!'

My friend, it seemed to me, was also discouraged. All he said was, 'I should have preferred sky on my canvas; but there will be no room for sky.'

We were on top of the world, yet we were in a deep hollow. The sky was merely a silken canopy, of which we saw only a tiny strip, stretched high above us on invisible poles.

He worked swiftly. In a trice he stroked in the yellow path that must have cost months, perhaps years, of toil to carve from the cliffs. He hung the bridge over the side ravine, a bridge built centuries ago with effort and ingenuity. He traced the house that must have cost a great deal of time and energy to construct.

Who, I thought, has the right to paint a house? A house is where someone lives. It is built by hands to house a family, to house love, to house children, to house sorrow and hopes; this particular house had been lived in a long time. The tempests had driven over it for decades. The snows had piled up around the door. But here it was on canvas in half a dozen simple easy strokes.

The mountains, reared aloft geologic ages ago, had caught the storms of the centuries, had been blanketed by the snows of a million years, had fed the streams which flowed into the Amazón — four thousand miles to the sea — all crowded on a little square of canvas. At their foot, my friend put the great yawning abyss, that had been cut down for untold ages, out of pure rock, by tireless water.

When he finished, he lifted a despairing face. Confronted with that majesty, his canvas seemed to him so inadequate, so pitiable a thing. The blue granite block of mountain shouldered across the picture; the steep slopes of the other two rose up along the two sides of the frame, crowded their way off and over the canvas.

The violet flowers, the red roof, the green willow, the gray-green eucalyptus, the yellow road — they were like a symphony, but here on canvas — though my friend has a genius for color, and no one could have reproduced them more exactly — the super-bright tints jostled and clashed, refusing to mingle at all at such close quarters.

We looked up at the sky. It was pale shimmering blue, a blue that filtered over the whole landscape, giving it vibrant subtlety. But the sky was not, could not be, in the canvas. Yet the subtlety of tone it imparted to the landscape was lost when the latter was brought into the canvas, had no meaning without the sky's own presence there also.

A road engineer, whom we had met in Huánuco, came by in leather leggings, sun helmet, and corduroy breeches. He looked at the painting. 'It's good, but it doesn't make sense at all.' He cocked his head to one side. 'This world ... well ... it's just too damn big for any canvas.'

The artist nodded ruefully.

Presently one of the Indians who had been beside the fire at the inn came by in his bright poncho, his flecked sombrero. After greeting us with elaborate courtesy, as is the wont of his people, he leaned his big eagle nose — one needs a lot of air at this altitude — over the canvas to look at the painting.

His high cheekbones glowed; his black eyes shone. In the firelight they had seemed lusterless, dull; now they shone like bright new silver dollars.

'It is beautiful!' he cried. He pointed with a seamed finger at the block of blue granite: 'That's the Blue Devil, where the tempests strike. There below in the ravine we go to pray when the *tuco* cries. It is all beautiful.'

'But not my painting.'

The Indian gravely stood erect. 'You do not understand what you have done,' he explained. Suddenly he pointed delightedly to a drift of white stones depicted near the bridge. 'You don't understand what you have done. It is good. It is beautiful. Those stones. Our feet have gone there and our fathers' feet before us. You see, we live here.'

CHAPTER XIX

Where Atahualpa Died

MARQUIS Alvaro de Bracamonte y Orbegozo of the Perú coast city, Trujillo, is dead. So are his Great Dane dogs which terrorized the whole community. He was the choicest flower of an epoch that is almost gone now. No more picturesque madman ever lived than Don Alvaro.

For four centuries the Orbegozos were masters of Trujillo and its surrounding sugar and cotton fields. Ever since Pizarro founded the place early in the sixteenth century, and named it in memory of his home town in the province of Cáceres in Spain, the Orbegozos, made wealthy by grants from the Crown, had driven Indians and negro slaves and Chinese coolies to their tasks on the broad fertile acres of the Moche and Chicama Valley lands. Now, though a few members still own broad acres, the family has decayed. One relative, Victor Raul Haya de la Torre — outstanding leader of the new revolutionary Apra movement — is hated by the remainder, who live, somewhat straitened, from the remnants of the family peculium; the larger estates have passed into the hands of foreigners — Grace and Company, the Gildermeisters, etc. — and Trujillo has changed from a feudal fief into a seething center of revolutionary peasant proletariat.

The millionaire Bracamonte y Orbegozo represented the last great arrogance and extravagance of the family and of an era. The pride of his heart was his ten Great Dane dogs. Like their master, they were perfect gentlemen at home and wild beasts abroad. At home each was cared for by a special servant and slept on silk, had a gold jeweled collar, and ate delicacies out of a silver plate. The Marquis's chief pleasure in life was to loose them on the populace. The great iron-studded doors of his house would swing open, and the huge beasts would rush baying and barking into the street. Ferocious animals, they did not hesitate to attack man, woman, and child.

'The dogs of Bracamonte are out!' would be cried out from all sides, and people would hurry indoors.

Bracamonte, if he did not follow in the wake of his pets, would post himself on the roof to watch the sport. Woe betide any neighbor dog that had not scurried to safety. The Great Danes would pounce on it and with a single crunch of its neck, fling it aside dead, sometimes devour it alive. On occasion, lacking anything else to attack, and excited by their freedom, the Great Danes would turn on one another. A spectacle indeed! The frightened neighbors would peer out from their balconies or the roof tops at the ferocious battle until the servants could rush up to pacify their charges. Often Bracamonte and his troops of servants led the dogs to the market to unleash them. The Indian folk selling their wares would scutter for safety with screams. The huge dogs would dash through the market in all directions like minions of hell. Over would go the stands of potatoes and other vegetables, grown by the poor Indians on the icy slopes of the Andes, and carried for hundreds of miles down to the city on their backs. The dogs would glue themselves on fish and meat from the stalls, finishing some poor soul's livelihood for the entire year. Once one of the Great Danes caught a twelve-year-old Indian lad unable to escape quickly enough by the throat and shook him to death as though he were a rat. Bracamonte laughed and considered the morning a huge success. Since he was so wealthy and powerful, nothing was ever done to him. The people were afraid to do anything to his dogs.

At night the Great Danes could often be heard baying at the moon from the Bracamonte house. The blood-curdling sound sent shivers down the spines of the good burghers of Trujillo. All hated the arrogant feudal lord, but one and all, priest and prefect, business man and trader man, they fawned at his feet. Several prefects did remonstrate with him. He had them promptly removed and demoted. One, more importunate, he punished by drawing his pistol and making him eat a whole basket of raw cucumbers. 'Eat them!' shouted the Marquis, and the man who represented law and order in Trujillo knelt down and began eating, till he almost burst. He left the Bracamonte house holding his stomach and took to his bed. He himself asked to be changed to a post elsewhere.

It took an Orbegozo to tame an Orbegozo. Prefect Carlos Samuel Leyva, a relative of the family, finally put a stop to it all. A new government had come in against the will of the feudal lords and had not yet been corrupted by them. Leyva sent sharp orders to Bracamonte to keep his dogs at home. Old Bracamonte laughed loudly in his throat and immediately launched them on the street. Prefect Leyva went with his men to shoot them. Ten Great Danes wallowed in their blood. Bracamonte was heart-broken. He rushed into the street and knelt down and wept over their dead bodies.

He challenged Leyva to a duel. Leyva refused to fight a relative and a man older than himself. But when Bracamonte became insulting, Leyva had him dragged off to jail to lie among the vermin-covered Indians he had abused so long. Bracamonte raged, threatened a thousand things, so Leyva had him marched on foot all the way to his distant Paiján estate and told him if he ever set foot in Trujillo again, he would be shot on sight.

Prefect Leyva not only killed the Great Danes, he killed a whole epoch of feudal lawlessness and abuses.

2

One gets an idea of what the region was before the Spaniard came by visiting the Pyramids of the Sun and Moon and other ruins, now mostly covered by great drifts of white sand, over toward the mountains beyond near-by Moche; and by visiting the many miles of ruins in Chan Chán, twenty minutes by car from Trujillo toward the sea.

The finest pottery in all Trujillo is dug up from under the sand where once stood the mighty Mochican city. The Mochicans were a great people who flourished in the dawn of Perú's history — from before Christ till some five centuries after. Their artefacts are superior aesthetically to anything since.

They had built great aqueducts about the Moche and Chicama Valleys, utilizing every inch of cultivable land, reclaiming great stretches from the ever-encroaching desert. One single fragment of aqueduct in the foothills of the Chicama Valley — about fifty miles of it remain — required the moving of five million tons of earth. The Mochicans built viaducts on raised piles through the desert above the level of the restless sands. Later the Mochicans were conquered by the Chimús from the north, who founded a great dynasty and built the city of Chan Chán, which numbered a hundred thousand inhabitants. From the carved palace of the Great Chimús with its bas-reliefs of textile motifs and formalized fishes and pelicans, it stretched for miles of great courts and athletic fields and reservoirs. The city was divided off into wards by huge triple walls. Along the sea ran a mighty parapet to protect wide meadows of irrigated land.

The old place has crumbled. Trujillo, now with a beggarly twenty-three thousand inhabitants, is thus the third known metropolis to stand on this balmy shore of eternal spring. Strangled by the surrounding foreign estates, it drowses dilapidated and sullen, with a pathetic sort of shimmering beauty from the reflected tints — soft blue, pink, green, rose — of its calcimined houses. Old carved Spanish balconies — seraglio style — sag over the cobbled streets; old church spires tilt above the flat roofs.

The pageant of history suggested by the pyramids of Moche, by the bas-reliefs of Chan Chán, and by modern Trujillo led me over the trail of the old Spanish conquest which broke the earlier peoples and put the Orbegozos and others of their kind in the saddle for so many centuries. If the assassination of the dogs of Orbegozo was symbolic of the ending of an epoch, so Pizarro's assassination of Atahualpa, the last of the independent Inca emperors was likewise the death-knell of an epoch; it was more — the death-knell of a whole civilization.

The trail to the site of the clash of these two great personalities — the illiterate ex-swineherd Pizarro, clad in shining mail, and the great Inca, head of the greatest empire of the New World — leads to Cajamarca in the high sierras above Trujillo.

The passenger car to Pacasmayo was to pick me up at the

patio of my little hotel at eight in the morning. At nine a messenger said we should not get off until eleven. At eleven-thirty he
told me we were leaving right away. At one I had lunch. At
three the messenger came to tell me we were leaving at once.

At four we were off.

Our way wound out through tree-shaded lanes of a little village
of barking dogs, past the crumbling walls of Chan Chán. First
we passed through rolling, shingly country, sparse of vegetation
— a few cacti and false pepper trees; then we plunged into the
desert along a twisting track of sand where once went a magnificent Mochica highway, but which now is a shifting zigzag,
scarcely passable, the proud result of Seligman loans to Dictator
Leguía. After rising country, we slid down into the rich Chicama
Valley, through the great German Casa Grande sugar estates,
and once more across the vague road through the sand.

Nothing is more majestic, fantastic, and fear-inspiring than
the Peruvian desert that stretches fifteen hundred miles, from
the jungles of Ecuador to the Chilean waste on the south which
runs on for another thousand miles of desert! Through this
narrow coast strip of barrenness some thirty perennial streams
move down to the sea, green bands of cotton and sugar, coffee and
coca fields, of canebrakes and algarrobo trees in an expanse of
desolation.

We passed through wind-smoothed hills, round and bald, without the tiniest vestige of vegetation, a fluid roundness in which
the eye seeks in vain for some straight angle, some harder projection of rock. It is a landscape akin to primitive sea-life, to eels
and jellyfishes — gigantic hills without bones or vertebrae.
When in the midst of them, one feels as if wrapped around by the
digestive tract of some primordial pulp, save that they are dry
and sterile, dead — all except their outlines, which are fluid, living, seeming to roll into one another like molten metal, a series
of heaving ellipses and hyperboles and pear-shaped domes, like
the cupolas of buried temples, like the smooth sombrero crowns
of buried giants.

We came to an expanse of pure sand dunes, rippled with the
wind, a tracing so fine and symmetrical as to seem the work of

a conscious engraver, ripple on ripple as on the straw-colored flounce of a dancing girl; designs beautiful but apparently meaningless. Here in the Peruvian desert one may encounter the supreme idealization of form — form for form's sake. Beneath the form is death — bones of animals, horses, mules strewn about, half-covered. A human cranium and a femur emerge, telling a mute tale of desperate black-mouthed strangling death. But aside from such interruption, Nature here devotes herself, with cruel indifference to everything else, to the task of creating pure form and line. Nature here has turned into a masterful modernist painter of the abstract.

Far up on the Andes, several thousand feet above the sea, the sand has accumulated in great white or tawny drifts. From the great sifted mounds poke the stony flanks of harsh mountains, silent iron crags, buried in a torment of eternal sands. How many centuries has it taken to sift and lift those fine particles into the heights, turning the crags into little coral reefs among a forlorn sea of powdered dust?

Most astounding was a vast red plain, strewn with tiny seaweed-like plants scarcely visible. Around each of these plants, sand, caught from the air as it whirls by, slowly collects in tiny crescents. Thus begin mountains of sand, great cones, smooth save for the wind-ripples in front, but steep and concave behind — all of them perfectly white above the level of the red plain, as though the desert had grown fecund, breeding half-moon baby crescents that would grow up into white monsters of beauty. In the dying light of the afternoon, and seen from a hundred different angles, these take on as many different white plastic combinations of spherical design; some look like writhing white bodies torn with love or torment. For a moment I had the impression of strewn corpses whose blood had run out to tint the plain, which in the last flame of the setting sun seemed turned to a bright scarlet. As twilight deepened, the landscape grew even more fantastic, by nightfall had become grotesque, Dantesque, terrifying; as eerie as the scenes one beholds by palming the closed eyes.

Farther on we came to a dead lake bottom, choked with dying vegetation and huge drifts of sand. Once every twenty-five years or so, the warm Del Niño current, which sweeps out of the Gulf of Guayaquil from the north, edges down along the coast and pushes aside the cold Humboldt current flowing up from the Antarctic.

The meeting of those two currents, one hot from the tropics, the other icy cold, causes vaporization, and across the desert drives a tempest of rain that washes away adobe houses and brings péstilence to the population. For a few brief months the desert blooms like a rose. Corn and other crops can be grown anywhere. If such rains continued, the coast would soon be converted into a dense jungle, like that of Ecuador or Colombia, but in three or four months the unexpected plants wither away; in a few more months the desert sands blot out all trace.

In this particular spot the high coast dunes had blocked the escape of tons of water, a lake had spread out. About six months before, it had evaporated, but the water had lasted long enough to give rise to a curious flora. Strangely enough, among the plants that burst forth at such a time are spore-bearing varieties of species belonging in evolution to the primitive ages of the world — queerly distorted, grossly bloated. Out of the desert, apparently so sterile, so utterly barren, had sprung — at the touching wand of rain — life. Now, the lake having dried up, great white loose drifts of sand were flowing in — our car could scarcely plow through them. It was terrifying now to see the canebrakes and other vegetation nearly all dead, the moisture gone, the roots buried, the stalks broken and withered, all this plant life awaiting complete extinction. In a few months more the desert would again extend over it all, barren, implacable, in monstrous silence with all its flowing curves of meaningless beauty.

The desert is a symbol of time in these regions, time without beginning or end. Far off against the mountains poking up above the sand beyond Moche are the Mochica pyramids; there by the sea is Chan Chán; there stands modern Trujillo. Over them have flowed the cycles of history in curves of death no man may decipher; over them time has flowed like the immutable breath of the desert. Man's history here seems like the story of this dead lake that bloomed for a brief span and now fades into the emptiness of silence.

3

Pacasmayo is a little town of steep muddy streets beside a river on the sea where the long swells of the Pacific break gentle with a smoke of surf. My hotel room hung over the little river; all night the sound of its gurgling waters made an undertone to restless sleep during the hot hours that cooled only toward dawn. Now and then footsteps echoed along the balcony bridge before our doors. Now and then a prostitute would stop to whisper through the shutters, offering bargain rates. Presently the feet no longer came and went, and only the endless river whispered through the shutters.

On the cane seats of the little train we wound toward the Andes, again across the desert, weaving through its mysterious dunes. At dismal little stations Indians in ragged European clothes sold cheese and wizened fruit and candies. Negroes, sons of slaves, lounged on the platforms. Heat and dust piled up with every passing hour. The line ended in a scraggly town of shacks, tin roofs, and flat adobe and thatched houses in a river bottom of sugar-cane field. Ahead, the river had washed out the highway for miles. We secured bony half-sided horses and clambered along the edge of river cliffs.

By five o'clock that afternoon we clattered across a high-flung bridge to where some twenty passenger automobiles were waiting, and began the process of bargaining for the ride to Cajamarca.

Fate landed me in a car with an ill-mannered army officer, his frail abused wife, in a torn black dress, three squawling babies, a three-hundred-pound woman with a loose tongue, a Chinaman with five smelly fish speared on a pliable branch, and heaps of bags and bundles.

It was dark before we got started. The last glimmer of desert sands had died away. The little farms along the ravine looked dark and cheerless despite the faint curls of smoke still visible. For hours we climbed up, leaving a black abyss behind us, which — fortunately for our nerves — we could not see. The road became more twisting, the hairpin curves more frequent. About midnight we stood on the crest of the first cordillera of the Andes. We stopped there at a little spring to replenish the boiling radiator.

Below, in the vast ravine, lay a sea of fog. Over this was just rising a big silver moon. Along its swollen face still floated wisps of mist. Finally it broke free. It was uncanny to see the moon actually rising thousands of feet below us, as though it had somehow emerged from the bowels of the earth itself. Soon it shed its bright rays over the white roof of billowing cloud, which looked more like a tumbled Arctic ice-floe swamped with the drifts of countless blizzards than a harsh Andean valley a few degrees south of the Equator. But above the snowlike expanse were now visible the steep brusque flanks of the Andes; here and there the moonlight changed to a flame of coppery gold on a bald precipice flung up from nowhere into nowhere.

We nosed over the crest of the mountains and dropped down on the other side into a pea-soup fog. The chauffeur slowed down with a screech of brakes and edged his way along the precipices. The automobile lights made the road visible only a few feet ahead. More than once he gave a soft, musical Spanish curse as he almost missed the way at some sharp curve.

The road, descending now, was all the more dangerous, and the fog, instead of lifting, grew even thicker until the road was practically invisible. We managed to creep up to a little inn. There the chauffeur refused to risk any farther advance until the fog lifted. Other cars were also waiting.

We sat at the little oilcloth-covered tables while the Indian proprietor prepared us hot cinnamon tea. With the dampish mist bellying in through the open door, we huddled over our steaming cups and, shivering and miserable, waited as patiently as we could. An American salesman snored with his head against a hole in the plaster. The Chinaman sat with his dead fish in front of him and mumbled to himself. The fat woman 'Ahed!' and 'Ohed!' A congressman, taking a short respite from special sessions deciding the fateful questions of war, was hastening back to his constituency to lay the wires for his re-election in elections that were never to be celebrated. He was talking with the engineer of the rutted track of a road over which we had just come. The engineer was bewailing the lack of funds — everything was going for war preparations. The road was being washed away more every day. The patchwork to preserve it was inadequate.

He told heartrending stories of Indians torn away from their homes, their families, and fields, and forced to work indefinitely on other roads without pay. He refused to be a party to such methods but feared he would lose his job.

Another passenger produced a guitar and with a little group in one corner played and sang popular songs. For three hours we drowsed while the throaty voices sang on and on. Occasionally the chauffeur went to the door and scanned the fog, but each time came back shaking his head dismally.

Not till two in the morning did he decide to risk it. Half-frozen, our heads sunk deep in our heavy overcoats, we clambered back into the car. Painfully we edged on down, curve after curve, through the fog, still thick. After about half an hour we left it behind. We had swung around a crest of mountain above the valley of Cajamarca. The night was now clear, the moon riding overhead casting silver glory over far reaches of gigantic mountains. Behind us we could just see the billowing mist through which we had come; it lay in a broad belt on the mountain-side, like a gauze bandage on the chest of a negro. Far above projected the sharp saw of the Andean peaks, one tipped with the silver fire of snow.

Whirling about another turn, we saw the lights of Cajamarca — far below. In about half an hour we had dropped down into the valley itself.

Here, four centuries before, Pizarro with a handful of followers had toiled over these lofty crags and down upon the lost Inca city that once stood here — into a world unknown and legendary. To the right of where he had entered, at the famous hot springs, he had seen the gleaming tents of Atahualpa, emperor of all the peoples from Ecuador and Colombia clear to northern Argentina. Forty thousand strong were the Emperor's immediate cohorts. It is told that Pizarro's stout heart sank at the sight of such a host. But taking their courage in hand, the little band unfurled its pennants of Cross and Crown and galloped in armored array across the fertile upland city toward the stone city — just as a rainstorm closed about them with the fall of cold night.

We joggled over cobbled streets to the entrance of a little hotel. A sleepy-eyed concierge took me up to a beatific room recently papered in pink, its furniture so new it was still odorous from the mill. But sheets and pillowcases were lacking. He sniffed and said he was sorry. They were locked up, could not be got at until tomorrow; I could sleep between the blankets and put a towel over the pillow.

I was awakened early in a cold morning with a feeble sun by a large black spider scuttling across my face. He escaped to haunt my memory unpleasantly all that day. That night as I lay down I spied him on the ceiling right over my head. I killed him by a shoe well hurled. To my dismay the shoe broke a hole in the new pink wallpaper; the ceiling, instead of being solid as I had imagined, was made of stretched muslin. I amused myself by thinking how Pizarro had come into these fearful heights to conquer an empire, but that my most furious battle would probably be this one with a black spider, though it seemed to me at the moment a very important one.

The outlines of the old Inca city can only be imagined, for one must discount the Spaniards' glowing accounts of its massive splendors. They saw it after months of toiling up the Andes through snow and ice, suffering deprivations, misery, sickness, and for many of them death. Any sort of place would have looked grand. But the few stones that do remain, huge hewn blocks of six-foot dimensions, indicate that it must have been an impressive metropolis. In Cuzco and elsewhere the older ruins have remained; upon them and with them was built the newer Spanish city. But in Cajamarca they have inexplicably disappeared. The Spanish city is mostly a thing of flimsy adobe. The churches, though, are massive enough, but with smaller movable stone blocks; perhaps the later builders sawed the old Inca stones into pieces.

Modern Cajamarca is not an achievement in civilization. Open stinking drains run down the centers of the streets. The broken cobbles are grass-grown from the heavy day and night rains that make the town dreary and cold — a penetrating cold because of the thinness of the upland air. There are no cafés or places of amusement except the club for a handful of aristocrats and officials; there is not even a moving-picture house. The stores are flyspecked cubbyholes with a dismal array of odds and ends.

My attempt to purchase a hundred sheets of typewriter paper caused a flurry of excitement. I acquired eighty-six sheets painfully counted; these exhausted the town's entire supply, and this though Cajamarca is one of Perú's more important centers. And yet, I reflected, human happiness, except for perverted creatures like myself, does not necessarily consist in buying typing paper.

But there is not even a bookstore, though a youth in a doorway was selling out a dirty stock of cheap second-hand paperbound novels and dusty theological tomes. On the other hand, Cajamarca goes in for journalism phrenetically. Two daily papers come out with fresh smudgy ink, impregnated with venom and vitriol, one run by a priest and supported by the local landlords, the other by the revolutionary Apra Party. But most of the news from the outside world consists of cribbing from the Lima papers, rewritten according to the respective bias of each editor. The Aprista paper has since been suppressed.

The only real art in the place, though an occasional modern exhibit is held in the local club-rooms, consists of saintly carvings in one of the convents, a frieze of medieval figures rudely shaped but with immense vitality and feeling; but even these have been daubed over by some later-day hand with horrible flaming colors, a fact which is said to have made Juan Leguía, son of the dictator, so furious that he got drunk instead of attending the official banquet prepared in his honor. Certainly it was an admirable excuse.

Nowhere else did I encounter such poverty as in Cajamarca. The natives there are a sorry, poverty-stricken lot. These, I reflected, are the descendants of the people whom the *conquistadores* eulogized for their proud bearing, their beautiful textiles, their prosperity.

Now they are diseased, alcoholic, doped with cocaine, in dirty rags. In the ill-kempt market they huddle in the upland cold with their meager wares; scrawny potatoes, yams, roots, sugarcane, coca leaves, and occasionally stacks of beans, but they have no artistic handicrafts as in central and southern Perú.

In the broad barren plaza an Indian procession marched around — rag-tailed folk following a saintly image and blowing mournful notes on the reed *quenas*. One fairly husky Indian carried a fifteen-foot bamboo horn, from which with lung-splitting effort he occasionally emitted a deafening, shrill blast — an instrument once probably used by the Incas for calling signals across the vast ravines of the Andes in ancient days of power and glory.

In this very plaza Inca rule had been destroyed, an empire had been shattered and the golden fragments handed over to the Spanish Crown. Here in a now-vanished palace Pizarro had camped with his adventurous followers. Here Atahualpa, surrounded by his crimson Canari guards, rode in his silk litter to confront the strange white captain from over the sea.

Here Dominican Friar Valverde had argued with him to accept the rule of that unknown king and the dogmas of the Christian religion. Here the Spaniards had suddenly beset with indescribable butchery the Emperor's forces and had taken his haughty person prisoner.

For months the Emperor was held in captivity, though permitted the outward symbols of his authority. He dressed in his imperial robes — some were of the finest bat-skins — he kept his concubines, received emissaries. He learned to speak Spanish, became an adept at chess. One day he asked a Spanish soldier to write the word 'God' for him on his fingernail and was hugely elated that all whom he met could tell him what the strange hieroglyphic meant — except Pizarro. The Spanish commander never forgave Atahualpa that glance of scorn when the Emperor discovered he could not read. Little by little the native ruler realized that the leader who had treacherously seized him was more boorish, more ignorant, than even most of the men about him.

Atahualpa learned that, next to God, the chief interest of the newcomers was in gold. He offered to buy his way to liberty with a room full of gold. There, buried in the inner patio of an old convent school and now used as a classroom, is perhaps the only authentic remnant of the Inca city. The large treasure room is of hewn stone. Gradually Atahualpa's messengers heaped it high, up to the red line the Spanish drew near the ceiling — perhaps the line still traced there — to mark the necessary quantity, the equivalent in modern money — prior to the New Deal —

of fifteen million dollars. Adjoining this room were formerly two rooms which he also filled, with silver. But though Atahualpa kept his promise he was not released, instead was treacherously executed on trumped-up charges. The Pizarro forces, augmented by reinforcements, moved on to Cuzco, the imperial capital, amid scenes of growing disorder and desolation as the Inca empire crumbled rapidly into chaos.

Out beyond Cajamarca, fifteen minutes by car, are the old sulphur baths, boiling hot, now occupied by modern pavilions with individual swimming pools. One pool, possibly Incan, still remains intact — the size and shape unchanged, the same huge stones in their places, the same broad platform steps leading down to the deeper part. There, where perhaps Atahualpa himself had bathed, I reclined or swam about — minus the concubines.

They had been loyal to the Emperor in his hour of doom. They had tried to fling themselves into the flame when he was to be burned at the stake. Because of his last-minute conversion to Christianity, the Spaniard snatched him from his fiery death and rewarded him by the kindlier strangle knout. One and all his concubines committed suicide. Not so the holy Virgins of the Sun. The conquerors burst in the doors of their sanctuaries and raped them. They became either the mistresses of the white men or passed on into common prostitution.

4

The rain continued in Cajamarca; endlessly it sluiced down over the sagging red-tiled, moss-grown roofs — colder and colder. Two more road-bridges high above the town were washed away. Cajamarca, once an imperial city, now a dilapidated town of misery, sank into more dismal isolation as it was cut off from all modern communication from the outside world.

As I rode horseback through the storm, back over the lofty Andes toward the coast, I felt still closer to the hardships and adventures of the early *conquistadores*. Something of that epic violence seemed to dog the steps of my horse through those majestic crags.

And the terrorizing Great Danes of Bracamonte now seemed all one piece with the spirit of the early conquest. For four centuries that spirit has ruled, a ruthless, fantastic, almost super-human violation of Perú.

Atahualpa died long ago. Now the Great Dane dogs are also dead. But new violences are knocking at the doors. Painfully, slowly, or again swiftly and fiercely, Perú, the nation, goes through the labor of being born into modernity — a violent amalgamation to form a country neither Spanish nor Indian, but welded of both. The old feuds, the old oppressions, will disappear. New ones will take their place. In spite of its present old-style, illegal dictatorship, the country slowly stirs and pushes toward freedom. After four centuries a new page is being written.

Four centuries hence, perhaps some other traveler will pass through here to record the romance of the coming struggle, which seems to promise brutality and sordidness of its own variety, but which is also charged with new hope and the promise of justice, strangled now these four centuries.

CHAPTER XX

Battles in the Jungle

BOLIVIA is on the high rim of the universe. La Paz, the loftiest capital in the world, is twelve thousand feet above the sea. Four snow-clad peaks, Illampu, Illimani, Sajama, and Chacacomani, tower more than twenty-one thousand feet into the limpid sky. Eighty per cent of the population lives above the ten-thousand-foot level.

Here on this great upland plateau, swung between two great ridges of the Andes, was probably the original home of one of the oldest civilizations in the Americas, the Tiahuanaco culture, from which evolved the later Inca empire. Fifty-five per cent of the present-day inhabitants are pure-blooded descendants of the old race; and forty-four per cent are mixed. It is an Indian-mestizo land *par excellence*, with the Indian decidedly dominant. The official language is Spanish; the real languages of the country are Quechua and Aymará.

They are a strong race of people, and, perhaps through a selective process over thousands of years, have a lung capacity larger than that of most human beings. This accounts partly for their successful survival at such lofty levels. The folk are noted for their longevity; the Bolivians claim a higher percentage of centenarians than any other country in the world.

On the Peruvian side to the northwest, across great Lake Titicaca, and the Inca islands of the Moon and the Sun, the plateau narrows to Cuzco, the later Inca capital, and loses itself in the wild tangle of the Peruvian Andes. To the south, the fertility of the great upland valley diminishes until the land turns into vast saline marshes and deserts. To the north and northeast, the land drops away to the upper jungle reaches of the Amazon — the Yungas — and to the southeast, to the tropical Chaco, setting for the recent war with Paraguay.

Though Bolivia is usually thought of as a mountainous highland country, its tropical rivers, which lead into neighboring Brazil and Paraguay, provide a great navigable network of twelve thousand miles.

From Bolivia come some of the most strategic products of the world. In the provinces above Villa Bella on the Madeira River is found some of the finest rubber produced. Bolivia annually ships out some two million pounds of quinine bark, besides the large amounts internally consumed. It is one of the world's major tin countries. Antimony (it rates next to China) and wolfram (tungsten) are plentiful. Bolivia could also supply the bismuth needs of the whole world. But both bismuth and tin output have been rigidly held down by international cartels controlled by Great Britain.

Besides such strategic materials, Bolivia is rich in all tropical and semitropical products: sugar, cacao, coca, tobacco, cotton. With effort its production of vanilla could equal that of Madagascar. Hard woods abound.

Potosí, southeast of La Paz, in the great Cordillera Real, drew the early Spaniards like a magnet. It was one of the outstanding Spanish centers of the New World, famous for its new-made millionaires, its wild licentious life, its great ecclesiastics, its famous adventurers. In a glacial arid site, the high town soon became a city of a hundred and fifty thousand inhabitants, four times the size of Madrid of that day, and thirty-nine times the size of the one great trading port of Spain, Sevilla. For three centuries the mines there, originally owned by Gonzalo Pizarro, poured vast wealth into the Spanish exchequer. The city spent eight million *pesos* on Charles's coronation and six million on Philip III's funeral.

Potosí still pours forth wealth. From there still comes silver, from the same mines worked by the Spaniards. From there comes part of the tin which customarily provides over seventy per cent of the country's exports; there is mined lead, bismuth, antimony, zinc. Farther south from Potosí, mostly near the

Argentina frontier, gush the new oil wells (confiscated from the Standard Oil Company), one of the main causes of the war with Paraguay.

Over the plateaus and the valleys roam several million head of cattle, more than five million head of sheep, several million head of llamas and alpacas. Its high, rocky western cordillera is the home of the fur-bearing chinchilla.

The two hundred thousand inhabitants of La Paz live in the deep canyon of the Chuquiapu River. It is a red-roofed city, with towers and church domes, and tilted cobbled streets. Despite its impressive public buildings, its great cathedral where twelve thousand people can worship, its beautiful parks and gardens, it has a rural sleepy atmosphere that well corresponds to its name, 'Peace.' Actually it has been torn by more war and revolution than any city on the continent, except possibly Quito in Ecuador.

Soldiers are always in evidence in La Paz, green or khaki uniforms passing under the old arcades, up the slanting streets. But more typical are the crowds of Indian women in their woolen skirts and flat-crowned felt hats, trotting along with their wares, pottery, vegetables, and bread. The dapper business man follows up the steep thoroughfares beside long files of donkey trains or llamas, driven by Indians in such regional costumes. The business man is quite likely himself a full-blooded Indian, though he does not think of himself as such, because he is clad the same as was Mr. Morgan in his New York office. The moving-picture theaters are always jammed, by all classes from the sandal-shod Indian to the smartly clad señoritas; and all classes, including the more primitive, attend the soccer games in the vast stadium; ten thousand can crowd into the place. Perhaps the Indian wins the price of his ticket by sifting placer deposits in the rushing Chuquiapu River that threads the city.

2

The most dramatic episode in the life of the country in recent times was the bloody four-year war with Paraguay, when the Indians of the country were rounded up and herded into battalions to fight in the steaming jungles of the Chaco, long a disputed area between the two countries. There, like all true highlanders, they moved into the fray with the sudden energy of such folk going to lower levels. But the impetus would fade away, and in the unusual hot climate their energies would flag, apathy would result, strange diseases attacked them readily, and their huge lungs fell partly into disuse in the lower altitude, so they died like flies from pneumonia. The Paraguayans are tropical people *par excellence* and already had pushed their settlements far up into the Bolivian-claimed Chaco, which the highland folk had done so little to develop.

The Chaco is worth coveting. Much of it is underlaid with oil deposits. Here are great forests of *quebracho*, used in the tanning industry. Here, in the near future, will probably be grown a great portion of the world's cotton supply, to the further disaster of our own industry and the South. The average yield of lint cotton in the Chaco is three hundred and fifty pounds per acre, as compared with the United States average of a hundred and sixty-seven pounds. It is a great cattle country. At least a hundred thousand cattle roam wild there.

But the basic cause of the conflict was not so much the Chaco as an oil pipe line, and the fact that Bolivia, once a maritime country until Chile seized her coastal areas, is landlocked.

As is the case with most conflicts, however, no single cause corresponds to reality. Between the highland-lowland areas of South America ancient feuds have always arisen. The ways of the highlands are not those of the coast or the jungle. This conflict is ever-present in Ecuador, where the political struggle frequently hinges on the rival claims of the politicos of Quito in the mountains and Guayaquil in the tropical lowlands. It has been a factor in such countries as Guatemala and Colombia, Venezuela and Perú. As a rule the more vigorous folk come from the highlands and repeatedly impose their rule over the coastal areas. Los Altos, the upland region of Guatemala, has nearly always provided the revolutionaries and the political control of the country. Perú, it is true, is governed by the mild lax *Limeño*, the man of Lima on the coast, but this is because the country still retains old Spanish ruling traditions. The conquerors founded

Lima, not on the site of an earlier Indian metropolis, but about a low desert hill, as a military beach-head on a narrow coast for a footing to conquer and control the highland Quechua empire. But even in Perú, when there is trouble, it is Arequipa, midway up the sierra, which most often has provided the revolutionary *Putsch,* to attempt to break the hold of the little greedy plantation clique that ordinarily runs the destinies of the country.

Were Bolivia and Paraguay one country, they would likely be smitten by frequent civil war, because of this highland-lowland duality. The folk of Paraguay are Guaraní, and *Guaraní* is the prevailing language of the country. They are a fierce, proud stock, a martial and fearless people. Time and again they have battled to the death. During the last century, ringed around by invaders, they fought all their enemies to a standstill, although at the end of the terrible war, only a few thousand male Paraguayans were left alive.

It was a nation with such a tradition that Bolivia, egged on by outside elements, provoked to war. Bolivia at that time had far superior resources; it was getting heavy Argentine and Brazilian investments, many of them disguised Italian and German capital; it was well heeled with American loan money; it was well stocked with Vickers munitions and American planes; its army was officered by a German World War general; it had an unusually large civilian (German-owned) and military aviation system. And Bolivia probably had the better paper claim to the Chaco. Paraguay had the better squatter claim.

The Paraguayans, if relatively poor, have a martial spirit lacking in Bolivia; also they had every advantage of terrain and communications. Too, they had the direct support of Argentina, trying to get hold of Standard's oil. The war was probably promoted chiefly by Argentine intrigue. The Argentine Government, following the military seizure of the government by the Conservative Party, in the hands of the brutal Uriburú and next of the brutal Justo, had been working on a program of economic autarchy, and was particularly desirous of gaining full control of the country's whole oil output, not in itself sufficient to provide entire needs. This had brought it into conflict with an American company in an attempt to force the selling of all output to the government at a determined price. Argentina was also anxious to gain control of Bolivia's new oil output, likewise under American control. An effort was made to build a pipe line through the Chaco and Paraguay for shipment abroad.

This immediately revived the whole issue of the Chaco. To what point in the Chaco did Bolivia have a right to grant a pipe-line concession? What should Paraguay get out of the deal? Through Argentine influence, Paraguay was persuaded to block the Bolivian-American effort to gain an outlet. This was coupled by an effort of Argentina to gain economic control also over a vast tropical and farming region in Bolivia, an effort the Bolivians had long resisted. But now, blocked by Paraguay, Bolivia was easily persuaded by interested parties to resort to arms.

And so, behind the scenes were sinister and obscure machinations, secret and evil diplomacy, imperialism, and private greed — all twisted in a confused tangle. If they did not start the war, nevertheless powerful foreign interests sought to reap the benefits. Both countries, to carry on and get ready cash, granted rich concessions in the disputed territory. Gamblers in the game of imperialism and get-rich-quick artists staked fortunes on either side.

The American stake was mostly in Bolivia. From there comes our tin supply (to the extent British control will release it) and our wolfram supply, which provides tungsten — both, essential materials for the waging of war. There, American oil interests had sunk wells. There, American bankers had made extraordinary loans, optimistically guaranteed up to ninety per cent of Bolivia's total income.

Paraguay was more especially a field for Argentine, British, and Italian capital. Millions of Argentine money are invested in forests, grazing lands, and other activities. Argentine interests control the steamship connections. They control much of the rich iron deposits. They control the *quebracho* and *mate* tea industries. They control lumbering.

And so airplanes ranged over the Chaco jungle, dealing death. Bolivia got most of hers from the United States. Paraguay apparently got most of hers from Argentina. The Bolivians used to say angrily that whenever they scraped the paint off a Paraguayan plane they found an Argentine army plane underneath.

If a Bolivian plane was scratched, the trade-mark read 'Detroit.'

Argentina backed Paraguay heavily in the war. Later, during the peace conferences, Argentina, posing as a humanitarian neutral, was zealous in promoting Paraguayan interests. One of her statesmen, who had done more than anybody else to promote the war and to keep it going, was — ironically — given the Nobel Peace Prize when he finally settled the conflict the way Argentina wanted it settled. From Argentina also came the cunning maneuver to set up an independent country — Santa Cruz — in the conquered territory. Another puppet buffer against both Brazil and Bolivia, and also between Brazil and Bolivia, would have suited Argentina even better than a large and too powerful Paraguay.

Through Pan-American efforts, which repeatedly broke down till Argentina was ready, the affair was finally settled, largely in favor of Paraguay, whose armies were more victorious in the field. But it was not settled until Argentina got control of the bulk of Bolivian oil, through Bolivian confiscation of Standard Oil properties. Later pipe lines were built, not through Paraguay, to service the outside world, but south to Argentina. Argentina moved into control of the Bolivian fields, through a masked Bolivian government agency.

3

Few big armies in history have been successfully demobilized. Most have worn themselves away in attempted conquest. Or, held in readiness for a new conflict, they have turned their guns on the state they fought to protect, either to attempt to set up a new social order or to conserve their own special privileges. Our own Civil War armies were an exception, although generals for a time became the only Presidents. The frontier was still at hand to absorb energies and violent instincts. Demobilized troops could be put on free lands.

World War I saw Fascism put in the saddle by the *arditi*, or shock troops. Out of World War I came the Russian Communist régime, the army surging from the front to overthrow tzardom;

also, more belatedly, Naziism and dictatorships in Turkey, most of the Balkans, and eventually revolution in Spain. All were régimes of force, not of democracy, though some had mass backing. There were no free lands in Europe; no more frontiers to be fought for.

In both Paraguay and Bolivia there is still plenty of undeveloped frontier land. But it is wholly monopolized. Or else unusable because of lack of communications. Or else suited only for semitropical production, requiring capital and concerted community effort and planning. The soldiers were not given land to any extent in either country. Instead, they turned back to capture their respective governments. Even before the final peace settlement, in Paraguay an army *coup* was led by Rafael Franco. It had two major objectives: to allay the discontent in the country itself, attendant upon the suffering occasioned by the war, and to conserve the victory won at the point of the bayonet. Other *coups* followed in both countries. And so to each, the war brought great exhaustion and a series of bloody military *cuartelazos*. In both countries, popular disillusion was great long before the war ended.

In Paraguay the military grab was partly to forestall a popular revolution that would have meant peace at any price and perhaps the loss of the territory in the Grand Chaco, won after so many years of fighting. The negotiations of the previous government, headed by Eusebio Ayala, seemed ready to endanger the victory. Paraguay, already nearly twice the size of England, with the new territory won by war and the peace treaty, became the size of Germany after World War I. The militarists cut the Gordian knot of threatened popular revolution, the threatened peace treaties, the international intrigue, by setting up a dictatorship openly called 'a totalitarian state.' Such a régime still rules the country with terrorism.

Actually, since in Paraguay 40 per cent of her exports are accounted for by forestal products, 35 per cent by animal products, 25 per cent by agricultural products, and the country is scarcely industrialized at all, this régime, rather than being Fascist (a symptom of industrialized lands), is a belated militarized feudalism.

And so despite the use of the phrase 'totalitarian' the phenomenon was merely a recrudescence of century-old militarism in a land traditionally militaristic, ever since the semi-military state organized by the Jesuits in the sixteenth century.

Also Paraguay has a long tradition of dictatorship, from the time of the notorious Doctor Francia, who ruled from 1814 to 1840, and of Francisco Solano López, with his absurd Napoleonic aspirations, to many later impositions. In more recent times, as the result of modern improvements, the building of roads, increased education, Paraguay seemed entering upon a more democratic phase. This has proved to be an illusion.

The constitution arbitrarily promulgated July 10, 1940, set up a system definitely borrowed from the Fascist corporate model. The President is appointed for five years by a Council of State composed of the Archbishop, the Rector of the University, one representative of commerce, two of agriculture, one of industry, two of the army and navy, and the President of the National Bank. This council — aside from the Archbishop — is wholly a creation of the president in power, so that for all practical purposes he can reimpose himself or name a puppet successor. Such have been some of the tragic consequences of one of the most tragic and futile wars of the many on the South American continent.

4

During previous years, Bolivia had suffered with the collapse of the American private-loan system. In no country in Latin America had loans been placed on a more advantageous basis, but being loans for nonproductive purposes, they could not possibly ever be repaid. Repayment would have required more than Bolivia's total national revenues, a patent impossibility, even had the country shown marvels of industrial expansion. Much of the loan money went for armaments from Vickers', which then laid the basis for well-prepared Bolivia to declare war on Paraguay in expectation of an easy victory.

Following the war and the revolutionary upsets in both countries, the Bolivians definitely flirted with the Axis. German influence had always been strong in the country. Now both Germans and Japanese were favored.

Steady pressure from Washington, the cutting off of European and Oriental markets, and the promise of financial aid from the United States Government finally turned the scales. German interests in the country were strangled. The German air services passed into the hands of Americans, and Bolivia became overnight one of the strongest backers of Pan-American policy, a position undoubtedly corresponding to popular sympathies. Even so, La Paz was probably still more of a center of German espionage and propaganda than was Chile or Argentina when openly accused by Sumner Welles.

For a time there developed considerable resentment toward the United States. Bolivia felt that in whole-heartedly backing the American policy she should have received the expected assistance that would have enabled her fully to support that policy. Instead, her newspapers soon teemed with articles pointing out that whereas the more powerful neighbor countries had been greatly helped, Bolivia had been forgotten.

The sum of $16,962,000 was allotted to Bolivia through the Export and Import Bank on condition that Bolivia would make payment to the Standard Oil Company for the expropriation of that company's properties. The Bolivians had claimed that the company had no legal claim upon the government, because the concession terms had not been fulfilled, because of evasion of taxes through secret pipe lines, and various other peccadilloes. The properties, the authorities claimed, rather than having been confiscated, had reverted to the government in accordance with the contract clauses. Nevertheless, Bolivia acceded to the American official demand for compensation and put up the money, but up to late 1942 not a cent of the credits allotted to Bolivia had been released, and no materials sent her.

Temporarily, Bolivia, being a source of tin, rubber, and wolfram, has prospered from the war. Her goods are piled up in Mollendo, Arica, and Paraguayan river ports, awaiting transshipment. She is getting excellent prices. There is no unemployment. In fact, plantation-owners of the rich Santa Cruz region are complaining bitterly because all their labor has run off to the jungles, to the Guapore and Acre regions, to gather rubber, at which they earn sixty instead of twenty cents a day. Whole villages in the most fertile part of Bolivia have been completely abandoned; much of the rich region has been left empty and desolate.

But the prosperity soon began to slip. The purchase of all Bolivian raw products by the United States threatened to bankrupt the country, the reason being that Bolivia was cut off from securing essential products and machinery from this country. Her factories have been running down; mining expansion is hampered; her agriculture is blocked by lack of farm machinery; replacements are not at hand; automobiles are disappearing. Bolivia, more than most countries, far more than even Chile or Argentina, has suffered from lack of priorities, and not being so obviously a key country in continental defense, not being a maritime country, and having no shipping, space allotments in vessels plying southward were not made for her.

In the meantime strong pressure was put on Bolivia for ratification of secret provisos rumored to have to do with oil, tin, rubber, and so on, as the condition for receiving any aid. In October, 1942, President Enrique Peñaranda asked a storm-tossed Congress to ratify unanimously secret terms demanded by Washington. He advised that body that the United States would grant nothing till *all* parties agreed to its demands — no loan, no supplies, no machinery.

The aftermath for some months was no agreement. Instead, Bolivia turned abruptly to Argentina. On October 31, word came through that Bolivia had signed up with her strong neighbor, who has so many more means than has the United States with which to influence Bolivia's domestic policies, to grant her, in return for credits, the right to develop more of Bolivia's oil resources and to extend her rail system. The machinery, it was promised, could be obtained from Great Britain; and in March, 1943, Argentina, in return for materials and machinery of various sorts, agreed to manufacture ammunition for British arms. And so behind the scenes in Bolivia is an international battle for the control of tin. And so, the complicated imperialist struggles which helped precipitate the bloody Chaco War have continued on their wearisome way.

Fortunately some of the differences between Bolivia and the United States have been ironed out. Concessions have been made by both sides. American credits finally were made effective in actual goods on condition that Bolivia agree to make an open declaration of war on the Axis. Such a declaration, like that of Chile, it was felt, would be another blow at Argentine prestige and her policy of isolated neutrality. And so, just as Argentine influence in Paraguay was earlier broken — by American credits and naval displays — so it has been blunted in Bolivia. The war declaration by Bolivia was dramatized by arranging the visit of Vice-President Wallace and thus giving it the appearance of a sudden and spontaneous popular demand. The effect is mostly moral, for Bolivia, lying landlocked in the highlands, can have little to do with the war effort beyond the great efforts the country has already made in behalf of the United States. The actual declaration of war had more to do with South American continental politics than anything else. On Bolivia's side, it was seen that such a declaration would put the country among the more favored nations. American supplies and equipment have streamed into those southern lands declaring war. Those which have merely broken relations play second fiddle. On the side of the United States, the war declaration by Bolivia was much desired as a further blow against Argentina's policies. The choice of Wallace to raise enthusiasm in countries adjacent to Argentina was also apparently deliberate. Unfortunately no man in American public life is more anathema to the ruling wheat and cattle barons of Argentina, who, though they enjoy a system of agricultural paternalism very similar to that established in the United States by Wallace, nevertheless sense in him a socialistic heresy that might easily undermine the pillars of Argentine authority.

PART SIX

West Coast

CHAPTER XXI

Jungle, Desert, and Ice

BEND over the continent of South America on the line of the Equator and lay it flat on North America, and the tip of Tierra del Fuego (beyond the Straits of Magellan) would just touch the southernmost point of Alaska. It would fall above James Bay in the middle of Labrador.

Or impose the same inverted part of South America on Europe, and the tip of Cape Horn would just about hit Edinburgh and lie on the same latitude north as Copenhagen, or Memel or Moscow. It could be made to coincide with the southern tip of Sweden. But it would miss Finland and Norway entirely. It would almost coincide with the northern tip of West Prussia.

Impose it on Asia, and the southernmost extremity would then cut into the lower part of eastern Siberia. Moved over slightly, it would hit about the middle of Kamchatka. Or it would fall just above the northern tip of Sakhalin Island. Or it would touch the city of Omsk. It would be just a little beyond the northernmost fringe of Manchukuo.

The climates of the various South American centers do not necessarily correspond to places of the same latitude elsewhere, north or south. Various factors modify climate: ocean currents, nearness to the sea, the location of mountain barriers, rainfall, altitude, etc.

Quito is almost exactly on the Equator, but as it is ninety-five hundred feet above the sea (not a coastal city at all), it has an eternal spring climate.

Along the narrow South American coast lowlands, the major factors in the climate are two ocean streams: the Humboldt and the Corriente del Niño. The Humboldt Current, coming out of the Antarctic, is an icy stream, so that it cools off the whole coast as far north as Ecuador, and what otherwise would be a jungle region, suffering the torrid heat of Central Africa, enjoys the finest climate. Lima and Callao in Perú are places of eternal spring. Valparaiso in Chile enjoys a climate very similar to that of Southern California.

The two ocean currents also condition the topography of the region. Due to the Humboldt Current, and the high Andes behind the narrow strip of coast, the whole region from northern Perú down to below the central part of Chile has practically no rainfall, and is all desert save where the numerous rivers cut through from the high mountains — some thirty streams in Perú. For endless miles the sands roll on, in many places without the slightest vegetation, and the driving winds from the sea lift up great columns of dust and in some places drive the loose drifts several thousand feet high in the foothills.

Only far south in Chile do climate and soil and vegetation change. Valdivía, the shipbuilding center of Chile, near which is located most of the German immigration, is humid, the vegetation dense. Farther south is the lake region, rivaling Switzerland in beauty, a place of crystal-clear inland waters and beautifully wooded mountains, cloaked in snow a good part of the year. Still farther south stretch wide grassy plains given over to cattle and sheep and the growing of wheat, a climate — except for the terrific and constant winds of Patagonia and Tierra del Fuego — less severe than most of the inhabited portions of Canada. In the upper levels of this region heavy snows fall, and winter sports (during what are our summer months) attract tourists from northern Chile and neighboring countries. Chile is the one country in South America that has a ski force in its regular army.

One must go north of Perú to find any real tropics along the coast. The hot Current of the Child swings out from the Gulf of Guayaquil, and meeting the Humboldt Current, pushes it out from the coast. The meeting of the two streams causes dense fogs and great precipitation. As a result, the coast of Ecuador and Colombia is humid hot jungle.

But in Perú and Chile the best climate is on the coast, and

there are located the capitals of the two nations. Chile is largely confined to the coast, for in the south the plateau regions of the Andes belong to Bolivia and Argentina. On the Chilean side the Andes rise swiftly, cut by steep ravines, and only here and there in the foothills or the folds of some valleys is agriculture possible at higher levels. Chile is therefore almost wholly a coast country, a long narrow sliver of land — between the Pacific Ocean and the Cordillera.

The other countries having a foothold on the Pacific are more complicated geographically. In each instance, geographically they are really three different countries: coast, mountain plateau, and interior jungle. The great barrier of the Andes has made communication between these different regions extremely difficult. Not one has a railroad or a good highway leading from the coast to the eastern jungles. The overland trip from the coast to Iquitos on the upper Amazón requires a month of difficult, dangerous travel on muleback. During the near war with Colombia over Leticia, Perú had to send her forces clear around the Straits of Magellan and up the Amazón to get them into action with equipment. For all practical purposes, she was much farther from the scene of hostilities on her own soil than the United States is from India. These later years airplanes have served to eliminate some of the isolation of interior points, although flying over the Andes, with their frequent storms, is not yet an overly safe or easy jaunt.

The interior jungles of Ecuador are little developed, and in the Putumayo region still roam head-hunters and possibly cannibals. Much of the interior of Colombia is a vast, little-explored region.

Thus, of the four Pacific Coast countries, Chile has the greatest geographic unity. Its long narrow expanse is reminiscent of the Nile region, except that no river ties it together. But there is the sea and also a railroad almost the entire length of the thin land, built for strategic reasons of defense, for since shipment by sea is less costly, it is anti-economical to operate.

2

Colombia straddles the Isthmus of Panamá, with ports on both the Atlantic and Pacific sides. Primarily it is an Atlantic coast country, for most of its commerce is with the United States and Europe. But Buenaventura, the only port of international importance on the Pacific side, has increased its traffic steadily. Whereas it takes nine days by road, rail, and steamer from Barranquilla on the Caribbean to reach the remote and lofty capital, Bogotá, from Buenaventura, only two and half days, by train and over a fine highway, are required. The Caribbean ports of Barranquilla and Cartagena are old historical cities, Cartagena particularly — one of the most interesting places in all Latin America. But Buenaventura on the Pacific side is new and raw, a small mud-hole of less than thirty thousand inhabitants. It has fine modern docks on the river, through which pass the products of a rich tropical valley — especially coffee, gold, and platinum — but otherwise it is one of the stink-holes of the world, a frightful medley of impoverished and diseased Indians and negroes living in muck and filth, dragging about with yaws, malaria, syphilis, leprosy, hookworm, and other maladies.

From Buenaventura one sails south for six hundred miles to the next port of call, Guayaquil, thirty miles inland on the Guayas River in Ecuador. Usually the ocean is calm; there are few storms in this area, although Pizarro, the early *conquistador* of Perú, suffered some bad ones in his frail vessels. At the mouth of the Guayas, the steamer, if of any size, must wait until high tide to go up. The traveler here is just a few degrees south of the Equator, and the climate is hot and humid, although from May to December, when there is little rain and the nights are cool, little discomfort is experienced. As the vessel moves up the river, all the portholes are screened against mosquitoes and other insects, which swarm toward the lights. As the boat rides in the harbor before the city, the spectacle is impressive: massive buildings and arcades, picturesque villas and walls, covered with densely flowering vines and climbing up the hillside to the west. From certain vantage points on clear days may be seen the snow-clad eminence of lofty Chimborazo, to the left of the northerly road to Quito, the mountain-perched capital.

Apparently Guayaquil is a marble town, solid and enduring, but the marble is fake — merely stucco laid on wire lath. Strike any of the massive columns a stiff blow with a cane, and they will puncture or crumble. The place seems built, like a World's Fair, not for permanence. But it is a leisurely attractive city, dominated by flowering balconies. Except for a few hours during the day, there is little traffic, but the traffic policemen — small fellows in white uniforms and big sun helmets — gesture the occasional vehicle on its way with majesty.

The fine appearance of the center of the city breaks down on the eastern side to terrible dirty slums and tumbled shacks. Evil smells blot out the overwhelming fragrance that sweeps through the city from the surrounding jungles.

Hardly is one out of the Gulf of Guayaquil than the desert of Perú begins, a long, desolate coast that stretches clear to the central part of Chile. Out of the northernmost sands pokes the modern little oil town of Talara, a successful and banal effort of frontier Europeanization, now occupied by American troops. Near-by is the old Spanish port of Payta, center of Perú's growing cotton industry (now an adjunct of Wallace's crop-subsidy plan) and an export point for the famed Panamá hats (a name the Peruvians resent) and for hides and skins.

Farther down the coast stands Trujillo, the third largest city of the country, with only thirty-three thousand inhabitants. It is entered by rough launch passage at Salaverry, another pest-hole, set in drifting sand and marsh, where you will likely be vaccinated against bubonic plague, which is endemic. A toy railroad with a gargantuan whistle leads to near-by Trujillo. The latter is an ancient Spanish town, with beautiful old buildings and carved balconies, but now down at the heel. Its famed university has less equipment than a small-town high school in the United States. Yet whatever the lack of test tubes and decent classrooms, or perhaps because of those shortcomings, from this institution came the first students' revolts that after World War I moved all South America, out of which grew the famed Aprista movement, which for ten years and more fought unsuccessfully to establish political democracy and economic justice in the country. There in Trujillo students died before the machine guns of Sánchez Cerro. Those who are left of that movement are now mostly in exile, while a usurping president, never elected by the people, holds the reins of power, able to do so in good part because of our federal-loan money, furnished by the American taxpayer.

Four miles west of Trujillo stand the ancient ruins of Chan Chán, once the center of the great Chimú empire, and in its day an impressive place inside high triple walls enclosing eleven square miles. There are the broken-down remains of temples, palaces, streets, gardens, canals, and reservoirs. It was undoubtedly a far more populous and prosperous place than modern Trujillo; and from the surviving artefacts, a place far more cultured and artistic.

3

The main Peruvian port is Callao (twenty minutes by automobile from Lima, the capital), a plain flat-roofed little city of no beauty and shunned as a residence by nearly all but the laboring classes. Save for a few colonial edifices such as Real Felipe fortress, its shabby buildings have no architectural distinction.

A few years ago, boats had to anchor far out, and passengers and baggage had to be rowed ashore through a sea swarming with huge orange-colored jellyfish. Today the vessels land passengers and cargo at new modern docks, built a few years ago by an American company.

Few people tarry in Callao (though they could enjoy some marvelous sea-food restaurants there), but hasten on to near-by Lima. Poor folk take the run-down interurban streetcars or the tipsy little buses. Better-heeled folk hire a car that whirls them over one or another of several fine new boulevards, already showing the cracks of grafting contractors.

The City of Kings, founded by Pizarro, the Spanish conqueror of Perú, is both very ancient and in spots modern. It has an old cathedral (sans towers owing to earthquakes), an electric cross on San Cristóbal, one of the first foothills of the Andes, colonial carved balconies, fairly tall offices and apartment buildings, a rococo marble palace known as the Hotel Bolívar, a very narrow main street, *El Girón de la Unión*, vaguely reminiscent of the cramped streets of Havana, beautiful parks, where vandals constantly rip apart the trees (difficult to grow and scarce in the bone-dry climate), fashionable bungalow suburbs, volunteer fire companies (as in Constantinople or New England villages), a racetrack, cockfights, horrible slums, ugly markets without handicrafts, a bullring, dog-races, soccer and cricket fields, an enormous red-light district, a sumptuous American country club, sixty-seven churches, some quite magnificent, and last, but not least, the tomb of Pizarro.

Some time ago I read a novel of early buccaneer days, in which a pirate crew sailed up the Rimac and anchored off Lima. Such is the danger of trusting the word 'river' in the atlases! Rimac has never been more than a good-sized creek; most of the year it is but a small trickle of water tumbling over sun-blanched stones. The poorer parts of the city lie along its lower course, in the shadow of the bridges; there lies the *Barrio de Cantagallo*, generally known as the ward of the thieves and murderers.

The prevailing tone of Lima is European. It does not pulse with native life, like an inland capital such as México. It has a large Indian, *cholo* (mestizo), and negro population, with many Chinese (who monopolize the meat business) and Japanese (who monopolize the barber business), but all these elements soon conform to European habits of dress. Thus Lima is a coastal city singularly isolated from the hinterland in spirit and habit, even though it lies at the foot of a trans-Andean railroad. Lima, therefore, preserves the spirit of the Spanish conquest; in that spirit it still rules the rest of the country.

Out through imposing residential districts, through orchards and vineyards, grown by the effort of constant irrigation, avenues lead to pleasant surrounding spas and suburbs, where the sandy beaches are nearly always sunny and warm, but the water icy from the Humboldt Current. There is rarely any rain the year 'round, often not for years on end, although in winter there are heavy drizzling mists.

In winter, which is like a cool spring day, the people of Lima go up in the Andes nearly three thousand feet to Chosica, which can be reached in thirty minutes. Above the winter mists and the chill of the Humboldt Current, it has a semitropical languor.

To the south, along the coast, lies Pachacamac, a few crumbling walls and piled-up bones on a hill overlooking cotton fields and the sea. Here one of the Pizarro brothers raided, soon after the conquest, and bashed in the doors of the famous temple in the search for gold.

Below Callao the coast stretches on very desolate. The black and brown hills are often without a spear of vegetation, and the sand piles against them in great drifts. But a hundred and thirty miles south at Pisco (which has given its name to the famous Peruvian brandy) a green fertile valley breaks through. The town, not a major port of call, is still ancient in spirit — old buildings about a typical Spanish plaza. Through a valley of puffy white cotton boles, railroad and highway run inland forty-five miles to Ica and there butt against the iron wall of the Maritime Cordillera of the Andes.

Once more the coast stretches on south, dreary and forlorn. Here and there are small half-abandoned ports. Two hundred miles below Pisco on a rockbound coast lies Chala, from which cattle from the interior meadows are shipped. Seals lounge on the rocks, and big-pouched sea birds dive into water teeming with fish.

Another two hundred miles and one reaches Mollendo, facing an open stormy roadstead, the gateway to lofty Bolivia and to Cuzco, the archeological capital of the Americas, site of the old palaces of Atahualpa. From the sea Mollendo looks like a picturesque town, white and glistening, climbing up the side of the hills; but actually it is merely a dusty and dreary place, lacking all distinction. Soon, probably, it will sink into insignificance, for fifteen miles south has been built the new modern port of Matarani.

4

The most northerly port of Chile is Arica, a dry rainless place at the foot of the Morro headland and hemmed in by high sand hills. It is the terminus of a rail line, up through the fertile, but little cultivated, Azapa Valley to La Paz. Formerly Arica belonged to Perú, till Chile tore it away in a brutal war of aggression.

A hundred and thirty miles farther south along the arid desert, between the Colorado and Cavancha headlands, lies a much more modern metropolis, Iquique, product of the iodine and nitrate industries. And now that war makes synthetic nitrates insufficient, Iquique is abustle with British and American ships, stinking with nitrate cars, and full of new cabarets and prostitutes.

A number of undistinguished, dry, dusty nitrate and copper ports line the coast — Pisagua, Tocopilla, Cobija — but the outstanding port of the whole north is Antofagasta, a fairly modern city behind a big breakwater. It not only ships out mineral products, but, being connected by rail with La Paz, is one of the major transshipment points for Bolivia. To it flow down much of the tin, wolfram, wool, and other products from the inland country. Another railway, being pushed from Antofagasta over the Andes to Argentina, will tap rich mining, cattle, and oil regions of the latter country.

More typically Latin and graceful is Coquimbo, four hundred miles on south on high slopes about a small bay. Though also a port for nitrates and copper, it is more of an agricultural center, being in the heart of a fine wine industry. Near it are resorts, thermal springs, casinos, and a racetrack to cater to wealthy Chilean and Argentinians seeking a warm winter spot. And at near-by Andacollo is the annual pilgrimage to the Virgen del Rosario, where Andean Indians come down and perform their ritualistic pre-Pizarro dances.

Valparaiso, the leading commercial center of the whole west coast of South America, is one of the most modern ports in the world, with up-to-date loading devices, wharves, and warehouses. But it is much more than that. 'The Pearl of South America' is one of the most majestic ports on earth. Behind it rise up tier on tier the snow-clad peaks of the Cordillera, among them the highest crest in the Western Hemisphere, Aconcagua, nearly twenty-three thousand feet. Half a dozen others nearly as high shoulder into the soft azure sky. The city itself rises up quickly in a series of terraces — a great amphitheater by day, glisten-ing with lights at night. The city is definitely broken into two parts. The lower portion has only a hint of colonial times about the church of La Matriz. Its narrow busy Prat Street and its heavy modern buildings are of today. Funicular railways and winding roads lead to the upper town. There, down Esmeralda Street, the shopping center, promenade some of the sprightliest and most independent women of La America, for Chile, more than most of the southern countries, has cast aside old Moorish sex concepts. It is a city of fine schools, a naval academy, and an excellent engineering university. Along the shore to the north stretch beautiful bathing beaches and resorts, of which Viña del Mar is famous throughout South America.

Santiago, the capital, 116 miles inland and 1706 feet above the sea, stands in a wide plain astride the Mapocho River, the Andes behind it. It is a garden city ringed by snow-clad ridges; a modern city of tall buildings and with traffic crammed over the five steel bridges crossing the river. It is a showy city of fine modern apartment houses, of gala residences, beautiful parks. In the center of the metropolis rises the Cerro de Santa Lucía, ornamented with gardens, balustrades, and lookout points that provide a magnificent panorama; behind, rises a still higher hill, the Cerro de Santiago, ascended by a funicular railway and sur-mounted by the huge statue of the Virgin Mary.

On the coast south from Santiago, a number of small ports serve some of the richest agricultural land in Chile. Out of Constitución, a summer resort, with a fine beach encircled by high rocks, flow lumber and wheat. The coastal ports of Talca-huano and Concepción (six miles up the navigable Bío Bío River) send out two million tons of coal a year, some of it north to the iron foundries of Coquimbo and some south to the industries of Valdivía. Concepción is one of the more beautiful cities of Chile, with its fine Paseo curving around the Cerro Amarillo, its Inde-pendence Plaza of impressive buildings and parks. Two hours distant are the famous Laha Falls and numerous lakes, Cerro Caracol, of pine woods and beautiful gardens — as grand a bit of scenery as may be found anywhere.

Valdivía, one of the main industrial centers, is a shipbuilding port. Many of its people are of German descent. Here begins the beautiful southern lake country — deep purple waters set against majestic mountain scenery. Numerous rivers tumble into the sea over flashing cascades and past verdant islands.

Still farther south is Puerto Montt, the terminus of the Chilean Railway, set upon a magnificent bay, backed by forest-clad mountains and the beautiful Lake Llanquihue. Still beyond rises the snow-clad Osorno, and in its shadow are half a dozen other lakes.

From here on stretches the wild, wintery southern sea of Chile, broken by rocky headlands, great unused harbors, thousands of islands. The Gulf of Peñas with the short river to Lake San Martín cuts a waterway the whole width of Chile. Far south on the Straits of Magellan is Punta Arenas, 1427 miles from Valparaiso, and farther from San Francisco than is Australia. An outpost sheep town, once merely a convict colony, today it has fine buildings about a central plaza.

Of late years Chile has felt the boom of a general frontier movement, a colonizing exodus to the south. New farm homesteads have been carved out of the southern wilderness; new sheep and wheat farms have been opened up. As a result, Punta Arenas, with its adjacent coal mines, has steadily grown in importance. A cool place, but not too cool: the thermometer rarely gets above sixty degrees in summer, rarely goes below freezing in winter. All winter long, outdoor sports — horse-racing, athletics, and soccer — are played.

Such is a cursory picture of the South American coast — jungle, desert, and ice — a long narrow lane between sea and mountain ranges much loftier than our Rockies. Every type of agricultural product is produced; it is the world's greatest source of natural nitrate and of iodine. From the adjacent heights come down platinum, gold, silver, copper, tin, tungsten, vanadium, zinc, molybdenum, bismuth, and numerous other minerals. Few regions of the world send forth such a plenitude of these strategic materials which today are the essence of the war-making power. Yet in few nations of the world — in contrast to this outflow of wealth — are the populations in a more miserable state, remote indeed from the four freedoms enunciated by F. D. R.

5

What is the political and cultural significance of the region? Chile, almost entirely, except for her lofty copper mines, a coastal expression, is the only country besides Brazil and Venezuela that has large iron deposits, also coal. It is destined to a high degree of industrialization. A mestizo country, it represents a unique and powerful expression in the Latin-American concert of nations.

But it also shows many bad and festering wounds in its social system.

Few countries of Latin America are more progressive and more disciplined than Chile. It has not been easy to wrest a living from that arid land; it has not been easy to create a unified society along the narrow strip of desert. Chile has done more with her resources than many a neighbor country more bountifully supplied.

Yet the extremes of individual wealth and poverty are tremendous. For all her limited farming areas, the land of Chile is monopolized by a few leading families, and an almost wholly feudal system prevails, with miserable semi-serf hirelings. There is a modern industrial Chile — but until recently, practically all the public utilities, mines, nitrate fields, and other sources of wealth were in foreign hands. Beginning with the world-wide depression, private ownership was gradually hedged about until today Chile has a system of government-holding companies, that has resulted in a peculiar form of state capitalism.

The Popular Front government has concerned itself in a superficial way with the status of industrial workers, and the country has a most enlightened labor code, but it has done little to alter the feudal landholding system, and the mass of Chileans remain in a propertyless state, cut off from the soil.

President Aguirre said, 'To govern is to educate.' President Ríos has recently stated, 'To govern is to produce.' But for all its industriousness and the hard-working character of its people, Chile cannot produce efficiently with existing low living educational and health standards.

In a recent number of *Mercurio*, the leading daily, Doctor Arturo Corbalán, speaking in behalf of the Chilean Medical Association, declared that the country has one of the highest infantile death rates in the world. *Fifty per cent of all children die before the age of nine.* The average life span in Chile is twenty-five years, compared to sixty years in the United States. Owing largely to the health conditions, only 22 per cent of the population is productively employed, as compared to 50 to 60 per cent in most countries.

The chief cause is malnutrition. According to Doctors Bragon and Burnet of the League of Nations, 49.2 per cent of the population customarily lack enough to eat, and only in Morocco is the amount of food consumed so low, its quality so inadequate.

The Chief of the Department of Child Welfare, in the *Medical Bulletin* of August 2, 1941, declared that 'in addition to the great deficiencies, observations in our hospitals show many children literally and unmistakably dying from hunger.'

This condition, declared the writer, is in good part due to government protection of the large landowners, who monopolize land and crops and set prices that make it impossible for the mass of the people to acquire even the minimum of necessary food.

In Chile and Perú, the coast region is dominant; in Ecuador and Colombia, the highlands. In Chile, the coast will always be dominant; for the coast is Chile — its deserts, lakes, narrow valleys, and windswept sheep and wheat regions in the far south. There are mines in the Andes, making Chile the second copper country of the world, but mostly the Andes are merely a great barrier, shutting Chile off from her neighbors, dooming her to a hardy and lonely post in the southern Pacific. The coast, therefore, is Chile.

But the political dominance of the coast in the case of Perú is merely a temporary historical accident, a falsification of her true destiny. Perú will achieve her traditional position and her richer destiny when control shifts back to the older highland centers. Perú, then, will assume its normal place and life, as part of the great Indian mestizo bloc of highland nations — Colombia, Ecuador, Bolivia, possibly Venezuela, in South America; México and Central America to the north.

CHAPTER XXII

The Thin Land

T HE racial homogeneity of Chile, which a certain known image of Chile evokes,' remarks Mariano Picón-Salas, a scholar who made that country his lifelong residence, 'is never a spiritual or political homogeneity.'

Perhaps he refers to the deep cleavages of Chilean society, the wide extremes of wealth and abject poverty. But, whatever the schisms in Chilean life, few Latin countries have greater national unity with respect to the outside world. The Chilean himself, if curiously a rampant, individualistic soul, nevertheless is among the most disciplined persons of the West.

Contradictions lurk in these generalizations, but they are explained by the geographical, historical, and racial determinants of the country. Two outstanding factors have moulded Chile's personality over the centuries: isolation and the long narrow desert coast between the Andes and the Sea. Part of the desert's feature is climate — the monotony of twelve months of rainless skies, limpid and achingly pale blue eternally.

Both factors have tended to produce identical social and political results. Chile, despite the goodly number of New Creoles (non-Spaniards of European descent) who have become prominent in its public life, has never been exposed to the same amount of immigration and outside influence as the countries of wide plains, such as Argentina, Brazil, or even Venezuela.

This isolation, plus the fear of its being broken down, partly explains Chile's long embrace of neutrality after most of Latin America had ended relations with the Axis and Japan. The long, unprotected coastline, a distance greater than from New York to San Francisco, a littoral at most half as wide as Nebraska, accentuated fears and caused reluctance to join in the United Nations' crusade. Not until Guadalcanal and the fall of Buna, which indicated that the Japs had perhaps reached the limit of their South Pacific expansion, did Chile fully toss in her lot with the other Western Hemisphere nations.

Also, this isolation, both physical and intellectual, until recently has meant, more than in any other country except Perú, the continued rule of a small feudal caste through strongly centralized government. So well intrenched was this so-called aristocracy of the plantation that it acquired a liberalism lacking in some other southern lands where its tenure was more doubtful. It could afford to be statesmanlike on occasions when similar groups elsewhere felt constantly the fear of being dispossessed and the need to be cruelly oppressive.

The long coast, which offers such a monotony of geographical expression (except in the far south, only now being opened up), tinctured political life with a similar monotony. Just as the high Andes and the remote southern sea long isolated the country, so the desert, while of one piece, has meant also the isolation of the various communities within the country from each other. The cosmos in a grain of sand is not so far astray in Chile's case. There was no Nile to thread the beads onto one chain. Unity required stern effort, the development of sea travel, the establishment of railroads and roads parallel to the sea which could never be profitable but had to be maintained at high expense on the ground of military and national necessity.

Of late years, since the discovery of nitrates and copper and iodine, the pull of the outside world upon Chile for raw materials, instead of bringing the nation as a whole nearer to other lands, has tended rather to make each community a little independent world that looks straight to the seacoast rather than to Santiago. Each locale became in turn an isolated realm exporting raw materials and importing a minimum of manufactured goods.

Whereas previously localism did not menace the rule of the plantation aristocracy, the new order did. This lack of articulation produced, during much of this century, a ruthless centralization to offset growing local independence, a centralization that imposed discipline and authority just as relentlessly as the desert itself. Creole aristocratic rule had been an undisputed tradition, but now it was forced, by the impact of the machine age, into sterner measures. As it repressed, it also readjusted itself to the new facts. As in our own South, where the soil has been largely exhausted over extensive areas, so in Chile (where the landed aristocracy has been limited to a few large central valleys) to survive, it had to make its peace, not with the people of the desert but with outside capital, by cooperating with foreign concessionaires, public-utility monopolies, shipping concerns, mining companies, etc.

In Perú the problem of maintaining such rule — by the so-called Civilistas — has always been the problem of Creole versus the Indian and the mestizo, always the problem of coast versus the highlands. In Perú there is extreme racial heterogeneity and geographical heterogeneity. In Chile there has been little heterogeneity except that of class.

This long made Chile a land of deadly uniformity, of military discipline. It was long the militaristic state *par excellence* of South America, the Prussia of the southern continent. Even before the Spaniards arrived, the most warlike folk of the whole continent lived there: the Apaches of the south, the famed Araucanos, who gave the *conquistadores* so many headaches, who had never been conquered by the Incas. Chile became a captain-generalcy, a purely military colony, as distinct from the vice-royalties of México and Perú. Its government and its life during the colonial period had little of the grace and splendor that shone forth from Lima and México City. It was a stern, austere, barracks-room colony.

This same sternness and austerity remain part and parcel of Chilean psychology. Chilean culture is not lyric, not romantic; it is stiff and formal; the country has produced many grammarians, lawgivers, statisticians, jurists, and of late, scientists; its poets have been mostly severely classic; or if they have broken through to original expression, their verse, like that of Gabriela Mistral, however deep its emotion, has a determined, hard-edged pattern. Life in Chile is more a system, though not entirely a pretty one.

Hence, in time of crises, its politics have had few really outstanding personalities. There has been far less opportunity than in Perú, México, or Central America or Venezuela, or in any of the truly Indo-American countries, for bold individualistic leaders to rouse masses, classes, or races in discordant warfare. Etiquette has been more binding. Hence Chile, with its stern discipline, its racial homogeneity — the mestizo (Spaniard and Araucano) — has been more orderly, less dramatic, its leaders more tailored to pattern.

2

Outstanding was Manuel Portales y Palazuelos, but in a thoroughly traditional way. A member of the wealthy creole class, he was in no sense a military *caudillo* or popular leader; he was a philanthropist and scholar; above all, an organizer, an organizer of the aristocratic class, its most efficient and valuable lawgiver, the Lycurgus of the cattle barons, the wine-growers, the raisers of wheat and cotton. Chile has rarely produced strong types who have swept across the social scene violently to impose their individual wills as in so many of the countries. Militaristic Chile has had an orderly, fairly pacific and unbroken rule. It has been praised for this excessively, especially by those who have personally profited from it, but there is little doubt that it has hampered Chile's creative processes. For it has been a rather drab class rule without many high-lights; it has been the rule of an undisturbed smug minority. It has had little whatsoever to do with democracy, as our good professors a few years back were so fond of telling people.

Up until about 1920 Chilean governing technique largely operated in two ways. Ordinarily innocuous but capable politicians were chosen to head the government — men of wealth and culture, such as José Joaquin Pérez or Ramón Barros Luco. When popular discontent threatened to shake the system down, a man outside the narrow governing clique was selected on the basis of his vulgar following, but always one who had been well dressed down by the feudal group, one they already knew they could depend upon, and who once in power would eat out of the proper hands.

Such a man was Manuel Montt, a powerful personality taken under the wing of the aristocracy. He governed sagely and long and firmly. He was of those who step forth from the stirrings of democracy, gather democratic following behind their personalities, then re-establish the suave upper-class rule so that it can follow comfortably in its accustomed grooves.

Chile was thus saved from that kind of unruly militarism that was long the curse of México, Ecuador, Bolivia, and much of the Caribbean area. It was a militarism nearly always well controlled by the feudal group, never allowed to overshadow the state except as an instrument of the group.

The extravagant titles and pompous eulogies which were bestowed upon or demanded by such fantastic types as Santanna in México, Rosas in Argentina, Santa Cruz in Perú, Guzmán Blanco in Venezuela, Melgarejo in Bolivia, were never bestowed upon or demanded by Chilean military or civil rulers. The Chilean commanders would have considered such ostentation as cheapening, childishly ridiculous, and so would their people. Something hard and dry, like the land, like the air, like the mountains and the sky, inheres in the Chilean character, in rulers and ruled. In his national statue, the great Montt, for instance, is not even dressed in his uniform but as a sober provincial judge — the lawgiver, not the military hero. All this has been the result not merely of a physiographic determinant but of long-standing class dignity and of traditions more ancient than the Spanish conquest. In a country like México there is a certain spirit of democracy; always there was that spirit, because the submerged, through violent and daring deeds, could emerge. However lowly, however raven black their hair, they could rise to the top, become all-powerful. But in Chile, the gulf between the aristocrats and the *rotos*, as those of the lower class are called, has ever been tremendous, almost impassable. *Roto* means literally 'a man in rags.'

As the Chilean man of action rarely expressed himself openly and boldly, the sternness of Chilean character has had another less obvious side, that of sinuosity, of cunning within set rules. The more the outer form is rigidly determined, the more ingenuity is required — as in the writing of a sonnet. The leader in Chile has had to work cautiously, with dissimulation. The Chilean vocabulary, above all others on the continent, is rich in special words and phrases expressing the idea of concealing one's hand, of putting on a false front, such as *apequeñarse*, 'make yourself little,' *hacerse el leso*, 'seem the fool.' The politician, so to speak, has to sneak into power, without too much noise or personal show of himself. One of the reasons the prominent and capable Vicuña Mackenna could not go far in the path to power was precisely because he was unable to reduce the apparent large dimensions of his personality. When Lastarría, another remarkable man, declared in Congress boldly, 'I have talent, and I let it shine,' he signed his political death-warrant. This, the Chileans felt, was to act like the inferior Argentinian; for in contrast, the Argentinian nearly always seems bold, exaggerated, and bombastic.

As one writer has said, 'In the tragedy of [José Manuel] Balmaceda — the greatest drama in the whole of Chilean history — this resistance of the social group against the outstanding individual operated. Deserting the mold of his caste, Balmaceda wished to follow a personal policy, based on the promotion of important public works and the popular aspirations of the masses, much like Pisistratus. But Chile was not Athens but more like Sparta, and Balmaceda was sacrificed.' He could do nothing and was thrown out of office and committed suicide. He was replaced with Montt, a dutiful marine official, and later by Barros Luco, the typical member of his class and close to the well-tailored norm, hence phlegmatic, unobtrusively dressed, but lacking in sensitivity and imagination.

The people were almost entirely absent from the long political banquet. They were successively calmed down. Portales, in the early days of the Republic, looked upon them as half-barbarous children who wanted food, drink, and amusement. Though an aristocrat he was obviously a good politician, hence did not find it beneath his dignity to participate in the popular festivals, go to bullfights, dance the *cueca* with the buxom many-skirted peasant women, eat barbecues under the *ramadas*, and swallow down his glass of rude *chica*. It was not democratic participation, however, but kingly noblesse oblige.

So far as any popular ideas went, these circulated only in the small cities and towns, rarely reached out to country districts. There was always a certain eagerness for small pamphlets with fantastic stories, such as those by Ramón Pacheco, and simple polemical ideas on the order of the French feuilleton and in the manner of Eugene Sue. Through such media and the popular leadership of Bilbao, in the fifties, Chile, as most of Latin America, was miraculously struck by a brief wave of anti-clericalism. In countries like México, Guatemala, Salvador, Ecuador, this became a mighty current; in México it led to the Reformation and the great social upheaval of Benito Juárez; in Central America, of Rufino Barrios.

But in Chile the Church was too closely wedded to the sure-handed Hoch-Aristocracy for such a movement to gather much headway. Also, as were other state institutions, the Church in Chile was better organized than in most of the southern countries; and so, if the new Jacobin ideas gave a certain turbulent enthusiasm to the *tertulias* in the cheaper cafés, they never moved out into the remote isolated countryside to foment any basic revolutionary reaction. The little hard-crusted local cells that honeycomb Chile remained sealed in their remoteness, the routine of tradition. The first feeble societies of artisans discussed some of these things heatedly in the taverns; that was all. The hint of a storm passed over, like the Chilean desert clouds, dropping no rain. The state centralism in this narrow strip of land made it impossible to recruit sufficient following behind the popular hero to menace the rich solidity of a city like Santiago.

3

Balmaceda was a harbinger of the twentieth century, the first stirring of a new plutocratic class, half-aristocratic, half-commercial, with a new type of ostentation. He prematurely foreshadowed the aristocratic-capitalist alliance later consummated. That alliance brought many changes. The twentieth-century type of ruler in Chile became semi-urban and semi-rural. The small governing clique lived wholly in the club (as the same group does in Nicaragua). The merits for political preferment were gradually lowered as an even greater obedience was demanded

not long change; that the hard uncommunicative upper crust of Chilean society would never budge a centimeter to give him a toe-hold.'

The local particularism, the slender desert realm, with little chance for complicated maneuvers, permitted him no revolutionary escape, as in a mountainous México. Ideas might come like the wind, sweeping men's minds chaotically, but the social order would bend a bit like a well-balanced cedar tree, then right itself little changed. The *roto* therefore looked out at the world through the magic fatalism of *tinca* — 'luck,' but even 'luck' was, in his concept of it, something almost as predetermined as a Calvinistic dogma. The *roto* learned to doubt everything: personal security, the worth of study, of sustained effort — nothing he could imagine in the realm of realism could help him escape his fate or dominate that other vague world intrinsically ruled by chance. The man who succeeds, the *roto* says, merely has *tinca*. He got where he is by one bright day 'following his nose,' listening to a secret 'hunch.' It could not have been otherwise. All this is a part of the heritage of the gold-seeker, an idea that came into Chile with the gold-lusting of the Spaniards. The lucky cache! Miraculous visitation — this is the psychology, in good part natural, of mining folk. The oldtime prospector of Arizona can understand the Chilean *roto's* mind perfectly. When the Chilean nitrate business blew up because of German synthetic chemistry, it was not science that did the trick; the unemployed *roto*, submerged then in unusual misery, shrugged and said, '*Tinca*.'

Politicians also believed in *tinca*. Having largely neglected the national economy and being without foresight, they also shrugged. And so the *roto* at last began to listen to socialist and communist discourses. This too, curiously enough, jibed with his psychology: that this doctrine of earthly utopia should magically appear before his eyes at a moment of need was another proof of *tinca*, something fallen like an asteroid at his feet.

Suddenly seventy thousand nitrate workers, thirty thousand copper workers, thirty thousand coal workers, any number of sailors and dock workers, mostly unemployed, trekked from all over the country across the sterile desert, converging on Santiago, to a city now boiling with new ideas of liberty. Railway workers, textile workers, bakers, what not, were now in solid unions, only too eager to strike. Nothing like it had happened in Chile since the struggles for independence.

The *rotos* brought to this crusade their frontier psychology, their spirit of adventure, of *Wanderlust;* but now they marched over the sands not as desperate lone soul-explorers, but shoulder to shoulder in an expedition. Chile was at last finding a new unexpected sort of unity, not one imposed by class rule or a disciplined army or a long coastwise state railway, but a human unity.

President Alessandri tumbled down as a result of this first *Putsch,* and the danger was staved off by the quick military dictatorship of Ibáñez, posing as a reformer, who implanted a species of colonial fascism; later he was to found a native uniformed Nazi group. But in those days he was touted to the world as a great leader, and American bankers gave him lots of money, and in the north many Americans bought bonds in blind faith of what we were falsely told about this new glittering uniform in the palace. American magazines produced myriad articles praising the new dictator, who was soon ruling with a hand of iron and putting an end to civil liberties. Ibáñez, all told, was more the braggadocio *caudillo* type of the less ruly mestizo countries, a bit too high-keyed in color and tone for traditional Chilean rule, but soon he was dutiful enough to the aristocracy, particularly the New Departure aristocrats who combined plantation-owning with modern business. He was even more dutiful toward foreign capital, hence represented a more open shift away from traditional Chilean feudalism to the puppetry of foreign financial penetration.

As the world depression deepened, a series of unprecedented revolutions swept over Chile, liberal, pseudo-socialistic, pseudo-communist. The strange name of Marmaduke Grove, sounding like that of an English lord, suddenly struck out as a Communist leader.

But when the smoke cleared away, the mild and suave but firm bourgeois Alessandri, a man molded with all the true subtlety of Chilean dissimulation, was back in power and now cannily enacting social legislation of a new unwonted nature, carefully canalizing the discontent. There are even good-will and smiles in the effort to ameliorate the situation, for it is serious and the feudal caste is frightened. There is now a poetic and intuitive effort to accomplish something, for the country is truly in danger. There is now a canny instinct to promote at long last the awaited diversification, to create new Chilean industries.

But Chile, once a strong military entity within the lines of traditional caste rule, for all of Alessandri, had become a country without a rudder. All was now hasty improvisation. Behind the edifice of reform he erected out of utter necessity, he sought to work back to normal colonialism and the safe old traditions. A new armament contract was made with the British; new funds were provided to modernize the air force.

Yet the new changes were amazing enough. Millionaire Minister of Finance Gustavo Ross worked out an intricate plan of state capitalism, the more astonishing for his being an arch-conservative. He began forcing industries, light and power, nitrates, mining into participation in mixed, government-controlled holding companies. All profits were rigidly apportioned for taxes, social security, reinvestment in the country, and private gain. If he avoided the international hostility that would have come with overt confiscation, nevertheless he established far-reaching controls. But Chile was harder hit by depression than any other country in the Americas, and the efforts, whoever wielded power, had to be correspondingly drastic.

Such reforms put out the immediate flame of discontent, but they did not meet the pressing needs of hunger and unemployment due to the depression; diversification of industry, also, is a slow process. And so, the fire of discontent, as in a coal mine, ate steadily through the souls and brains of the Chilean people.

In mighty fear of what might happen, the middle class, mainly composed of bureaucrats and small shopkeepers, formed its Fascist Falanxes, with the approbation of the government. But there was not a big enough budget to give them their place in the sun, not enough government posts to go around, not enough employment to stave off small-business bankruptcies.

The situation did improve somewhat through rigid **autarchy,** prohibition of many imports, an import quota system, rigid control of international currency and trade, the barter system, etc. But the older governing elements, still honeycombing the bureaus, lacked initiative and the firmness to promote any large-scale national transformation with ruthless energy, such as México had done with her Six-Year Plan, or even to the extent that the clique of cattle and wheat barons of Argentina has done. Inevitably, however, lacking in a philosophy or a real program, the government was forced to take ever more steps in the direction of economic nationalism, control of foreign capital, control of exports and imports. But the knack of governing was departing from the hybrid feudal-bourgeois group — they could not improvise readily or make the necessary concessions, were basically without any real desire, energy, or capacity to renovate the country. They could not even appreciate the brilliant Gustavo Ross, whose bold strokes had organized industry in chaos, who had promoted new industries, and at the same time had left untouched the patrimony of the six hundred families who controlled sixty-two per cent of Chile's arable land, and the best of it; probably over ninety per cent of it in the rich central valleys.

4

It was in this general atmosphere of suffering from long depression, of bewildered upper-class fumbling, of hostility to foreign enterprise and foreign-loan merchants, of growing international uncertainty in a world heading toward war, of local Communist, Nazi, and imperialist intrigue, and pressure from the American and British foreign offices, that the elections of November, 1938, took place. It came at a time of Popular Front experiment in France and Spain and during the civil war in the latter country.

Gustavo Ross was pitted against Pedro Aguirre Cerda, an Indian-like mestizo, leader of the Radical Party (a center group) and a wealthy but liberal landowner. Ross had the backing of the outgoing Alessandri Government, of the large landowners, and in spite of his coercion of capital and industry, the help of native and foreign capital, which feared worse. Aguirre Cerda was backed by the Radicals, Socialists, Communists. To add to the paradox, the Nacistas or Nazis jumped on the Popular Front bandwagon. So did the Ibáñez elements.

In Chile there is a hundred-peso fine (five dollars), a sum in excess of the monthly income of many a poor agricultural *roto*, exacted from those who do not vote, so Chile has about a hundred per cent turnout. This, coming at a time when popular feeling was so high, meant — despite the coercion of the army and bureaucracy, and the mass voting of many docile plantation and mine serfs — a victory for the Popular Front. One of the first acts of Aguirre was to release all imprisoned Nacistas.

This was practically the first time that diverse groups with totalitarian philosophies had been able to get together on a non-totalitarian basis. True, the Soviet Union had early made a strong trade alliance with Mussolini, and at the time of the Abyssinian invasion had hastened to supply his forces with oil when the United States was establishing a boycott. Mussolini and Hitler had shown signs of working together, but the Chilean election preceded the great alliance later consummated between Nazi Germany and Soviet Russia, subsequently ruptured when Hitler struck and Russia was forced to turn to the 'imperialist capitalist democracies' for aid. There was, therefore, perhaps nothing particularly anomalous in the earlier Chilean Nazi-Communist electoral collaboration. The glue, as in all the other instances, was not common ideas or moral principles, but expediency and national interest.

For when any movement proceeds from the realm of the propagation of ideas in accordance with conceived truth to that of direct participation in the struggle for power, group safety and immediate advantage soon supersede intellectual integrity, and even the freshest slogans lose their intrinsic validity as they are converted into instruments of attack and counterattack. Tribal and party and other loyalties supersede the search for the truth. Truth falls into the poisonous embrace of opportunism.

With the Popular Front victory in Chile, a wildly shouting populace of *rotos*, uprooted *pampeños* from the once prosperous northern nitrate fields, surged into Santiago, crying, 'The New Order! The New Order!'

Aguirre Cerda appointed a Communist to govern Santiago, the capital, and a Socialist to govern the near-by fashionable race-track spa, Viña del Mar, and arbitrarily cut the price of bread and foodstuffs fifty per cent or more. The army and diplomatic corps were purged.

It was certainly a new note. Many a politician previously had talked of building up industry and helping the people. Few had ever cited concrete measures and enterprises. Now the effort, apparently, was really to be made. But Chile obviously lacked the material resources and capital for these undertakings. The capital could come from only two sources: confiscation of foreign investments or an outside loan.

Fears were universally expressed that foreign capital was in for a bad trimming. But no precipitate moves were made, and the more acute fears of the more conservative elements, who had been hurriedly selling their blooded race-horses to American buyers, gradually subsided, although their antipathy to 'the new order' was not thereby diminished.

By May, 1939, Chile's Minister of Finance Robert Wacholtz found himself in the United States dickering for a loan of eighty million dollars with which to carry out some of Aguirre Cerda's grandiose program. Curiously enough, the radical elements of the country, which previously had been so anti-imperialistic and anti-American, were now wholly in favor of this move; now the conservative and commercial interests, enticed by Germany's great strides in mass-purchasing of Chilean goods and the shipping in of cheap German merchandise, saw this as merely a battle for world markets in which Chile should play a very cautious rôle. Certainly previous loan experiences had been catastrophic. Although Chile had got the money and the goods practically free, the loans had stopped when they were most needed. The depression in the United States (which country had formerly dominated the Chilean market especially for the export of copper, nitrates, etc., and above all with manufactured goods brought into the country) had precipitated the country into economic ruin, and this had brought long-enduring political upheaval.

Germany, Italy, Japan stepped into the picture precisely when the economic situation in the United States was worst; and now, the activities of the Axis private-state merchants provided the Chilean authorities with a leverage to help persuade the United States to grant more funds. Brazil, by alternately flirting with the Axis and Washington, had been most successful in winning enormous credits. The previous administration of Alessandri had been obliged to get arms, ammunition, war planes, electrical and railway equipment from Germany because of lack of credits in the United States. Germany was decidedly willing to barter her goods for strategic Chilean materials. Already her exports to Chile were nearly equal to our own.

The new Aguirre Government showed a certain antagonism to the Hitlerian régime by rounding up and deporting Nazi agents, among them twelve Britishers on the Hitler payroll, but unless Chile could get help, it might have to depend on the Germans for needed supplies.

But Chile was not so strategic geographically as Brazil; besides, the norm of the State Department is stability. Brazil under the iron personal rule of Vargas appeared quite stable, whereas Chile had a Center-Leftist régime. It is true the State Department had reluctantly made its peace with such a régime in México; but it had helped oust the popular Grau coalition government of Cuba, and it had universally been most sympathetic to the more reactionary feudal régimes of Latin America. In any case, Chile did not get the loan. Shortly after, the government there served notice on the Standard Oil's West Indian subsidiary that the government would take over nine million dollars of oil tanks, pipe lines, and refinery installations.

The new régime found hard sledding. Its budget was strained at the outset by relief needed for the terrible earthquake in Concepción. Although Chile's strategic materials (especially copper and nitrates) were now in heavy demand as the nations girded for war, the internal financial and political situation was unstable. Not only did the numerous Popular Front groups jockey constantly for power, but the Conservatives kept up constant pressure. Former dictator Carlos Ibáñez returned and formed a new fusion, taking in most of the Nacistas and many Radicals and Socialists — the Partido Unico. This, although

Ibáñez gave his 'warm support' to Aguirre, increased the tension. The new grouping, which split the Socialists, gave Ibáñez, through the affiliation of the Alianza Popular Libertadora, six seats in the national chamber.

The general aims of the new régime were stated by Arturo Bianchi, Minister of Commerce and Industry:

'Our twenty Latin-American republics are largely branches of foreign capitalism. It is true that we possess political independence, but this is greatly limited by our economic slavery to foreign interests.

'We are nothing but markets for foreign powers and providers of raw materials for these same nations, because the Latin-American republics lack a comprehensive and constructive economic and industrial policy. Our labor which we furnish these foreign interests is sweated and undernourished.'

Sr. Bianchi added that Chile is now entering upon a new phase of its international economy by striving for economic as well as for political independence. As means to that end, he declared that it would become necessary for his Government to have a firm and clear policy to create and to keep for itself all the means of production and distribution of the nation.

Despite stormy moments, Aguirre rode through his period without the expected upset, although he carried out few of his promises. The gradual improvement of state revenues was due more to the previous activities of Gustavo Ross than to his own régime. The grandiose electricization program could not be put through. Some small new industries were started. But the large landholders were not molested, although the state forced some improvements in the conditions of workers and peasants and kept the cost of living from rising too rapidly by the superficial and artificial, although ever costly and in the long run negative, exercise of rigid price controls.

5

Now, as new elections approached, Alessandri returned to the scene. The Popular Front put up Juan Ríos, a fairly colorless politician of the Radical group. Ibáñez had broken with the

Popular Front, so that now its chances looked fairly slim. But Ríos went in by a small margin.

The outbreak of war and the impossibility for Chile to gain outside equipment for new industries and enterprises largely put an end to the government's program of industrial expansion, even if it had been sincerely pushed. Public attention was diverted by the bitter controversies over the war, the struggle between the pro-Axis elements, the neutral elements, and the pro-war elements favoring the United Nations.

The government itself, fearing the Japanese advance, worried over Chile's long, unprotected coast, desired assurances of proper protection, but at the same time was unwilling to cede to the United States demanded air and naval bases in Chilean territory. Also, a price for war-participation was set: shipping quotas, guaranteed supply of industrial and manufactured goods, guarantees for Chile's copper and nitrate market; a demand that the United States refrain from developing beyond a certain point the fabrication of synthetic nitrate and agree to acquire the product from Chilean sources after the war.

At the same time the Ríos Government was harassed in these negotiations by the growing demands of the Communists and Socialists that the country sign up with the United Nations. Part of the picture of these undercover negotiations was the sudden sharp warning by Sumner Welles — on the eve of President Ríos' visit to Roosevelt — that several neutral southern countries (Argentina and Chile) were harboring Nazi agents, who were endangering, by information sent out, the safety of American ships at sea, and were carrying on other nefarious activities.

This resulted in a sharp protest from the Chilean Foreign Minister and the cancellation of Ríos' voyage. Ríos was now in a difficult position. The majority of his own party backers favored breaking with the Axis, and it was perfectly evident that Washington did not intend to accede to the demands Chile had set for her participation in the war effort. In general the opposition Conservatives were against Chile's breaking with the Axis, but a large group, for opportunistic political reasons, were pot-shooting at the government for its neutrality policy, merely in order to embarrass Ríos. At the same time the economic outlook was bad.

Although Chile's copper mines, nitrate fields, and other enterprises were running full blast, so there was little unemployment, nevertheless the cost of living, despite price controls, was creeping up; although Chile's strategic materials were being rushed over seas, few goods were coming in. There were shortages on every hand. This was generally ascribed to Ríos' antagonizing of the United States. Ríos bowed to the inevitable.

The Foreign Minister who had criticized the United States was removed and replaced by the Chilean Ambassador to Uruguay, known to be friendly to the United Nations. He passed through Buenos Aires, where the Argentinean officials tried to influence him to remain neutral by staging splendid celebrations and banquets, but the farewell given him was somewhat cooler. Chile rounded up many more Fascist agents, and finally in January, 1943, broke off relations with the Axis.

PART SEVEN

Plains of
The Far South

CHAPTER XXIII

Uruguay

THE Palacio Salvo sticks up above flat-roofed Montevideo like a sore thumb. It is the city's one skyscraper — a nightmare in stone. Although only an atrociously overadorned twelve-story edifice, a huge fourteen-story tower, bulging topheavy in the middle, rises from one corner.

Aside from that, Montevideo boasts of some of the finest modernistic architecture in South America, and is also one of the handsomest of Latin-American cities, with its broad clean avenues, its wide palm-dotted squares and parks, its eternal scent of orange blossoms, its massed flowers.

This is the country's one large city, and not so large, a little over seven hundred thousand people, but even so more than a third of the population of the little country. But if Uruguay is small in terms of South America, compared to certain more compact areas of the world it is fairly large. It is half again the size of England and almost seven times that of Belgium, but with only a fourth of the latter's population.

The most numerous inhabitants of Uruguay are cattle and sheep. There are four times as many cattle and nine times as many sheep as there are citizens with printed birth certificates.

The four-legged population roams over a hinterland very similar to that of the Argentina pampa, but more rolling and with even more succulent grasses. It is a country without mountains or deserts or lakes, except for enormous Lake Mirím, which forms most of the border with Brazil. It is a country without ancient ruins, had few aborigines and has practically none at all at present. It is just a vast cattle and sheep range, and Montevideo is the grange.

But despite this suggested monotony, little Uruguay is one of the most distinguished of all the southern countries. Its life has plenty of variety; its people are independent and alert, and it is one of the most positive expressions of the continent in terms of government, education, health, and social justice. It is customarily called 'the Switzerland of the South,' not for its topography but for the wisdom of its institutions.

Part of this achievement is due perhaps not to any unusual qualities of the inhabitants (although the population, largely of European origin, has been freed from the cultural and economic clashes of Indian-mestizo countries), but to the fairly genial continuous prosperity that the country has enjoyed. When that prosperity has cracked, Uruguayan liberties also have cracked. It is true that the modern Uruguayan is chiefly a descendant of the Basque, with considerable Italian infiltration, and the Basques came from the same stock, the cleanest, hardiest, most industrious, best educated, most liberty-loving element of modern Spain; but easily garnered prosperity due to so much roving gold on the hoof, the balmy and healthful non-tropical climate, and the close ties with the European world, plus Uruguay's general ethnic homogeneity, have been mostly the cause of the well-ordered institutional life of the country.

Its spirit of independence, its desire to demonstrate its superiority by actual deeds, may also have been fostered by the fact that it is a proud little land between two powerful neighbors who have long contended for possession of the country, either by outright annexation or by control over domestic affairs. The retention of independence, in the face of such difficulties, has also depended on a voluntary national discipline which is reflected in the Uruguayan way of doing things.

In colonial times, though Uruguay, or the Banda Oriental, was chiefly under the government of Buenos Aires, it was more than once occupied and held by the Portuguese, either by force or voluntary cession by the Spanish Crown. To this day, the Spanish language of Uruguay, especially in the eastern provinces, is interlarded with Portuguese expressions and has an intonation distinct from that of near-by Argentina, which is so influenced by the Italian. Certain frontier folk actually speak an argot that is almost as much Portuguese as Spanish.

This early shuttle between two sovereignties undoubtedly promoted a consciousness among settlers there that they were different from either of their neighbors; so was produced a growing sentiment of nationalism and independence.

Uruguayan pride and self-reliance were greatly fostered in 1806. When the British, after Trafalgar, seized Buenos Aires, the Spanish Viceroy Sobremonte and his forces ran away, whereupon the Uruguayans, rising in arms, recovered the city. This, in fact, was the beginning of Uruguayan independence, for by this voluntary uprising and victory the people sensed their power, and their leader declared, 'Men born in America are not inferior to Spaniards or Europeans, and none can surpass them in courage.' The grateful Spanish Government awarded Montevideo a coat of arms and the title of 'Most Loyal and Reconquering City.' But the Creoles or Americans still remained in an inferior political, social, and economic status before the law, and felt this irksome condition had to be abolished. Viceroy Sobremonte was scornfully ousted by the Argentineans and Uruguayans, and the liberators named their own Viceroy — this in itself was astounding independence of action.

The British, however, quickly retaliated, and in 1807, after a costly assault, laid waste to Montevideo. They were not driven out till six months later, but driven out they were. This battle, too, the Uruguayans largely had to fight alone. And also, when the final break with Spain came, the Uruguayans, under the great patriot José Artigas, a thoroughgoing republican, had similarly to paddle their own canoe, with little aid from the Argentineans. The first important Uruguayan victory was won in 1811 at Las Piedras, a Silasian monastery center, now in a rich wine and ostrich region. The whole Banda Oriental was fired by this victory, and it gave the patriots courage to go on, for, soon they were to discover, they had to fight not only the Spaniards, enjoying the resources of a vast empire, but the Argentineans, who frowned on the independence of the Banda Oriental, and at the same time imperial Portugal; for the colonial rulers of Brazil saw this as the supreme opportunity to get hold of the wealthy region so long coveted.

The Portuguese invaders were expelled in 1814, but for fourteen years more there was a seesaw over Uruguay between Brazil and Argentina, till finally both (Brazil herself having become independent in the meantime) recognized the little country as a sovereign state. Part of this outcome was due to British intervention. The English, apparently realizing that further attempts to seize New World territory would result in disaster, now assumed a paternal rôle. They saw in Uruguay's struggle the opportunity to set up a puppet buffer state as a leverage against both Brazil and Argentina. The British Empire agreed to guarantee Uruguay's independence 'forever,' certainly a Godlike gesture not without considerable realism.

From 1839 to 1850 Uruguay was torn by civil war and by repeated Argentine invasions. The country turned to Brazil for aid, and both nations then overthrew the Argentine tyrant Juan Manuel Ortiz de Rosas in 1852.

In 1863 civil war again broke out, precipitating both Argentine and Brazilian invasions. In 1864 Brazil imposed a puppet president. In 1868 there was another serious uprising. Subsequently Uruguay was involved in the terrible war with Francisco Solano López, the Napoleonic tyrant of Paraguay, and marched in with Brazil and Argentina as allies.

In 1903 the Colorados, a major party made up of the more middle-class farming and urban elements, particularly the latter, a movement somewhat resembling our own Populist Party of the nineties, won the elections and put into office Uruguay's greatest modern president, José Battle y Ordóñez. It took a year of civil war to establish his government.

Battle was born in 1865 and educated in Europe. In 1885 he founded the daily paper *El Día* to spread his ideas of political reform. He joined the Colorado Party (so named originally out of sympathy with Garibaldi's Red Shirts), as opposed to the Blancos, the conservative cattle and wool elements. Above all else, Battle stood for political freedom and the end of dictatorship. He pondered long and deeply on the best way to limit executive power so as not to destroy efficiency yet prevent tyrannical rule.

He himself gracefully relinquished power to his elected successor at the end of his term and went to Europe again. There he studied Swiss politics at first hand, in which a group rather than a single man exercised executive responsibility, a collegiate system.

Battle was re-elected in 1911 and announced his new ideas in the columns of *El Día*. They were too startling, and as a result the Colorados were in a minority at the constitutional convention he called for 1917. But in spite of this, his ideas made rapid headway even among his opponents and were largely utilized in framing the new structure of government.

Executive power was now divided between a President and an Executive Council of nine, also directly elected by the people. The proper functions of each were precisely defined. Every two years three members of the Council, who enjoyed six-year terms, were automatically replaced by those having received the next largest number of votes, one in any case to be of the minority party. The Council, not the President, was to appoint the Ministers of Public Instruction, Finance, Industry, and Public Works. Each department, moreover, was to be governed by an administrative council, including minority representation.

Church and State were separated — for the first time in South America. Primary and normal instruction, posts and telegraphs, industrial education and the electoral court (named by Congress), were given autonomous powers apart from the President and the Council.

This was the first time, except for short-lived monarchical efforts, that any free country in the Americas had abandoned the conventional tri-part balance of power system of the original United States Constitution, although actually in most of the countries that system had quite failed to work because of the repeated usurpations of dictators, the constant encroachments of executives greedy to concentrate all power and every function in their own supposedly capable hands.

Social reforms were not neglected by the Constituent Assembly, and these were greatly expanded during succeeding years. Up until the military *coup* of dictator Gabriel Terra in 1933, these included pensions for the aged, invalids, and government employees; a minimum wage graduated according to the size of the family; a weekly rest day; a maximum eight-hour day; special protection for women workers; rural credits.

The government embarked on the operation of the Bank of the Republic, the Loan Bank, the administration of all port facilities, railroads, electric light and power, telephones and telegraphs, the making of cement, the distribution of alcohol, petroleum, etc., and it set up rival meat-slaughtering establishments. The government banks charge lower interest rates than private banks. Railroad rates are a third cheaper than on private lines, and have done much over the years to encourage small independent farming and crop diversification.

2

Much of the Battle governmental structure came to an end with the military *coup* of General Gabriel Terra in 1933. He was a depression product, part of the crop of dictatorial assaulters of the power which grew out of the 1929 collapse in the United States, which so affected Latin America and which so destroyed democratic progress in so many countries. Terra had been duly elected in 1930, but as the depression had already bitten deep, he faced a difficult situation of much unemployment and straitened government finances.

His first act, after seizing power by a *coup* against his own government, was to abolish the National Council. One of the notable leaders and statesmen of the continent, ex-President Baltasar Brum, rather than face arrest, disillusioned by the turn of events, committed suicide in protest. Members of Congress were arrested and in general a reign of terrorism was instituted.

It was into this whirlpool of terrorism and death and the destruction of Uruguayan liberties that the delegates of the Pan-American Congress of December, 1933, had to come to hold their meetings for the good-neighborliness of the continent. The foreign correspondents present, naturally, were unable to tell the truth of the situation, and even their dispatches about the international congress were censored.

Terra ruled by a personally appointed junta, which in turn

created a deliberative assembly of ninety-nine members. Terra ruled by absolute decree. However, many of his measures were wise. He had, above all, to handle the situation derived from the collapse of foreign markets and the resulting widespread depression. He ordered compulsory cultivation of land and the planting of trees. Owners of more than seventy-four thousand acres had to construct a dwelling on each seventy-four hundred acres and maintain families therein. The land tax, in compensation, was reduced twenty per cent.

Also Terra felt obliged to permit a new constitutional convention, although the delegates were restricted as much as possible, through the abolition of civil liberties, to his own followers. Nevertheless, the document which resulted was by no means a reactionary instrument. It established women's suffrage and penalized non-voters of both sexes. The President was required to include in his cabinet, in given proportions, representatives from both major parties. Congress was given disciplinary powers over the cabinet, and in case of a full vote of censure, new elections must be called. If thereafter there is another vote of censure, the President and his entire cabinet must resign. The Senate of thirty members is divided equally between the two parties receiving the largest number of votes.

The bulk of the social legislation was retained, even expanded to include more child welfare, state attention for the poor, accident insurance, cheap workers' dwellings. The right to unionize and declare strikes is specifically recognized. Illegitimate children are given the same rights as those born in wedlock.

Thus within a short time, while greatly strengthening executive powers, Terra found it advisable to restore at least part of the party and parliamentary system, although many elements continued to be excluded from political activities and failed to recover their civil liberties.

Terra remained in power until 1938. In the elections of that year the voters were given the choice of two relatives of Terra as candidates for President, and his brother-in-law, Alfredo Baldomir, was shoved into office, June 19, 1938. Aside from this, the elections were relatively democratic, although certain oppositionists were subsequently not allowed to enjoy office. The

Chamber was made up as follows: Colorados, 64; Blancos, 29; Socialists, 3; Catholics, 2; Communists, 1.

3

The modern era in Uruguay has tended to see substituted for Brazilian or Argentine military aggression a wider pacific economic penetration. The territorial and imperialistic greed of her two large neighbors has largely ceded ground to capitalist enterprise and diplomatic maneuvering, although as late as 1941-42, Argentine troops were briefly massed on the Uruguayan border. But the American battleships rushed to the scene clearly showed that the dual usurpations of the two powerful neighbors were no longer the only strong outside factors influencing Uruguay's destiny.

In the process of economic penetration, British capital long took the lead in buying up Uruguay's public utilities, meat-packing industries, and broad acres. Not until after World War I did American capital make some inroads. By 1940, when such investments had been scaled down, the water squeezed out, and a more realistic estimate made, the score sheet stood: British, $200,000,000; the United States, only about $14,000,000.

The years just prior to World War II saw considerable Brazilian and Argentine capital flow into the country. Argentine capital was usually masked British and Italian capital. Brazilian capital was often masked German and Italian investment. These imperial financial forces created many a political seesaw.

Such was the setting for the world conflict. At the time of the Pan-American Conference, Uruguay was, in an economic sense, pretty definitely hostile to the United States. Although her officials signed agreements, as at Lima, to abandon all new trade barriers, except tariffs, the depression had seen Uruguay's exports to the United States dwindle to almost nothing. To bolster their hard-hit economy, the Uruguayans celebrated five-year barter deals with Italy and Germany, at the same time announcing that such stabilization of trade was necessary because of the anarchistic and chaotic trade methods of the United States. Some years American buyers might take the whole wool clip; the next year, if they could get wool a quarter of a cent cheaper in Australia, Uruguay would be forgotten. This would mean economic disaster for one of the two major industries of the country. No country, the Uruguayan argument ran, could enjoy stability or prosperity without some regular guarantee for the major industries. This the Axis countries were willing to give, thereby promising more continuous production and a surer market.

The present war, which threw all this into the discard, brought serious schisms in Uruguay, particularly over the question of ceding bases to the United States. The deals for these, though denied by the Uruguayan Foreign Office and our own State Department, were finally dragged into the light by the opposition to Baldomir and were made the football of internal political commotion.

The Baldomir Government had been trying to ride two horses: extreme friendliness to the United States, while giving as little offense as possible to Germany and Italy. Opposition elements, not so much because of their concern over international affairs as because of the chance to embarrass the government, took two lines: one group fought the granting of the concessions being demanded by the United States and of these elements some were honestly neutral, others pro-Axis; and another group demanded sterner measures against Axis fifth-columnists.

The people, smarting from the Terra-Baldomir abuses, were increasingly against the Axis as a symbol of dictatorship which they themselves suffered, if nothing more; and as war-clouds came closer they grew more whole-heartedly in favor of the democratic nations. But this enthusiasm did not draw in a majority favoring the granting of bases on Uruguayan territory. Also, a neutral group entrenched in government posts obstructed any decided stand. The chief leader was Luis Alberto de Herrera, the strong man of the Blanco Party, the pro-Catholic conservative group. The 1934 constitution gave heavier representation to the Blancos than was warranted by the voting — half the Senate and one third the Chamber, plus cabinet representation.

The Herreristas fought rapprochement with the United States, particularly the granting of defense bases, and gave ground only when promised these would become inter-American or Pan-

American bases and on condition that every step taken be first submitted to the Blancos for approval. However, in many subtle ways the Blancos obstructed and won over — on patriotic grounds of national sovereignty and territorial integrity — enough of Baldomir's own followers to defeat his candidate for the presidency of the lower house of parliament.

Baldomir, then, in violation of the constitution, and as a foretaste of the *coup* he would later make, ousted the three Blanco members from his cabinet, and distributed their portfolios among the five remaining members. This arbitrariness created such a hullabaloo that on April 5, he had to put three Blancos back in his cabinet, although he selected men more in line with his own policies. In the meantime the government had arrested many Nazi agents. A supposed wholesale Nazi plot to seize the country was discovered. It was mostly created in the minds of the op-positionists, although there was not the slightest doubt that the Nazis were using Uruguay as a base for many of their sabotage and propaganda activities there and in adjacent South American countries. Such alarming disclosures were pushed in Congress chiefly to embarrass Baldomir, who was playing a waiting game, apparently to bid up the price for which his loyalty could be obtained by the United States. Actually these moves played right into his hands, for they permitted him to call on the United States now for protection against the supposed Nazi *Putsch*. American battleships were rushed to the scene. Chief of Staff Marshall made sensational declarations. Scareheads flared across the tops of American newspapers. Thus Baldomir used the very sword of the opposition group against it. Heartened by American battleships and the promise of large credits, he rose up with iron hand to handle the situation. On the grounds of national security, all public assemblage was forbidden, the newspapers were suppressed, part of Congress was driven into the streets, and universal conscription (which Baldomir had opposed during his campaign for the presidency) was imposed — in an effort to promote the Democracies' cause against Uruguayan elements in opposition, both those desiring neutrality and those desiring a stronger pro-Allied stand. All this rough and tumble probably had more to do with the intrigues of Uruguayan domestic politics and Baldomir's dictatorial instincts than with foreign relations or the Nazis.

Public riots broke out in protest. Pro-neutral and anti-Axis elements battled. The students called a general strike, demanding the ousting of all pro-Fascist-Nazi and Falangist professors, the expulsion from Congress of Deputy Alejandro Kayel, publisher of the pro-neutral newspaper *La Libertad*, the suppression of all newspapers 'constituting a threat to national sovereignty.' In Trinidad troops with drawn sabers had to drive off a mob attacking an Italian restaurant.

July 30 the Chamber of Deputies suspended Kayel, and *La Libertad* had to fold up. In August the Minister of Interior closed down the Spanish Falanx organization, Fundación Española. September 11, ignoring Italian official protests, the government seized two Italian and Danish steamships idle in Montevideo harbor.

A congressional investigation of totalitarian activities had begun in 1940 and still continued. It now extended its inquiry into the personnel and activities of the army and police. A Fascist veterans' organization was raided.

This drive on totalitarianism was taken in close cooperation with the United States. The American legation was raised to embassy status, and William Dawson named Ambassador. July 12, 1941, the first Uruguayan and naval mission arrived in the United States to buy arms, for which the southern government had allocated 7,500,000 pesos in accordance with promises of American financial and technical assistance, and by August 19, the Baldomir Government accepted a seventeen-million-dollar arms credit from the United States Export-Import Bank. Through the close of the year and on into 1942 (over German-Italian protests before the break came), punitive action was taken against numerous Axis agents and representatives.

All, however, was still not smooth, and following a vote of censure by Congress, which he had been unable to override on the question of granting bases to the United States, Baldomir on February 23, 1942, followed the example of Terra and made a complete *coup d'état*. Both houses of congress were dissolved arbitrarily, a state council on the Terra model was set up, and the coveted bases were then granted to the United States. Followers of Herrera were arrested, including members of Congress. The Battlistas (Colorados on the left) were also harassed.

More public riots broke out. Baldomir had succeeded in arousing such hostility that he found difficulty in finding members for his new dictatorial and illegal council to replace the suppressed Congress. United States planes arrived, and public attention was somewhat diverted from Baldomir's tyrannical acts by new drives on totalitarian elements. Police officials, accused of pro-Axis sympathies, some pro-Axis and some merely followers of opposition leaders, were ousted. An American loan was finally arranged for twelve million dollars, and July 4 was declared a national holiday.

In October J. J. de Amezaga (of the government faction of Colorados) and Doctor E. Blanco Acevedo (of the regular Colorados) announced themselves rivals for the presidency. Rumors grew that the elections would be suppressed, but the most serious development seemed to be merely lipstick. Women were warned that any lipstick marks on ballots would nullify them.

And so, after some delay in turning over the power, March 1, 1943, Amezaga was inaugurated. His first act was to restore political rights and to set up a cabinet composed of representatives of all major parties. This is the first time in ten years that the Battlistas, ousted by Terra and Baldomir, have been allowed their legal place in the government and have been free from persecutions. The swing now is back to democracy.

But the new President faces a serious situation in his country. The intense drouth has decimated sheep and cattle herds. There is serious fuel and gasoline shortage, a lack of shipping; promised supplies from the United States have not arrived; and the public debt (aside from that contracted with the United States, which is, of course, a gift from the American Treasury) has mounted dangerously. Despite heavy taxes, it has been impossible to balance the budget.

CHAPTER XXIV

Pampas Riders

THE pampas (or open plains) of Argentina and Uruguay are vast, sparsely settled. After four centuries of colonization, great cities, great factories are only beginning to rise above the face of that mighty empire. Man, the individual, be he gaucho (cowboy), the oldtime cattleman, or ordinary European settler, is still the hub of a vast physical circumference. The hub rotates under an open starlit sky; from him, the individual, the spokes ray out, and he knows not how far they reach. He is the pivot of the slow-wheeling frontier.

To the eye the pampas are a great circle. The circle is the oldest human symbol, without beginning or end. It is the rolling snake with its tail in its mouth, as pictured in prehistoric American carvings and codices. It is the horizon; it is the sky; in the Argentine pampas, it is the universe.

There gaucho and artist alike are dominated by the enclosed curve, the flat round disk of their world. In México and Central America — tilted volcanic regions — the dominant motif, from ancient times to the present, has been the pyramid, whether revealed in the art of the Mayan stone-worker or the modernistic paintings of Carlos Mérida and Diego Rivera.

The pyramid is a thrust of mingled supplication and defiance. It is the symbol of finger-pressing, praying hands that rise up in search of the godhead appealingly, and end with the frustrated thrust of clenched fist — for Aztec and Mayan pyramids, like so many of the surrounding volcanic cones, are truncated and blunt.

But the circle is the symbol of completeness and perfection, of universality, of dull dominion and self-confidence; also of wariness, of a man facing ready all ways. At the center is the fierce overproud pampa dweller, his poncho wrapped around his left forearm, his fighting knife in hand, and pivoting on his heel, ever ready for man or beast.

The bellicose occasion is rarely concerned with money or property — for the Argentinean is the free-handed spendthrift of the world, but the fray may be over a woman, a point of honor, or due merely to a sarcastic word; for with ready insults, the pampa drifter hastens to test out the mettle of any newcomer. '*Que pavo!*' ('What a turkey!') is the Argentine expression for too stupid pride. But by such *bravatas* friends and enemies are quickly made. And if the man of the pampa dies, in the very face of death he sings nonchalantly:

> Burying man, I come to demand,
>   Don't stick my body in the cemetery;
> Bury me, with my guitar in my hand,
>   Out on the open prairie.

The circle impresses itself on thought and conduct and deeds. When the exiled Peruvian writer, Manuel Seone, crossed the Argentine plains for the first time, he recorded in his *Rumbo Argentino* the following vivid impression of the pampa dweller.

> Round, without psychoanalytical angles, is his face, with thick ruddy cheeks. Round is his sombrero, flat-crowned like the pampas, but with the front brim turned up as a man who has nothing to conceal but wishes to know everything. Round is the traveling lasso, a dancing and acrobatic halo. Everything seems influenced by the curve of the landscape, enslaved by the soft distortion of the horizon.

Actually the vastness, the essential immobility of those grassy plains, so flat and apparently insipid, definitely delimit human and animal and vegetable life. At first glance, man and beast and tree seem to have no individual significance except to break the monotony; about them is the aura of sad isolation.

'In the pampa,' remarks novelist Ricardo Güiraldes, 'impressions are rapid, quickly blotted out by the amplitude of the setting, leaving not a trace. This is why all faces become impassive.' Only when man and beast fling themselves loose from the soil do they become something in and for themselves. As Güiraldes puts it in his *Don Segundo Sombra*, 'Animals and persons move as though enslaved by a single fixed idea: to go on and on and on.' Even though motion seems without purpose, a lost effort, like the futile racing of the Red Queen, men on the pampas constantly feel the need desperately to dash on and on, to perform gargantuan exploits. The men of the plains, the ordinary men and even some of the ruling landholders, are mestizos, of mixed blood, and the restlessness from the surge of two conflicting blood streams, is added to the restlessness born of the flat expanse.

The Argentinean, self-centered and wary in his circle, is otherwise the most self-confident of all Latin Americans — even to the point of petulancy. He is the hub of his wheel; and his great individualism and self-reliance are accentuated by the persistence, in many parts, of semi-frontier conditions, plus the knowledge that his country is the most productive, wealthy, and puissant of all Latin America. Life may often be harsh, but it does not preclude sturdy survival, great deeds, and lusty crude enjoyments. And a turn of the wheel may still bring great wealth and the sybaritic joys of Buenos Aires and (before the war) of Paris.

2

The man of the open world of the Argentine has limitless gusto. He is still a hearty meat-eater. In remote parts wild game varies the diet: the ostrich, the succulent armadillo, the soft-fleshed *lagartija*, the tinamou partridge. But as these have been increasingly killed off, more and more the pampa dweller has been reduced to a crude carnivorous beef and sheep diet. Now, modern commercialism and diversified crops reverse the process, adding new elements to the menu, but in remoter sections, an all-beef or all-sheep diet is still common.

The rope slides under the wild forehoofs, the animal is quickly slaughtered in the shade of the *ombú* tree. From a belt glittering with silver coins and plaques the long keen blade is drawn from its strap to slice off the skin deftly with a few strokes. The carcass is hoisted to a limb, the intestines carved out with another flourish, and the fresh-killed meat eaten in the fists red and dripping a few minutes after it is put to dangle from the tripod over the sizzling campfire. When the meat is dried into *tasajo*, the gaucho must tear at it fiercely to shred the toughened fibers. The cattle, too, except the thoroughbreds in lush alfalfa fields of the provinces closer to the capital, are obliged, when the bunch grass gets tough and spiny, to jerk at it sharply lest it cut their mouths.

In the old days cattle were slaughtered only for their hides and for food. The gaucho then disdained all but the choicer parts. He might cut out only the tongue and the *criadillas* and leave the rest to the vultures. But today when herds are branded, and Argentina helps feed the British Empire, meat is never wasted.

But before all else, even before meat, the modern Argentinean must have his stimulating *mate* tea — either 'sweet' or 'bitter,' and scarcely is he off his horse, abroad or at home, when he proceeds to *cebar su mate*. He sucks it blistering hot from the gourd through a silver tube — the *boquilla* — he always carries. If others are present, the gourd goes the round with much polite ceremony, any disregard of which, even among intimates, is quickly construed as deadly insult and may lead to violence and a knife fight.

Around the bare squat ranch-houses sometimes are grown a little horehound and other necessary plants, but rarely do vegetables accompany the meat diet, except onions and garlic, bought at stores, where are also obtained bread, rice, *mate* tea, oil, vinegar, raisins, cinnamon, pepper, cumin seed, or whatever other seasonings can be afforded to make the steady diet of beef and mutton palatable.

At his home, the gaucho — now, except in a few outlying sections, little more than a modern peon — eats at a crude table, lit by candles or smelly oil lamps. Only during the First World War boom did the great ranch-houses really put on much splendor. Except for the Big Houses of the huge *estancias*, the homes of the pampas are still mostly humble, of burnt brick or adobe, the floors of hardened mud. They are always low, often one has to stoop to get through the squat doors; and unless they are surrounded by eucalypti, these habitations are scarcely visible more than a mile and a half — as though the folk were afraid to break the level aspect of the plain, and wished to keep it wholly free and open, unobstructed by anything immovable.

Even the occasional far-spaced towns are laid out flat and low, with dull drabness, insipid, without imagination, as though set in their places without any rhyme or reason whatever — 'dusty and blunt,' Güiraldes describes them — melancholy places largely devoid of cultural significance, steeped in primitive isolation. The larger centers in more distinctly farming areas are newer, crude, sometimes briskly commercialized, a-bustle with buyers, sellers. Farm societies worry about seed, weather, and market prices. Like many of our Midwestern communities, they are very heavy-handed places.

The vast pampa circle is broken by little growth except the even grass far and wide, carpetlike and changing color with the wind, from gray to silver. Often there is nothing for the casual traveler to see except this endless silver-green, for a short time in the year, quite flowerless. Sometimes he will go hundreds of miles without encountering a single permanent watercourse. There are places, as in our Dakotas, where a plow can be driven for twenty miles through the fertile loess without striking a tree, stone, marsh, or ditch. 'The only undulations on the pampas,' says the Argentinean, 'are the breasts of our women — our beautiful fierce women, soft yet defiant.'

Although from May to September, in years of exceptionally heavy rainfall, some of the pampas turn for many days into shallow lakes, for the most part, so nicely is rainfall adjusted to the absorbency of the soil, there is little runoff, yet no stagnant water. More often, in the drier western sections, there are whirling dust storms, so dense the head of your horse is invisible.

Near the sea are sometimes great salt mud marshes, infested with gigantic crabs. Horses and cattle that have strayed there have had their legs progressively devoured as they struggled out on their bellies to die.

3

The only tree natural to the pampa soil is the *ombú* of the rare Phytolacca family. It tries to spread out like the pampa itself —

perhaps because of the wind, perhaps because of the paucity of subsoil water — for it has an immense girth, in some instances forty or fifty feet.

As a rule not close together, the *ombúes* seem, like the human beings, to require space, and thereby to acquire solitary grandeur, to be complete individuals, to be also the hub of a vast circle. It is a bungling pachydermic sort of tree, the subject of sarcastic songs. Concealed in the round pudginess of the slow-growing trunks is the same sort of lurking violence, apparently in contrast to the pacific vastness about — for their sap is full of venom. This in part accounts for their survival, for although mostly useless for human needs, except as shade, they are one of the few species not eaten by pests or cattle. Native doctors often pluck the poisonous glossy dark leaves to steep a brew for patients who require a violent remedy. The wood is so spongy it can be easily cut with a knife, hence is not even fit for firewood, for it refuses to dry, simply 'rots away like a watermelon.'

Another growth, in more upland parts, is the *algarrobo*, or acacia, which has a delicate edible foliage. The beans are chewed up by both cattle and sheep. There are various drouth-resisting bushes, such as the widely disseminated *chañar*. Some shrubs are beautifully flowering or have brilliant foliage. The chinaberry tree — an importation — does well because it is not devoured by the eternal locusts; other trees in the drier stretches are often tough-barked, spiny, almost leafless. In more recent years, the eucalyptus, brought from Australia, has flourished widely, lifting its graceful lanky shape high above the flat plain everywhere — the only truly vertical note.

Worst of all is a thistle year, so vividly described by Hudson. The giant thistles, ordinarily restricted in area, suddenly spring up everywhere and cover much of the land — thick as sedge to a height of nearly ten feet, a dense mat of big jagged leaves, stalk touching stalk, an eternal rustle as cramped stiff foliage crackles free. These thistles cage in the world and block the movements of horsemen at work on the range; and the gaucho in his flat mud hut grows restless as his view on all sides is hemmed in.

By the end of hot November the sea of thistles has dried up, but often fires then sweep on for miles, destroying houses, herds, and humans. To stop these roaring conflagrations, the gaucho sometimes lassos a few sheep and drags them at a gallop back and forth to smash down the dead growth and make a firebreak; but more often the wind drives the sparks over and past him. The sun, in that late spring, sears the whole world, and the traveler then, as the river beds dry up, may see the water-mirage, a mocking surface, dancing in flickering transparent waves, tinged with silver gray.

Now and then one comes across great herds of cattle, horses, or sheep. Occasionally a horseman gallops over the plain, perhaps whirling his *bola* to wrap it about the forelegs of some racing steer, and perhaps quite unaware that he is using one of the most prehistoric tools ever devised by man in the Americas.

At long intervals a small grove of trees — palms or eucalypti — may mark an *estancia,* or sheep and cattle farm — a little island on the sea-like flatness. Closer inspection reveals the house to be a boxed rectangle, with columns, perhaps a big veranda and a corridor that looks down a thin avenue of trees to the empty pampas. The flat roof is immediately the center of the limitless circle all about. This dwelling is the residency of the 'aristocracy' as contrasted to the little mud huts of the modern gaucho, or indentured ranch hand. Not far from the Big House, though at other times miles away and quite alone, may be a windmill from the base of which radiate long lines of galvanized troughs — the ensemble looking like a spider in a high hat with a revolving rosette. More often the land stretches empty, gray-green, and vacant.

4

No one knows where the pampas begin or end. One writer says 'It extends from Buenos Aires to the mountains of Córdoba, seven hundred miles from the sea and sloping up to the Andean foothills.' But south, too, are grassy plains, far into Patagonia; and north, far into the Chaco. Even in the highlands are many isolated grass plains of big extent that carry the pampas, like a series of steps, closer to the sky.

Somewhere lie the borderlines of mountain, desert, jungle,

Antarctic snow, but the change is very gradual. Nearer Buenos Aires, the old free wild pampas no longer exist at all in the tangle of railroads, barbed wire, and European colonists, who have changed the face of the land over into compact horse- and cattle-breeding farms, neat truck gardens, and fields of blue-green alfalfa. Somewhere one comes to the deadline of such settlement and of intensive cultivation. The farther advance of settlement there comes up against the wall of the vast cattle and sheep kingdoms, the big landholders with thousands of acres, who refuse to break up their holdings. When occasion demands, they will sometimes lease some out for a rotation of corn, wheat, and finally alfalfa, for feed. This cycle completed, the settler is pushed back beyond the barbed wire, back toward Buenos Aires or Santa Fé.

Somewhere toward Córdoba and Tucumán, the cow country gives way to intensive sugar production; and in Mendoza to the long sun-clad slopes of vineyards which provide grapes for some forty million gallons of wine annually; and on certain foothills, the line changes over to tobacco and coffee growing.

But vast areas remain relatively unpeopled. Besides natural pasture lands, good for little else, Argentina has at least 212,500,-000 acres susceptible of cultivation. Of this empire but 65,000,000 acres have been broken to the plow, and of these 25,000,000 are devoted to alfalfa, an adjunct of the cattle kingdom. Large land-holding, despite islands of small colonizers, sets the major pattern. Even in thickly settled Buenos Aires and Santa Fé Provinces, farms of over twenty-five hundred acres represent sixty-seven per cent of the total area, a percentage that has varied little for forty years.

Although Argentina produces and exports nearly as much as the rest of South America put together, under present economic conditions its progress remains limited, and with the spur of war, Brazil is likely to surpass it in all lines except wheat raising. The system of large landholding, of chiefly a wheat and meat economy, has held Argentina, despite all its wealth, at a standstill agriculturally for decades.

The equation is this, says Luis E. Heysen, in his able study of Argentina agriculture: 'Three million square kilometers of territory with but ten million inhabitants, badly distributed. The pampa as deserted as it is fertile is but a remote geographic expression — a beautiful Venus de Milo without arms. Large landholding smothers it.' The country is made over into a great cow pasture, and settler needs are largely subordinated.

But once more, war changes the picture. This time, unlike World War I, it brings little wealth for the exporters of wool and hides, meat and wheat, for with the semi-Anglo-American boycott, the lack of shipping, and *en masse* buying which holds down the price, the bonanza days of the early conflict have not put in an appearance — instead, with glutted warehouses, Argentina is rocked by economic difficulties.

But the war and semi-boycott push ahead — what the depression started — an attempt at greater autarchy, an effort to multiply and utilize all possible domestic resources to cut down the amount of imports, to make the country less dependent upon foreign materials and sources and foreign-imposed prices. And so, diversification has made great headway. Gradually this or that ministry of the government has forced more and more land under cultivation.

5

The pampas feel the pull of other life at the edges. The pull at the northern end is from the highlands, from Indian Bolivia and mestizo Chile; from Araucano and Quechua and Inca traditions. Pale between-worlds Jujuy, in a low fold of the Andes, seems to belong to neither region. A bit south, Salta, where the cattle fair blossoms, and oil wells gush, is a rough-and-tumble outpost of the pampas. In Cuyo, save for herds traveling over the divides to west coast markets, the pampas are practically forgotten. Cuyo lives in the shadow of the Santa Madre Cordillera — 'The Holy Mother Divide,' under the two greatest snow-clad mountains of the Western Hemisphere. In Cuyo those of the pampas are called *abajinos*, 'those from below,' as contrasted to the *arribanos*, 'those from above.'

> Those who come down from the heights
> To show off in the town,
> Come down with mighty shouts,
> And return . . . oh, so very tame!

Out of the northlands also comes the Zonda, the balmy August wind from the realm nearer the equator, to announce the coming of spring and to make the buds open. 'The Zonda brings us the warmth of life.... It is like the fusion of man and condor, the mighty winged bird of the Andes, and brings us messages from our ancient Indian Sun' — that is, from Viracocha, from the god himself.

At the northeast corner, the pampas shrink back from the tangled jungles of the Chaco, the *quebracho* regions, and the thick sweaty verdure of the upper equatorial reaches of the big rivers. And in the south the Patagonian pampas shrink back from the wild storms of the Magellan Straits, the snow and ice of the Antarctic.

But there is still another important aspect of the pampas. As the winds rush over the high grass, often they seem not of earth, but sea, ever moving, advancing in steady tide, a geographical expression that only certain Mississippi Valley dwellers or the denizens of the steppes can understand properly. Although mostly level as a billiard table, nevertheless the Argentine plains then seem to advance along the giant La Plata River, down myriad streams, fed high in Andean snows or from heavy tropical storms in the deep jungles, from Bolivia and Perú and Brazil, from Chile and the Antarctic — down toward the Atlantic.

For centuries the pampas had their life keyed in with the mining centers of Chile, Bolivia, and Perú. The pull was toward the thriving gold, copper, and mercury mines, where flourishing new towns demanded supplies. Today those places provide a small market indeed compared to the beef-eating British Isles. This century, with the decline of European agriculture, the flow has been through Buenos Aires — beef and corn, flax and wheat, wool and hides — across the sea to Europe. Today the real movement of the pampas is with the rivers, away from the mountains, down to the sea.

Indeed the whole pampas seem almost to move with the wind down to Buenos Aires (Port of Good Airs), to Montevideo (Mountain View), to Mar del Plata (Silver Sea), to Bahía Blanca (White Bay), to Viedma; and there, in the ports, the bluff pampa winds wrestle with the blander feminine breezes from the mild sea — another vast circle — and therein lies the secret of the strange persistent duality, the eternal conflict, in Argentine life.

6

Argentina, like the gaucho himself, is rooted in the center of its vast circle, but it looks outward in all directions, out over the gray green pampas, out over the seven seas. The spokes on that hub are indeed indefinite. Thus, Argentina is peculiarly provincial, yet more cosmopolitan than any other Latin-American country. The city of Buenos Aires is the focus of the Argentinean's world outlook, the symbol of the national dualism. Where the opposing currents of pampas and port meet and swirl, there the man of the plains battles for supremacy with the bureaucrat, the international diplomat, the foreign capitalist, the shippers of wheat and meat to far places, with labor unions and strange international sects, whose words have an alien flavor that greatly irritates the brusquer man of the plains. Into Buenos Aires focus the forces of Europe and the Atlantic, and there they meet the land-tide of the vital forces of South America.

The pampas are a great corridor to the sheep highlands of Antarctic Patagonia, to the upper-river tropic jungles, to the Indian plateaus, to the mines of the Andes; and all those places also live in and for themselves — their homes, their families, their wives and children, the beauty of their particular soil, their own peculiar modes of life — and often resent the demands of the great world they feed and clothe. Buenos Aires is the center of the conflict. And thereby, with its hordes of strange immigrants, its quick sensitivity to international life, and at the same time as spokesman for the pampa, is a dramatic city, one of the most dramatic in the New World.

This division between port and pampas existed from the earliest days, even when Buenos Aires depended on limited Spanish trade supplemented by colossal smuggling activities, whereas the interior provinces truly looked toward Lima and Santiago, clear across the Andes. This division was present in the very hour of revolt against Spain. As a result, Argentina today celebrates two national independence days: May 25, when Buenos Aires threw off the Spanish yoke; and July 9, when deputies of the great interior Congress of Tucumán declared the United Provinces free.

Probably the true and more vital independence was born there, far in the interior on the rim of the pampas. The Tucumán deputies listened gravely to a motion to give the new nation the form of 'a limited monarchy under the dynasty of the Incas,' though the shadowy rulers of the old highland empire had been gone for three centuries. The local George Washington, Manuel Belgrano, actually proclaimed 'the restoration of Inca rule.' It was necessary to minister to the pride of the half-breed gauchos and the upland Indians of Bolivia and the jungle Indians of Paraguay.

But as elsewhere on the continent, the popular revolution that independence represented — the gaucho revolution in this case — was soon smothered by the wealthy creoles, the *Porteños*, the men of Buenos Aires, who contrived very quickly to take over the management of the country. Naturally this led to a reiterated struggle. For out of the pampas thereafter came hard-riding gaucho armies to subdue the port city, to right injustices and create new and worse injustices, to force the wayward metropolis to look homeward whenever its gaze strayed too far over the seas.

The struggle was similar — equally violent, but more national — to that of our own Middle Border farmers of the nineties, when home-spun wisdom matched its own teachings and faith against the academicians, politicians, and financial middlemen. The Middle Border revolt, coming to a head under Bryan, was sidetracked into conformity with post Spanish-American War prosperity; but in Argentina the gaucho chieftains (as portrayed in Sarmiento's novel, *Facundo*) successfully overran Buenos Aires time and again; and time and again Buenos Aires embraced the wild invaders, till they grew soft and forgetful and pliable. Then the storm would blow up anew.

The ruthless *Porteño* dictator, Juan Manuel Ortiz de Rosas, who ruled for a generation, finally broke the might of the gaucho chieftains and stamped out pampas revolt. Men of the pampas, such as Roca and the great Sarmiento themselves, then sternly shaped the national life to order, established schools, helped build railroads, linked the country together. Settlers, barbed wire, schools, new industries made law and order effective. Came the airplane, and the man of the far northern *quebracho* kilns was brought to within a few hours of the port. The sheepmen of Rawson and the miners of Jujuy and the oil drillers of Salta were made over into suburbanites. Except on the fringes the wild free cattle-hunter, the gaucho, was tamed to a peon, a hired hand. Now he is chiefly a literary legend.

The great duality of the pampas and of Buenos Aires, the one big city, persists, perhaps always will persist, but it is no longer the armed and shooting duality of earlier days, but that of two necessary and complementary ways of life. The pampas have increasingly forced Buenos Aires — its thought, its habits, its officialdom, its culture — over into a truly Argentinean expression; have obliged it to think more in terms of an integrated democracy and a whole people. Buenos Aires, on its side, has obliged the pampas to meet the challenge of the modern world.

7

This readjustment has not been easy, and many an individual has suffered. Out on the plains the struggle is reflected repeatedly in domestic tragedy — this provides the theme for several of the best dramas of the famous Florencio Sánchez. There the feudal, patriarchal life of the *estancia* is repeatedly shattered by the demands of each new generation. The youngsters go off to the city and learn new ways. Their traditional servility to their father, the master of the household, often even elementary respect, is destroyed.

Such was the tragedy of Don Eulogio, a big but very provincial cattleman southeast of Córdoba, whose *estancia* stretched from the level plain to the rolling country of the *chañar* bushes. He felt only anger and frustration in the presence of his own grown son, Don Ramón, when the latter returned for his vacations from the medical school. His son had become a Nietzschean and Voltairian, talking nonsense the old hard-headed father could not understand and found wholly unimportant except that it was derisive and heretical. Don Ramón sneered at the old ways of home and church. It riled Don Eulogio, with his traditional ideas of filial respect and absolute mastery over his household, because the boy tried to treat him as hail fellow well met instead of practicing the old bent-knee, hand-kissing attitude. As much as anything Don Eulogio was riled because in the morning his son had to have sweetened chocolate — a female drink without virility — and refused to drink the bitter *mate* brew, which is the delight of all true country folk. Chocolate-drinking was a symbol of decadence and foreign infiltration as opposed to the sound Argentineity of the true son of the interior.

In due time the son disgraced a girl protégée living in the house, then refused to marry her. 'Why should a lifetime of unhappiness result from a moment of thoughtless passion?' he demanded loftily.

'A man without character,' Don Eulogio warned his son, 'is merely a dead man walking.'

'You mean, a man without money,' retorted his son cynically. On top of this Don Eulogio's daughter, Celestina, refused to marry the designated suitor, a rich neighbor *estanciero* — unheard-of rebellion.

Don Eulogio, beaten on his own ground, fell desperately ill. Bitterly then he turned his back on 'drugstore remedies,' and reverted to local superstition. He called in Doña Rita, the native priestess doctor, who gave him queer stinking brews and made many crosses on the edges of the first advancing shadows of morning.

But the old feudalism has given ground to modern commercialism all along the line. Slowly habits become interfused as the country becomes more closely woven together. Buenos Aires still looks out on the seven seas, as it will always do. Into it have poured millions of new immigrants; into it have come new languages, new ideas, new gadgets of civilization; but now, what Buenos Aires gains and learns flows more easily out over the pampas. The latest cowboy songs, shouted at the fiesta, to the thrum of guitar and the pacing of dancing feet about the sizzling barbecue, now tell of the ruthlessness of Hitler, of the good cousins to the north; and into Buenos Aires in turn come the song and dances of the gaucho world to be built up into sophistication, as was the tango — folded into a dress suit and sent out over the world.

Now, out to the pampas go the great reapers and electric motors and farm machinery; new rolling mills turn out steel; new meat canneries creep out toward the great herds; textile mills move on to Rosario and Santa Fé and San Luis; settlers tame new regions where a few years ago the herds ran wild or the jungle encroached. Slowly but surely the omnipotent power of the cattle king gives way to newer needs and the claims of national greatness. The old duality that brought only conflict and blood and tears now fructifies the life of a great modern nation, building itself, even in a world at war, into strength and prosperity.

Newer conflicts are engendered. Argentina, today, is ruled by a combination of capitalist entrepreneurs and great cattle barons, set off against the people, the small farming class, the vintners, the coffee and cotton growers. The monopolization of vast acres holds much of the country in an economic vice. It is a struggle of democracy against the peculiar ruling combination of industry and rural feudalism — a structure similar to that in our own south. On the outcome of that struggle — and the Argentine people are now very submerged — will depend whether Argentina remains frozen in a backward pattern, unable to meet the challenge of the modern world, unable to maintain its present economic superiority over all the rest of Latin America, or whether it opens its arms to new progress, new economic strength, and achieves a moral leadership it is rapidly losing.

CHAPTER XXV

Proud Argentina

SOMETIME prior to the war, as a gesture of good-will, President Roosevelt directed the Navy to purchase Argentina corned beef in preference to the domestic product. Instead of appeasing Argentina, this merely concentrated more resentment in the form of strong political opposition to the United States because of our general policy toward her leading national product, beef. In effect President Roosevelt's order was that of a carpenter ordering a half-dozen nails from a wholesale hardware house. The insignificant amount we then wanted to buy meant nothing to Argentine economy; it quite failed to face the long-standing cause of Argentina's resentment toward the United States.

Moreover, whatever good-will there was behind our order was canceled when vociferous American cattle interests shouted from one end of the country to the other. Argentineans asked themselves what likelihood there would be of a normal, full-sized beef trade with the United States if such a mighty clamor arose when we ordered a virtual thimbleful — and then only because we had hardly enough of the domestic product to supply our own needs. As though to underline our feeling on this question, we refused to allow Argentina even to include displays of chilled beef at her exhibits in the San Francisco and New York Fairs. That was like inviting a peacock to a beauty show and ordering him to leave his tail feathers home.

Technically, we exclude Argentine chilled meat on 'hygienic' grounds; we want to guard against the possible spread of the hoof-and-mouth disease. Actually only at certain past periods has the hoof-and-mouth disease widely threatened Argentine cattle; even then, not the whole country. Our attitude has been as though England were forever to refuse to buy American meat because the hoof-and-mouth disease had once hit Oklahoma. Argentina has repeatedly offered to submit her beef to as strict medical examination as we might require; on the ground, if we so desire. Actually, of course, we merely wish to protect the home growers against competition from abroad. Argentina argues quite justly that our ban is hypocritical and unfair. In addition, it violates one of the sacred Pan-American agreements, signed at Lima, that the various nations would impose no trade barriers other than tariffs. Nevertheless, our ban continues — an obstacle, then, to Secretary of State Hull's trade-reciprocity program; now, to Argentine cooperation in the war effort.

Argentineans never took the ban lightly. 'We'll run our last year's cars and trucks down to the rims before we'll buy American,' a prominent Argentinian cattle-breeder threatened. 'We'll buy our new cars in Europe,' was another familiar cry.

Nor were these empty threats. Prior to the war America's automobile business in Argentina dropped off thirty per cent. And while American motor-car manufacturers wrinkled their brows over these figures, German and British automobile officials gleefully planned to convert our loss into their gain. Now, since we have temporarily destroyed our automobile industry, and we don't want to export anything to anybody except for war purposes, it matters little — but it may matter greatly sometime in the future.

America's unpopularity in Argentina has long been widespread. For Argentina — quite aside from her resentment over trade policies — is suspicious and even jealous of the United States. Desperately anxious to maintain her position as the leading nation of South America, she looks askance at any help or manifestations of friendliness by the United States toward Chile or Brazil. When in 1939 the United States completed arrangements under which Brazil would receive a substantial loan and military equipment, Argentineans shouted to high heaven. Officially, the Argentine reaction to our assistance to Brazil took the form of sweeping new import restrictions against American goods — and of new barter arrangements with the totalitarian powers. The fine hand of Argentina was also seen by many experts in the confiscation of Standard Oil properties by Bolivia.

There are other factors, some of them largely psychological. More than any other nation in South America, Argentina — like the United States — has a population largely European in origin. Argentina's climate also is much like ours. The combination has helped develop a country in many respects similar to our own. Her railways, schools, industrial organization, press, even her habits, show advanced development.

In all this progress, Argentineans have taken great pride, a nationalism intensified by the up-to-now condescending attitude of the United States, with whom Argentina considers herself on a par. Our exclusion of her leading export on false sanitary grounds is a blow to her dignity which she has never intended to take without retaliation.

It was not surprising, therefore, to find that the United States, in tense pre-war days, became the favorite football of keenly nationalistic organizations in Argentina and even of the lunatic fringes. The Nationalistic Youth Alliance and the Spanish Phalanx, both Fascist organizations — whenever the ban against demonstrations connected with foreign affairs grew a bit lax — paraded and demonstrated against the United States. Placards were posted to emphasize the contention that our good-neighbor aims were a blind for ulterior purposes, that our real intention was to foist a 'Jewish-Protestant plutocratic' rule on all South America.

2

But even were we to open our markets to Argentine beef, our professions of good-will would still sound hollow to many Argentineans. We don't want Argentina's wheat, wool, cotton, corn, fruit, rice, peanuts, sugar, apples, or grapes. We don't want them, because we either have them already or have commitments to get them from other nations. Will Rogers once remarked that Argentina exported to us wheat and gigolos, that we received too little of the former, too many of the latter. But with our north-central granaries bursting with several years' supply of wheat and no place properly to store the 1943 surplus, we can far better accept the gigolos than we can accept almost any of Argentina's major products.

Argentina does have a number of minor products, however, which the United States could use to advantage: linseed, vegetable oils, tannin, furs, tin, wolfram, and vanadium. Previously we lacked the ability of the totalitarian powers to direct purchases abroad, and the United States could only hope that our importers would buy enough of these minor commodities to make up for the major commodities we do not buy, and thus create trade parity. Now, of course, when our foreign trade is as controlled as by the commissars in Russia, it is possible to favor any country outside the circle of Japanese and German conquests that Washington chooses to favor or to put the economic spurs into any country it wishes to influence.

At the moment when this might have altered the economic relations with Argentina, it is being used rather to harass that neutral land as much as possible. And yet so great has been America's need for raw materials that trade trends have overridden this shortsighted, petty, and hostile bureaucratic attitude. In 1941 we took 37 per cent of Argentina's exports as opposed to 18 per cent in 1940 and 7 per cent a few years earlier. Of course, much of the increase percentage is due to the falling off of Argentine totals owing to loss of European and Asiatic markets, and it is likely that the 1942 figures will show a very definite setback.

Previously, in invoking the plea of our self-sufficiency as an excuse for not buying Argentina's leading goods, we could hardly expect that Argentina would not use the same argument against us. Thus, of late, her oil, iron, steel, building, lumber, cotton, sugar, textile, and shoe industries have received ever-increasing government aid in their development. Argentina has even taken to the manufacture of railway locomotives and ammunition for the British Isles. Industry is to be diversified, imports controlled ever more. This has rapidly increased the pace of this trend.

Previously the totalitarians capitalized on difficulties between Argentina and the United States and are still doing so. Earlier, Germany completed barter arrangements with Argentina and adjacent countries and accompanied her political and economic 'missionary' work with a propaganda campaign. A great many Argentineans soon showed worry over the German threat. Nazi agents were placed on trial in Buenos Aires on charges of attempted arson of non-Nazi papers, and of violence and property destruction. At one time Argentine Nazi groups were said to be plotting an armed filibuster into Chilean Patagonia. Chilean Nazis and Spanish Falangists, working on a similar Putsch from the other side of the Andes, issued posters declaring the whole of Patagonia had been stolen from Chile, and that 'the liberating Falanx will free Chilean Patagonia from the Argentine yoke.'

The charge that the Germans were planning to take over Patagonia was in the air a long time. It became concrete when Heinrich Jurges, a German émigré whose wife had been sent to a Nazi concentration camp, produced documents in the liberal press. The storm was so great the government had to act. Alfred Mueller, the local German Fuehrer, was arrested amid protestations by the German Embassy that the documents were false.

In the end, the federal prosecutor released Mueller, stating that the evidence was 'insufficient to warrant prosecution,' and strongly recommended the punishment of Jurges for perjury. The Ortiz Government, moreover, apologized to Germany.

From the first the Ortiz Government either took little stock in the charges or did not want them aired. It made repeated assurances to Germany that the investigation and any limitations that might be placed on local organizations in no way affected Argentina's friendly feelings toward the Reich and had no bearing on existing trade agreements.

Even today numerous Nazi and Fascist organizations, both foreign and native, continue to flourish, and *El Pampero*, a Nazi-subsidized daily, openly attacks the United States.

3

Nazi efforts to embroil Chile and Argentina ran counter to Argentina's efforts the last few years to build up a set of alliances against Brazil. Argentine capital, inextricably mixed with that of England and Italy, later with that of Germany, has penetrated

Uruguay, Paraguay, and Bolivia, long satellite nations, constituting a 'Caribbean area.' Argentina has her own 'imperialism,' a definite policy of economic pentration and political tutelage in adjacent countries. She has watched carefully Brazil's efforts to exercise similar economic and political influence in those countries; she has observed bitterly the expansion of American capital in Brazil; the increasing aid we were giving to the latter country even before the war; the enormous aid we are now giving.

Brazil certainly has made successful economic counter-raids upon Uruguay and Paraguay, and has been striking toward Bolivia with roads, railroads, and new plane services. Argentina feels herself encircled; so does Brazil.

In this tug of war, Chile has occupied a peculiar position. Chile and Brazil, both fearing aggression by Argentina, the big-navy country, until recently the best armed and boasting the biggest array of war planes, were long close allies. Only a few years ago, border clashes occurred between Brazil and Argentina, also between Chile and Argentina. When landslides occurred on the trans-Andean railroad, Chile, to discourage any possible attack, delayed repairing the damage. Chile had spy jitters, arrested Argentineans, even forced a high diplomatic personage to leave the country under suspicion of such activities. Brazil's efforts were also directed toward bringing Bolivia into the Chilean-Brazilian alliance.

Argentina strove desperately to combat all this petty power politics, and her success before the war in gaining the economic and political upper hand in Bolivia may partly explain Brazil's eagerness to turn toward the United States for loans and armaments. Argentina also made closer connections with Perú, and strove to break Chile away from her alliance with Brazil. A long-smouldering boundary dispute with Chile was arbitrated in friendly fashion. New trade treaties were made. Soon after, the rise of the Chilean Popular Front government cracked intimate ties with dictatorial and totalitarian Brazil. Not only has repair work on the trans-Andean road been pushed, but a new line is now being driven through the Andes. Until January, 1943, Chile and Argentina, closely allied, stood apart from the continental war attitude.

Brazil, cut off from the Chilean alliance, frustrated considerably in Bolivia, frantically rushed armaments to match those of Argentina, an activity which we, the Germans, and the Italians helped to promote, but which, now that Brazil has gone to war against the Axis, must somewhat chagrin the latter for all its long and, for a while, apparently successful efforts to win over Vargas.

And so before the war South American power politics cut across the whole pattern of the American good-will policy. It is only partly in abeyance, and helps explain the present war alignments even though war has now put most of the southern countries in the same boat, and has brought about new rapprochements. But jealous though Argentina may be of both Brazil and the United States, now, because of the lack of shipping, she has had to turn more and more back to us and to Brazil for goods and markets. With Brazil she has concluded ever more liberal trade agreements.

Last year the growth of commerce between the two countries — coal, wheat, textiles, leather goods, shoes, etc. — was literally phenomenal. Argentina exports to Brazil and other neighbor countries increased 22 per cent; imports 41 per cent. The two countries, one temperate, the other tropical, are naturally interdependent, as are Brazil and the United States, and this interdependency should redound to the greater prosperity and friendship of both, if, in the future, they can be persuaded to abandon futile local power politics in servile imitation of European models, jealousy over leadership, and competitive armaments.

With the entry of Brazil into the war and Argentina's confirmed neutrality, new rifts have appeared. The invitation of Brazil to ex-President Justo, who aspired to return to power and who was an open enemy of the existing Argentine administration, 'to fight the Axis in Brazilian ranks' had little to do, actually, with the war against the Axis but was a direct slap at President Castillo of Argentina. According to the *New York Times*, Justo was received with great *éclat* in a public demonstration by Vargas and Ambassador Jefferson Caffery. Although Justo, when in power, was very anti-American, in order to get back into control of his country he espoused the United Nations cause strongly and became the white hope for overthrowing the present régime and bringing Argentina in on the American side. His sudden death early in 1943 eliminated the one strong contendant against the Argentine neutrality policy.

4

The election of President Ortiz in 1936 seemed to promise a new deal in Argentine-American relations, and led to a brief interlude of back-slapping. Former President Irigoyen, for almost a generation the political boss of the country, had always been anti-American. His successor, the blood-soaked Uriburú, who seized power by armed *coup*, was briefly more amenable, but soon turned against us, and even promoted Brown-Shirt movements. President Justo, the next Executive, leaned heavily on these and similar Fascist elements, and prevented all other factions from exercising democratic rights. Only toward the end of his period of bloody repression did he seem to look with more friendly eyes on the United States.

Ortiz, who promised to restore civil liberties and in good part did so, seemed a perfect choice from the viewpoint of American diplomacy. Known to be a capable administrator in previous high government posts, he had, as Minister of Finance, reduced Argentina's debt (to the delight of long-despairing American bondholders), had improved and beautified Buenos Aires, and had so expanded and modernized port facilities that, by comparison, New York's harbor facilities were an old-fashioned junk heap. A self-made millionaire, he was closely tied up with various British, American, and Italian business interests.

And so, six United States super-bombers flew down magnificently in record time to welcome him into the presidency. Soon after, eight American army aviators became instructors to the Argentine air force. Sure enough, the onerous trade-quota system was abandoned, and though exchange restrictions still forced our merchants to pay a twenty per cent premium over nearly all other countries, our exports to Argentina crept up and up, finally outdistancing even those of Great Britain. New roadbuilding created demand for American automobiles and trucks. Ortiz' nationalistic program of creating diversified industries, for the

time being, called for the importation of more American machinery.

Brazil now found the shoe of friendship on the wrong foot —
for some time that country had been looking doubtfully at our
growing friendship with her rival, and resentfully coquetted with
Germany. Then, when we swung back to Brazil, Ortiz cooled
off toward us. Thus the two jealous South American rivals have
long made a difficult team for the paternalistic good-will policy
of the United States to drive in tandem.

In Brazil resentment at our cordiality toward Argentina, plus
surplus cotton, plus a very active German colony, plus fine transatlantic steamship and air service, had drawn the country constantly closer to Germany, whose doctrines of government were
in any case more agreeable to Dictator Vargas than were our own.

The situation was growing serious, for German trade had out-
distanced ours; German air lines were weaving a brown pattern
over the whole country. The State Department hurried down
clever Jefferson Caffery to Brazil to outwit the Nazis. Successive
offers of loans, battleships, trade assistance; army, navy, and
aviation experts; gifts of quinine seedlings, promises to buy
Brazilian rubber, numerous and ceaseless gestures of military
strength and friendship, presently gained us more nearly equal
rights in Brazil with the totalitarian powers, presently turned
Vargas, cautiously at first, against the Nazis, presently carried
the dictator into war on the side of the United States.

But Argentina's cordial sentiments toward us then froze up
correspondingly step by step. Soon she was sending us a sharp
protest against our efforts to dispose of our subsidized surplus
wheat in the Brazilian market. All Argentina's feelings of wariness toward us revived. She heeded a British warning that she
would lose her best market unless she bought more goods from
the Empire; she gave ear to the Nazis; and so, even before the
Lima conference of American nations, Argentina had announced
— though she there signed a promise to the contrary — that she
would restore the quota system so distasteful to us. It was resumed eight days after the ink was dry on her Lima pledge not
to put up any new barrier of this nature against our trade and to
reduce any already in existence. But then, neither did we live up

to the Lima pledge. Our 'sanitary' embargo on Argentine meat was not revoked and still stands.

With the sickness of President Ortiz, the reins of power increasingly fell into the hands of Vice-President Ramón S. Castillo, strongly conservative, nationalistic, and anti-American. Presently Ortiz had to resign; presently he died. Castillo has taken ever stronger measures to prevent all popular demonstrations in favor of the United States. In accord with a Pan-American proviso to curb outside propaganda, he first utilized the new measure to suppress a Roosevelt radio broadcast at a public pro-United Nations assemblage. All discussion of the war is forbidden in the press, and even debates of Congress with regard to Argentina's international attitude may not be reproduced in periodicals.

The United States has brought ever-increasing pressure on Argentina to break with the Axis. She has been cut off from many needed supplies, prohibited from purchasing armaments, denied priorities, denied shipping; American meat purchases have been given to Great Britain to handle to force Argentina into line on prices. Argentina has been very hard hit economically. Her meat and wheat have piled up in storage. In the last war, Germany was really blockaded and the Allies were feeding most of Europe. Today the European market for foodstuffs is practically cut off. To piece out, Argentina has made barter deals with Spain, by which she will get naval vessels; she has promoted trade with the most of Latin America in an able manner; and for certain raw materials — especially rubber — she is outbidding the United States.

5

Argentina's high agricultural development, her great wealth, place her at the head of all other independent American nations except the United States. Greater Buenos Aires is now larger than Chicago, and one of the most beautiful of cities. Argentina has the best and largest public-school system in Latin America. She is the only South American country with an authentic theater. Her writers merit international attention. She has pro-

duced some of the world's leading authorities in jurisprudence
and international law. Argentine painters, if mostly unknown in
New York, have long been hailed in Paris. Musical attainments
are considerable, the gaucho melodies providing an inexhaustible
source of folk music. Argentine film production increased more
than a hundred per cent in 1938. Buenos Aires has seventy daily
newspapers — some with millions of circulation — and seven
hundred and thirty-five periodicals in all. Argentina's spirit is
cosmopolitan, her outlook wide, her international contacts numerous, and her pride too great to permit her to depend for leadership on the United States or any other country.

In late years, however, a shadow of doubt has spread over the
country. The depression hit Argentina hard. She came to realize
just how dependent she was on foreign markets and on world
prices she could not control. She saw that her purely agricultural
rôle was hazardous. World competition in her products was
getting constantly keener.

The result was a nationalistic determination to achieve greater
economic independence. This also explained her increasing
interest in Bolivia, where she has secured amazing railway, oil,
and agricultural concessions, for in many ways Bolivia's economy,
like that of Brazil, supplements that of Argentina. Particularly
it meets the latter's lack of certain mineral and tropical resources.
Argentina's program of economic nationalism, her moves to take
over foreign-owned railways and oil concerns, her nationalization
of the great stock-growing and meat industry to benefit Argentine growers rather than the foreign-owned packing companies,
her determination to control foreign trade exclusively in her own
interest, her manipulation of international relations with a care-
ful eye on Brazil and the United States, her determination not
to cut off her contacts with Europe and the Orient — many
of these developments should not have been taken as antagonism
toward the United States or any other foreign land, but merely
as an indication that Argentina was more than ever proud of her
own heritage, determined not to accept outside paternalism,
and assured that she could take her place among nations as an
equal, not as a semi-colonial appendage.

But now in wartime, the differences between Argentina and the

United States have led to new moves by Argentina in South America that, from our viewpoint, are extremely irritating. These are partly against us, but even more are a desperate effort to extract herself from her difficult existing economic situation. Thus in all markets, Argentina is bidding sixty cents a pound and up for rubber as against our contract arrangements for forty-five cents a pound; and naturally, Argentina is getting rubber. In October, 1942, she scored a *coup* in Bolivia — where we had made great promises of loans and funds, but with secret provisos, exceedingly distasteful to Bolivia. Argentina stepped in and granted Bolivia urgently needed assistance for oil and railway development. The machinery and supplies, unobtainable from the United States, are being secured from England in return for ammunitions production.

It is indeed unfortunate for us that Argentina's proud attitude and our own failure to cooperate have led the two strongest nations of the Western Hemisphere into covert antagonism, that it has isolated Argentina from the New World concert of nations. It is unfortunate that at a time like this it should have led to any international scheme to overthrow the present Argentine government, for that would have proved merely a boomerang, something never to be pardoned by the Argentine people, and in the long run frightening to all Latin America. All this is even less unfortunate from a war standpoint than it is for the future development of continental economics, good neighborliness, and solidarity.

Certainly this is no time for petty speeches of recrimination, petty harassments, bickering, and secret plots. It is a time for more than usual broad statesmanship. Perhaps another Morrow is needed — though his task would be greater than that in México — but a Morrow who would not seek to alter Argentina's domestic régime and policies; who would be able to cut across the tangle of blundering on both sides, and to find a solution that would recognize Argentina's national dignity and freedom from improper coercion, which would reach a commercial agreement for both the war and post-war periods, on meat, wheat, shipping, and needed supplies. This would provide a lasting basis on which to complete and round out the good-neighbor policy.

6

The *New York Times* for January 26, 1942, contained a front-page article by Charles E. Egan in which he reported that American importers and exporters urged a boycott of Argentina to force it to break with the Axis. The piece was pretty obviously a State Department trial balloon, and it was subsequently refuted by leading business men engaged in Argentine operations. But this, unfortunately, was not the first proposal from varied sources that harsh punitive tactics be used against Argentina by the American Government; and indeed a number of very Fascistic and aggressive acts, which need not be enumerated here, have already been perpetrated against Argentina.

If some acts by Argentina seem to us in our present passionate mood almost unfriendly, we should not forget that Argentina has her own rights, her own needs, and has also made numerous wartime concessions to us. The United States is not treated as a belligerent, which means that although Argentina is theoretically neutral, she gives us favors which are not granted to the Axis. She has lightened many previous trade restrictions to favor us, and various American military missions have been hospitably received there.

Any attempt to browbeat Argentina would be Hitleristic and a colossal blunder. Naturally war itself is force, and its favorable outcome depends primarily on the use of force. But it is sometimes forgotten that friendship or enmity, the nature of international relations, economic facts, and national psychology are tangibles which influence the outcome of battles. To substitute coercion for other methods is sometimes a mistake. Perhaps by means of our superior economic power and our control of the seas, we might force the present administration in Argentina into taking the warlike steps that we desire, but such action might be a gun with too powerful a kickback. The Argentineans are a proud people, and they and their government would be unified in bitter resentment. Certainly, in any case, we should not have won a voluntary ally any more than Hitler has won a voluntary ally in the case of Bulgaria. Very likely we should get merely a nominal status, no open cooperation, and perhaps even secret trouble. In fact folded arms and the placing of hidden obstacles owing to such resentment might offset all the advantage gained. We should harvest ill-will for the future.

Third, to use overt coercion would rupture the spirit of Pan-American solidarity. It may be argued that Argentina has ruptured that solidarity and should be punished for following a more independent course. But in recent years we have attempted to make Pan-Americanism a symbol and an actuality of international cooperation of voluntary association. Many things, above all shortsightedness in economic matters, may possibly be checked up against the manner in which Pan-Americanism has operated, but whatever its defects it is today the brightest example of union among a large body of sovereign nations, and the steps taken to bring this about may well serve as guidance in the attempt to re-establish political stability in the world after the war. For us to depart from the spirit of continental cooperation, although we may feel that Argentina has done so, would be, it seems to me, a grave mistake. Even friendly Latin-American nations, who now condemn Argentina's present position, would fear, as of old, that they had no security for their internal decisions and mode of life unless they conformed slavishly to the needs of the United States. Such a change of policy on our part should be taken only with deep trepidation and as a very last resort.

To attempt to browbeat another, friendly republic would be in open violation of repeated declarations by our leaders that Pan-Americanism as now constituted rests upon non-interference in the domestic affairs of our neighbors. Sumner Welles has categorically stated that whoever wounds that basic principle is endangering the whole structure of continental relations.

I fear that in this clamor, that we, a powerful nation, browbeat Argentina into the conduct we desire, is quite a little of the stupidity that featured the tactics of George III and his clique against the American Colonies so long ago. It was Burke who at that time pointed out that the true course was conciliation. If conciliation fails one can always use force, but the converse is not true.

Some have gone so far as to call Argentina pro-Nazi and to

argue that to placate her in any way would be merely another disgusting example of appeasement. But the application of justice, understanding, and economic fair play is never appeasement. Appeasement is giving the bully and the thief a deed of title to ill-gotten gains or the possessions of others not your own. Argentina has stolen nothing, has committed no aggression, and is merely anxious for her security and prosperity.

Have we attempted to cooperate with Argentina in any fundamental sense? Have we attempted to find out what her interests are and how they may be safeguarded in war and in peace? Or do we merely want her to conform to our immediate requirements regardless of the effect upon her economy and her future? Perhaps we should make every possible attempt at cooperation before we utilize punitive methods.

We blithely refuse to face the economic fact that Argentina is a competitor of the United States in nearly all her important products on which her national prosperity depends. Chief of these are wheat, corn, hides, and meat. Many of Argentina's major markets have been cut off by the war, and in the markets remaining, measures have been taken to force Argentina to sell products needed, especially meat, at the terms we dictate.

It would seem that the present time is most favorable to guarantee to Argentina a proper outlet for such products, both during the war and for a considerable period after. With the rigid production and price controls that now exist in this country, with full control over distribution to all the United Nations, the element of competition for our products no longer exists. Cost of production, supply and demand, automatic price levels — all the usual play of forces has been wiped out by wartime controls.

What Argentina fears, perhaps more than the terrific economic pinch she is now suffering, is the post-war period. With present plans of the Washington New Dealers to establish a milk route at every jungle crossroads of the world, this will mean that we shall have, through post-war lend-lease methods, through our control over the rehabilitation of Europe and Asia, an assured outlet for all our farm products, which will squeeze Argentina far worse than now. We shall supply the world, and if we take any products from Argentina, it will be at the terms we dictate.

I have recently queried some three hundred Argentine intellectuals, and I find that these are real fears. Argentina wishes guarantees that will safeguard her future. We have been unwilling or too shortsighted to meet this problem.

A brilliant stroke could be made by making Argentina a partner in our war enterprise and in our rehabilitation projects. The basic economic principle at the root of the efforts of the United Nations is the pooling of resources. It should not be difficult to ascertain, on the basis of Argentina's normal production, over a period of years, the minimum share that her products, in any pooling arrangement, should have; the same holds true for a long post-war period. In other words, if we honestly took Argentina into national partnership, we might not even have to ask her to join more fully in the war effort.

Another matter might also be worked out: that of the Falkland Islands. These should pass under Argentine sovereignty, where they rightfully belong; and this would push ahead another step the policy of 'America for the Americas.' To transfer the long-claimed islands to Argentine's control as part of the rectification needed for her to come whole-heartedly to the support of the cause of the United Nations would not restrict their use in war-time by the United Nations, and after the war, the bases there, it could be stipulated, should become Pan-American bases, thus furthering the eventual solidarity of the Americas.

Of course, eventually the artificial war-controls and the post-war controls will break down unless they are in accord with economic realities. The competition of Argentina's products would then reassert itself. But this need not be a barrier to continued solidarity. For if the standard of living of the tropical Americas is in the meantime raised to levels similar to our own through the proper development of new industries, then more than enough purchasing power will be created to absorb Argentina's temperate-zone food products.

Efforts along these various lines will be far more productive of genuine Argentine support, will have a more sterling effect on the war effort, will promote our ideals of democratic methods, will put Pan-Americanism on a more worthy and durable footing, will offer more hope for the future in every way, than merely

resorting to hobnailed methods which have at least the outward aspect of those we are accustomed to see used by the totalitarian war lords. No one is more unhappy than I am over Argentina's absence from the united American front, but I would rather
see her absent than that any of our international methods should
wear the ugly garb that makes our enemies such a good target for
decent minds.

Whenever we are prepared to get together with Argentina,
not merely on the basis of what we want her to do, but in an
attitude of fair play, with serious consideration for her problems,
and to put into effect a joint economic program, we shall not have
to worry very much about her attitude. If, furthermore, we
carry on a program throughout Latin America on the economic
front which will make possible the general raising of Latin-
American living standards to civilized levels, we shall scarcely
have to worry about any country's absenting itself from a common front in the Americas. This, certainly, is the logical development for the good-neighbor policy, and the direction it is
already beginning to take. Already that policy has brought us
many benefits at a time of great need.

CHAPTER XXVI

What Does Latin America
Expect from the War?

SEVENTY-FIVE outstanding intellectual leaders of Latin America have written me their opinions on what their respective countries and Latin America hope to accomplish as a result of the war. Specifically they were requested to state what they believed Latin America's rôle should be in the future peace conferences for establishing a workable post-war pattern.

Four of those replying, among them the Bolivian journalist Fernando Díez de Medina, and Alejandro Córdova, director of *El Imparcial*, the leading Guatemalan daily, thought the question premature. First, win the war, said Dardo Régules, the Uruguayan lawyer, professor, and education expert. Four answers stressed the desirability that all Latin America should act as a common unit in the conferences; quite a number felt that this united action should also embrace the United States, as for instance, J. E. Lefevre, former Foreign Minister of Panamá. A few felt that this common action with the United States should be undertaken only on condition that none of the Latin-American countries would be considered as 'inferior satellites.' Several Cubans, among them the essayist Juan J. Remos, felt that their country should act in full cooperation with the United States regardless of the attitude of other Latin-American countries. The Cuban historian, Elías Entrealgo, declares that his country should demand a place in the conference 'more respectable and useful than it occupied at Versailles'; or, as another writer and diplomat, Antonio Iraizoz y del Villar, puts it, 'more than a chorus, as at Versailles.' The Salvadorean lawyer and ex-presidential candidate, Enrique Córdova, remarks that the Great Powers will impose the peace, but 'if it has been pleasant for the United States and England to have Latin America with them in the struggle, they must not commit the discourtesy of not remembering it when the bases to preserve the peace and harmony of the world are established.' 'To exclude Latin America from the peace conferences would be to place her in everlasting slavery,' writes the Peruvian-American educator, Victor Cano.

One correspondent believes that only the democratic New World nations should have a vote in the final proceedings. A number, including Raul Maestri, Assistant Director of the *Diario de la Marina*, the oldest daily still published on the American continent, believes that participation should be in accordance with the promptness with which the various countries identified themselves with the efforts of the United States and the degree of sacrifice of each, as well as the importance of their position — in the case of Cuba, that of the leading or 'metropoliton' state of the Antillean world.

The prominent Peruvian feminist and author, Magda Portal, now in exile in Chile, believes that to prevent a repetition of the present 'horrible experience' and the 'errors of Versailles,' the peace negotiations should be conducted by 'not merely the politicians, rulers, and financiers, but also intellectuals, teachers, and other free individuals who have carried out some labor for progress and culture.' The one hundred and thirty million people of Latin America, she remarks, must have a leading place in the negotiations, but for this to be effective 'there must first be a sincere and profound reform of democracy in those countries now professing it.' 'Don't repeat the errors of Versailles,' says Doctor Manuel Castro Ramírez, former head of the Central American Court of Justice.

Various answers emphasize that Latin America's participation should be restricted to purely continental questions. For the most part those replying showed little or no interest in Europe or world problems. Nearly all were chiefly concerned about the future status of their own countries and of the Americas. The opinions revealed rather sharply that the people south — always said to be for the most part culturally and economically closer to Europe than to the United States — are pretty definitely thinking in terms of the Western Hemisphere; that above all else, their interest lies in clarifying and improving the future relations between Latin America and our own country. Nearly all now realize that their destinies, for better or worse, are closely linked with ours.

But an outstanding Uruguayan poet, Gastón Figueira, who has published at least eighteen volumes, writes that since Latin America is such a melting-pot of all races, 'nothing in the world is or can be alien to us.'

Of the twenty-two persons concerned primarily with European or world conditions, five — among them the famous international Haitian jurist, Dantes Bellegarde, and that excellent novelist, now Mexican Ambassador to Cuba, José Rubén Romero, believe that the Atlantic Charter is the perfect guide to future world peace, or, as a sixth, Ignacio Mariño Arizo, former Colombian Consul-General in New York, puts it, 'the reality of the Rooseveltian ideal.' Bellegarde also stressed provisions of the declarations of the representatives of the United Nations. 'Defense of a general democratic thesis,' writes the Mexican archeologist, Enrique Juan Palacios. 'Consolidate democracy and liberty,' writes Cuban Senator Demetrio P. Santovenia.

Doctor Alejandro Alvarado Quirós, Rector of the University of Costa Rica, fears that the peace conferences may fall into the hands of men made military-minded by the war, but is hopeful that 'our independence and democratic habits and our wealth will be an efficacious contribution to the equilibrium of the Old World.' Quite a number, among them the famous Peruvian feminist and folklorist, Dora Mayer de Zulén, feel that Latin America can contribute a spirit of 'fairness and equanimity' impossible in those countries that have borne the direct brunt of the struggle. A similar belief is expressed by Cayetano Betancur, Colombian lawyer, economist, and philosopher, with many published works to his credit.

One correspondent feels that the Americas are the central continents of the world, the tie-up of East and West, North and South, a sort of geographical cross, and that therefore it must be

America's rôle to crucify itself for the good of all humanity. Doctor Alberto Demicheli, Uruguayan aviator, former head of the cabinet, and the author of numerous works on jurisprudence and government, shares this view. Since the New World has inherited the benefits of the westward march of civilization, it must now be 'one and indivisible in the permanent service of mankind and peace.'

'A united America can form a front able to dictate sensible and just conditions to the rest of the world,' writes the Peruvian painter, F. Cossío del Pomar. And Mauricio Razzetti, a Colombian journalist, says that the Americas are 'called to maintain the peace of the world.'

The Mexican musician, Antonio Gomezanda, believes that to establish a proper basis for a just peace, the first necessary step must be 'to aid and reanimate the victims of the war (orphans, widows, crippled, etc.), without distinction of races, religions, or political creeds.' Enrique Córdova of Salvador quotes the Cuban liberator Martí: 'America must promote all that brings nations nearer together and abhor all that separates them.'

One correspondent wishes the enemies of democracy disarmed. An Ecuadorean painter of international note, Germania P. de Breilh, desires that in the political and economic reconstruction of the peoples, 'firm bases be established to prevent the rebirth of the enemy and the creation of another conflagration.' An Ecuadorean of German-Jewish extraction wishes to exterminate all Germans. 'Chastise the Axis with a hand of iron,' writes the Colombian poet, Ciro Mendía, who is a fervent admirer of Archibald MacLeish.

Three persons, among them the outstanding Cuban jurist, Cosme de la Torriente, and Justo Prieto, former Rector of the University of Asunción, former Minister of Education in Paraguay, but now in forced exile in Argentina, desire a new and better League of Nations, but it is fairly obvious that this idea is distasteful to nearly all the others.

World peace should be the aim, writes Carlos García Prada, editor of the *Revista Ibero Americana*, but as this will be achieved only in the remote future, the immediate goal should be to create three great political economic zones: (*a*) Europe and Africa, (*b*)

Asia, (c) America, on the basis of historic divisions, each to follow its own destiny. It shall then be the rôle of the Americas to reconcile world interests in behalf of all humanity.

Uldarico Urrutia, a prominent Colombian author and member of the Catholic Society of Jesus, lays down a five-point program antagonistic to communism, totalitarianism, the abuses of capitalism, the Hegelian state, the Rousseauan social pact, but favoring a just equilibrium between individualism and collectivism, a purified League of Nations, an evangelic crusade for the principles of Christ, and the re-establishment of the solidarity of Christian peoples, reunited under the authority of or at least the moral influence of the Pope.

One Mexican writer, among others, called for a planned world economy. Other suggestions are for 'a better international law,' 'freedom of the seas and of commerce,' 'the lowest possible customs barriers,' 'proper economic opportunity for all peoples.' 'Give to all peoples the right to live and the elements for labor that there shall be no pretexts for future calamities,' writes the Mexican engineer and astronomer, Joaquín Gallo.

Only one writer, an Ecuadorean novelist, is concerned with the liberation of India. Another correspondent feels that all peoples now under imperial tutelage should be freed. A Chilean physician favors the freeing of the three American Guianas.

The majority of answers were concerned mainly with perfecting Western Hemisphere solidarity and New World conditions. 'The ideal for which the Americas should fight in the conference,' writes the Ecuadorean dramatist and novelist, Humberto Salvador, 'should be to implant a régime of authentic and real economic justice.' If that is done, 'the future of the Americas will be truly glorious. They will perhaps represent the future of Humanity.'

Most replies stressed the need for greater continental solidarity. As Octavio Méndez Pereira, founder of the University of Panamá, puts it, 'Let the good-neighbor policy become permanently embodied in the foreign policy of the United States, and Pan-Americanism after this second world war be a union grounded on juridical equality and on the independence and democracy of the member nations, all acting collectively for peace and progress.'

The Ecuadorean lawyer, Olmedo del Pozo D., editor and mem-

ber of the Department of Agriculture, would have the Americas
act as 'one and indivisible,' a common front of peoples based on
economic cooperation and political solidarity. Their effort should
be to give 'to each people that which rightfully belongs to it,
recognizing its inalienable and unabridgeable rights, seeing to it
that imperialisms have no place in America.'

A number suggested that long-pending Pan-American agreements, some dating back to the first conference in the eighties, be
adopted and put into effect. Doctor Fermín Peraza, the eminent
Cuban bibliographer, feels that the peace conferences will provide
the opportunity to implant 'a true American policy' and 'to face
the various problems that have kept a large part of American
territory isolated from progress.' The conferences must contribute 'to the American utopia,' writes Felix Lizaso, Cuban
essayist. Latin America 'should be the least insistent upon material compensations; the most insistent upon everything that
refers to a secure peace and the survival of the ideals of America,'
writes Agustín Basave y del Castillo, the Mexican architect
who constructed México's most model prison. This sentiment is
also held by Mariano Azuela, the dean of Mexican novelists.

Four correspondents favored a New World confederation of
nations; one reply favored it on the basis of annual democratic
congresses. One of the strongest backers of this idea of an American League was Peruvian painter F. Cossío del Pomar; and
Manuel Toussaint, Rector of the National University of México,
calls such an organization 'an overriding necessity.' Clodomiro
Picado Twight, the Costa Rican zoologist and writer, desires a
separate confederation of México with the whole Caribbean area,
this to follow the imperial scheme of Emperor Iturbide, except
that it should see the elimination of all dictatorships and be on a
socialistic basis. Still another writer, from México, suggests a
number of regional confederations on the two continents, to be
based on common economic interests, in order better to balance
the strength of the United States in future negotiations.

Quite a few argued for the improvement of democracy and for
an end of Latin-American dictatorships. One went so far as to
propose joint intervention by the democratic members of the
continent to impose democracy on the others. 'Rid the insides

of Latin America of the factors that upset it,' writes the former Bolivian Minister of Education, Gustavo Adolfo Otero. Among these disturbing factors is Bolivia's lack of territorial access to the Pacific, from which she was excluded by previous aggression by Chile. Other Bolivians also stressed this point.

The vast majority had definite economic proposals for the New World, such as a single customs union, free trade, a single monetary unit, a New World bank, proper regulation of monetary tariffs. Victor Hugo Escala, a leading journalist, at present Ecuadorean Minister to Panamá, mentioned most of these points, and in addition, urged the rapid termination of the Pan-American Highway. Gerardo Gallego, the notable Ecuadorean novelist, believes that in the Americas, regardless of 'race, religion, or level of culture,' every person should be a citizen in every country, with equal rights everywhere, 'through the abolition of immigration quotas, work restrictions, national discriminations.' Our loans have had 'too immediate objectives.' Rather should they serve 'as the basis for a plan of continental Americanism.' For 'while the conflict between the agricultural countries, producers of raw materials, that comprise Latin America, with the ... strong Anglo-Saxon competitors continues, there will persist the old rancor against the so-called "imperialism of the North."'

Alfonso Toro, the leading contemporary historian of México, feels that the guarantees of free peoples in Latin America must be the equalization of wages with those of the United States, plus 'greater socialization of wealth and wider diffusion of education.' Quite a number emphasize the necessity of equalizing United States and Latin-American living standards. Ignacio García Téllez, Secretary of Labor and Social Welfare in the present cabinet of President Camacho of México and one of those advocating a planned world economy, writes, 'See to it that the great monopolies do not convert the means of production into instruments of conquest and of violence; demand that the peace treaties lead to an elevation of the living standards of all producing classes.'

The foremost Mexican anthropologist, Manuel Gamio, declares that, above all, the indigenous population of Latin America must be raised to a civilized standard. This is echoed by the leading Peruvian anthropologist and archeologist, Luis E. Val-cárcel. 'In the post-war conferences, it specifically corresponds to countries such as México, Perú, Bolivia, Ecuador, etc., to raise the question of the social condition, in all its aspects, of the great Indian population of eighty millions that lives outside our "western" world, the victim of oppression and its fatal consequences. We cannot speak of justice and liberty if millions of human beings cannot aspire to its benefits.' Haitian leaders, such as Doctors Dantes Bellegarde and Price-Mars, emphasize racial equality as a peace norm. The great Mexican editor, Felix Pala-vicini, who founded *El Universal* ('the *New York Times* of México') and so served the cause of the Allies in the First World War, desires that drastic measures be taken to prevent the future competition in the Americas of slave labor and slave-produced products in the imperialist areas of Europe, Asia, and Africa.

Alejandro Córdova, Guatemalan editor, thinks a fruitful peace must create a new order and equilibrium in the Americas, which will take into account the ideals and aspirations of each of the New World republics and rest upon a proper solving of the problems of education, tariffs, industry, commerce, agriculture, and currency, among others.

Justo Prieto, exiled Paraguayan educator, puts the goal for the Americas as 'the right to work, socialized services for food, shelter, and health; insurance against sickness and invalidism, unemployment, and accidents; freedom from abuse by authorities and by oppressive monopolies; right of free speech, unabridged by the terrorism of secret police; equality before the law; a necessary minimum of education; the development of individual abilities with which to contribute to the progress of civilization.'

A certain element is somewhat wary of a too powerful United States in the future. Alfonso Toro sees the great danger of the future to be that the United States be converted 'into a modern Rome, a great unopposable military power, which will always try to impose its will, even contrary to justice.'

Victor Polay of Huancayo, Perú, former director of the daily *La Tribuna* of Lima, and now editor of the magazine KUNTUR (A Quechua Indian word), states that it is 'of vital importance not to forget that in spite of good faith, the strongest nation economically and militarily always becomes, if not at the present, in the future, the oppressor. Therefore Latin America should not merely participate in diplomatic banquets of cordiality and emit beautiful speeches lacking the flavor or vibration of the peoples, but its function must be effective, for the organization of a common economic, military, and cultural plan in order that thus in our continents, the two forces, Saxon and Latin-American, will be so perfectly balanced that there need be no fear of any subjugation whatever from within or from overseas, a set-up that will benefit all mankind, and we then — why fear to say it? — can intervene in the other continents where there are tyrannies and slaveries, for we shall not be blessed with liberty and justice if these do not light up the whole world.'

'Define the Monroe Doctrine,' in order to establish continental unity on a durable basis, writes the Honduranean author, Rafael Heliodoro Valle, recent winner of the Maria Cabot Lodge prize. American business men 'must change their attitude,' writes a Brazilian. 'Replace dollar diplomacy with psychological understanding,' says a Bolivian. 'The Yankees are good business men, but are incapable of understanding other peoples.' Foreigners, remarks Palavicini, can no longer expect to enjoy extraterritorial privileges and greater protection in a given country than the nationals or citizens. After reciting past abuses, he pleads for the abolition of diplomatic protection. Let outsiders abide by the decisions of the national courts as they must do in the stronger countries.

Avoid continental Fascism masked as a democracy, hints a Peruvian. Luis Alberto Sánchez, the leading literary critic of the continent, and head of the largest publishing house in Chile, Ercilla, sees this Fascism as taking the character of forcing Latin America to become merely a purveyor of raw materials rather than developing necessary domestic industries. He predicts that such a course would soon bring about a new world war.

Nearly all stressed the need for greater guarantees for national sovereignty. 'Let no country in the Americas,' writes Fernán Silva Valdés, 'the national poet of Uruguay,' 'benefit by taking advantage of the sacrifices of its neighbors, even if any country has been unable to contribute by its own sacrifice for the con-

quest of Victory and Peace,' The stronger nations of the Americas should protect the weaker ones, says an Ecuadorean, 'without intervention in their national affairs so that all may enjoy
equal rights in international life.' Díez de Medina of Bolivia sees
the seeds of future war in any continuation of the present United
States policy of favoring some Latin-American countries at the
expense of others. 'Effective guarantees for the sovereignty of
the peoples of this hemisphere,' writes the Bolivian journalist and
diplomat, Gover Zárate M. 'Protect weak nations against those
believing themselves superior races seeking to dominate the
world,' says the Mexican journalist and author, Alfonso Tara-
cena. 'Let no one interfere with our internal problems, even
with the worthy desire of helping us,' writes the Cuban author
Iraizoz.

The fine Peruvian novelist, E. López Albújar, calls the future
peace negotiations 'the second war,' an effort to balance conflicting interests among the allies. Unfortunately many of the
countries will go to the conferences 'with the prejudices of their
potential racial, cultural, and economic importance, ... an idea
of superiority, ... which naturally they cannot strip off as one
would change one's shirt.' The basic principle should be that of
'equality of treatment.' The reality may be far different, but
the lesser nations should struggle for such equality. One important question must be that of deciding the fate of 'all the peoples
now under imperial tutelage.'

The replies from Argentina and Chile have special interest.
Doctor A. H. Roffo of Buenos Aires, one of the world's cancer
experts, and a man who has done a great deal to build up Pan-
American scientific and medical contacts, writes: 'The rôle
which my country should carry out at the peace conferences
after the war will be logically that which corresponds to its place
in the concert of South American voices, and in relation to the
active importance it will have had in the defense of American
peace.'

The well-known writer and literary critic, José Gabriel, who
advocates an immediate declaration of war on the Axis, limits
himself to the cry, 'Long live America, free and united!'

'Argentine professor,' finding it inconvenient to permit publication of his name, writes that Latin America's rôle in deciding on post-war problems should be 'that of cooperation with the United States, but not as a satellite. Without relinquishing its independent judgment in matters such as international trade and other economic questions, Latin America should in the future contribute to the reconstruction of the world along lines parallel to the Pan-American spirit and understanding.'

The Argentine neurologist, Gregorio Bermánn, who did so much, at the cost of much personal hostility and injustice, to modernize the universities of Cordoba and Buenos Aires and who served as head of the Loyalists' front-line psychiatric hospital during the Spanish Civil War, believes that in future peace conferences, Latin America should act as one unit, 'to collaborate in the renovation and reconstruction of the world on broad bases of economic and social justice. To do this Latin America should sweep away the residue of its semi-feudal politics and economy and put itself squarely on the road of development and growth. It should act as a sovereign, free of the suspicion that as a whole or that any of its governments, is a vice-royalty of Yankee or British imperialism, as has been charged in the past.' Thus free, Latin America can play 'a dignified rôle, along with the United Nations, in their blood and sorrow, among them our sister, the United States of North America.'

The outstanding novelist and essayist, Victoriano Lillo Catalán, believes that although Latin America should have a voice in the conferences, only México, Cuba, Venezuela, and Brazil should have a vote. In his opinion all the other southern governments are dominated by feudal ecclesiastic or landlord elements, and represent 'a grave obstacle to the peace of to-morrow, the Peace of Victory.... Only those countries that sacrifice to save the hard-won conquests of human progress, should shape the peace. That peace should be based on a juridical structure reflecting the legal norms already accepted in the internal national life of the most democratic peoples.' This implies full disarmament and 'a new adaptation of the economic order,' and he warns that the complex problem of human peace 'cannot be solved in a few hours over a table soaked with the blood of the tremendous struggle.'

From Chile, the economist and former National Socialist leader, Carlos Keller, as might be expected, casts the questions aside with the curt remark that before talking of peace it will first be necessary to see who wins the war.

The leading caricaturist of Chile, 'Coke,' by name Jorge Delano, who is also the leading movie producer of that country and who constructed the first Chilean studio, is whole-heartedly with the good-neighbor policy, but somewhat pessimistic about peace. 'Agreements are the product of the moment in which the conferences are organized, and with the passage of time, . . . such agreements are not in tune with the new rhythm gained by events or with the ideas of the men who must face them.' Frankly I should prefer that there would be 'no necessity to celebrate any such peace conferences, for in them lies the germ of war.'

The outstanding Chilean economist, Enrique L. Marshall, declares that in case Chile is called to the conferences, it should promote 'the principles of American solidarity which serve as the basis of our international policy.'

The head of the Chilean Institute of Radium, Doctor Leonardo Guzmán Cortés, who is also a world cancer specialist, declares that Chile and Latin America, acting as one body, should 'defend the liberties of which Roosevelt and Wallace have spoken, and the integrity of the Americas.' He favors a customs union of all the Americas, a single monetary standard to do away with all currency exchange problems. It is he who calls for the liberation of the three Guianas. He supports the bill of rights of the American Constitution — a concept 'as old as Aristotle and Zeno.'

The railroad authority, engineer, and banker, Raul Simón Bernard (literary pseudonym César Cascabel), one of the outstanding and constructive minds of his country, believes that the southern nations should act in the peace conference both as individual sovereignties and collectively, and in case their war-participation has been passive, merely with Western Hemisphere affairs. They should seek to have legally defined the relation of the small countries to the zones of influence 'which eventually will be recognized by the Great Powers surviving the war.'

In contrast to Chile, so long neutral, and Argentina, still neutral, what are the opinions of the people of Brazil, the one country of South America, and potentially the most powerful, which has declared outright war on the Axis?

The notable physician and poet, Jorge de Lima, quotes the first Emperor of Brazil, Dom Pedro I: 'It was not for nothing, Senhor, that the Supreme Architect of the Universe put the Ocean between America and Europe. Those who serve Europe can create the happiness of Europe but cannot create the happiness of America.' De Lima advocates that henceforth Brazil — and it will be a miracle if the country continues to consider itself leagued with the Old World — should dedicate itself to tightening the bonds of American fraternity and should increase the production of continental weal as a species of cooperation on the grand style. 'The salvation of all demands the solidarity of all. ... Brazil should defend its liberty in common with the peoples who are its neighbors, without offending the liberty of others.' He advocates the establishment of 'pure law,' never the law of groups or races.

The novelist Alfonso Schmidt (one of whose most notable works, *Reino de Ceu*, is a fictionalized version of the life of Saint Francis) advocates the application of the doctrines of primitive Christianity. He believes that the program and policies of Henry Wallace are best adapted to the establishment of an improved social and international system.

> The civilization which has just crashed was anti-Christian ... periodic wars, enslavements, humanity divided into classes, the satanic division of production in which few remained with food and many with hunger. A civilization terminating in a manner offensive to God and man: in an infernal holocaust in which were burned billions of sacks of coffee, countless herds, mountains of wheat, worlds of manufactured products, all this to maintain commercial prices above a world of human misery.... And the holocaust was so great and so insulting that it has ended by devouring continents, men, lares, all that it reaches to. Happily this is passing. There is still time to take another road, the only road. Let God have pity on his children and inspire us in the forthcoming peace.

The Brazilian pianist, Guiomar Novaes Pinto, so well known to the concert halls of Europe and the United States, declares that all the New World nations will 'do everything possible to establish absolute guarantees of lasting peace.' One of the main foundations for such a peace will be 'the fullest liberty of the seas and of commerce, freed as far as possible from customs barriers. Free countries like ours need the freest interchange for their best progress.'

The prominent civil engineer, Virgilio Corrêa Filho, authority on the great Matto Grosso region, presents a four-point program:

1. Formal condemnation of armed conquest of alien territories.
2. Arbitration of international disputes, as provided for in Brazil's very first constitution, and as exemplified by the two notable arbitrations by President Cleveland.
3. Equality of the rights of nations, weak or strong.
4. Intensification of economic, sentimental, and cultural interchange among the American peoples, so that they may be able to act as a homogeneous bloc, capable of radiating their pacifistic and humanitarian idealism to the entire world.

Jonathas Serrano, an authority on law and a distinguished author, declares that in the peace negotiations, Brazil 'should defend with the same energy as at present, the policy of good relations and sincere collaboration with each and all of the states of the continent, to the end that the ideals of democracy be constantly strengthened, in a spirit of cooperation in an atmosphere of peace and with full respect for juridical norms.'

Doctor Arthur Moses, outstanding scientist and neurologist, feels that Brazil, as well as the American countries as a unit, should participate in the conferences equally with the British Empire, Russia, and China. Proper application of the Atlantic Charter should be the yardstick for a just, enduring peace. No country of the Americas will be able to escape Pan-Americanism, which should be strengthened as soon as the world returns to normalcy.

Perhaps the most outstanding woman of Brazil, and probably its most noteworthy woman poet, is Anna Amelia de Queiroz Carneiro de Mondonça. Once 'queen of the students of Brazil,' she is today President of the Casa do Estudiante do Brazil and active in many other institutions. The wife of a prominent manufacturer and historian, the mother of a number of children, but still active in sports, she has been sent to nearly all international women's conferences, once to Turkey, and is the only woman ever named as a member of a national electoral commission in her country. She believes that Brazil's rôle will be that of the rest of the continent — 'to give a blood transfusion to weakened organisms. We should carry new blood and a new social and political mentality to Europe, devastated by the sanguinary horde of the Axis, as a new breath of life — stimulus and faith for reconstruction; and for the heroic peoples which, with England at the head, battled against the barbaric avalanche, the American family, youthful brothers, created in the wider atmosphere of democracy and liberty, will stand with open arms.'

The explorer and copious historian, Mario Melo from Recife, believes that the New World nations should form 'a Political Confederation ... a Demo-Republican Confederation of America, the President of the Great Republic to be elected by all the countries of the continent, in indirect manner, one vote from each country, and to be chosen in rotation from each country. She should leave European questions to Europeans and form of America an indivisible bloc, as a military power, with political, economic, and currency uniformity.'

The most renowned ethnographer of Brazil, with many volumes to his credit, and now President of the Brazilian Folklore Society, Luis da Camara Cascudo, who lives in Natal, an exposed point on the Brazilian bulge, declares that 'peace can exist only in normal minds. It does not automatically follow victory. It cannot be created at "peace tables" by minds still dominated by war psychology.' There is the danger that documents signed under such circumstances may 'become the engendering force from which springs a new conflict even more horrible.'

To be lasting, peace should be the result 'of conferences and studies begun by the winning nations even before the close of hostilities. ... The surest way to provoke resentments and subsequent revolt is to have a peace treaty flow from the pens of international politicians interested solely in the future of the strongest nations.'

Brazil has a real contribution to make. His country, 'with four centuries of civic education, with its pacific and Christian mentality, devoid of any taint of wars of aggression and conquest, can bring to these preliminary peace studies, factors never recognized and consequently impossible of evaluation by those who measure countries in terms of material riches and balance of trade.'

Here, he believes, is the crux not only of the peace but of the good-neighbor policy, both of which can be successful and enduring if 'national characteristics will be respected in this fusion of interests, and if the thoughts of no one nation be taken as a mold into which all others must fit.' And in that common effort, Brazil can bring 'its collective traditions of friendship, industry, peace, and moderation.'

Perhaps the most noteworthy aspect of these replies is the general sense of remoteness, not in terms of struggle, but in terms of ideas and ideals, from Europe. Before the outbreak of war, probably most of South America, besides its strong economic ties with Europe and the Orient, looked to the old continent, rather than to the United States, for cultural inspiration.

Possibly this is only a temporary shift of interest. But the nature of the arguments set forth suggest that, just as we are becoming far more interested in Latin-American affairs, so the southern peoples are gaining certain enduring interests, not only in the affairs of the United States, but also in those of the other Latin-American republics.

There still lurks considerable fear of an all-powerful United States, the insistence that Latin America be treated, not as a mere satellite of ours, not merely as a crude warehouse of raw materials, not merely as a dutiful echo of Washington policies. These writers are convinced that if the rights of nations are respected, if sound plans are made for a firm economic basis for hemispheric unity, if closer ties are really cultivated in a spirit of equality, if the good-neighbor doctrine is made a permanent part of North American foreign policy, then the western union of peoples will not only be able to promote its own prosperity, but will be a basic factor in the establishment of an enduring peace.

If anything, the writers are more critical of the shortcomings of Latin America than those of the United States. There is recurrent criticism of Latin-American dictatorship, a consciousness of the low standards of living prevailing to the south and the need to improve them, and a universal desire for the extension of democratic practices where they do not now exist.

In general the writers showed themselves in accord on the following points: a strong economic and political bloc of the Americas in which the needs of each country would receive due and fair consideration; an end of previous business imperialism; an end of previous military and political imperialism; the proper development of Latin-American resources to serve the needs, primarily, of the Latin-American peoples; a free world of free individuals and free nations; a more intensive and extensive practice of democracy in local, national, and international affairs. All felt that Latin America should have a larger voice in world affairs, particularly with regard to matters of the Western Hemisphere. There was considerable harsh criticism of the caliber and conduct of many of our good-will emissaries and the ignorance of fly-by-night journalists and writers who pontifically set themselves up as Latin-American authorities. Yet, on the whole, aside from a few bitter notes, the letters were remarkable for their spirit of tolerance, their belief in the workability of the ideals of human freedom, the necessity to approach all problems on the basis of free discussion and cooperative effort. After reading these communications, I had the sensation of a fresh and vital world, fully confident of itself, moving without fear toward its destiny.

THE END

INDEX